The Scandal of Leadership t
church today—the promulga
this problem as more than just a matter of individual leaders g
rather of broken systems of formation and imitation.

MATTHEW CROASMUN, associate research scholar, Yale Center for Faith & Culture; author, *The Emergence of Sin: The Cosmic Tyrant in Romans*

With the help of Girard, Wink, and Stringfellow, JR makes an important contribution to imagining how we dwellers in institutions can live in them self-critically. Through his enriched understanding of the principalities and powers, he offers religious leaders, or those who would become such, a realistic and dynamic set of criteria to judge by which "other" they are being run and so learn to avoid dysfunctional and destructive patterns of church life. Highly recommended.

JAMES ALISON, Catholic priest and theologian

Looking over the current landscape of US Christianity, one wonders how it may have gone so wrong. The church in the West has fallen victim to diseased narratives perpetuated by dysfunctional leadership. In this text, JR Woodward not only presents a necessary postmortem of this dysfunctional leadership, but he also shines a possible way forward that releases the church from cultural captivity. Through the possibility of positive imitation of previously unexplored models and examples, Woodward offers a hope beyond the scandal of leadership.

SOONG-CHAN RAH, Robert Munger Professor of Evangelism, Fuller Theological Seminary; author, *Prophetic Lament*

What has happened to our leadership? An entire "leadership industry" has cropped up in the last forty years, but we still have rampant abuse, bullying, and control techniques that have come to light in the church. JR Woodward offers a sharp, intriguing, carefully researched analysis of the dynamics at work that often hide themselves in our systems and souls. This book is a leadership-paradigm-shifter! *The Scandal of Leadership* brings together theology and multiple sciences to expose "the Powers" at war. Even better, JR himself doesn't merely write as a disruptive academic but also as one who actively practices a radical self-emptying form of leadership.

DAN WHITE JR., author, *Love Over Fear*; cofounder, The Kineo Center, Puerto Rico

At every level and in every sphere, especially the ecclesial, we are witnessing authority gone awry, wreaking havoc and leaving traumatized people and shame in its wake. If you ever wondered why it is almost impossible to uncouple God-given authority from the lust for power, why authority and power are so often conflated even in the church, and if "sheep may safely graze again" this book is a must-read. With careful theological work engaging key discursive writers on power, Woodward pulls the wool off our eyes and helps us see the ultimate personalities behind the oft lapses into building personality cults—the principalities and powers of Pauline theology, the spirits behind institutions, the "structuring structures," to use psychospiritual language. The antidote is not more programmatic attempts to shore up the character of leaders, nor even engaging in spiritual warfare with the spiritual Powers but the call of the master to the cruciform life that spills forth in ministry as cruciform. May sheep now safely graze.

REV. ESTHER ACOLATSE, PhD, professor, Pastoral Theology and World Christianity, Garrett-Evangelical Theological Seminary; author, *Powers, Principalities, and the Spirit*

This book is a sensation! Instead of allowing the raft of recent high-profile leadership scandals to be put down to a "few bad apples," JR Woodward unmasks the subtle ways the Powers try to misdirect church leaders' affections and manipulate them to mimic their patterns of domination. The answer, he reveals, is nothing less than a fresh call to "the kenotic journey"—the giving up of oneself to the cause of Christ. Every Christian leader should read this.

MICHAEL FROST, Morling College, Sydney

Over twenty years ago, I first heard JR Woodward discuss "the Powers" in relationship to leadership in ministry. Shortly after he finished, I relayed to him that what he shared was so profound, not only did I think it would become one of his life messages but that it was also one of the most important for the church. In this time of upheaval, I commend this book to anyone who is giving deep consideration to the nature of the church in our day.

CHRIS BACKERT, director, Fresh Expressions North America

This is a book for our times! In *The Scandal of Leadership*, JR exposes the deeply spiritual elements at work in the assumed culture of leadership of the contemporary church. Readers are summoned to a deep self-searching that calls for metanoia in their personal as well as their collective lives. We resonated deeply with this book. A must-read!

ALAN AND DEBRA HIRSCH, authors; cofounders, Forge Missional Training Network and Movement Leaders Collective

JR uses his prophetic voice to diagnose deep problems within Christian formation that plague the church today. He offers theological tools to help identify malformed powers in leadership, and then offers pathways for healthier, life-giving solutions.

ROHADI NAGASSAR, author, *When We Belong*

"Imitate me, just as I imitate Christ" (1 Corinthians 11:1). Leaders are imitators, but there is a subtle competition for their souls. The question is not whether they are being influenced but what kind of influence they are under. Is it the powers of sin and death that conform us to the fallen ways of this world, or the power of the Spirit that transforms us into the image of Christ? In this profound interdisciplinary study, Woodward invites us to wrestle deeply with matters that lie at the heart of all discipleship and mission. If leadership is about influencing others, then leaders must have lives worthy of imitation, for the health of the church and its witness in the world. A hugely important contribution to missiology, for a time such as this.

DR. PHILIP R. MEADOWS, Sundo Kim Professor of Evangelism, Asbury Theological Seminary, KY; international director, Inspire Movement; author, *Remembering Our Baptism* and *The DNA of Discipleship*

JR artfully weaves a tapestry of biography, Scripture, academics, and theological engagement to illuminate how the principalities and powers thread through our leadership consciousness. *The Scandal of Leadership* should be read by all who feel called to the work of ministry, in the hope that by JR's unmasking of the powers that influence us, we might be a better witness and hope to the world.

JESSIE CRUICKSHANK, founder, Whoology

JR Woodward's book offers a comprehensive, missiological understanding of the problem of domineering leadership. He then provides the solution to the problem through the development of a kenotic spirituality that moves us from death to life. This book is unique. It is the first one to synthesize the work of some of our greatest spiritual masters of the late twentieth and early twenty-first century. Woodward's application of their insights on the powers and principalities can help us model positive leadership. As a friend of Henri Nouwen, Walter Wink, and René Girard, I can say with confidence, they (along with Stringfellow) would herald this profoundly prescient work. It could change *your* life.

STEVEN E. BERRY, DD, DMin, author, pastor, and teacher; producer; director, Global Meetinghouse Enterprises, LLC

Finally! An academically robust and comprehensive missiological study into why so many pastors and church leaders have fallen to scandal. This isn't a book of anecdotes or pithy leadership one-liners. This is a deep analysis of how we've come to the place we're at and what role the powers have played and continue to play in our lives.

DANIEL IM, lead pastor, Beulah Alliance Church; podcaster; author, *You Are What You Do*

If unseen Powers are most powerful when we don't talk about them, then this book will seriously unsettle those Powers. In this timely and rigorous examination of why leadership so often corrupts good leaders, JR Woodward invites us to discern who we're imitating. Such a deep, spiritual investigation will disrupt the forces of domineering leadership and help us name our temptations, transforming us from the inside out and restoring integrity to individuals and systems and to our mission.

MANDY SMITH, pastor; author, *The Vulnerable Pastor* and *Unfettered*

If you care about the future of the church, then you clearly care about church leadership. The domineering presence that has infected the church has spread like a virus, and this book is a critical cure. Highly recommended for generations to come.

TIM SOERENS, author, *Everywhere You Look*

Finally, a book that takes us beyond naming the "what"—that toxic leadership is prevalent—and helps us grasp "why" it exists and "how" we can seek healthier structures here forward. Wise leaders should read this book and heed JR's invitations.

AJ SHERRILL, Anglican priest; author, *Being With God*

The Scandal of Leadership is a prophetic trumpet blast from the watchman's wall. JR Woodward has given the church a scholarly yet vibrant portal into a primary issue few up to now have seriously dealt with at the roots.

LANCE FORD, coauthor, *The Starfish and The Spirit*

Not for the fainthearted, this book urges leaders to engage faithfully with complex theories, theologies, and practice. Practical and academic, it is a theological remedy to abuses of power. It offers profound hope that we can be *re*-formed by faithful imitation of the praxis of Christ and engage in missional lives that scandalize the world for Christ's sake. Woodward's sweeping exploration takes us from the pervasive realities of the powers and principalities at work in the Western church and its leadership models to the depths of Christ-centered character. Read, weep, and be challenged.

REV. DR. DEIRDRE BROWER LATZ, principal, Nazarene Theological College, Manchester; researcher and coauthor, *Church on the Margins*

Poetry has been described as an un-American activity. JR Woodward shows how a robustly orthodox Christian faith and its embodiment in a faithful, well-led church is also an un-American activity, if that means prophetically challenging a culture that prefers climbing the ladder to carrying the cross. Scholars and saints from the Americas help Woodward to open up the Bible and the heart and hence a world of new possibilities. Christian leaders seeking the renewal of their vocation, ministry students beginning to shape theirs, and everyday Christians struggling with "the Powers" in an increasingly post-Christian America all owe Woodward a close reading.

SCOTT COWDELL, Australian Anglican priest and theologian; author, *René Girard and the Nonviolent God*

It's one thing to chronicle and bemoan the failures of leaders in Christian circles. There are plenty of books and social media posts for that. It's another—and more helpful—thing to chart a path forward. JR Woodward helps to chart that path by explaining the forces that derail some leaders and discussing what can be done differently. *The Scandal of Leadership* is not a screed but rather an engaging exploration of leadership for Christian communities. Churches and other Christian organizations would do well to read and engage with Woodward's analysis.

DENNIS R. EDWARDS, dean, North Park Theological Seminary; author, *Humility Illuminated*

JR Woodward is a rare combination of a theorist and a movement leader, which brings a unique perspective to this book. He goes beyond the distorted leadership of our age that is driven by power and the Powers and instead shows true leadership rooted in Christ and kingdom values. This book presents a paradigm shift in leadership that encapsulates key elements for faithful and fruitful missional movements. I highly recommend this book to anyone looking to deepen their understanding of leadership and gain valuable insights from an experienced movement-builder. It is truly game-changing.

SANGHOON LEE, PhD, president, America Evangelical University, Gardena, CA; president, Missional Church Alliance, Gardena, CA; author, *Re-Form Church*, *Re-New Church*, *Re-Think Church*, and *Re-Fresh Church*

JR has a way of saying things we are all thinking and feeling, and he doesn't disappoint in *The Scandal of Leadership*. He challenges the church to think deeply and honestly about shifting from a domineering leadership to a missional leadership that imitates Christ.

REV. DR. JEREMY SUMMERS, missional leader; author; affiliate professor; director of training, Groundswell www.groundswellmovement.net

The work and writing of JR Woodward cannot be overlooked. Through a lived experience of serving the church and her leaders, Woodward has shown he is not only a tested practitioner but also a brilliant thinker. *The Scandal of Leadership* represents not only a book. It's a manifesto of hope for the church to live into her God-given glory. Highly recommended.

A. J. SWOBODA, PhD, associate professor of Bible, Theology, and World Christianity, Bushnell University; author, *After Doubt*

Dr. Woodward reminds us of the critically important call for leaders to imitate Christ's humility and resist the Powers that seduce us into patterns of abusive dominance. In the process, he weaves together the historic intellectual contributions of Walter Wink, William Stringfellow, and René Girard. His biographical summaries of their lives and the life of Archbishop Óscar Romero are vivid and inspiring descriptions of men who taught and incarnated this message. Other scholars will need to build on this work to explore the applicability of this theoretical framework to women and North American communities of color, strengthening the role of shared power and communities of accountability. Still, this book raises timely questions and provokes deep reflection about issues that concern us all.

REV. DR. ALEXIA SALVATIERRA, academic dean, Centro Latino and associate professor, Mission and Global Transformation, Fuller Theological Seminary; coauthor, *Faith-Rooted Organizing* and *Buried Seeds*

Fabulous book on power and leadership! Drawing on renowned theologians and philosophical anthropologists alike, Woodward surpasses the common narratives for why leaders morally fail with a deeper examination of desire and imitation. Rather than a "do better" appeal, this book charges the reader in expanded and fresh ways to reconsider imitating Christ, thereby incarnating true missional leadership. Robust, compelling, and genuinely impressive, *The Scandal of Leadership* is an essential book for every Christian leader.

LISA RODRIGUEZ-WATSON, national director, Missio Alliance; contributing author, *Voices of Lament* and *Red Skies*

In this hugely important book, JR Woodward examines the very real temptations faced by today's leaders. In an era where leadership challenges can be overwhelming, Woodward offers a way to lead with a Jesus mindset while avoiding the unseen pitfalls that can destroy the life of a leader and ultimately all those around them. If you are leading and you want to truly understand how to be more Christlike in your leadership, pick up this book!

DAVE FERGUSON, lead visionary, NewThing; author, *BLESS*

Many bemoan today's crises in leadership but point to little more than personal failings as the cause. JR Woodward demonstrates how imbibing worldly leadership assumptions have—surprise!—made church leaders worldly. He cogently explains how the solution to "the leadership scandal" lies right before our eyes in what is often eloquently preached behind pulpits but ignored behind executive desks. What does it mean for a leader to deny oneself, take up their cross, and model Jesus? Woodward takes this question seriously, and you will, too, after reading this book.

R. TODD MANGUM, PhD, academic dean and clemens professor, Missional Theology, Missio Seminary, Philadelphia

Having the personal experience of missional communal praxis in both local and translocal ministry for over thirty years, Dr. Woodward amalgamates not only his observation and diagnosis of, and prescription for, domineering leadership in Western Christendom but also his own desire to imitate Christ into life-giving servant leadership. While some have attempted to identify pieces of triumphalism and its impact on the church today, Dr. Woodward has accomplished a thorough survey of domineering leadership in the past, its brutal claim over the present, and a practical hope—founded on grounded spirituality, missional theology, and movemental ecclesiology toward imitation of God— for our future. This is, undoubtedly, not only Dr. Woodward's magnum opus but also the work of every Christian leader in our time.

REV. DR. EUN K. STRAWSER, lead pastor, Ma Ke Alo o, Hawaii; movement leader, The V3 Movement; author, *Centering Discipleship*

Ministry flows from the inside out. From the heart, good, healthy, and vibrant ministry emerges. But also from the heart, damaging and harmful ministry emerges. We must attend to the heart. In a world that too often glamorizes ego and willful power, Woodward reminds us that ministry must follow a different path: the humble, emptying, way of Jesus. This book is theologically rich and insightful. It offers the ministry leader practices that not only cause us to imitate the ways of Jesus but also allows Jesus to transform us. This is an essential book for ministry leaders. It will encourage us to examine our own lives, our patterns of ministry leadership, and guide us along a new, deeper, heart-shaped path.

KURT FREDRICKSON, DMin, PhD, associate dean, Professional Doctoral Programs and associate professor, Pastoral Ministry, Fuller Seminary

This is a major work on leadership—leadership generally (theory and practice) and particularly leadership in the church, with a strong missional focus. Woodward helpfully engages the key issues of the Powers, an important biblical theme. He unpacks the nature of dominance models and advocates instead for what he calls an "imitation-based framework," reminding leaders (and Christians generally) of the lure and subtle temptations of power. Woodward focuses on biblically authentic ways of exercising Christlike maturity and upside-down leadership. We don't so much need theories of leadership as we do examples—examples of people who lead through who they are, their characters, their honesty, their humility, and their practice. Woodward helpfully points us in this direction.

HOWARD A. SNYDER, author, *The Problem of Wineskins*, *Community of the King*, *The Radical Wesley*, and *Salvation Means Creation Healed*

The Scandal of Leadership may be a tough read for some, not because it's harsh or scathing—far from it—but because parts of it describe leaders we all know, including, potentially, the one looking at us in the mirror. But I am very glad JR did this research and is calling us to a better way. His work is guiding us to a kenotic way of life and leadership found in the very example of Jesus. It is not so much novel as much as it is untried and untested in our modern leadership paradigm. And it makes me excited and hopeful for this generation of leaders that are emerging.

DANIEL YANG, director, the Church Multiplication Institute; coauthor, *Inalienable*

Moral failures, domineering leaders, bullying, and abuse of power are some of the all-too-common phrases that fill Christian headlines these days. Sometimes I wonder if there are any "good leaders" left. Christian leaders of any kind must reexamine their relationship with power. JR Woodward names the powers and principalities that corrupt once-good-leaders and invites us to rediscover the gift of power through the lens of Jesus and Scripture. Finally, a book that doesn't just deconstruct the tired framework for leadership but reclaims a Christ-centered vision for leadership that reflects the goodness of God. This is the book we've been waiting for.

TARA BETH LEACH, pastor; author, *Radiant Church*

THE
SCANDAL
OF
LEADERSHIP

THE SCANDAL OF LEADERSHIP

Unmasking the Powers of
Domination in the Church

JR WOODWARD

100
MOVEMENTS
PUBLISHING
ACADEMIC

First published in 2023 by 100 Movements Publishing
www.100Mpublishing.com
Copyright © 2023 by JR Woodward

Library of Congress Control Number: 2023902452

Credits are continued on page 377.

ISBN 978-1-955142-24-3 (print)
ISBN 978-1-955142-25-0 (ebook)

Cover design: Jennifer Phelps
Interior illustrations: Dan White Jr.
Interior design: Revo Creative Ltd.
Copy-editing: Heather Campbell
Proofreading: Sarah Giles

100 Movements Publishing
An imprint of Movement Leaders Collective
16 Absoraka Drive
Cody, Wyoming
82414

www.movementleaderscollective.com
www.catalysechange.org

To those who are willing to follow the scandalous way of Christ.

CONTENTS

LIST OF FIGURES AND TABLES

LIST OF FIGURES

LIST OF TABLES

FOREWORD
DAVID FITCH

It is clear that the Western church of Jesus Christ is in a crisis of leadership. In the midst of devastating moral failures by church leaders of every kind, our structures of leadership have clearly betrayed us. Our ways of thinking about power and authority have failed to meet the challenge. How could so many good leaders go bad? How could our most "successful" churches promote and sustain horrifically abusive leaders? Amid these ruins, we are looking for answers to these questions.

Over the past thirty years, we have witnessed an explosion of publishing around the topic of leadership in the church. Thousands of pages of wisdom have been offered by leaders in government, business, and education as well as by successful megachurch pastors. We have seen leadership conferences attracting thousands of pastors and leaders of Christian organizations. We have been told we must learn from the best and most successful leaders among us, whatever that might mean. It has been assumed that leadership is leadership, wherever it may be found. And this, too, has born ill fruit, as the very sponsors and speakers of these conferences and books have fallen to scandal. We have tried to manage leadership more effectively or better guide the character of leaders, but these solutions have also failed. The church of Jesus Christ stands jilted by its fallen leaders and is shrinking in all its traditional forms.

So after hundreds of years of Christendom, the church finds itself at a crossroads regarding its leadership. We need more than just another Band-Aid. We require a profound reevaluation of leadership, a deep searching of the Scriptures, and the seeking after the person of Jesus Christ for another way to lead God's people.

It is at this juncture that JR Woodward's *The Scandal of Leadership* arrives. In it he offers us a remarkable unraveling of the complexities of leadership. In doing so, he describes a picture of leadership that challenges all things American, including the markers of success to which we have become so accustomed. He guides us through the theological problems of leadership as currently conceived. He leads us through the insights of great theologians and social thinkers, the Scriptures, and some stories of heroes of the faith. When we finish, we will have not only reexamined the foundations of what leadership has been, but we will have also reconstructed a whole way of understanding leadership in the way of Jesus, under the Lordship of Jesus, out of relationship with God in Jesus and what he is doing in the world for his mission. Woodward offers us so much more than a Band-Aid.

We can often be tempted to put guardrails around our leaders, try to keep them in line, or perhaps encourage a set of spiritual disciplines to keep their character in check. But there is no putting a Band-Aid over the problem of domineering leadership in the church. Beneath the problems of our leadership lie more insidious forces at work. These forces work against the very way God works. The apostle Paul labels them "principalities and powers." And we cannot simply manage these forces; we must, in the words of Walter Wink, name them, unmask them, and engage them. Woodward refuses to put a Band-Aid over these issues of leadership. Instead, he dissects "the principalities and powers" at work among institutions and the idolatries that lie waiting within.

None of this excuses us from examining our leaders' characters. Over and over, we have seen the character of good leaders go bad. But instead of simply proposing some spiritual disciplines for our leaders to use, Woodward probes more deeply. Using the works of René Girard, Woodward helps us to understand how a person's desires can get twisted within the matrix of power and "the Powers." Interacting with Girard and then William Stringfellow, he demonstrates how a leader becomes captive to the Powers, how good things become idols, and how good leaders become twisted toward abuse of power and injustice. In a church culture that consistently pushes the Christian to seek success, self-fulfillment, and purpose in one's own achievements, Christian leaders are deeply susceptible to these powers and their idolatries. There is no managing our leaders out of this. Band-Aids simply won't do. Woodward rips off the Band-Aids and uncovers what we must first see before we can even begin to heal and walk in a different way.

Spiritual formation, of course, is important for Christian leaders who choose to face the Powers and the malformation of desire. But this must involve more than attempting a few disciplines or adopting some practices of personal devotion; it must be a whole way of life. More and more, I am convinced that there can be no true leadership in the kingdom apart from what Woodward calls "the kenotic journey," the giving up of oneself to the greater purposes and work of God in Christ. I am grateful to Woodward for giving us a marvelous description of this journey through Scripture and for illustrating it so well through the life of one of Christianity's greatest modern leaders: the Latin American priest and martyr Óscar Romero.

The result of all this is an account of leadership that is truly scandalous to all of us who have subscribed to the standard account of American leadership. And yet it is the way we are called to go. So I encourage the reader of this book to take their time reading through what can only be a total upending of their understanding of what it means to lead in Christ's kingdom. If we dare, and if enough of us join with Woodward on this kenotic Christocentric way of leadership, I believe a revolution of sorts lies ahead: a renewal of the kingdom of Jesus in our midst, for our time, in North America. In these most challenging of times for the church in North America, it cannot happen soon enough.

PREFACE

The issue of domineering leadership holds personal significance for me. Over the years, it has been a great privilege to be a part of various leadership teams, and it was while serving in one particular national team that a few of my fellow team members began to see signs of controlling leadership in our primary leader.

Within this context, I had been thinking and praying about the idea of power. So when I was asked to speak at our annual gathering of pastors on the theme of spiritual warfare, it seemed more than a coincidence. Spiritual warfare is primarily about the struggle of power. There is worldly power, which Jesus eschewed, but there is also a holy power, brought by the Spirit. In preparation for this talk, I stumbled upon the work of Walter Wink, who explores the Powers from a different and deeper perspective.

The aim of my talk was to help leaders better identify the fingerprints of the devil in our own lives, the lives of our churches, our movement of churches, and the world at large. I used Wink's framework of naming, unmasking, and engaging the Powers as an outline.

I began with an excerpt from *The Screwtape Letters*. In the section of the book titled "Screwtape Proposes a Toast," author C. S. Lewis describes a fictional scene in hell. It is the annual dinner of the Tempter's Training College for young devils. The principal, Dr. Slubgob, has just proposed the health of the guests. Screwtape, the guest of honor, rises to reply,

> *Mr. Principal, your Imminence, your Disgraces, my Thorns, Shadies, and Gentledevils:* It is customary on these occasions for the speaker to address himself chiefly to those among you who have just graduated and who will very soon be posted to official Tempterships on Earth. It is a custom I willingly obey. I well remember with what trepidation I awaited my own first appointment. I hope, and believe, that each one of you has the same uneasiness tonight. Your career is before you. Hell expects and demands that it should be—as Mine was—one of unbroken success. If it is not, you know what awaits you.[1]

Later in his toast, Screwtape educates his audience about how they are to use structures, principles, ideas, and influencers so the demons do not have to use their energy for personal temptation. They are taught to instead utilize the systems already in place to lead people to "Our Father Below," or the devil, and to keep them from following the "Enemy," or God. The toast continues:

As the great sinners grow fewer, and the majority lose all individuality, the great sinners become far more effective agents for us. Every dictator or even demagogue—almost every film-star or crooner—can now draw tens of thousands of the human sheep with him. They give themselves (what there is of them) to him; in him, to us. There may come a time when we shall have no need to bother about *individual* temptation at all, except for the few. Catch the bell-wether and his whole flock comes after him.[2]

I shared about how Screwtape then makes it clear that the lowest demons are given the role of personal tempters and that the greater demons are those that influence whole systems and world values. Screwtape's goal is to keep leaders from following the "Enemy," for if Screwtape could get them to become a part of these evil systems unaware, he could win over many more.

As my talk continued, I began to explore some lessons I learned from Walter Wink as well as from life experiences. We looked at how the Powers were at work, not only in the city in which I was planting but also in our movement of churches. As I closed the talk, I posed the following questions to my fellow church leaders, questions I often ask myself:

- Are you involved in joining God to bring about his kingdom or your own kingdom?
- Are you confronting the demon of being driven to other people's ideas of success, or are you resting in the Lord, trusting in God and in his promises and his timing?
- Are you creating systems in your ministry that mirror the systems of the world, or are you creating systems and structures that mirror the kingdom of God?

Many at the gathering seemed to be deeply challenged by those questions. People were positively impacted by the message and talked about it for some time. Weeks after the talk, leaders continued to share with me how much they had received from the message. Some even said they believed it was my "life message."

As our church continued to be fruitful, I could sense how power and the Powers were at work in my life. There were times in my ministry when God made it clear to me that my love for ministry was greater than my love for him. This was deeply troubling for me. I felt the spiritual battle for my heart, and this war within gave fresh motivation for further studies.

In one of the organizations I served, I was saddened to discover that my fellow national leaders thought the head of our organization should move on, due to a "soft case" of controlling leadership. Although I did not experience this firsthand, when I heard the concerns of other leaders, it was difficult to deny there was a problem. So we made the difficult decision to give a "no confidence" vote, which led to the resignation of our leader. In time, I was devastated to learn of other, earlier leaders who had also been asked to quietly move on.

I could not help but wonder why good leaders seem to become less good the more time they spend in this particular role. Is there something in our very structures that makes us more vulnerable to domineering leadership?

God was prodding me to make room for further study. I eventually pursued a master's degree at Fuller Theological Seminary, with a focus on missional leadership. Part of the preliminary findings, which were also being worked out in our local context, can be found in my book *Creating a Missional Culture*. In that book, I make the case for polycentric leadership, as opposed to hierarchical or flat models; I also state that we both create structures and structures recreate us.[3]

I was hungry to develop my understanding even further, so I went on to complete my doctoral studies at the University of Manchester (UK) in 2013, under the supervision of Phil Meadows. In the summer of 2020, I was awarded my PhD after defending my thesis, *Missional Leadership, Mimetic Desire, and a Theology of the Powers*.

Along my journey, there were opportunities to share my findings with various leaders around the world. Wherever I share about this topic, it seems to deeply resonate with those who hear it, providing language for an unspoken intuition. All the while, as my studies continued, it seemed that through the fall of significant leaders, God was revealing this problem of domineering leadership in the church. As soon as I recovered from the heartbreak of one leader falling, another revelation soon followed. News of the fall of leader after leader after leader continued. Sadly, it seems to have become an epidemic. In this context, it seems some church planters and pastors would prefer to resign or find alternative work than risk being in a leadership role. In significant portions of the church, a cynical spirit has surfaced within both leaders and members.

A variety of media have highlighted the problem of domineering leadership in recent years, including the popular podcast *The Rise and Fall of Mars Hill*.[4] These are good and useful tools, but if we are to deal effectively with the issue, it will require a deeper diagnosis. I believe that as we develop a more robust theology of the Powers, we will better be able to *name* the Powers of domination and unmask their subversive work in our lives. In this way, we can better engage them and ultimately prevent the tragic "falls" we have seen of late. This is not an issue we can simply ignore. When we, as church leaders, succumb to domineering leadership, people get hurt, Christ is misrepresented, and the witness of the church is damaged.

My desire is that *The Scandal of Leadership* would offer theological immunity to the disease of domineering leadership in the church. Primarily based on my PhD research, this book is an attempt to deeply diagnose this problem and point a way forward. Although I take an academic approach in these pages, my intention is to publish a couple of popular-level books in the future.

My prayer for you is that God would grant you the wisdom to understand what he wants you to know, the grace to receive what he might offer you, the discernment to cast aside anything that is unhelpful, and the courage to lead in the way of Jesus. As you read, you will discover that each of us will either follow the scandalous way Jesus led or become a scandal. There is no neutral ground.

INTRODUCTION

Life is a paradox. We are all a mix of good and bad; we are beautiful and broken. We often have mixed motives. Sometimes, as leaders of families or churches, we become controlling. However, when we start to become domineering leaders in the church as a way of life, it leads to our fall, where we are either fired or compelled to step down. Falling does not have to be permanent, "for though the righteous fall seven times, they rise again" (Prov. 24:16a). Our fall does not have to fully define us. But if we fail to repent, it often will.

I write this book with hope for the fallen and as a vaccination for those who have not fallen but are capable of doing so (which includes us all). I want to describe a reality where we, as flesh-and-blood people, recognize the unseen dark forces that work against us, because if we fail to name, unmask, and engage them, we are likely to fall.

The stories of those who have fallen—those I mention by name in this book—do not have to be the last word for their lives. In order to give a deeper diagnosis to concrete realities, I share what is public knowledge for all, in the hope that we can build immunity against the plague of domineering leadership.

For those of us who have been hurt by the leadership of others, we do not have to allow that hurt to define us. We can forgive even if we cannot reconcile with others, for forgiveness takes just one person, but reconciliation takes two and involves repentance from the wrongdoer.

Although I end this book with a sense of hope, we must first confront the brutal truth of our current cultural moment.

In July 2011, C. J. Mahaney, former president of Sovereign Grace Ministries, took a leave of absence after confessing to "expressions of pride, unentreatability, deceit, sinful judgment and hypocrisy."[1] In April of 2013, he resigned from his role.

Steve Timmis, former Acts 29 CEO and pastor of The Crowded House in Sheffield, UK, resigned in February 2020. "Fifteen people who served under Timmis described to *Christianity Today* a pattern of spiritual abuse through bullying and intimidation, overbearing demands in the name of mission and discipline, rejection of critical feedback, and an expectation of unconditional loyalty."[2]

And in August 2014, Mark Driscoll, founding pastor of Mars Hill and cofounder of the Acts 29 church-planting network, was asked to leave the leadership of Acts 29. He was also forced to resign from Mars Hill in October 2014. In his resignation letter, he confessed to "past pride, anger and a domineering spirit,"[3] as well as admitting to paying a company to purchase his book from enough key markets to get him on the *New York Times* Best Seller list.[4]

These are but a few of the most high-profile cases of domineering leadership in recent years. Most of us are aware of this recent spate of pastors publicly "falling." In their wake there have been books, articles, and podcasts that have sought to identify and understand the underlying causes of such leadership. This is an important moment for the church. Cases that may once have been swept under the rug are now being exposed, and we have an opportunity to change. However, this is only possible if we get to the root of the issue. Dandelions may be nice-looking flowers, but they are weeds, and the only way to remove them is to deal with them at the root. Dandelions have taproots that can extend several feet into the soil, so simply pulling them out at the surface will never solve the problem. In the same way, if we are going to deal with domineering leadership in the church, we need to move beyond the presenting surface issues and get to the root of the problem. To do so will require a robust diagnosis of the issue.

In this book, I not only seek to link the fall of church leaders to patterns of domination, but I also hope to demonstrate a link between imitation and the Powers. I want to explain how leaders who uncritically imitate patterns of power seen in the fallen world are liable to fall into patterns of domination. These patterns can vary in intensity and impact, and it is easy to assume that such domination tendencies happen to "other people" in "other places." Yet, to one degree or another, we are all fallible in this area. If we exercise any degree of self-reflection, each and every one of us can no doubt identify times in our lives when we have wielded power inappropriately, whether that be manipulating people for our own gain, intimidating others, or being overly defensive. Indeed, I have felt the grip of power in my own life—seeking people's applause is a temptation with which I continue to struggle. This book was born out of a desire to help myself as much as to help others. There are too many heartbreaking stories and too many people who have been hurt as a result of this form of leadership. I am passionate about seeking preventative measures that deal with the problem of domineering leadership in the church.

THE SUBTLE DANGER OF CROWDS

The North American church has, by and large, assimilated with contemporary culture, and we now subconsciously assume that those with the largest churches are the most "successful." "How many people attend your church?" is the first question pastors ask of one another, as if this is the primary way to discern the faithfulness of ministry. I have never been asked, "How many people in the church you serve reflect the fruit of the Spirit?" Or "How many people in the church you serve seek to live in the world for the sake of the world in the way of Christ?" Taking our lead from wider culture, our churches have become obsessed with celebrities, and we put our pastors on pedestals. Either implicitly or explicitly, we have believed the lie that our key aim is to "build a crowd" and that all of our best efforts should be geared toward this goal. But rarely are we aware of the subtle dangers this presents.

It would seem that Jesus was not impressed by the crowds. His first message recorded in Luke ended with him escaping the crowd before they were able to throw him over a cliff (Luke 4:28–30). In an article titled "Jesus and Crowds—An Unhappy Marriage," Karl Vaters notes that "Jesus didn't value crowds. He didn't even trust them (John 2:23–24). But he valued the people in them."[5] Vaters makes the point that the largest crowd recorded in Scripture was the one present at the feeding of the five thousand, which is sometimes used to justify the importance of spending the majority of our time, talents, and resources to build crowds so we can be like Jesus. However, Vaters challenges this logic, pointing out that on this particular occasion, Jesus was actually trying to escape the crowds, but they followed him to a remote place. Because of his love for the people, he had the disciples feed them.

Jesus frequently tried to escape the masses, and his message was never defined by them—he regularly said things that made the crowds dwindle, to the point of asking his disciples if they too were going to leave him (John 6:67). His identity was grounded in the Father—not in how many came to hear him speak.

When we become infatuated with the crowds, we become possessed by our image instead of possessing our image in God. Infatuation with the crowds has formed pastors who look and act like rock stars, and it has created a celebrity culture within the church. This seems to be a breeding ground for domineering leadership. We are taken by the charismatic personalities that draw the crowds, and the more the crowds flock, the more we deify our leaders. In such scenarios, leaders are viewed as beyond reproach, and domineering leadership often ensues. This has only been accentuated with the dawn of social media and the elevated platforms that come with it.

In his memoir, *The Pastor*, Eugene Peterson—the antithesis of the domineering styles of leadership prevalent in the North American church—recalls how he once wrote to a fellow pastor who was drawn by the appeal and prestige of the crowds. Philip, the pastor in question, had been part of the "Company of Pastors"—a group Peterson had helped form as a way of bringing mutual encouragement and development for the pastors who were part of it.

Philip announced one day that he was leaving his congregation in order to pastor a church with a thousand members—three times the size of the church he was currently pastoring—because it was "more promising."[6] Despite the ethos of the group, Peterson recognized that Philip had "absorbed a concept of pastor that had far more to do with American values—competitive, impersonal, functional."[7] This bothered Peterson, not because Philip was changing churches, but because "Phillip's reasons seemed to be fueled by something more like adrenaline and ego and size."[8] So after meeting with him one-on-one to no avail, Peterson wrote Philip a note. Within this letter, Peterson gives some wisdom regarding the crowds. Recalling their personal conversation, Peterson shares his concerns about how Philip seemed too enthralled by the prominence of this church, and he warns of the dangers it poses. He talks about how size is the "great depersonalizer," quoting Kierkegaard's wisdom: "the more people, the less truth."[9]

Peterson goes on to note how Christian maturity comes through "intimacy, renunciation and personal deepening. And the pastor is in a key position to nurture such maturity."[10] Maybe that is why Jesus devoted himself to the Twelve instead of to the crowds, and maybe it is why he commissioned us to make disciples rather than host large services. We are wise to take heed of Peterson's reflections. The following was penned in his personal memoir toward the end of his life:

> Classically, there are three ways in which humans try to find transcendence—religious meaning, God meaning—apart from God as revealed in the cross of Jesus: through the ecstasy of alcohol and drugs, through the ecstasy of recreational sex, through the ecstasy of crowds. Church leaders frequently warn against the drugs and the sex, but, at least in America, almost never against the crowds. Probably because they get so much ego benefit from the crowds.
>
> But a crowd destroys the spirit as thoroughly as excessive drink and depersonalized sex. It takes us out of ourselves, but not to God, only away from him. The religious hunger is rooted in the unsatisfactory nature of the self. We hunger to escape the dullness, the boredom, the tiresomeness of me. We can escape upward or downward. Drugs and depersonalized sex are false transcendence downward. A crowd is an exercise in false transcendence upward, which is why all crowds are spiritually pretty much the same, whether at football games, political rallies, or church. . . . But I really do feel that crowds are a worse danger, far worse, than drink or sex.[11]

Few churches in North America have drawn crowds like Willow Creek Community Church in the northwest of Chicago. In its heyday, it reported a weekly attendance of twenty-five thousand people.[12] In a recent case of domination and control, cofounder Bill Hybels resigned from Willow Creek on April 10, 2018, amid allegations of sexual misconduct. His story is important

for at least two reasons: First, Hybels hosted a prominent annual conference—the Willow Creek Leadership Summit, which has influenced leaders
and pastors worldwide. Second, an independent report on Hybels showed
how his domineering leadership led to sexual misconduct.

The Independent Advisory Group issued a seventeen-page report detailing
their review process, observations, conclusions, and recommendations.[13] The
first observation stated, "Allegations were made in two areas, overlapping at
times: sexually inappropriate words and actions in relationship with individuals; abuse of power and position."[14] Other relevant observations included
how the "descriptions of Bill Hybels' leadership role as reliant on power,
celebrity and position to implement his personal preferences and personnel
management are widespread."[15] His approach to leadership was described
as "command and control," which "contributed to executive and leadership
turnover."[16] "Board members expressed recurring difficulty in holding Bill
Hybels accountable for his leadership and management style."[17] The conclusion of this independent report was that the allegations were credible and
that "the credibility of the allegations [was] not based on any one accusation
or accuser but on the collective testimony and context of the allegations."[18]

THE TIP OF THE ICEBERG ON WHY LEADERS FALL

High-profile "fallen" leaders often share common characteristics: pride,
manipulation, seeking status, isolation, a lack of community to hold them
accountable, using status to push an agenda, love of the crowds, an abuse
of power and role, a push to "succeed," and a sense of self-importance.
For example, the influential podcast *The Rise and Fall of Mars Hill* gives
a glimpse of what was happening behind the scenes of the church Mark
Driscoll was leading. In one of the podcasts, Jesse, who was hired by Mark,
confesses how he used his social media skills to promote the brand of both
Mars Hill and Mark.[19] His efforts were extremely successful, and because
of this, Driscoll allotted more and more money to help him build the brand.
Driscoll's podcast rose to the top of the charts. With his successful podcast
and a growing church, Driscoll was less willing to allow others to mentor
him. In time, his team realized his preaching seemed to be more about Mark
than Jesus.[20] At one point during a Mars Hill training day, this became
particularly evident, as Mark shared for an hour, at one point saying, "I am
the brand."[21]

When leaders fall to domineering approaches, there typically is a flurry
of articles written by teachers, counselors, and practitioners who attempt
to explain why the leader has fallen and how to address it.[22] Some attribute
a leader's personal behavior and attitude to issues of identity: self-compar-
ison, seeking acclaim, the cessation of a vibrant walk with the Lord, and

a false sense of infallibility. Others relate an unbearable level of stress and pressure on leaders in their relationships with congregations. Scott Sauls writes,

> It's easy to put pastors and other public figures on a pedestal. But when people do this, they turn pastors and public figures into objects instead of subjects, personas instead of persons, celebrities instead of neighbors, untouchable heroes instead of the frail image-bearers that we are. This tends to widen the community gap between congregants and their pastors, which in turn isolates pastors significantly. This can be especially true in larger churches.[23]

In *Pastors at Greater Risk*, H. B. London Jr. and Neil B. Wiseman ask pastors to recognize that there is a crisis in progress. They offer practical suggestions for attending to marriage and family life, including understanding how to recover from stress and burnout, finding freedom from sexual addiction, and pursuing the practice of personal holiness.[24]

Licensed professional counselor Michael Todd Wilson and pastor Brad Hoffmann, along with the CareGivers Network, have spent thirty years working to care for "fallen" and hurting pastors, missionaries, and other paid Christian workers. Through collaborative wisdom, they identified three distinct themes of concern for leaders: who the leader is, what the leader values, and how the leader relates. In looking at who the leader is, they address the lack of genuine intimacy in relationship with God, spouse, and others, as well as a distorted sense of calling. Building on this foundation, they then examine what the leader values. Here they address inadequate stress management skills, lack of appropriate boundaries, and the failure to prioritize recreation. Finally, in exploring how leaders relate, they speak of insufficient people skills and underdeveloped leadership skills.[25]

Pastor and author Alan Roxburgh primarily developed what I refer to as the three contours of leadership: identity, praxis, and telos, although he uses the term *work* instead of *praxis*. Others, including myself, prefer praxis.[26] I will explore and develop these contours throughout the book. But for now, it is enough to say that these terms will help us to understand how the praxis of the leader is significantly informed by the leader's identity and telos. In the context of leadership, these terms can be defined as follows:

Identity (being) refers to a sense of self and how it is established.
Praxis (doing) deals with the practice of leadership as it takes place within the cycle of thought, action, and reflection.
Telos (becoming) is indicative of the end goal of leadership, both for the

leader's life and where they are leading the church. Telos signifies the true end.[27]

In many ways, the three distinct themes of concern that Wilson and Hoffmann identify reflect the three contours of leadership. (See table I.1.)

Table I.1 Contours of Leadership and Areas Needing Healing

Contour of Leadership	Area Needing Healing
Identity	Who the leader is
Praxis	How the leader relates
Telos	What the leader values

In the CareGivers report, the authors address the unique challenges of vocational ministry.[28] Two stressors they highlight relate to the identity of the leader. The first occurs when the congregation tends to put the leader on such a high pedestal that they are considered godlike and are no longer seen "as human beings with feet of clay."[29] The second is when ministers with a personal sense of inadequacy "put on an air of confidence," presenting a "perfect" public image.[30] Therefore the identity of the leader—who the leader is—is foundational in forming strategies to prevent abuse.[31] This study suggests that the symptoms found in high-profile leaders are not unique to their levels of influence but seem to be common struggles for leaders at many levels of influence.

The diagnosis and remedy of these various resources are extremely helpful, as they encourage a healthier psychology, relationality, and spirituality. However, this is merely the tip of the iceberg.

A DEEPER DIAGNOSIS OF DOMINEERING LEADERSHIP

My hope is that this book will offer a more comprehensive missiological understanding of the problem of domineering leadership. Missional theology begins with the metanarrative of Scripture that moves from creation through the fall to new creation and the *missio Dei,* which is the work of God in making all things new.[32] A critical but often overlooked part of that narrative is how the fall not only affected humanity but also social and cosmic realities.[33] From the garden to Christ's temptation in the desert all the way to the beast and dragon in John's revelation, there are Powers manifest through social realities that actively warp God's intentions for the world. But the good news is that the life, death, and resurrection of Jesus represents the victory of God over the Powers.[34] In an attempt to understand how this dynamic shapes the present and dictates the future, some missiologists have sought to retrieve the biblical language of the Powers.[35] This book deals with both power and the *Powers* (Satan, the demonic, principalities, and powers). The Powers as a catch-all term will be capitalized. When speaking to just one aspect of the Powers—such as the principalities and powers, the demonic, or just the term *power*—capitalization will not be used.

I will take these incipient arguments and apply them to leadership, in both its fallen and redeemed states. "Fallen" leadership occurs when leaders forsake the mission of God in the way of Christ through the Spirit and instead move (knowingly or unknowingly) toward imitation of the Powers to achieve the leader's agenda.

I will demonstrate the link between leadership, imitation of desire, and the Powers. As this link is developed, it will become evident how the Powers seek to subvert us in shrewd ways and easily influence us to "fall" into patterns of domination. In addition, I seek to make the case that "fallenness" is driven by malformed desires and that the reshaping of our desires should be at the heart of leadership formation. After the link between imitation and desire is made, I suggest that the primary way to reshape our desires is through imitating the desires of Christ, who found his identity and telos in God and the mission of God. Finally, as leaders, if we seek to imitate Christ and live our lives in God, our desires can be reshaped, and we can subsequently become positive models for imitation in the church, which leads to genuine discipleship and healthy multiplication.

When leaders fall to domineering leadership, it does not always lead to a resignation or removal from leadership. However, I argue that domineering leadership does always lead to rivalry, chaos, and scapegoating in the congregation and thus a poor witness to the world. Redeemed leadership is reflected in the apostle Paul's appeal to the Corinthians to "be imitators of me, as I am of Christ" (1 Cor. 11:1 ESV). Thus, the central question I seek to address is the following:

> How might a theology of the Powers help us as missional leaders practice
> a spirituality that reshapes our desires for the sake of discipleship,
> community, and mission?

Domineering leadership hurts people and damages the witness of the church, so it is therefore important to develop a proper diagnosis. Albert Einstein reputedly once said that if he had only one hour to solve a problem in which his life actually depended on the solution, he would spend the first fifty-five minutes determining the proper question to ask.[36] If he knew the right question to ask, he could solve the problem in less than five minutes. This book focuses on the fifty-five minutes of that hour, seeking to ask the right questions and uncovering what is below the tip of the iceberg.

I seek to make a missiological contribution to the study of missional leadership from the perspective of a theology of the Powers. Missiology as a methodology, described by Bruce Ashford and Scott Bridger, "is a theological discipline, that is undertaken in conversation with Scripture, church history, and the social sciences and in consideration of its cultural context."[37] Each of these areas is addressed in this book, with emphasis on Scripture and the social sciences relating the Powers in the cultural context of the Euro-tribal Western church, in particular the North American church.[38]

My research approach for this book involves developing a conceptual framework, which I refer to as an *imitation-based framework*. A conceptual framework performs "as the overarching argument for the work—both why it is worth doing and how it should be done."[39] Such a framework not only shapes the argument but provides a methodology for the construction of this book. The beauty of this approach is that it can "provide the researcher with *theoretical frameworks* to advance the argument beyond where previous researchers have taken it, or to introduce new questions, considerations, hypotheses, or explanations into the inquiry."[40]

The conceptual framework (see figure I.1) I am seeking to advance incorporates the leader, mimetic desire (imitation), a theology of the Powers, and imitation of Christ. But due to the emphasis on developing a deeper diagnosis of the problem of domineering leadership, this book will focus more on the missional leader, the Powers, and mimetic desire. The focus of how the missional leader is connected to the Powers via mimetic desire will help us recognize that we are all captive to imitation. *I am proposing that the only way to overcome the Powers is through imitation of Christ, in particular his desires, which always leads to how we act.*

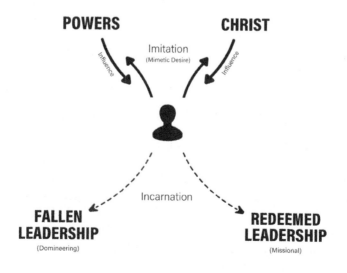

Figure I.1 The Imitation-Based Framework

Although this imitation-based framework is simple, it is not simplistic. Looking upward from the center where we, as leaders, stand, we will ultimately either imitate the desires of the Powers or the desires of Christ. If we imitate the desires of the Powers, the result will be fallen leadership characterized by egotism, pride, and a command-and-control approach to leadership. Our imitation shapes how we incarnate our leadership, which in turn shapes others. If we imitate the desires of Christ, it will result in true missional leadership, evidenced by others-centeredness, humility, and a *kenotic* (self-emptying) approach to leadership.

My approach is both theological and missiological, since the life of the leader greatly shapes the formation and witness of the church. In section one, after exploring a preliminary understanding of the Powers, I examine the current missional church conversation and demonstrate the need for this imitation-based framework as an alternative approach to leadership theory and practice. The fruit of such an approach may stimulate deeper self-reflection among leaders that will help to avoid fallenness and to adopt a spirituality that leads to redeemed missional leadership in the church. An imitation-based framework invites leaders to a spirituality that shapes the three contours of leadership, which

- grounds their identity (being) in the life of the triune God;
- orients their telos (becoming) toward life in God, the mission of God, and new creation; and
- ultimately reshapes their praxis (doing) as they seek to imitate Christ in identity formation and telos.

The hypothesis that this book seeks to confirm is that a robust theology of the Powers enables leaders to better imitate Christ and resist the temptations common to fallen leadership. Leaders are thus enabled to participate in the life and mission of God through the power of the Holy Spirit; through this, they will develop lives worth imitating.

PRIMARY INTERLOCUTORS: WINK, GIRARD, AND STRINGFELLOW

Developing this imitation-based framework will take a multidisciplinary approach. Jeanne Stevenson-Moessner paints practical theology[41] as an orchestra "of musicians in relationship," which is different from the performance of a "soloist" or a "guest musician," because "practical theology plays in concert with other disciplines or areas in theology."[42] Because practical theology can dialogue across a wide array of disciplines—from biblical theology to cultural anthropology, from sociology to emergent science, from psychology to systematic theological reflection—the interlocutors chosen for this study have expertise that spans various fields.

Walter Wink was a New Testament scholar adept in psychology, biblical studies, philosophy, and social ethics. He was not only a scholar but also an activist—someone who put his life at risk as he married theory with practice. His seminal trilogy on the theology of the Powers demonstrates that leaders will face personal, social, and cosmic temptations that seek to subvert the three contours of leadership—identity, praxis, and telos.

René Girard was a literary critic, cultural anthropologist, and historian who wrote in the fields of theology, mythology, sociology, and philosophy. His mimetic theory demonstrates the link between the Powers and imitation and desire (*mimetic desire*). Mimetic desire suggests that humans are the most imitative creatures on earth and that we imitate the desires of our models. This can be seen in all sectors of society—from Madison Avenue to the fashion industry to the network effect in stock trading to keeping up with the Joneses. Although our physical needs for sex and food are instinctual, our wants are mimetic. Girard helps us to understand our "hidden models" and how they shape our desires. Mimetic desire eschews individualism and speaks to the reality that we are relational creatures. Mimetic theory ties together the imitation-based conceptual framework of this book, because through Girard we learn that, ultimately, we will either imitate the Powers or Christ. There is no neutral ground. And our ultimate model will determine the nature of our incarnational leadership.

William Stringfellow was a practicing lawyer, incarnational activist, political analyst, and social critic who engaged in empirical theology.[43] He was an early incarnational practitioner who discovered the Powers while living in Black and Brown Harlem in the 1950s and '60s. Stringfellow will add to our understanding of the Powers and enable us to identify the specific ways that the Powers seek to subvert our leadership.

Although my research led to these primary interlocutors because of their seminal works in these given areas, I also recognize their inherent limitations. They represent diverse Christian traditions, but they do not represent diversity of ethnicity or gender. As a White male, I have sought to bring in a number of other voices that offer more diverse perspectives, but it nevertheless remains a limitation. Because I am a White male, my life experience is different from men of color, so it is important for men of color to contextualize this message based on their lived experience. And it's important to acknowledge that the topic of abuse throughout the history of the church mainly relates to male abuses of power. Sadly, the story of women's leadership has not been documented in the same way as men's. I've heard from female friends in leadership that the cautions I share about dominating leadership are not necessarily speaking to the temptations they often face—the temptation to avoid power altogether. Referring to this very issue, author and pastor Mandy Smith says in her book *Unfettered*,

> When childlike faith leads us to follow, childishness will bind us in our inadequacy. Rather than leading to childlike dependence, our childish sense of limitation can lead to shame, despair and passivity. We see this temptation in every Bible character who says "Who am I?" as a way to avoid God's call—every way that Esther hesitated, every way that Moses rested in his lack of eloquence, every way Jeremiah used his age as an excuse. Underuse of power can be just as much an abuse of power as overuse. It feels Christlike because it doesn't grasp for power. But we've created a caricature of Christ. His childlike reliance led to obedience which expressed itself in surprising authority. He was childlike and adult-like—free to be powerless and free to be powerful.[44]

Such an exploration is beyond the scope of this project, but I pray that we all have more opportunities to learn about and from women's ways of leading.

Another limitation to my research is that although Wink, Girard, and Stringfellow all address a number of other themes, these lie outside of my conceptual framework and therefore the scope of this book. Thus the imitation-based framework guides my argument as well as helps to strengthen my focus.

In sections two and three, I will explore the life and work of Wink and Girard to help deepen and connect the elements of the imitation-based framework. In section four, I will look at the life and work of William Stringfellow, and I will uncover how the Powers seek to subvert the missional leader at the three contours of leadership: identity, praxis, and telos. In section five, I offer a synthesis of Wink, Girard, and Stringfellow as well as others, and I consider a theological immunity for the disease of domineering leadership and prescribe the remedy of formation of desire through positive mimesis. In this section, I also seek to interpret the book of Philippians through a Girardian lens, and I examine the life and work of Óscar Romero as a recent example of kenotic spirituality.

It is likely that as you read, you will come across new terminology, because some of my interlocutors develop their own vocabulary. I seek to define terms the first time they are mentioned. However, the use of the words *myth* and *mythology* are used differently depending on the context. When Girard uses the word *myth*, it is typically in the negative sense: the stories we tell about ourselves that hide the truth of our complicity to violence. However, I also use *mythology* to refer to the *reality* of the Powers. Theologian Rudolf Bultmann seeks to demythologize the Powers, but I, with Croasmun and others, seek to remythologize the Powers. In other words, Satan, the demonic, and the principalities and powers are real creatures, remythologized through an emergent ontology. This will become clearer as the themes are developed within the book.

With the help of these interlocutors, I hope it will become clear that we are all captive to imitation. Who we choose as models determines our desires; and ultimately, either Jesus or the Powers will be our arch-model. Because there is much misunderstanding on the nature of the Powers, we do not tend to take them seriously enough. Although a psychological and social analysis are helpful, a full analysis requires a theological exploration of the Powers, so let us get to the work of unmasking the Powers of domination in the church.

SECTION ONE

THE CHALLENGE OF
MISSIONAL LEADERSHIP

Domineering leadership in the church is not just a
current problem; it is a historical issue, as old as the
church itself. In the introduction, I noted that a deeper
diagnosis of this prevailing problem will require more
than a psychological and sociological analysis—we need
to see it from a cosmic viewpoint. I will start this quest
in chapter one by exploring the various interpretations
of the Powers (in particular, the principalities and
powers) in our context. In chapter two, I will examine
how missional theology has sought to deal with a
colonialist and triumphalist approach to mission and
why missional leadership is key for the church today.
Not only do we need a missional theology that informs
our practice as missional leaders, but we also need a
missional spirituality that forms us to become more like
Christ. This is particularly important in light of how the
Powers seek to misshape the contours of our leadership—
identity, praxis, and telos. In chapter three, I will explore
Graham Houston's understanding of Peter's approach to
dealing with domineering leadership in the early church.
From there, I will develop and examine an imitation-
based framework. This framework will enable a deeper
diagnosis of the issue of domineering leadership so we
can move toward a more robust remedy.

1

A DEEPER DIAGNOSIS OF WHY LEADERS FALL

At the center of J. R. R. Tolkien's The Lord of the Rings series is the One Ring. Created by the evil Sauron, this ring mesmerizes all who encounter it, and those who wear it are overcome with a desire for domineering power. The ring poses danger to even the simplest and most kindhearted of all creatures: the hobbits of Middle-earth. One of these hobbits, Frodo, volunteers as the lead ring bearer of the fellowship that embarks on the quest to destroy the One Ring. As he journeys to Mount Doom, we discover that not even he can withstand its temptation. All who place the ring on their finger feel its power—often with deadly consequences.

Sadly, this fictional tale mirrors the reality of the church. Leaders are falling to the lure of domineering power in epidemic proportions. Like those who encounter the ring in Tolkien's story, we are aware of the dangers of power, and yet we, too, are drawn to it. Rather than respecting this power and keeping a safe distance, we often succumb to the temptation and too willingly place the ring on our finger. Although no one is immune, leaders are particularly vulnerable. And when a leader falls, it often has a devastating impact on the whole church and undermines our witness. Speaking of the reasons for the decline of the church in the West, Gerard Kelly notes, "Of all the charges laid at the door of the church by many disaffected young people . . . the most frequent and damning is the charge of *controlling leadership*. . . . Stifling creativity, stunting innovation and imagination, forcing uniformity, silencing dissent."[1]

Although there are a number of extremely helpful books, articles, and podcasts that explore domineering leadership in the church today, I believe the current diagnosis of the problem doesn't analyze the issue deeply enough, failing to examine it mythologically from the viewpoint of the Powers.[2] When I say *mythologically* here, I am using the word in its positive sense, defining it as "the actual state of affairs."[3] In G. K. Chesterton's novel *The Scandal of Father Brown*, the protagonist, an amateur detective, says while working on a case, "It isn't that they can't see the solution. It is that they can't see the problem."[4]

Only when we adequately diagnose the root of the problem can we find the right solutions. This requires a theological framework that helps diagnose *and* prevent the fall of leaders. And although no remedy is foolproof, a deeper diagnosis of the problem has the potential to make a positive difference.

A ROBUST THEOLOGY OF THE POWERS

Albert Einstein writes, "The formulation of a problem is often more essential than its solution . . . To raise new questions, new possibilities, to regard old problems from a new angle, requires creative imagination and marks real advance in science."[5] Hermeneutics is the science and art of interpreting Scripture. If we hope to develop a deeper diagnosis of abusive power in the church, we need a theology of the Powers that has a high view of Scripture and the story of God *and* is faithfully contextualized. I will explore the Powers in detail later in this chapter and throughout the book, but for now, I simply want to draw attention to the Powers as a reality in our twenty-first-century world. In brief, the term *the Powers* refers to Satan, the demonic, and the principalities and powers mentioned in Scripture. My hope is that as you read this book, you will better see the unseen forces at work in our world so that you are able to name, unmask, and engage the Powers. For they are currently wreaking havoc in the church and in our world, bringing divisions, perpetuating polarization, and cultivating violence. If we fail to develop a robust theology of the Powers in which we add a mythological analysis to the current biological, psychological, or sociological analysis, our solutions to the problem of domineering leadership in the church, although instructive, will not bring the deeper transformation we desire both for individual leaders and for the culture of leadership in today's church.

Developing a theology of the powers involves making sense of passages such as the following (emphases mine):

For I am convinced that neither death nor life, neither *angels nor demons,* neither the present nor the future, *nor any powers,* neither height nor depth, nor anything else in all creation, will be able to separate us from the love of God that is in Christ Jesus our Lord.

ROM. 8:38-39

None of *the rulers of this age* understood it [the hidden wisdom of God], for if they had, they would not have crucified the Lord of glory.

1 COR. 2:8

Then *comes* the end, when He delivers the kingdom to God the Father, when He puts an end to *all rule and all authority and power.* For He must reign till He has put all his enemies under His feet. The last enemy *that* will be destroyed *is* death.

1 COR. 15:24-26 NKJV

That power is the same as the mighty strength he exerted when he raised Christ from the dead and seated him at his right hand in the heavenly realms, *far above all rule and authority, power and dominion,* and every name that is invoked, not only in the present age but also in the one to come.

EPH. 1:19B–21

As for you, you were dead in your transgressions and sins, in which you used to live when you followed the ways of this world and *the ruler of the kingdom of the air, the spirit* who is now at work in those who are disobedient.

EPH. 2:1–2

Put on the full armor of God, so that you can take your stand against *the devil's schemes.* For our struggle is not against flesh and blood, but against *the rulers, against the authorities, against the powers of this dark world and against the spiritual forces of evil in the heavenly realms.*

EPH. 6:11–12

For in him all things were created: things in heaven and on earth, visible *and invisible,* whether *thrones or powers or rulers or authorities*; all things have been created through him and for him. . . . For God was pleased to have all his fullness dwell in him, and through him to *reconcile to himself all things,* whether things on earth or things in heaven, by making peace through his blood, shed on the cross.

COL. 1:16, 19–20

And having *disarmed the powers and authorities,* he made a public spectacle of them, triumphing over them by the cross.

COL. 2:15

Power can be positive—it was through the power of the Spirit that the church was birthed, disciples were made, the world was blessed, and the message of the gospel spread rapidly. But power can also be destructive. The unholy use of power has damaged the church's witness, crippled her mission, and aided her decline.

Many people have experienced the damaging repercussions of dominating forms of leadership, and many have seen and felt the Powers through the systems and structures of the local and translocal church. As a result, an increasing number of people are deeply suspicious of all organizations that might interfere with their self-agency, especially the church. There is a growing resistance to institutions. But the church relies on people being a community, which requires organization, politics, systems, and structures. The answer, therefore, is not to demonize all forms of power and structure— for all living things have structure, power, and the capacity to cultivate a flourishing life. A more robust understanding of the Powers will give space to articulate an institutional imagination that critically affirms structures as part of the created order that were designed to serve us, while also recognizing that most of the Powers are radically fallen. Fallen principalities are not benign; they seek ultimate allegiance and promise freedom. However, any allegiance that does not center on God is idolatry and leads to death.

FAITHFUL CONTEXTUALIZATION

In order to comprehensively diagnose the problem, we need a *contextualized* understanding of the Powers for today. A term developed from the mission field in relation to our presentation of the gospel, contextualization can be under-applied, resulting in a gospel that makes no sense in its context. As British theologian and missionary Lesslie Newbigin describes, "It can fail by failing to understand and take seriously the world in which it is set, so that the gospel is not heard but remains incomprehensible because the Church has sought security in its own past instead of risking its life in a deep involvement with the world."[6] Conversely, we can over-contextualize, creating a gospel that presents no challenge to the culture in which it resides. Newbigin notes that this happens when we allow the world to dictate the issues in such a way that the world is not challenged but domesticates the gospel for its own purposes.[7]

Although "every communication of the gospel is already culturally conditioned," we need to discern how to share it with true contextualization.[8] Understanding how to contextualize the gospel takes discernment. And it is the same when seeking to recognize the Powers. So how can our understanding of the Powers make sense in the culture in which we find ourselves? And does it issue the correct challenges that are faithful to God and how he calls us to live? For Newbigin, faithful contextualization helps the gospel "come alive" in particular contexts. He writes,

> True contextualization accords to the gospel its rightful primacy, its power to penetrate every culture and to speak within each culture, in its own speech and symbol, the word which is both No and Yes, both judgement and grace. And that happens when the word is not a disembodied word, but comes from a community which embodies the true story, God's story, in a style of life which communicates both the grace and the judgement. In order that it may do this, it must be both truly local and truly ecumenical.[9]

In many ways, my task in this book is to faithfully contextualize the Powers for those living in the Western milieu while remaining cognizant of how the Powers are understood globally. In doing so, we can more effectively unmask the Powers of domination in the church. Faithful contextualization makes sense of the Powers in our current time (context of reception) in a way that is aligned with the writers of Scripture in their time (context of production).

Translating the Powers in today's context presents a difficult hermeneutical challenge. This may explain, in part, why the current diagnosis of the problem of domineering leadership in the church so rarely shows any awareness of the Powers. American theologian Marva Dawn writes, "Scholars' interpretations of the original meaning of the biblical concept of 'the principalities and powers' vary widely, ethical formulations frequently ignore the hermeneutical gap between original meaning and present application, and most theological analyses have failed to apply the concept to human psychology or to other dimensions of reality besides the state."[10]

Thus, if authors or podcasters try to bring up the Powers in their diagnoses, those reading or listening may dismiss them altogether as an alien concept in our contemporary worldview. A premodern understanding causes some, consciously or unconsciously, to dismiss the Powers because their understanding of the Powers does not tally with their everyday lives. This is not just a recent phenomenon. In fact, for a significant season in the history of the church, the Powers were disregarded by most scholars as unimportant.

THE REDISCOVERY OF THE POWERS

W. A. Visser 't Hooft and Marva Dawn make the case that the "Powers" language "fell out of use during the time of the Reformation, when various apocalyptic sects made Martin Luther and John Calvin cautious about eschatology."[11] Bill Wylie-Kellermann writes, "In fact, for most of its history, the gods of this world have blinded the Church to its own scriptures with respect to the 'principalities and powers.' In the hermeneutical history these terms have been excised, suppressed and obscured."[12] Walter Wink and William Stringfellow locate the loss and hiddenness of the Powers in the fourth century with the "Constantinian Arrangement," when the church "became the darling of Constantine."[13] Wink writes,

> Called on to legitimate the empire, the church abandoned much of its social critique. The Powers were soon divorced from political affairs and made airy spirits who preyed only on individuals. The state was thus freed of one of the most powerful brakes against idolatry, although prophetic voices never ceased to be raised now and again anyway.[14]

Although different scholars locate the disappearance of the Powers language at different times, there is agreement that the rise and fall of Hitler and Nazi Germany brought a renewed scholarly interest in the Powers. The Enlightenment project had failed; theologians needed a more holistic and comprehensive way to articulate the power of evil.

Amos Yong, Marva Dawn, and Robert Ewusie Moses each give excellent histories of the theological engagement with the Powers (in particular "the principalities and powers").[15] Thus I bring them into the conversation as I analyze a few approaches to this hermeneutical task. But before I analyze three ontological perspectives of "the principalities and powers," it is important to note some significant theologians who helped reintroduce the Powers in recent history.

Karl Barth and Paul Tillich, two influential theological voices in the 1930s, made it palatable for academics to reengage and develop a theology of the Powers. Barth, at the rise of Hitler and Nazism, was not only the primary author of the Barmen Declaration for the resisting church, but he also wrote *Church and State* (1938).[16] This book was written to help the church navigate its life when the state becomes demonic by absolutizing itself, as did Nazi Germany. Barth, agreeing with the reformed theological understanding of the state as part of God's good, created order, affirmed the church's need to be *for* the state. Barth provided a way for the church to minister to the state by helping it remember its divine legitimation comes through Jesus, the Lord of lords, not itself. So when the state seeks self-deification, the church must remain faithful to its Lord through passive and active resistance, and at the same time, it should continue to pray for the state and respect its leaders. In this way, the church can help the state live up to its divine role.

Tillich named nationalism and authoritarianism as demonic. "Tillich was acutely aware of the fact and the function of the demonic in human existence."[17] In *The Eternal Now*, he talks about the importance of casting out demons. And when reflecting on the "body of sin" addressed in Romans, Tillich identifies the cosmic tyrant of Sin: "Paul seldom speaks of sins, but he often speaks of Sin—Sin in the singular with a capital "S," Sin as a power that controls world and mind, persons and nations."[18]

G. B. Caird's *Principalities and Powers: A Study in Pauline Theology* is another significant early work, drawn from his lectures at Queen's University in Kingston, Ontario, in 1954.[19] Marva Dawn writes, "G. B. Caird emphasizes that salvation in the NT is always 'a past fact, a present experience, and a future hope.' The same threefold character, he continues, can be seen in all the NT passages about Christ's victory over the powers. Those three-time references are marked by the resurrection, the Parousia and the time in between."[20] Also, Gordon Rupp, a Methodist minister who famously challenged the charge that Martin Luther was the spiritual ancestor of Hitler, wrote *Principalities and Powers: Studies in Christian Conflict in History*, pointing out the many parallels and similarities between the early church and contemporary times.[21] Marva Dawn writes, "Gordon Rupp extensively discusses . . . the following parallels between biblical times and the present:

a world which became too complicated too fast; a world in which the 'little people' feel themselves as playthings of great forces."[22]

Though others were writing on this topic in the 1960s, two of the most significant authors were William Stringfellow in the United States and Jacques Ellul in France. I will engage Stringfellow in chapters eight and nine to bring some clarity to how the Powers seek to subvert our leadership. And I will draw on Ellul when, in chapter ten, I analyze the temptations of Jesus.

THREE ONTOLOGICAL PERSPECTIVES OF THE POWERS

With this brief history, it is important to analyze three key voices: Clinton E. Arnold, Rudolf Bultmann, and Hendrik Berkhof. As Yong writes, they represent the "three contemporary interpretations of the New Testament powers: a traditional (spiritualist) view, a demythologized (reductionistic) model, and a dual-reference option."[23] The primary question I am asking in this analysis is the following: *What is the nature of the Powers?* Although the term *the Powers* refers to Satan, the demonic, and the principalities and powers, in this current analysis, I primarily focus on "the principalities and powers." In the course of this book, I will be discussing each of these.

CLINTON E. ARNOLD

In his work *Powers of Darkness: Principalities and Powers in Paul's Letters*, Clinton E. Arnold critiques views of the principalities and powers as impersonal social, economic, and political structures rather than organized, personal, spiritual beings led by Satan, whose aim is to lead humanity away from God and oppose the people and work of God.[24] Arnold argues for a traditional threefold understanding of the nature of evil, involving the flesh, the devil and his entourage, and the world. He sees the sources of evil as interior (flesh), exterior (world), and supernatural (devil).[25] As James Beilby and Paul Eddy remark, "This triumvirate has become one common way of expressing the primary foci of spiritual warfare."[26] Arnold believes that Paul was a man of his times and that both he and his first-century audience believed in the ontological reality of personal spiritual beings. Arnold states,

> I would suggest, however, that it is erroneous to equate the powers with the structures. As I will argue, we ought to distinguish between the powers of darkness and the structures of our existence. The two categories are ontologically distinct. One is personal, the other nonpersonal; one possesses intelligence and the ability to will, the other does not. Truer to Paul's letters is to say that the powers exert their influence over the structures of our existence than to make the powers coextensive with the structures.[27]

Arnold considers the principalities and powers in Paul's writing to represent personal demonic spirits with ontological reality. This leads Arnold to a classical evangelical approach to spiritual warfare.

Arnold believes that Paul, in his letters, emphasizes the powers working to prevent people from becoming Christians and to stall a disciple's character formation. "The major issue of concern for Paul, therefore, is not so much the relevance of the powers with regard to social justice, but their implications of salvation history and Christian behavior."[28] For Arnold, Paul does not direct Christians toward "reforming the social or political order."[29] The gospel proclamation is important "because it has otherworldly, eternal implications."[30] In Arnold's analysis, "the institutions of this world (*kosmos*) and the structures of the present age (*aiōn*) are destined to perish."[31] Consequently, as Christians focus on seeing individuals changed and to the degree that those individuals are changed, institutions will become more liberating.

Arnold is effective in considering the message in its given context; however, there are several critiques to make. Robert Ewusie Moses, whose PhD dissertation is titled "Powerful Practices: Paul's Principalities and Powers Revisited," analyzes Arnold, noting, "The main deficiency of this approach is that it falls short of offering the church a comprehensive view of the nature and methods of the powers, and arming the church with the adequate tools needed to combat the powers."[32] Moses rightly indicts Arnold's understanding of the principalities and powers as simply being personal spiritual beings: "The church needs to come to terms with the complex and myriad schemes and methods of the powers. In the end, one wonders if the purely personal interpretation of the powers has not itself succumbed to the 'powers' of modern individualism and Romanticism."[33]

Although Moses seems to miss Arnold's mention of social structures, he is right to note that such structures hold trivial importance for him. Arnold's view simplifies the Powers to only malevolent spirits, whereas Paul seems to hold a wider interpretation (Rom. 8:38–39). Berkhof makes the case that "Paul observes that life is ruled by a series of Powers. He speaks of time (present and future), of space (depth and height), of life and death, of politics and philosophy, of public opinion and Jewish law, of pious tradition and the fateful course of the stars. Apart from Christ man is at the mercy of these Powers."[34]

In addition, Arnold deals inadequately with the reconciliation of the Powers mentioned in Colossians (Col. 1:15–20). On the one hand, "all things" reconciled through Christ in the passage "includes the heavenly entities, namely the principalities and powers," which he considers to be demons.[35] On the other hand, he writes, "Certainly the powers of darkness will not be redeemed in the same sense as Christians and thus experience a reconciliation with God as friends."[36] So although the principalities and powers are at first reconciled, finally, they are not. With Arnold, I would agree that the possibility of reconciliation for the devil and the demonic seems tenuous at best (Matt. 25:41; Rev. 20:20), but it does seem possible that the principalities and powers are redeemable. It is therefore important to distinguish between the devil, the demonic, and the principalities and powers, because although the principalities and powers seem redeemable, the devil and demonic do not. Arnold tries to deal with this tension by saying, "The powers will ultimately be brought to their knees before him."[37] The difficulty with this statement is that it sounds less like reconciliation and more like forced submission. Moses offers this helpful conclusion: "Paul's account of the powers presents us with comprehensive features of reality; and a purely personal interpretation of the powers is too simplistic to capture adequately Paul's complex presentation of the powers."[38]

RUDOLF BULTMANN

One of the most common interlocutors chosen to engage the theme of the Powers, either in a complementary or contrasting fashion, is Rudolf Bultmann.[39] Bultmann seeks to translate the Powers for an enlightened and scientific age, thus he demythologizes the powers. He does this by interpreting the Powers from an existential point of view.[40] In *New Testament and Mythology*, Bultmann begins by stating,

> The world picture of the New Testament is a mythical world picture. The world is a three-story structure, with earth in the middle, heaven above it, and hell below it. Heaven is the dwelling place of God and of heavenly figures, the angels; the world below is hell, the place of torment. But even the earth is not simply the scene of natural day-to-day occurrences, of foresight and work that reckon with order and regularity; rather, it, too, is a theatre for the working of supernatural powers, God and his angels, Satan and his demons. These supernatural powers intervene in natural occurrences and in the thinking, willing, and acting of human beings; wonders are nothing unusual. Human beings are not their own masters; demons can possess them, and Satan can put bad ideas into their heads.[41]

As Bultmann continues to share the story of the New Testament and the story of redemption, he speaks of it as mythical talk that can be traced back to Jewish apocalypticism and the Gnostic myth of redemption.[42] Bultmann contends that the New Testament authors spoke mythically, in the language of their context. But now, as we are living in a scientific context, "the task of theology [is] to demythologize the Christian proclamation."[43] For Bultmann, the Enlightenment and the development of science and technology means that to expect someone to believe in the New Testament world is to split from reality and live untruthfully.[44] "We cannot use electric lights . . . and at the same time believe in the spirit and wonder world of the New Testament."[45] He contends, "If the New Testament proclamation is to retain its validity, there is nothing to do but to demythologize it."[46]

Bultmann then goes on to describe the task at hand: "Demythologizing seeks to bring out the real intention of the myth, namely, its intention to talk about human existence as grounded in and limited by a transcendent, unworldly power, which is not visible to objectifying thinking."[47] For Bultmann, to demythologize is to interpret Scripture so that it speaks to the existential realities that humanity faces. The purpose is to reveal the truth of the *kerygma* behind the myth.[48] So when speaking of the principalities and powers, he writes,

> The spirit powers represent the reality into which man is placed as one full of conflicts and struggle, a reality which threatens and tempts. Thus, through these mythological conceptions the insight is indirectly expressed that man does not have his life in his hand as if he were his own lord but that he is constantly confronted with the decision of choosing his lord. Beyond this, they also contain the conviction that natural man has always already decided against God, his true Lord, and has let the threatening and tempting world become lord over him.[49]

In relation to the Powers, Bultmann believes that the heart of the *kerygma* is coming to an understanding that people live in a world that is beyond their control, one filled with struggle, temptation, and conflict—and they must choose to which lord they will submit their lives.

Bultmann is to be commended for seeking to translate the message of the New Testament regarding Satan and demons for those shaped by a scientific and materialistic worldview. Others have sought to accommodate to the point of disposing of these themes altogether. Kenyan scholar Kabiro wa Gatumu states, "Demythologisation compels interpreters to pay attention to their pre-understandings and assumptions as they read the text within its religio-cultural and socio-political context."[50] He goes on to say,

> It is by appreciating the context of production [the time the text was written] that we can re-contextualize the Pauline texts in the context of reception [our current context] without sneaking our default setting into the text and the context of production. . . . So, even if the New Testament can be interpreted today within a particular frame of reference, which may differ radically from what the text initially addressed, this does not mean today's interpretation is what the text originally meant.[51]

Gatumu reminds us it is crucial to interpret the New Testament so that the past comes alive, illuminating the present with new possibilities—but solid exegesis coupled with reflective hermeneutics is also vital.

In his critique of Bultmann, Moses refers to Barth, writing, "Karl Barth detects that the NT writers are less determined by their inherited cosmology than we are by our contemporary worldview."[52] Although "we may label the world picture of the NT authors as 'magical,' this 'magical' world picture did not prevent the NT authors from taking seriously the efficacy of the powers."[53] Quoting Barth:

> It would be better for us if we were to learn again with the same fearless-ness and freedom to see and to reckon with the fact that even today we still live in a world that has been basically dedemonized already in Jesus Christ, and will be so fully one day. But in the meantime it still needs a good deal of dedemonizing, because even up to our own time it is largely demon-possessed, possessed, that is, by the existence and lordship of similar or, at times, obviously the same lordless forces which the people of the New Testament knew and which have plainly not been broken or even affected, but in many ways intensified and strengthened, by the fact that our view of the world has since those days become a rational and scientific one.[54]

Moses describes what Barth is suggesting: "If we are to undertake a demy-thologizing, it should not be a demythologizing of the concept of the principalities and powers in the NT, but rather the myths of modern powers. What is needed, according to Barth, is for Scripture to demythologize our modern world picture, not the reverse."[55] Thus Bultmann's demythologizing project minimizes the reality of the principalities and powers in an unhelpful way.

HENDRIK BERKHOF

Dawn, Yong, and Moses all point to Berkhof's 1953 publication *Christ and the Powers* as a work that significantly shaped the ongoing conversation on the Powers.[56] After witnessing the rise and fall of Nazism, Berkhof seeks to explain how such evil could have taken place. Berkhof's basic argument is that Paul was, in a sense, demythologizing the concept of the Powers, ultimately identifying them with the structures of human existence and the invisible reality behind them. The nature of the invisible reality behind the social, cultural, economic, and political structures is more ambiguous for Berkhof. He was an early advocate of recognizing systemic, structural evil, which is one of the ways liberationist theologians understand the Powers. His ideas were later adapted and developed further by John Howard Yoder.[57]

First, Berkhof lays out all the Pauline texts that mention the "princi-palities and powers."[58] When Paul uses various terms such as *principalities, powers, thrones,* and *dominions,* Berkhof wonders whether they relate to their function, their names, or to something more inclusive. "If it be the case that their meanings are distinct, this is never made clear, and is therefore not essential for an understanding of Paul's message."[59]

Berkhof recognizes that the terminology Paul uses for "principalities and powers" was not his invention but was borrowed from Jewish apocalyptic writings.[60] And in the rabbinic writings, "two things were always true of the Powers: (1) they are personal, spiritual beings and (2) they influence events on earth, especially events within nature."[61] But Berkhof doesn't want us to assume that Paul is retaining this exact meaning. In reference to the verses "For I am convinced that neither death nor life, neither angels nor demons, neither the present nor the future, nor any powers, neither height nor depth, nor anything else in all creation, will be able to separate us from the love of God, which is in Christ Jesus our Lord" (Rom. 8:38–39), Berkhof states, "If we have begun to think of the Powers as angels or classes of angels, this text is somewhat embarrassing. The angelic names stand here side-by-side with other nouns which certainly do not designate personal spiritual beings."[62] He eventually concludes that Paul's emphasis was not on the principalities and powers being personal-spiritual but rather on how the principalities exert great influence over human affairs.[63]

Such an understanding is supported in Paul's letter to the Corinthians when he writes, "None of the rulers of this age understood it [the hidden wisdom of God], for if they had, they would not have crucified the Lord of glory" (1 Cor. 2:8). Berkhof sees the principalities tied to both religious authorities and the Roman state, recognizing both the visible authorities and the invisible powers behind them.[64] In continuing to emphasize that the principalities are the social realities, he examines the concept of *stoicheia* found in Colossians 2:8, 14, and 20, to which Paul connects the principalities and powers. The principalities to which Paul was concerned people would fall prey "are definite religious and ethical rules, the solid structures within which the pagan and Jewish societies of the day lived and moved. In verse 14 these structures are spoken of as the way in which the principalities and powers rule over men; or rather the powers *are* the structures."[65] Berkhof, in seeking to describe the nature of the powers, connects them with human life and events. He finds a similar pattern in Galatians 4:1–11 with the word *stoicheia*, where Paul is warning the people of Galatia not to return to the miserable forces that had enslaved them before their redemption.

Although the Jewish apocalyptic circles had angels in mind, Berkhof believed that Paul was broadening the nature of the principalities, pointing out that Paul does not emphasize their angelic nature, as in the list found in Romans 8:38.[66] In fact, when discussing the list in this passage in Romans, Berkhof questions why angels are even mentioned, stating that *angelos* simply means God's messengers and that in Luke 7:24 and 9:52 and James 2:25, *angelos* means ordinary human messengers. In addition, he asks whether the nature of these angels is good or bad. If good, how does one understand the texts that speak about combat with them or victory over them? If fallen angels, how can this be understood, considering the creation, preservation, and reconciliation mentioned in Colossians 1:15–20? He states, "The conclusion is obvious; we must set aside the thought that Paul's 'Powers' are angels. Whether they be conceived as persons or as impersonal structures of life and society, they form a category of their own."[67] This is a significant development when it comes to understanding the principalities, one which seems to be adopted by Wink, Ellul, and others.

Moving to Colossians 1:15–17, Berkhof makes the point that Jesus is the key to all of creation, and that creation consists of the visible and invisible, the earthly and heavenly. He says, "Creation has a visible foreground, which is bound together with and dependent on an invisible background. This latter comprises the Powers."[68] When he talks about *stoicheia*, the principalities and powers are the structures, but as he further contemplates the nature of the powers, they are the invisible reality shaping the social realities. Berkhof believes that Paul's understanding of the principalities and powers as not inherently evil is because they were designed to hold life together, to preserve life, and to serve as aids and intermediaries for the purpose of binding people to God. The powers correspond to the orders of creation. In Colossians, the principalities and powers are Christ-created structures designed to give order to life, be it the state, morality, religious rules, or ethics. So although they can be tyrants, they were designed to bring life.[69]

And although the principalities and powers were designed to bring life, humanity experiences them in their fallen state, where they seek to master us. No longer do the principalities and powers bind us to God; they separate us from God, seeking to be gods themselves. The principalities and powers still fulfil half of their role, preserving society from utter chaos, but "by holding the world together, they hold it away from God."[70] Berkhof then relates how, as a student in Berlin, he experienced the principalities and powers at work when Hitler took leadership in Germany. He sensed the powers "in the air" and saw how the principalities and powers grabbed hold of people and separated them from God. He observed,

> The state, politics, class, social struggle, national interest, public opinion, accepted morality, the ideas of decency, humanity, democracy—these give unity and direction to thousands of lives. Yet precisely by giving unity and direction they separate these many lives from the true God; they let us believe that we have found the meaning of existence, whereas they really estrange us from true meaning.[71]

Finally, Berkhof addresses the principalities and powers in redemption and consummation, where human redemption is not simply being relieved of guilt but being set free from the bondage of the powers, over which Christ triumphed. Berkhof brings attention to the fact that the legal demands and regulations mentioned in Colossians 2:13–15 correspond with Jewish and pagan regulations, which are both overcome in Christ.[72] Not only are the powers disarmed, but as Berkhof points out, their reconciliation is spoken of in Colossians 1:19. Berkhof talks about the reconciliation of the powers being strange because reconciliation is typically thought of as something between people, yet these "creatures" will return to their originally good functions.

Berkhof completes his work by writing about the present engagement with the principalities and powers. Although Christ has disarmed and reconciled the powers, there is still the "already and not yet" dimension of engagement; thus the battle continues, as followers of Christ work to help the powers live out their God-intended purposes, where nations function on behalf of the people, where the powers are unmasked, where the people of God in the power of the Spirit build multiethnic communities in which justice and mercy reign and social injustice is resisted.[73]

Berkhof's argument is compelling, which is demonstrated by the number of thoughtful people who have adopted his viewpoint.[74] He makes many contributions: he notices the variety of ways the Powers are talked about in Romans 8:38–39; he shows how "the rulers of the age" relate to the powers being visible and invisible; he connects *stoicheia* with the principalities and powers; and he makes the case through Colossians that principalities and powers are created good, experience fallenness, and are redeemed in Christ. Wink later borrows and develops Berkhof's convincing argument.

Although Berkhof's work is limited to Paul's view of the principalities and powers, one question left unaddressed is that of fallen angels: if they are not a part of the principalities and powers, where do they belong in Berkhof's understanding? Berkhof had no difficulty acknowledging Satan, as he writes when speaking on the persona of the Powers that "it is possible that [Paul] paints them with . . . personal traits because he sees them as tools of a personal Satan."[75] Berkhof does not seem to deny the reality of Satan or demons. He simply makes the case that the Pauline language of principalities and powers should be seen as a completely new creature, the invisible reality behind and connected to the visible reality of social structures. It is helpful to separate the principalities and powers from the devil and the demonic, because their telos is distinctly different. It appears the principalities and powers will be reconciled (Col. 1:15–20), but the devil and his angels seem to have a different telos. Jesus seems to indicate their final doom (Matt. 25:41). How do we seek to understand these divergent views related to understanding the principalities and powers, and what tools might help us better see reality?

A DYNAMIC TYPOLOGY OF THE POWERS

American theologian Hans W. Frei proposed the interplay of two "often contentious, but necessarily mutually exclusive" approaches to Christian theology.[76] One approach gives primary thought to exploring "theology as a philosophical discipline" within the accepted norms of academia.[77] The second approach gives precedence to approaching theology as a discipline within the faith community, an internal self-description.

Frei developed a fivefold typology on the interplay of these approaches. This was adapted by Cambridge professor David Ford as a continuum on which to place various modern theologians who seek to engage contemporary issues through current academic disciplines in conversation with theology.[78] I will use Ford's adaptation to place Arnold, Bultmann, and Berkhof on this continuum, using some of the terms developed by Anglican priest Les Oglesby (see figure 1.1).[79]

At one end of two contrary poles is type one—*the traditionalist*, who seeks to reassert traditional theology without regard for the knowledge humanity has gained in the interval; and at the other end, type five—*the reductionist*, who gives "complete priority to some modern or secular philosophy or worldview, and Christianity in its own terms is only valid insofar as it fits in with that."[80]

Within the center of the two opposite poles would be type three—*the correlator*, who seeks to give equal weight to theology developed within the church and other disciplines of academia (such as anthropology, sociology, and psychology), with the goal of connecting theology to the modern person in a way that makes sense to them.

Finally, there are the two mediating positions on the continuum, type two—*the interpreter*, who gives priority to Christian theology developed within the community of faith "but with serious engagement with its present-day intellectual and cultural context."[81] And type four—*the reinterpreter*, who sees "integration with modernity as more important and even essential to modern theology."[82] The reinterpreter seeks to develop a theological method in line with modern concepts or current concerns of the day (e.g., poverty, racism, ecology, oppression, violence, gender).

TYPE ❶	TYPE ❷	TYPE ❸	TYPE ❹	TYPE ❺
The Traditionalist	The Interpreter	The Correlator	The Reinterpreter	The Reductionist

Figure 1.1 The Ford/Frei Scale

This typology provides a way to analyze Arnold, Bultmann, and Berkhof. At one end of the spectrum is Arnold, who reasserts what he considers to be the first-century understanding of the Powers in continuity with the intertestamental period's fascination with the angelic world, without giving much regard to what has been learned about systemic evil. He sees the principalities and powers as personal spiritual beings. He may be located at one and one-half on the Ford scale, seeking to be faithful with the text, *without* a strong engagement with the current Western context, aside from the revival of the occult. As a result, Arnold minimizes evil found in social structures and fails to provide what is needed in terms of speaking truth to day-to-day social realities.

Ford places Bultmann on this scale at type four. Bultmann uses existentialism to interpret the Scriptures, starting with the human subject. He does this by demythologizing the Powers, thereby abandoning what may have been the original understanding of the Powers (context of production) in favor of explaining the Powers as a world that is beyond humanity's control. Although this view accommodates the scientific worldview of modernity (context of reception), it minimizes the text in context and does not apply so well in a postmodern setting, where a variety of views of reality are valued.

Berkhof, seeking to hold tightly to the text of production, sees Paul in "a sense" demythologizing the powers. Although Bultmann took a demythologizing approach to the text, Berkhof makes the case that Paul was *in some ways* demythologizing the principalities and powers. However, Berkhof does not simply minimize the principalities to the structure; he gives credence to the invisible spirituality behind the structure. Although Berkhof seems uncomfortable with those who emphasize angels, giving more preference to the principalities and powers as structures of society, he never reduces the principalities to just the structure. Berkhof's careful work at understanding the principalities and powers in the context and realities of World War II would be classified as a type three, where he is "devoted to shaping Christian practices and teaching in dialogue with modern philosophies, culture and social practices."[83] Figure 1.2 places each of these authors on the Ford/Frei continuum.

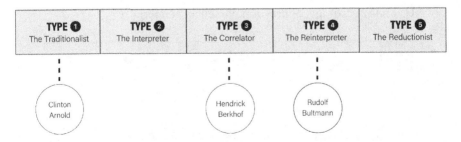

Figure 1.2. Arnold, Berkhof, and Bultmann on the Ford/Frei Scale

From this initial analysis, it is clear that faithfully contextualizing a theology of the Powers is a difficult hermeneutical task. And although this analysis has primarily focused on seeking to understand the principalities and powers, as we journey together, we will also be gaining a fresh understanding of Satan and the demonic in a way that brings the text to life and helps us to better engage the Powers that seek to subvert us as leaders. This will require an engagement with Walter Wink, René Girard, and William Stringfellow, as their corpus of work is centered on the Powers and offers great insight into diagnosing and unmasking the Powers of domination in the church.

But first it is important for us to understand the nature of missional leadership and how missional theology has sought to avert a colonialist and triumphalist approach to mission.

2

THE NEED FOR MISSIONAL LEADERSHIP

In 2010, missiologist Alan Roxburgh noted, "The word 'missional' seems to have traveled the remarkable path of going from obscurity to banality in only one decade."[1] More than a decade later, it seems we find ourselves in a similar position. The term *missional* is used in a number of different circles, with different understandings. Because the context for this book is missional leadership, it is important to clearly define the concept and explore some of the developments in missiology and the subsequent implications for missional leadership.

Examining missional leadership could be approached in a variety of ways. One method would be to conduct a wide literature review, seeking to synthesize the work of those representing the primary missional streams that author and professor David Fitch has identified: The Missional Network (TMN), which descends from the Gospel and Our Culture Network (GOCN); the missional evangelicals (MEs); and the neo-Anabaptist missional (NAM).[2] Another approach would be to conduct a deep literature review, focusing intently on texts that are both seminal and analytical. This latter method—a deep review—is preferable, because as the missional leadership conversation has developed and new books are published, they tend to elaborate and expand on the themes developed in the seminal work *Missional Church*, edited by Darrell Guder, which remains a highly influential academic work in missional theology and ecclesiology. In this chapter, I engage the work of Craig Van Gelder and Alan Roxburgh, both of whom contributed to *Missional Church*. Van Gelder later critically engaged *Missional Church* with the help of Dwight J. Zscheile in their book *The Missional Church in Perspective: Mapping Trends and Shaping the Conversation*.[3] This critical engagement not only maps out the evolution of the missional conversation since *Missional Church*, but it also seeks to expand the conversation in ways that intersect with the scope of this book. Roxburgh was the primary author of the chapter "Missional Leadership: Equipping God's People for Leadership" in *Missional Church*, as well as the coauthor of other missional books, including *The Missional Leader* with Fred Romanuk.[4] As noted by Fitch, both Van Gelder and Roxburgh are not only part of the original six researchers for *Missional Church*, but also through their prolific writing and consulting work with churches and denominations, they have significantly shaped the missional conversation across North America.[5]

THE MISSHAPING OF LEADERSHIP IN THE CHURCH

It is important to acknowledge the impact of Christendom on both mission and church leadership. Darrell Guder defines Christendom as a "system of church-state partnership and cultural hegemony in which the Christian religion was the protected and privileged religion of society and the church its legally established institutional form."[6] Though medieval monastic orders led by the likes of St. Patrick (432 CE) and St. Francis (1209 CE) remained faithful to mission, for many who lived under Christendom, missiology and ecclesiology were bifurcated and ecclesial leadership was reduced to maintenance mode.[7] In addition, the melding of the church with the state in Northern Europe opened the church to forces that malformed ecclesial leadership.

Van Gelder notes, "Within a Christendom worldview, the church and the world occupied the same location: the social reality of the church represented the same social reality of the world within that particular context."[8] It was therefore assumed mission was something that happened in other countries and there was no need for mission in the West. Van Gelder writes, "The developments that gave birth to the modern missions movement unfortunately led to the conception of church and mission as two distinct entities. This dichotomy was fully established within the institutional and organizational life of Protestant Christianity at the beginning of the twentieth century."[9] Author and missiologist Michael Goheen's description of this bifurcation of ecclesiology and missiology helps to clarify the nature of the problem and the need to reframe the church and leadership:

- Mission and church are separated. There are two different and parallel institutional bodies—groups committed to the missionary enterprise and local congregations who support it.
- This leads to churches without mission and missionary organizations that are not churches. Churches are reduced to their pastoral role and become introverted. Mission organizations carry on their work outside of ecclesial structures.
- The world is divided into the Christian West (home base) and the non-Christian non-West (mission field).
- There is no need for mission in the West. The West is already Christian and therefore only evangelism of individuals is needed. The critical or prophetic challenge to culture is eclipsed by a

Christendom mindset and ecclesiology where the church is seen as part of the broader Christian culture.[10]

Ecclesial leadership has been significantly shaped by the dichotomization of ecclesiology and missiology. Roxburgh writes, "History and culture affect our present understanding of church leadership, and in North America two movements in particular have dramatically informed our present understanding of such leadership rules. They are Christendom and modernity."[11]

CHRISTENDOM: FROM APOSTLES TO PRIESTS

For Roxburgh, Christendom reshaped ecclesial leadership from apostles to priests. The priestly religious order developed to the detriment of apostolic leadership. "Amid this transposition in leadership, then, rank and role increasingly displaced the New Testament experience of gift and charisma."[12] The apostolic band of missionary people "became a religious organization in which the means of grace were sacramentally communicated through an ordained priesthood and the reign of God identified with the church structures and its sacraments."[13] As Christianity became sanctioned by Constantine, and the church and state started to fuse together, "the practices and training of the church's leadership were significantly formed by the assumptions of the empire, even as the empire was itself transformed by the Christian presence at its center."[14] This place of privilege helped to institutionalize the church, further distinguishing clergy from non-clergy. The clergy "functioned as a separate order of society," and "membership in the church through baptism was concomitant with citizenship in the state. Thus mission was politicized and the *missio Dei* completed."[15]

Roxburgh notes that the Reformation did not substantially alter this trajectory. The focus on the marks of the church—"pure doctrine, pure sacramental administration, and pure discipline"—simply moved ecclesial leadership from priests to pedagogues, where teaching and preaching became the primary focus for ecclesial leadership.[16] A noted exception are the Radical Reformers, who refused to be co-opted by Christendom and sought to "recover a more apostolic and functional leadership based on neither a priestly-sacerdotal nor pastoral-pedagogue model of leadership."[17]

MODERNITY: FROM PEDAGOGUES TO PROFESSIONALS

The second shift was modernity. The introduction of the Enlightenment initiated the fall of Christendom, and according to Roxburgh, pedagogues gave way to professionals, where leaders became counselors, managers, and technicians.[18] He notes that these revised images of ecclesial leadership sought to keep church leadership at the center of culture and that the church "missed an opportunity to recover a missional identity. The problem with this move was not that it was adaptive to its cultural context but instead that its prime motivation was to regain influence at the center rather than engage the culture with the gospel."[19]

The professional-counselor approach reduced the gospel by centering on the human potential of private individuals; the manager sought to develop an organization "shaped to meet the spiritual needs of consumers and to maximize market penetration for numerical growth"; and the technician sought to control outcomes with the ascendancy of technique.[20] Roxburgh observes that as these professional forms of leadership began to displace older forms, they did so without any critical evaluation, and as a result, "their presuppositions and functionality, [drove] the agendas of church leadership and [became] operational ecclesiologies in and of themselves."[21]

A MISSIONAL CHURCH NEEDS MISSIONAL LEADERSHIP

As missional theology developed, it became apparent that ecclesial leadership needed reshaping. When the words *missional* and *church* are used together, they essentially note the reuniting of missiology and ecclesiology. Van Gelder outlines five primary theological developments that began to fuse missiology and ecclesiology back together. These five developments—in addition to the need to integrate missiology and ecclesiology (church and mission/missions)—comprise the roots of the missional church "tree" found in the introduction of *The Missional Church in Perspective*.[22] They include

- a Trinitarian missiology;
- *missio Dei;*
- the reign (kingdom) of God;
- the church's missionary nature; and
- a missional hermeneutic.[23]

Van Gelder states that above these roots sits the book *Missional Church* as the trunk, out of which grows four primary branches. Each of these branches describes how the missional conversation has been taking place in North America since the publication of *Missional Church*, as well as to what degree of accuracy they use the term missional:

- The *discovering* branch reflects the least understanding of missional church.
- The *utilizing* branch represents an understanding of some of the concepts.
- The *engaging* branch reflects a fuller understanding.
- The *extending* branch represents those who completely understand

the roots and are expanding and extending the missional conversation in positive ways.

Keep this missional tree illustration with the various branches in mind, as after examining the nature of missional leadership, I will refer to this metaphor again.

Besides the reconnection of church and mission, theological developments starting in the first half of the twentieth century focused on the *identity* of God, with the help of Karl Barth. A Trinitarian missiology and *missio Dei* speak to the social and sending nature of God, emphasizing that the starting point for mission is God, and the church participates in his mission to the world. The concept of *missio Dei* has two primary strains: one emphasizes God working through the church, and the other focuses on God working in creation and the church joining that effort.

Not only was there a growing understanding of the identity and nature of God and the church, but there was also a widening understanding of the nature of the good news through the quest for the historical Jesus, which started in the late nineteenth and early twentieth centuries.[24] Consensus was reached that the central message of Jesus' teaching was the availability of the kingdom of God. This broadened the focus of missional theology to include the reign of God, with its already/not yet dimensions.[25] God was not just interested in saving individuals; there was also a social and cosmic aspect to the good news. Finally, Van Gelder mentions a missional hermeneutic. It was "a transition from a 'theology of mission' to a 'mission theology,' where the larger framework of Scripture was beginning to be viewed from the perspective of the mission of God."[26]

It is within this historical context that Roxburgh seeks to speak to the nature of leadership and the ways in which ecclesial leadership needs to be reshaped and recover practices alien to its current experience.[27] Missional leadership is about "re-forming a collection of consumer needs-centered individuals to live by an alternative narrative."[28] This "alternative" narrative involves eschatology: demonstrating and speaking the "already but not yet reign" (kingdom) of God, the telos reshapes the identity of the church, and the work of leadership "takes seriously the creation of a covenant community as sign and foretaste, agent and instrument of the reign of God."[29] Roxburgh uses the metaphor "pilgrim people," because the church's identity ought not be defined in static terms but by its direction, which has both missionary and eschatological dimensions.[30]

Roxburgh makes a solid case for this community to contain a centered set as well as a bounded set. The centered set invites new people to participate in a journey shaped by the reign of God; the bounded set within the centered set is a covenant community whose identity as a pilgrim people shapes an alternative way of life.[31] This narrative in turn shapes the missional nature of the church and shapes the work of leadership in its context. "Missional leaders [should] focus their time, energy, and thinking on the formation of this covenant people" engaging in "spiritual disciplines of a common life, disciplines of learning, and disciplines of mission."[32] The centered set requires leaders to know how to welcome others on this journey and engage in mission contextually, while the bounded set requires leaders to form missional orders, that is, communities of sent people who are shaped by the reign of God.[33] Roxburgh says, "This can only happen as leaders themselves participate in such orders."[34] He notes that modeling is an important concept, pointing to Lesslie Newbigin's idea that Jesus did not sit in the headquarters and send the disciples out, but instead led them into battle, saying "follow me."[35] Thus "the location of the leadership in this process is at the front," leading the congregation toward the telos—life in God and God's reign.[36]

Roxburgh believes this leadership task requires a plurality of leaders.[37] He points out that the church needs apostles, prophets, and evangelists to come alongside pastors and teachers.[38] Roxburgh notes that "apostolic, missional leadership will be learned through apprenticeship within communities."[39] In addition, he suggests missional leadership is formed by a deep sense of vocational call, the development of character, and academic and intellectual competency; in this way the missional leader is "biblically informed and theologically grounded."[40] Finally, there is an essential need to develop skills for communal spiritual formation.[41]

THE IDENTITY OF THE LEADER

In their book *The Missional Leader*, after examining the context and challenge of missional leadership, Roxburgh and Romanuk explore the shape and work of the missional leader. The shape of the missional leader is based on the self-identity of the leader, which Roxburgh and Romanuk consider foundational, noting, "Self-identity is the foundation on which everything else is constructed."[42] They consider the leader's maturity, trust, and integrity to be of first importance. The work of the missional leader—which involves cultivating people (discipleship), forming mission environments, and engaging context—depends entirely upon the *identity* of the leader. For our identity comes from God and shapes our praxis. I explore the importance of our identity shortly.

The telos is also important. The chief end of the missional leader is to be found in the life of God, which in turn shapes the identity of the leader as well as the work of the leader. All three work together, as "leadership is about identity formed out of knowing the *telos*, which in turn can be known only from participating in the life of God."[43] Roxburgh and Romanuk warn leaders not to "borrow its categories for leadership from other arenas and impose them on its life. To do so is to borrow a purpose and end that are not shaped out of this fundamental participation with God."[44] Roxburgh makes the case that when leaders borrow from business or corporate governance, the character and identity of the leader move away from the individual being formed as God's person in the world for the good of the world. The implication here is that a leader whose identity and telos are distorted will inevitably lead to a malformed church as well. When missional leaders take their identity and telos from business, people in the congregation start to feel like cogs in a wheel or workers on an assembly line instead of beings formed by God for his purposes.

Having now gained a historical overview of the development of missional theology and how it helps us understand the nature of the missional church and missional leadership, I want to explore some significant themes that have surfaced and engage these themes with the help of other missional thinkers and practitioners.

SIGNIFICANT THEMES IN MISSIONAL LEADERSHIP

Together, Van Gelder and Roxburgh help to form an understanding of the nature of the missional church and the need for missional leaders. Yet it seems that the domineering leadership crises we currently face in the church accent the need for further development. Part of Van Gelder's motivation for writing *The Missional Church in Perspective* was to critique the book *Missional Church*, a book in which he contributes. Thus, after Van Gelder explores the roots of the missional church tree, which reunite missiology and ecclesiology, he brings three critiques. He points out the underdeveloped concepts, the concepts which seem to be in conflict with each other, and he seeks to address themes not explored in *Missional Church* that should have been.[45]

Van Gelder and Zscheile believe it was a mistake not to bring the social Trinity (the interrelatedness of the Father, Son, and Spirit and how that ought to shape the church) into the conversation, and they claim that in some chapters, *Missional Church* fails to pay attention to the Holy Spirit. This claim seems to have some validity. They also seek to make the case that those in the discovery and utilizing branches should (1) move from imitation of God to participation with God and (2) hold a more positive view of the culture/world.

I contend that both these viewpoints need to be challenged, and I explain why shortly. Before exploring this, it is important to note a key area that was unintentionally minimized in Van Gelder's own critique and until recently has been a key area that seems to have been neglected in the missional conversation at large: *missional spirituality.*

LEADERSHIP FORMATION NEEDS MISSIONAL SPIRITUALITY

As Van Gelder offers his constructive critique of *Missional Church* and its underdeveloped concepts and unresolved theological issues, there is near silence regarding missional spirituality, which involves an approach to spiritual formation where we ground our sense of identity in Christ by "embodying God's love from the inside out."[46] Missional spirituality is about the healthy formation of "sent ones." Van Gelder's work in the first chapter of *The Missional Church in Perspective* simply recalls the historical development of the missional church and identifies the theological concepts that make up the roots of the missional church tree. Van Gelder had the opportunity to examine the underdeveloped ideas of the earlier book and yet failed to explore the notion of missional spirituality. With that said, both Van Gelder and Zscheile believe that the roots of the missional tree must be embodied realities rather than mere theoretical theological understandings. In addition, they assert the precedence of identity in God, emphasizing the sequence of the being, doing, and organizing of the church: "The church *is*. The church *does* what it is. The church *organizes* what it does."[47] Both of these beliefs go some way toward acknowledging the importance of embodying inner beliefs, but missional spirituality itself is overlooked.

Although missional spirituality is not specified by Van Gelder as an unaddressed theme in the historical conversation, the final chapter of *The Missional Church in Perspective* does explore the idea of spiritual disciplines becoming more missional. This comes under the book's framework of extending and expanding the missional conversation.[48] Although giving space to missional spirituality in the extension of the branches of the tree is important, it also serves to minimize missional spirituality. Missional spirituality is not simply a branch or a root—it is the very soil in which the missional church tree ought to be planted. If missional spirituality is merely a branch or a root, the status, value, worth, and ultimately, identity of the leader might be found in how well they understand and embody the roots of missional theology. As missional leaders, our call is to be grounded in the Trinitarian life of God, which is embedded in the height, depth, width, and length of God's love (Eph. 3:14–19). In recent years, many thinkers, including Van Gelder, have begun to understand and appreciate the importance of missional spirituality.[49] But what remains undeveloped is helping missional leaders understand how the Powers seek to subvert leadership and a corresponding spirituality that can withstand the Powers' attack. In the pages to come, I seek to demonstrate the importance of missional spirituality in helping leaders overcome a domineering spirit.

THE IDENTITY AND CHARACTER OF THE LEADER

As I noted earlier, Roxburgh and Romanuk assert that the self-identity of the leader is foundational; the work of the missional leader is inextricably linked with his or her character. Considering the growing list of "fallen" pastors, this point must not be diminished. Yet stressing the character of the leader is not unique to Christians. In critiquing how ecclesial leadership in the modern business world has created a CEO approach to leadership—especially in megachurches—Fitch warns of danger when "Jesus becomes a leadership principle applicable across all working environments," as, for example, John Maxwell seeks to do with *The 21 Irrefutable Laws of Leadership.*[50]

Maxwell makes the point that leadership is essentially the same, no matter what occupation one has, whether "you're looking at citizens of ancient Greece, the Hebrews of the Old Testament, the armies of the last two hundred years, the rulers of modern Europe, the pastors in local churches, or the businesspeople of today's global economy. Leadership principles stand the test of time. They are irrefutable."[51] Although character is typically understood as important in all fields, Fitch makes the point that when "there is no direct link between character formed in Christ and what it means to pastor his church," there is no conflict in inviting Bill Clinton to speak at the Willow Creek Leadership Summit for pastors, as he did in 2000. David Staal of the Willow Creek Association said, "Who is better qualified than the president of the United States to talk about leadership?"[52] Fitch cautions that "the implicit bottom-line understanding here is that leadership principles are not determined in specific ways by the person and work of Jesus Christ that demand allegiance to him in order to make sense."[53] Christian leadership, in any realm, ought to connect leadership to Christ.

Roxburgh emphasizes that character is rooted in the narrative and telos of God. "In the Christian story, the *telos* of human life is neither to fulfill oneself in the modern sense of the individual nor the drive to self-actualization or even self-differentiation. Our *telos* is to know God. . . . To know God is to know the Good."[54] And to know God is to live in such a way as to bring him glory. Scripture reveals aspects of the world that would not be understood otherwise; therefore, when considering the nature of missional leadership, it is important to allow the narrative of God to shape our approach to leadership. Leadership in the church ought to be distinct from what is seen in the world. As Roxburgh writes, "Before anything else, leadership is about our identity as people who are participating in God's life and given work to be done in the world." For Roxburgh, telos shapes both identity and praxis, and "leadership is fundamentally about forming character and living a life shaped by virtue."[55]

Roxburgh solidly grounds missional leadership in Christ and the life of God. He demonstrates the ability to discern how leaders can become misshapen, but what remains undeveloped is helping missional leaders understand how the Powers seek to subvert leadership and develop a corresponding spirituality that can withstand the Powers' attack. Despite showing an awareness of the work of the Powers throughout his writing, Roxburgh rarely addresses the issue directly.[56] He recognizes that "any missional leadership must face the temptation to reduce the life of the church solely to abilities and skills offered by the principalities and powers" and that leadership requires a spirituality that allows leaders to faithfully follow Christ.[57] Yet he does not give concrete ways for leaders to name and unmask the powers, thus leaving leaders vulnerable.

As Roxburgh gets to the work of the missional leader, he highlights the importance of the spiritual formation of an alternative community. The imitation-based framework presented throughout this book is designed to help the formation of missional leaders, with the presupposition that spiritual leadership has its own unique challenges specifically related to the Powers. This is seen in the temptations that Jesus faced in the desert at the start of his ministry, where his identity, aims, and methods were tested. The instructions Paul gives Timothy regarding the appointment of leaders are also telling: "A church leader must not be a new believer, because he might become proud, and the devil would cause him to fall" (1 Tim. 3:6 NLT).

MISSIONAL LEADERSHIP AND THE VIEW OF CULTURE/WORLD

Our perception of "the world" affects how readily we acknowledge the Powers. In the second half of their book, Van Gelder and Zscheile extend the missional conversation by making the case that the missional church needs to view culture and the world more positively. "At stake is how culture and world are to be viewed: are they to be viewed primarily in positive terms or in negative terms?"[58] Part of their argument relates to how the *missio Dei* intersects with the reign of God. Van Gelder notes that there are five variations of how these terms relate; these are broken into the *specialized*, *generalized*, and *integrated* views, which are represented in table 2.1.

The *specialized* view includes two variants: first, "the church embodies the reign of God"; second, "the church witnesses to the reign of God."[59]

The *generalized* view includes two variants as well: first, "God's mission unfolds through secular history"; second, "God's mission unfolds in the midst of secular history."[60]

The *integrated* view, which Van Gelder prefers, is that "the church participates in God's continuing creation and redemptive mission."[61]

Table 2.1 *Missio Dei* and the Reign of God

View	Variant
Specialized	• The church embodies the reign of God • The church witnesses to the reign of God
Generalized	• God's mission unfolds through secular history • God's mission unfolds in the midst of secular history
Integrated	• The church participates in God's continuing creation and redemptive mission

Van Gelder points out how different chapters in *Missional Church* emphasize different views. Variations on the specialized, generalized, and integrated views of *missio Dei* and the reign of God lead "to confusion regarding how God works in the world in relation to the church and to the reign of God."[62] For Van Gelder, it seems apparent that adopting the integrated view leads one to have a more positive view of culture and the world.

Van Gelder and Zscheile believe that the work of the church is to discern—with the help of Scripture—where God is at work in the world through his Spirit and join him in his redemptive work in the world. In this, they seek to decenter the church and increase appreciation for the work of the Spirit, with the hope of cultivating a humble church that is less vulnerable to colonialism and triumphalism. Missiologist Michael Goheen writes, "The Christian faith became fused with political, cultural, social, economic, military, and religious elements in one theocratic system"[63] This fusion led to a domineering posture of the church, resulting in many atrocities. One way Van Gelder and Zscheile seek to bring a positive view of culture/world is by tying culture to creation through the Trinity, emphasizing God as Creator and incarnational Redeemer, actively bringing creation to its fulfillment. They write, "The world is by no means godforsaken, but rather charged with God's presence and movement and redeemed at the greatest cost: the cross."[64]

Although this is useful, their lack of delineation of the words *culture* and *world* is unhelpful, and they sometimes use the terms together as "culture/world."[65] In their critique of the book *Missional Church*, they point to how some chapters take a more positive view of culture/world (chapters six and seven), and another chapter (chapter five), takes a more negative view of the world. They feel the Anabaptist-inspired vision found in chapter five "portrays the church as a contrast society within a fallen world," in which the role of the church is "to develop an alternative culture to that of the world."[66] Van Gelder and Zscheile do not seem sympathetic to the Anabaptist approach to Scripture. This may be why they seem to de-emphasize the Powers in favor of viewing the world more positively.

The heart of Van Gelder and Zscheile's argument is that the church ought to join what God is already doing in the world through his Spirit, and our posture toward the world should value "the themes of reciprocity, mutuality, and vulnerability" found in the inner life of the Trinity. They contend,

> These themes also shape the missional church's engagement with culture and the world. To view the world as a place of hospitality (as in Luke 10) is to recognize the gifts that lie within it to be shared—gifts that inform and enrich our own experience and understanding of the gospel.[67]

Despite arguing for a more positive view of culture/world, they do not propose the church should see it uncritically. They write, "It is important to remember that culture is part of creation. Culture in all its diversity as such, is infused with the promise of God's creative presence and the Spirit, and at the same time liable to distortion through human sin."[68]

Although they aim to cultivate a humbler church and emphasize the ways in which God is at work in the world, Van Gelder and Zscheile seem to minimize what William Stringfellow describes as "the ubiquity of the fall." The pervasiveness of the fall not only affects people made in the image of God but also affects social and cosmic realities.[69] For Stringfellow, to minimize the fall is to live in an illusion without hope of true redemption. Stringfellow sought to "view this world with unflinching, resilient realism," recognizing the fall is greater than human sin.[70]

Van Gelder and Zscheile give a helpful history of the development of culture, noting that it is a "highly contested" concept with its "complicated history";[71] however, it seems a mistake to make *culture* and *world* synonymous. *Culture* is a concept developed relatively recently through anthropology; *the world* is a concept developed through Scripture.[72] In not taking the time to define the word *world*, and in their desire for the church to view the world and culture more positively, Van Gelder and Zscheile place greater emphasis on the positive ways Scripture uses *world*, with just a hint of caution regarding the ways the Scripture talks about *world* negatively. For example, after a long, eloquent argument of God's work in the world, they write that the world "is liable to distortion through human sin."[73]

Walter Wink, in his trilogy on the Powers, presents a nuanced view of the *world*, distinguishing between

- the good world God has made (creation);
- the world that he loves (people); and
- the world as "human sociological realms that exist in estrangement from God" (the Powers).[74]

A robust theology of the Powers can enable a view of creation and redemption that is both helpful and realistic. If, as leaders in the church, we have a fuller understanding of the Powers, we will have greater clarity on how to view culture and the world.

The need to understand the Powers is evident in the work of Newbigin, who is widely recognized as the father of the missional church movement; he inspired the writing of *Missional Church*.[75] Van Gelder does not give much attention to the Powers in his critique of *Missional Church*. He is critical of the sole chapter that emphasizes the Powers, primarily because of how the fallenness of the world is accented. This leads to a more negative view of the world as well as a seemingly more limited understanding of the *missio Dei* because it favors a specialized view as opposed to an integrated one.[76] Yet Newbigin devotes an entire chapter to the theme of the Powers in his groundbreaking book *The Gospel in a Pluralist Society*. His chapter titled "Principalities, Powers, and People" heightens awareness of how the fall included not just people but also social and cosmic realities. Reflecting on this neglected theme that finds prominence in Scriptures, he writes,

> I refer to the whole mass of teaching in St. Paul's letters about what are variously called principalities, powers, dominions, thrones, authorities, rulers, angels, and other names. With these we must also look at what the Gospels have to say about hostile spiritual powers, about Satan, and about what the Fourth Gospel calls "the ruler of this world." If I am not mistaken, most scholarly readers of the New Testament in the past 150 years have regarded all this language as something . . . which we have grown out of. . . . The domination of a reductionist materialism, which supposed that when we had discovered the atomic and molecular and biological facts about any phenomenon we had explained it, has prevented us from discerning the realities that Paul and other New Testament writers are talking about, and they *are* realities. . . . we find such words on almost every page.[77]

Newbigin saw the necessity of understanding the work of the Powers in relation to culture and the world, highlighting the prominence of the theme in the New Testament.

As I mentioned earlier, a renewed academic interest in the Powers took place after World War II, as people sought an explanation for its horrors. It has been argued that those in the German church who were complicit with Hitler had a very different theological approach from those who held to the Barmen Declaration.[78] It is important to note that those who led the resistance—individuals such as Bonhoeffer and Barth—were alert to the Powers. Although Newbigin's treatment demonstrates a solid understanding of the Powers and the importance of tending to them, his acknowledged debt to Wink is evident.[79] Thus it is important to engage Wink on the Powers.

Missiologist and theologian David Bosch lived in the context of South African apartheid, where the Powers of racism reigned. Noting this, Anabaptist and Bosch scholar George Van Wyngaard states that, for Bosch, "any ecclesiology that withdraws from society, on the one hand, or becomes indistinguishable from society on the other hand" is not a missionary ecclesiology, and that "the constructive argument for a missionary ecclesiology always takes into account the society in which we are to be church."[80]

It is evident that the Powers of racism shaped Bosch's careful understanding of the nature of the relationship of God-world-church—or perhaps more accurately, God-church-world. The evidence suggests that one's social location influences how alert one is—as well as how much weight one gives—to the Powers. Although the church in the global South recognizes how the Powers shape everyday life, many of us, with our comfortable lives in the West, seem oblivious to the Powers and how they are at work in our world. Newbigin registers a similar neo-Anabaptist sentiment in the following statement: "The most important contribution which the Church can make to a new social order is to be itself a new social order."[81]

Roxburgh, on the other hand, by drawing attention to how false narratives and an uncritically adopted telos can misshape a leader's identity and work, demonstrates an understanding of how the Powers work. He seems more sympathetic to the Anabaptists than Van Gelder does, and he notes how the Radical Reformers were able to resist being co-opted by Christendom. He emphasizes that the central work of the missional leader is forming the people of God for a missional future. He insightfully quotes Alan Kreider, an American Mennonite historian, who traces the changes of the "meaning and means conversion" from the early church to the time of Charlemagne (Charles the Great).[82] Kreider writes, "Conversion, which had made Christians into distinctive people—resident aliens—now was something that made people ordinary, not resident aliens but simply residents."[83] Roxburgh and Romanuk note how this shift changed the focus of leadership during Christendom "from formation of a people as an alternative society of God's future to oversight of orthodoxy, proper administration of the sacraments, and regulation of spiritualized and privatized ethical practices increasingly disconnected from any biblical or theological understanding of the *ecclesia* as the people of God."[84] Roxburgh displays an understanding of the work of the Powers but does not give enough assistance in helping missional leaders to clearly name, unmask, and engage the powers—to use Wink's language.

MISSIONAL LEADERSHIP AND THE IMPORTANCE OF IMITATION

Van Gelder and Zscheile assert that those in the discovering and utilizing branches of the missional tree put too much emphasis on a "mere *imitation* of God's life and mission."[85] They give two reasons for the need to move "from imitation to participation."[86] They write, "First the stress on human agency. It is up to us to realize the perfect trinitarian model of community or to enact the life of Jesus through our own performance."[87] They mention that this does not take our personal and corporate sin seriously enough. "Second, God's own Trinitarian involvement in the world . . . is rendered largely irrelevant. Mission is something humans do, rather than primarily an attribute of God in which humans (and the church) participate."[88] With the goal of correcting the imperialist and colonialist tendencies of the past and present, they are seeking to help those who have a renewed focus on Christology to have a more "fully trinitarian understanding of Christ."[89]

Although the larger argument has merit in the sense of fully participating in the life of God and appreciating the work of the Trinity, minimizing the imitation of Christ holds potential dangers. First, one of the underlying assumptions Van Gelder and Zscheile seem to make is that imitation is limited to external behavior. Per René Girard, humans are imitative by nature, but the primary way we imitate is internally, through desire, which is then expressed externally, through behaviors. Leaders will either imitate Christ, as exemplar of the *missio Dei*, or Satan, as exemplar of fallenness and rebellion. Instead of minimizing the need for imitation, I will explore the notion that the best starting point for participating in the full life of the Trinity is to imitate Christ. As disciples imitate Christ—not simply by their behavior but primarily through their desires, as Girard states—we will desire the Father as Jesus desires the Father. And as we participate in the life of God, our desire to imitate Christ is increased. Additionally, as we seek to imitate Christ, we will also depend on the power of the Spirit, as Christ did. In other words, true imitation *leads to* participation. Participation can also lead to greater imitation, both inwardly with our desires and outwardly through our actions. But without a concrete, incarnate Christ to imitate, leaders could easily co-opt the language of the "Spirit" to justify domineering leadership. For example, it has been pointed out in the *Rise and Fall of Mars Hill* podcast how Driscoll would often justify his actions, under the assumption that the Spirit had directed him, even if his actions did not demonstrate the fruit of the Spirit.[90]

Fitch, in his desire to bring the neo-Anabaptist perspective into the missional conversation alongside The Missional Network (TMN) and the missional evangelicals (MEs), offers some strengths and weaknesses to the missional stream identified with Van Gelder.[91] Fitch's argument lends itself to *maximizing our imitation of Christ*. He recalls that following World War II, debates regarding past Western missionary endeavors centered on two criticisms: *ecclesiocentrism* and *Christocentrism*. Ecclesiocentrism was blamed for "pervert[ing] mission into a form of cultural colonialism."[92] Christocentrism was charged with causing the church in the West to be "overly focused on the second person of the Trinity in terms of God's work in the world, almost to the exclusion of the other two persons of the Trinity."[93] In addition, "This focus worked to locate salvation in a past (somewhat static) event of God's work in Christ . . . This served to detach God from being active in the world today."[94] Some—most notably, missiologist J. C. Hoekendijk— even argued "that such Christocentrism was colonialist in impulse. It was the means by which other religions were excluded from salvation."[95] Fitch acknowledges that each stream of the missional conversation (TMN, MEs, and NAM) seeks to deal with the church's improper use of power.[96] But he explores how this can best be done through a comparison of the streams.

Fitch is on point when noting that Van Gelder's missional stream (TMN) deals with Christocentrism by prioritizing "the Spirit's work in the world . . . the church finds its location in the world through discerning the Spirit."[97] Here, in regard to ecclesiocentrism, they decenter "the church within the mission of God."[98] Thus, God-world-church is their preferred order of relationship.[99] Fitch believes that the strength of this missional stream consists in its ability to lead churches into deep engagement with their context. "They have shaped a new praxis for cultivating imagination in churches for the way God works in the world."[100] Yet he locates their weakness in their strength:

> The intense focus on the Spirit's work in the world, and locating the church in that work, can separate the discernment of God's work in the world from Jesus Christ. Shifting the starting point of ecclesial imagination . . . from Jesus Christ (and traditional practices of the church) to the Spirit in the world can leave the church open to losing itself in attempting to see God at work in the world.[101]

While giving other critiques, he asks two key questions: "Without the social formation of a church in its historical practices, how do we avoid getting caught up and absorbed in the world? How do we check ourselves from taking back the agency of mission from God and putting it on our own backs again?"[102]

The missional evangelicals—the second stream of missional writers Fitch highlights, headed by prolific authors Alan Hirsch and Michael Frost—have been prominent in the missional conversation. They, along with the TMN, view the *missio Dei* as their starting point, where they seek to overturn ecclesiocentrism with a renewed focus on Jesus. Fitch writes, "The MEs prioritize an individual discipleship in the ways of Jesus, from which the church is a result."[103] This is confirmed by how Frost and Hirsch articulate the methodological flow of the missional church. "Christology must determine missiology (our purpose and function in this world), which in turn must determine ecclesiology (the cultural forms and expressions of the church)."[104] For the MEs, the church follows mission because "ecclesiology is the most fluid of the doctrines. The church is a dynamic cultural expression of the people of God in any given place."[105] Thus communities are formed incarnationally in their cultural context.

Fitch believes the MEs' strength is in their ability to embody an incarnational approach to mission, which can connect to people groups estranged from current forms of church. He considers their weakness to be "in their Christocentrism and the individualism that lies at the heart of it. . . . and because this Christology is accessed through the individual encounter, the resultant mission is individualized."[106] For Fitch, this results in two further weaknesses: first, because ecclesiology follows Christology and missiology, "this individualism can undercut the development of a people as an alternative sociality, in a context that can give witness to Christ's Kingdom as a way of life. . . . the emphasis on incarnational living and church as an afterward development risks undercutting mission."[107] The second potential weakness Fitch points out is "the personal Jesus can easily become captive to a particular culture. The MEs assume an immediate access to Jesus for individuals if they just open themselves to Scripture."[108] For Fitch, the evangelical confidence in the ability to get "Jesus right" as opposed to adopting an enculturated form of Jesus brings concern of a new type of colonialism. He writes, "How do we avoid new colonialism that imposes our Christ on others?"[109] He suggests what is needed is a Christology "that has its bearings in a historic social practice, which extends Christ's real presence corporately, inhabiting and birthing communities unique to each new context."[110] Ultimately, the advice he gives to the MEs is that they "must avoid the colonialist temptation to universalize [their] own experiences and interpretations of Christ and to make them universal for all contexts."[111]

Fitch, in seeking to bring the neo-Anabaptist missional stream perspective, adopts an alternative approach to the "problems" of Christocentrism and ecclesiocentrism. Fitch recommends an "incarnation-centered Trinitarian theology," meaning that the incarnation is the "focal point for understanding how God works in the world."[112] The neo-Anabaptist missional perspective starts with the sending Trinity, the difference being the following:

> The emphasis falls on the Spirit extending the work of the incarnation through the twofold work of the Son into the world. First, there is the work of the Son over the whole world via the reign of Christ (through the Spirit), who now sits at the right hand of the Father as the lamb that was slain (a more specific version of *missio Dei*). In addition there is a second work of the Son through the Spirit extending the continuing presence of Christ via the church as his body in the world. The Incarnation becomes the focal point from which God launches a twofold work of Christ into the world. His reign over the whole world becomes visible via his presence in the church.[113]

One danger of this view Fitch names is that by locating a "special presence of Christ in the practice of church, the church itself may seek to exert human control over Christ and the benefits of salvation in the world."[114] This is the very critique the Reformation leveled against Roman Catholicism.[115] In countering this weakness, Fitch says that Christ cannot be controlled. In addition, "Christ's reign in the church can never be triumphalist because the community follows the logic of incarnation: humility, vulnerability, submission to God's work in the world. Apart from this submission to his work, his vulnerable nonviolent presence in the world, Christ's power and authority are lost. In this situation there can be no witness."[116]

To summarize his argument, this incarnation-centered Trinitarian theology "maintains Christ's center as Lord bringing in the Kingdom (Christocentrism) and the centrality of the church as the means of God's witness (ecclesiocentrism)."[117] At the same time, it does not limit the work of God to the church, nor does it lend itself to a sense of triumphalism "of a Christocentric church in the world (because he rules as the lamb, non-coercively, as one to whom the church must submit and be present)."[118]

Considering these options, Fitch's perspective seems most logical, for the telos of the church is to reach the full stature of Christ (Eph. 4:11–13 ESV), by the power of the Spirit. Fitch's argument lends itself to recognize the need to *maximize our imitation of Christ* through a historical, communal, ecclesial understanding of Christ instead of speaking in ways that might minimize this logic. For in Christ, Christians have God in concreteness. This might be why during Hitler's rise in Germany, where the Powers were clearly at work, Bonhoeffer (in his book *Discipleship*) makes a clarion call to imitate Christ. The need of our day is not to minimize imitation but instead to embody it in Trinitarian ways.

While Van Gelder and Zscheile seem to minimize the imitation of Christ, Roxburgh wisely accents the theme of imitation, as he calls leaders to lead in mission and in the spiritual formation of the community by example, living a life worth imitating. When summarizing the role of the leader to lead the congregation toward the reign of God, he writes, "Leadership is a calling that both engages the context with the gospel and leads in the formation of the disciplined community. Being at the front means that the leadership lives into and incarnates the missional, covenantal future of God's people."[119] In addition, he suggests the best approach for the development of missional leaders is through apprenticeship.[120] He writes, "Apostolic, missional leadership will be learned through apprenticeship within communities. Such leaders will learn firsthand how to live out the practices of community formation that require a profound involvement of the self and deep roots in Bible and theology."[121] As models of what could take place today, Roxburgh points to three positive historic examples of how this training has previously taken place:

- Bonhoeffer's seminary pre-World War II in Germany, "where students lived together in covenant community."
- The Catholic monastic orders.
- John Wesley's "weekly class meetings around a common set of disciplines and commitments."[122]

Proximity gives space for imitation. In this book, I will follow Roxburgh and accent the importance of imitation in developing missional leadership. According to Girard, disciples will model the desires of their leaders, so beyond the need for leaders to model methodology and theological understanding is the need to model a right heart toward God. In chapters six and seven, I develop this concept of mimetic desire, which provides additional motivation for missional leaders to be examples to those whom they lead.

WHY MISSIONAL LEADERSHIP?

Van Gelder and Zscheile and Roxburgh and Romanuk all make a compelling case that missional leadership is imperative in our post-Christendom context, asserting that ecclesial leadership needs to be reshaped. The need to move from solo leaders to shared leadership is not just affirmed by each of them but also by leaders of other missional streams, including the streams represented by Hirsch, Frost, and Fitch. Because this is such an important practice to reclaim, I take five chapters to make the case for polycentric leadership in my book *Creating a Missional Culture*.[123] Polycentric leadership creates a system for community that is neither hierarchical nor flat. Polycentricism assumes that there are many centers of leadership that interrelate. I give contextual, biblical, theological, emotional, and practical reasons for polycentric leadership.[124]

In a post-Christendom context, Roxburgh asserts the need to return to a more apostolic approach to leadership. The pastor/teacher is insufficient, for we now live in a context where apostles, prophets, and evangelists are clearly needed; mission is not solely expressed overseas but is also needed in our context. Hirsch concurs, as he writes, "Quite simply, a missional church needs missional leadership, and it is going to take more than the traditional pastor-teacher role of leadership to pull this off."[125] Fitch, Frost, and other voices consider a return to apostolic leadership (Eph. 4:1–16) to be an important development, not only in missional leadership but also in the missionary shape of the church.[126] I concur, and in *Creating a Missional Culture,* I give a chapter to each of the fivefold, listing their focal concern as well as the telos, or destination, they are seeking to bring the congregation.[127]

Roxburgh asserts that the missional leader fosters a missional imagination for the entire congregation. In other words, missional leadership seeks to unbind the clerical captivity of the church. Ed Stetzer, in a series focusing on the priesthood of all believers, mentions that "people create a religious hierarchy to outsource their religious obligations."[128] Missional leadership recognizes a move from professional "priests" to the "priesthood of all believers."[129] The combination of shared leadership, a reemphasis of apostolic leadership, and the priesthood of all believers helps decenter the leader in healthy ways—both for the leader and for the congregation.

There is a general consensus that identity and telos shape and inform both the work of missional leadership and the leader's posture so that the ends inform the means. These three dimensions of leadership (identity, praxis, and telos) are affirmed by others who have sought to address the dearth of literature about theological reflection on the concept of missional leadership.[130]

However, what is left unaddressed is how the Powers seek to subvert the leader at the contours of leadership. I will develop this throughout these pages, especially in the final chapters, with the help of Stringfellow. He provides a concrete way for missional leaders to name and unmask the powers that seek to subvert them. His understanding will also help us to see how the fallen Powers seek to reshape the very desires of the missional leader.

As I move forward, I will develop the imitation-based framework, and the first part of that framework illustrates how missional leaders are linked to the Powers via mimetic desire. The theme of imitation will hold significance throughout this book and will validate Albert Schweitzer's claim that "example is not the *main* thing in influencing others. It is the *only* thing."[131] In the next chapter, I will demonstrate how the apostle Peter emphasizes the need for leaders to be a good example. And through the work of New Testament scholar Graham Houston, I will work to uncover the imitation-based framework found in 1 Peter 5.

3

DOMINEERING LEADERSHIP IN THE FIRST-CENTURY CHURCH

Domineering leadership is not a new issue—it is as old as sin. Fortunately, it is an issue that is addressed in the New Testament by one of the pillars of the early church: the apostle Peter. Unlike some Christian hagiographies, the Gospels are candid in their portrayals of Peter and the other apostles. For example, we know from the Gospel accounts that Peter not only demonstrated great faith by walking on water, but he also had moments when his faith let him down and he sank. The Gospels highlight Peter's revelation that Jesus was the Messiah as well as Jesus' rebuke shortly after: "Get behind me, Satan!" (Mark 8:33). Peter, along with James and John, had the privilege of seeing Jesus transfigured, but shortly after, he naïvely offered to build three tabernacles for Jesus, Moses, and Elijah. And we know from the Gospel accounts that Peter made emphatic statements about following Jesus until the bitter end, only to deny him a few hours later.

It is interesting that one of the most common apostolic arguments centered on which of them was the greatest.[1] This was in part because each time they sat at a table together, they had to seat themselves according to their perceived rank, a cultural tradition of the day. Jesus constantly had to teach them that to be great is to be a servant—and to be the greatest is to be a slave. Jesus knew that more is caught than taught, so he also modeled this principle. All the way up to the Last Supper, we see the disciples arguing over who is the greatest. And we are told that "Jesus, knew that the Father had put all things under his power, and that he had come from God and was returning to God" (John 13:3). Jesus had all power, was certain of his identity, and wanted to show his disciples the full extent of his love (John 13:1). He did this by rising up from the table, taking off his outer garments, and washing the feet of those who had been arguing about who was the greatest. He then called them to follow his example (John 13:1–17).

Jesus' approach to leadership is not only distinct from the world but is also often distinct from his church today. What can we learn from Peter, who had the opportunity to walk with Jesus and learn from his own failures? I will first seek to summarize Graham Houston's study of 1 Peter. I will then proceed to analyze and engage Houston, suggesting that to strengthen the relationship between missional leadership and the Powers via imitation and desire, I will need to engage Walter Wink and William Stringfellow regarding the Powers and René Girard regarding mimetic desire.

HOW PETER DEALS WITH DOMINEERING LEADERSHIP

In his book *Leading by Example,* Graham Houston seeks to provide a way forward for the problem of domineering leadership that Peter likewise addressed in his day.[2] With thirty-five years of experience as a Christian leader as well as expertise as a New Testament scholar, Houston explores 1 Peter from a practical, theological perspective. He focuses on leadership in the church in Peter's day and how it should inform an approach to leadership today, reflecting on 1 Peter 5:1–9 as a key passage. Addressing the problem of domineering leadership, Peter calls the leaders (elders) of the church not to "lord it over" others but instead to be examples, following the way of Christ. Houston connects the problem of "lording it over" others with leaders' sinful desires to be in control and build their own kingdom. He then connects these desires with the work of the Powers.[3] Addressing the problem of domineering leadership, Houston notes how Peter calls the elders to follow Jesus' example: to live as *resident aliens* in the house of Caesar.[4] Because they are part of the household of God, they have a new identity and are therefore called to live transformed lives so that they might be witnesses of Christ and his way. Houston leverages this key passage to demonstrate how the themes of leadership, example/imitation, desire, and the Powers are found throughout the book of 1 Peter:

> So I exhort the elders among you, as a fellow elder and a witness of the sufferings of Christ, as well as a partaker in the glory that is going to be revealed: shepherd the flock of God that is among you, exercising oversight, not under compulsion, but willingly, as God would have you; not for shameful gain, but eagerly; *not domineering over those in your charge, but being examples to the flock.* And when the chief Shepherd appears, you will receive the unfading crown of glory. Likewise, you who are younger, be subject to the elders. Clothe yourselves, all of you, with humility toward one another, for "God opposes the proud but gives grace to the humble."
>
> Humble yourselves, therefore, under the mighty hand of God so that at the proper time he may exalt you, casting all your anxieties on

him, because he cares for you. *Be sober-minded; be watchful. Your adversary the devil prowls around like a roaring lion, seeking someone to devour.* Resist him, firm in your faith, knowing the same kinds of suffering are being experienced by your brotherhood throughout the world."

1 PET. 5:1–9 ESV, EMPHASES MINE

THE POWER OF IMITATION

Houston reminds us that authoritarianism is not a new problem in the church today, commenting that "'lording it' is singled out by Peter as quite a distinct problem, and I believe it is just as destructive to healthy Christian fellowship in the twenty-first century as it was in the first."[5] It is Houston's contention that when looking at the context of Peter's letter, the leaders in the first century uncritically sought to imitate patterns of leadership in Asia Minor in the same way leaders today uncritically adopt North American marketplace approaches to leadership. "Then, as now, authoritarianism was a real problem."[6] Houston writes,

> We shall try to follow Peter in his concern to avoid inappropriate ways of leading in the churches, especially those which are wedded to insights and influences that are not rooted in biblical modes and tend *uncritically to mimic imported cultural patterns, even when they arise from dominant sources* such as ancient Rome or contemporary America, with their attendant control of much of the communication media.[7] (Emphasis mine.)

Houston unpacks the theme of imitation here. He describes how Jesus both modeled and taught his followers that if they wanted to become great they would need to become servants, and even slaves.[8] "For even the Son of Man did not come to be served, but to serve, and to give his life as a ransom for many" (Mark 10:45).

Continuing to tie the theme of imitation/example with leadership, Houston considers how Peter, as a fellow elder, appeals to the elders to engage in ministry, not for their own gain or to dominate others but to *be examples of Christ*. Houston explores how leaders imitate not only the doing (praxis) of others but also the very being (identity) of others: "It is possible to derive appropriate ways of being and doing from the example of others."[9] He notes, "The Greek word for example found here [1 Peter 5:3] is *typos*, the root of the English word type."[10] To help unpack the meaning of *typos*, Houston uses the analogy of a typewriter: when someone hits letters on the typewriter, it leaves an impression, a mark on the paper. Likewise, "Peter is speaking of leading as making an impression on others, or of leaving a mark."[11]

Because leaders leave a mark (impression) on others, they need to think carefully about their approach to leadership. Houston writes, "In contrast to lording it over all, Peter promotes the imitation of God in Christ as the only valid approach to leading by example."[12] It is only when leaders follow the example of Jesus that they become "good news people."[13] Clarifying this pattern, Houston goes on to demonstrate how imitation operates in two different ways: first, the need for leaders to imitate Christ, and second, the need for leaders to be good models for others in their care.

MISSHAPED DESIRE

Houston highlights the fact that leaders will either be good or poor examples. There is no middle ground. Houston quotes from John's third letter: "I wrote to the church, but Diotrephes, *who loves to be first*, will not welcome us. . . . Dear friend, do not *imitate* what is evil but what is good" (3 John 9, 11, emphases mine).

Here, the theme of leadership and imitation is mentioned again, but this time it is also linked to the desire of the leader: Diotrephes *"loves* to be first."* Houston notes how Diotrephes's desire to be first is evil and should not be imitated. He writes, "So lording it, being overbearing, and loving to be first are all aspects of this problem we might term empire-building, which is the very antithesis of true Christian leadership. Yet such behaviour is often condoned and excused today, despite our claims to be part of the one true catholic and apostolic church."[14]

Houston considers it likely that Peter wrote this letter in Rome, "code-named Babylon (5:13)," under Nero's rule, just before Peter himself was martyred.[15] In this context, Peter felt an urgent need to exhort "the churches with a series of ethical imperatives,"[16] such as, "do not conform to the evil desires you had when you lived in ignorance [1:14] . . . Rid yourselves of all malice and all deceit, hypocrisy, envy and slander [2:1] . . . Abstain from sinful desires [2:11] Live as free people [2:16]."[17] On the positive side of desire, Peter writes, "Crave pure spiritual milk" (2:2). Peter frequently addresses the desires of the church throughout his letter, and therefore desire is a theme Houston repeatedly returns to in his own book, as he considers leadership through Peter's perspective.

As Houston explains why Peter chose to write the book, he draws upon Lauri Thurén's work on 1 Peter. Thurén believes that the "main purpose of I Peter is to intensify the Christian conviction and commitment of people who are tempted to conform to the surrounding society in one way or another."[18] Thurén is persuaded that Peter's audience is convinced of the message but lack the motivation to live differently—the issue here is desire. He asserts that Peter's aim was to give them fresh motivation, partly because of the unjust suffering they had to endure. "He believes that if he can enhance right attitudes and encourage them to be more steadfast in their convictions, this will produce the desired outcome of changed behaviour and lifestyle."[19] Houston consistently reminds us that Peter encourages the church to look to Christ as their example, especially amid spiritual warfare, where their desires could become malformed. "In I Peter the starting point is to focus on the attitude of Christ himself, as Paul does in Phil. 2:1–11, and then to exhort Christians not to live out their lives according to evil human desires, but rather to do the will of God."[20]

THE SUBVERSIVE WORK OF THE POWERS

Houston links these themes of leadership, imitation, and desire and then connects them to the Powers in his chapter "Authorities and Powers." For Houston, "Peter's warning and advice about the powers of evil, and how to handle them, are integral to his entire message in his letter about the place of suffering in the Christian life, and the standard struggles, which all believers must learn to survive."[21] Houston believes Peter's emphasis on the Powers has not been given the attention it deserves.

Houston devotes an entire chapter to the theme of the Powers because of the everyday spiritual warfare believers face and the suffering that leaders should expect—for leaders are no greater than their Master.

> [Peter's] ethical exhortation speaks about real struggles which typify the daily lives of his hearers and himself. Yet he is saying that behind the scenes there is another battle going on, in the spiritual realm. Inhabiting the structures of family, church, and society, as well as invading personal individual experience, there are other authorities and powers at work.[22]

Drawing from the work of Wink, Houston demonstrates how Peter understood evil at three levels: personal, social, and ecclesial.

Houston also chose to focus his attention on the Powers because Peter, like Paul and James, recognized that the Powers seek to subvert the desires of Christian leaders by tempting them to imitate the ways of the devil:

> There are great temptations awaiting all who seek to become teachers and leaders within the churches, and they are held especially accountable to God for the proper exercise of their powers. They dare not *mimic the work of the devil and dominate God's dear ones* but rather must follow Christ's example of servant-leadership and face up to the reality that "power must become incarnate, institutionalized, or systemic" as Walter Wink says.[23] (Emphasis mine.)

Here, once again, Houston makes a clear connection between the concepts of leadership, imitation, and the Powers. For Houston, when Satan is brought up in the context of domineering leadership, it is not a digression but is "part of [Peter's] strategy of exposing evil in the individual Christians, in the community of faith, and in the pagan world around. 'Lording it' is a pattern of behaviour, therefore, which Peter understands to be rooted in the machinations of the devil."[24]

Clarifying this pattern, Houston goes on to demonstrate two distinct ways that imitation should occur in healthy Christian leadership: first, leaders need to imitate Christ, and second, leaders need to be good models for others in their care. "Christian leaders who lord it over God's people are succumbing to the schemes of Satan, as well as failing to model their ministry on the servant-leadership style of Christ, the Chief Shepherd."[25]

Expounding on the aforementioned connection between Peter, Paul, and James on the theme of the Powers, Houston highlights Paul's teaching in multiple places (Eph. 1:21, 3:10, 6:10–20; Rom. 3:38; 1 Thess. 5:8) as well as James's teaching, specifically in James 3:1–4:7. Houston particularly observes the similarities in how Peter and James close their respective passages: "Submit yourselves, then, to God. Resist the devil, and he will flee from you" (James 4:7).[26] Houston reflects on James's understanding that many should not be teachers because they will receive harsher judgment, and he then proceeds to write about the role of the tongue:

> The tongue can be a vehicle for *bitter envy and selfish ambition*, warns James (3:14), but where does all this evil ultimately originate? In his first chapter, James had faced up to the weakness of people under temptation and tells them not to blame God for their own evil desires (1:13–15). But now he decides to *name the powers* which are behind such negative attitudes and actions. Christian leaders should demonstrate their wisdom and understanding, by living good lives in all humility, rather than by worldly wisdom, which "does not come down from heaven, but is *earthly, unspiritual, demonic*. For where you have *envy and selfish ambition*, there you find disorder and every evil practice (3:15–16)."[27] (Emphases mine.)

Houston demonstrates how *desire* and *imitation* are crucial in determining the health of leadership, and he highlights the role of the Powers as the source of worldly wisdom. In pulling together how the evil desires of envy and selfish ambition lead to the problem of domineering behavior by church leaders (all inspired by the Powers), Houston shows how these desires end up misshaping the community: "The situation in the early church is volatile, and human pride can lead to quarrels and fights, and push out humble prayer, so that intercessions and petitions remain unanswered by God. Why? You ask with wrong motives accuses James (Jas. 4:3; 1 Peter 3:6)."[28]

INTRODUCING THE IMITATION-BASED FRAMEWORK

Having examined Houston's exegesis of this passage, I will now analyze and engage his work. If we are going to develop a deeper diagnosis for the problem of domineering leadership in the church, it seems appropriate that the framework would emerge from a passage in Scripture that is addressing this issue head-on. The imitation-based framework—where ecclesial leadership is connected to the Powers through mimetic desire—holds promise in helping us, as missional leaders, to be alert to how the Powers seek to subvert our leadership. In this part of the chapter, I will analyze the various elements of the framework that emerge from Houston's biblical study of 1 Peter, namely the themes of missional leadership, imitation of desire, and imitation of Christ or the Powers.

THE THREE DIRECTIONS OF IMITATION

In relation to leadership and imitation, Houston makes several significant points. First, he establishes three different directions in which imitation can take place. The first two regard the missional leader and whom they seek to imitate: leaders can uncritically mimic what they see in the world (the Powers) *or* they can imitate Christ. The third direction, which he does not fully develop, is the necessity of the leader as an example because of the impression they leave on others. This third area needs clarification and development, as I argue in this book that leaders leave a significant impression, or mark, on others, especially those who look to them as models. Girard will help us to explore this in chapters six and seven.

Uncritically Imitating Triumphalism and Cultural Forms of Leadership. In his work on 1 Peter, Houston makes the case that when Peter is writing about the concept of Christian leadership, he is connecting his thinking with his own stories of leadership, featured in Mark's Gospel.[29] Jesus made a clear impression on Peter. Jesus called Peter to follow him, not just as part of the Twelve but as part of the intimate three, which also included James and John. Houston mentions how Peter has a strong presence in the book of Mark, but he is not cast as a superhero.[30]

As I noted earlier, his failures and mistakes are evident for all to see. Peter's weaknesses are not hidden. Houston writes, "There is no attempt to portray Peter and his friends as larger than life heroes in the Hellenistic traditions which they would have well known and understood."[31] For Houston, Christian leadership in the apostolic communities and those communities following "is not rooted in triumphalism."[32]

Houston contrasts this transparency with the triumphalism he observes in contemporary Western Christian leaders who proclaim themselves and their method of ministry as the answer and seek to have their model uncritically exported to other contexts.[33] He explores in depth the problems of egotism and of "selfism" and contrasts this with the humility that Peter stresses is required for leadership: "God opposes the proud but shows favor to the humble" (1 Pet. 5:5b).

Houston confirms what Roxburgh establishes in his examination of the history of ecclesial leadership. Roxburgh demonstrates how easily leaders tend to uncritically mimic the leadership style of the day, seemingly unaware that a leader's telos and identity not based on Christ will ultimately lead to unfaithful praxis. Peter, reflecting on his journey with Jesus, did not point people to imitate Roman or religious rulers. Peter was confident in pointing others to follow only one person: Jesus, the one who modeled a cruciform love.[34]

The Priority of Imitating Christ. In his study of 1 Peter, Houston confirms David Fitch's argument that the answer to colonialism and triumphalism is not to decenter Christ but to wholeheartedly imitate him. Peter was reminding people who were undergoing suffering that Christ also suffered for them and left them an example of how to live when facing unjust suffering (1 Pet. 2:21). Throughout his letter, Peter lifts Christ up as the concrete example.[35]

In his PhD thesis, "Christ as Example: The *Imitatio Christi* Motive in Biblical and Christian Ethics," scholar and author Soon-Gu Kwon highlights key figures in the history of the church who made a fresh call for God's people to follow and imitate Christ.[36] Starting with the words of Jesus and moving through the Pauline texts, Kwon focuses on Thomas à Kempis, author of *The Imitation of Christ*, which, for Christians, is one of the most-read books in history, second only to the Bible.[37] This book shaped significant leaders in the church, including John Wesley and Dietrich Bonhoeffer. The strength of this book is à Kempis's focus on union and communion with God, dying to self, and living humbly. Wisdom, in his view, is how one lives rather than what one says. Theology helps frame what we think of God, but only a strong missional spirituality can result in a transformed life. Kwon calls this the *monastic* interpretation of *imitatio Christi*. He then moves to Søren Kierkegaard in what he labels an *ascetic* interpretation: "In the ascetic understanding of the imitation of Christ, Christians are to pursue a slow death to the world as a way of imitating Christ."[38] Next, Kwon examines Bonhoeffer, in what Kwon calls a *political* interpretation of following Christ. Bonhoeffer wrote *Discipleship* during the rise of Hitler, when the Powers were in full force. According to Bonhoeffer,

> Discipleship is a commitment to Christ. Because Christ exists, he must be followed. An idea about Christ, a doctrinal system, a general religious recognition of grace or forgiveness of sins does not require discipleship. In truth, it even excludes discipleship; it is inimical to it. One enters into a relationship with an idea by way of knowledge, enthusiasm, perhaps even

by carrying it out, but never by personal obedient discipleship. Christianity without the living Jesus Christ remains necessarily a Christianity without discipleship; and a Christianity without discipleship is always a Christianity without Jesus Christ.[39]

Bonhoeffer gives clarity to the importance of following and imitating Christ and demonstrates the need to make a strong call to follow Christ, especially amid the Powers working so visibly. This rich history of calling the church to model Christ continues to capture the interest of scholars today.[40]

The Power of Imitation. As I noted earlier, in his explanation of Peter calling the elders to be an "example," Houston mentions that the word refers to leaving an impression or mark on others. However, Houston ultimately fails to develop this theme. Girard, in particular, is one of the primary interlocutors for this book because imitation is foundational to his project. Girard makes the case that there is only one way to overcome the Powers, which is to imitate Christ. An important contribution that Girard brings to the rich tradition of *imitatio Christi* is his understanding that imitation most profoundly takes place in the area of desires. In this way, it is evident how imitation of Christ leads followers into the life of the Trinity; for as Christ desires the Father, those who imitate him will desire the Father as well. In the same way, as Christ desires and loves the Spirit, those who imitate him will also desire the Spirit.

THE PREEMINENCE OF DESIRE

Houston demonstrates that desire is a central idea in the letter of James and reminds us of how Peter's entire letter was written to motivate leaders and other recipients to reshape their desire to imitate Christ. In addition, when talking about leadership, we saw how Houston refers to Diotrephes's desire to be first (3 John 1:9) as evil and not something to be imitated. This highlights an apparent link between desire and imitation as well as the contagious nature of desire. Although Houston gives attention to this theme of desire, he doesn't elaborate on the prominence of desire in regard to what it means to be human, nor does he fully integrate the theme of imitation with desire.

One of my goals of developing this imitation-based framework is to help us, as leaders, become aware of our desires, the way that the Powers seek to distort them, and how fully imitating Christ through embodied practices can reshape the telos of our desires toward God, his kingdom, and his righteousness.

In *Desiring the Kingdom,* philosopher and theologian James K. A. Smith articulates a philosophical anthropology that understands humanity not simply as people-as-thinkers, shaped by ideas; or people-as-believers, shaped by faith; but ultimately as people-as-lovers, shaped by desire, which is always aimed toward a telos.[41] In seeking to reframe how education takes place in learning institutions—especially those that are confessional—he asks, "What if education, including higher education, is not primarily about the absorption of ideas and information, but about the *formation* of hearts and desires."[42] Smith recalls that "what distinguishes Augustine's two cities (the earthly city and the city of God) is not ideas or beliefs but *love*."[43] To make his case in support of Augustine, he reviews some of the reasons education today is often approached with this reductive view of people-as-thinkers or people-as-believers instead of people-as-lovers.

Smith articulates how people-as-thinkers—a rationalist or intellectualist picture of humanity, as old as Plato—was revived by Descartes and cultivated through modernity. And although this perspective still tends to dominate a current understanding of human nature, it is ultimately reductive.[44] He believes this rationalist picture of humanity was "absorbed particularly by Protestant Christianity (whether liberal or conservative)" operating on an overly intellectual account of human beings.[45] He calls this "bobble head" Christianity because this approach is so focused on the cognitive, assuming a picture of humanity with "mammoth heads that dwarf an almost non-existent body."[46] In other words, when the church buys into a cognitivist anthropology, pedagogy becomes stunted. For if we just fixate on the mind without addressing the heart, we will not experience the transformation we desire.[47]

This overly cognitive approach to human beings has been contested, especially within the Reformed tradition. Smith describes this move from seeing people-as-thinkers to people-as-believers, saying, "In this alternative anthropology, human persons are understood not as fundamentally thinking machines but rather as believing animals, or essentially religious creatures, defined by a worldview that is pre-rational or supra-rational."[48] With this anthropological understanding, it is not what we think that ultimately defines us but what we believe—"the commitments and trusts that orient our being-in-the-world."[49] Although Smith sees this move as laudable, it fails to get to the heart of the matter. The clash of ideas moves to the clash of beliefs, and the person-as-believer still tends to be disembodied and individualistic.[50] Reflecting on the contemporary approach to education, he writes, "Is the 'believing' pedagogy really going to look much different from the 'rationalist' pedagogy?"[51] He considers both to still be in the *information* paradigm instead of moving to the *formation* paradigm. While not rejecting the importance of thinking and believing, Smith contends for a more robust anthropology that emphasizes embodiment.[52]

Rather than viewing humanity primarily as thinking or believing people, he states, "We need a nonreductionistic understanding of human persons as embodied agents of desire or love."[53] In this Augustinian model of humanity, the center of gravity moves from the head to the heart and considers "noncognitive ways of being-in-the-world."[54] For Smith, as with Augustine, people are ultimately creatures of desire. The anthropological picture of humans that Smith develops is people-as-lovers, with desires aimed at a particular telos, a specific vision of the "good life." The picture of this good life is built on assumptions of what good relationships look like, assumptions about just economics, vocation, how we relate to creation, the nature of flourishing families, and more. Our view of the good life, our telos, "governs, shapes, and motivates our decisions and actions."[55] A vision of the good life captures hearts and imaginations. Smith emphasizes,

> The telos to which our love is aimed is not a list of ideas or propositions or doctrines; it is not a list of abstract, disembodied concepts or values. Rather, the reason that this vision of the good life moves us is because it is a more affective, sensible, even aesthetic picture of what the good life looks like."[56]

What captures one's imagination and desire are pictures, which are "communicated most powerfully in stories, legends, myths, plays, novels, and films rather than dissertations, messages, and monographs."[57]

Smith articulates a robust philosophical anthropology—in the way of Augustine—that captures the fullness of what it means to be human, with desire at the center. Smith maintains that because people are primarily shaped by their desires, it is what we love that makes us who we are and forms our ultimate identity.[58] Honing in on the core of the issue, he writes, "Our identity is shaped by what we ultimately love or what we love as ultimate—what, at the end of the day, gives us a sense of meaning, purpose, understanding, and orientation to our being-in-the-world."[59] For Smith, to be human is to love, to desire—and one's ultimate love defines one's identity, because "our ultimate love is what we worship."[60]

Smith also seeks to diagnose what shapes desire. He talks about habits—in the way of Alasdair MacIntyre—as love's fulcrum, and embodied practices as the formation of loves.[61] Smith writes about the importance of liturgies as "thick" practices as opposed to "thin" practices. We all engage in the practice of brushing our teeth, but we don't call ourselves "toothbrushers" because brushing our teeth is a thin practice. "Thick" practices, on the other hand, shape our identity and telos, whether they be the liturgy of the mall or the liturgy of a church service. What is important to note at this point is that Smith makes the case that desire is central to what it means to be human. We become what we love. Our telos—what we ultimately love and desire—shapes our identity and praxis.

Although Smith gives significant wisdom on how desires can become misshapen and reshaped through secular and religious liturgies, Girard makes the case from anthropology, mythology, and the Scriptures that our models are most formative in the shaping of our desires.

UNMASKING THE POWERS OF DOMINATION

Houston notes that "Peter believed that he was struggling against spiritual opposition, as did Paul, and that he needed to prepare his people to engage in spiritual warfare."[62] Christian leaders should expect to suffer unjustly, just as their chief Shepherd did.[63] For the early church, suffering may have occurred through persecution by the civil authorities, as well as through difficulties at home in the family and within the churches themselves.[64] The temptation for them, as for us, was to return evil for evil, but Peter pointed them to Christ, who repaid evil with good. It was only through prayer and a Christlike attitude that they could learn to overcome evil.[65] Houston points out that behind the suffering, another battle was going on: "Inhabiting the structures of family, church and society, as well as invading personal individual experience, there are other authorities and powers at work."[66] According to Peter, "Your enemy the devil prowls around like a roaring lion looking for someone to devour" (1 Pet. 5:8). Peter tells them to resist the devil and stand firm in the faith (1 Pet. 5:9).[67] Houston believes that Peter's advice and warnings about the Powers is pertinent to his entire letter.[68]

Houston reminds the reader that Peter was acutely aware of the insidious influence of evil, for in response to Jesus going to the cross, Peter rebuked him; and in turn Jesus rebuked Peter, saying "Get behind me, Satan!" (Mark 8:33). Houston wisely refers to James, who has a similar admonition: "Submit yourselves, then, to God. Resist the devil, and he will flee from you" (James 4:7). James was addressing the teachers of the church and reminding them of the power of the tongue and that they are not to use it to curse others made in God's image; instead, they are to live good lives "in all humility, rather than by worldly wisdom, which 'does not come from heaven, but is earthly, unspiritual, demonic. For where you have envy and selfish ambition, there you find disorder and every evil practice' (Jas 3:15–16)."[69] Scot McKnight also acknowledges the importance of James and 1 Peter in relation to the theme of domineering leadership, which I will discuss when I examine Girard in chapter seven.

Houston believes, looking at these two letters holistically, "that we see how the problem of domineering behaviours by church leaders is of massive concern to the apostolic teams."[70] The battle is clearly with the Powers. In an effort to give a fuller picture of how the Powers seek to subvert us, he turns to Wink's trilogy, observing how the Powers inhabit "authorities in the real world, as well as infiltrating the church."[71] Because Houston, Newbigin, and others continually cite Wink as authoritative on the Powers, it is important to engage Wink to better understand the nature of the Powers.

Before moving on from the Powers, Houston takes "a closer look at *exousia*—and demonic domineering."[72] This is an important contribution from Houston, as it relates to leadership, authority, and the Powers. He first discusses two words pertaining to authority that are relevant to this book:

exousia ("authority," "ruling power," "bearer of authority") and *katexou-siazein* ("to exercise authority over," "to misuse official authority," "to tyrannize").[73] Essentially, "*Exousia* denotes the power which may be demonstrated in legal, political, social, or moral affairs, and is always linked with a particular position or mandate. Such authority can be delegated, and may also be illegally usurped by despots."[74]

Houston says that in the Septuagint, *exousia* denoted authority given by God, the Lord of history. Houston turns to Otto Betz for an explanation of *exousia* in the New Testament: "*Exousia* is that power, authority, and freedom of action which belongs (1) to God himself; (2) to a commission in the last days; to (3) a Christian in his eschatological existence."[75] The first application "links God's ultimate authority with his role as the Lord of history."[76] Though the Powers continually seek to usurp God's authority, he is still Lord. The second area Betz addresses "has to do with the fact that Jesus has been given *exousia*, in a special way. His earthly ministry uniquely heralds the coming of God's reign, and announces that evil powers have been dealt with definitively in Jesus' life, death, and resurrection."[77] Jesus demonstrated this in his ability to destroy the works of the devil, exorcise demons, and forgive sins—and he did it by preaching with an authority not found among the scribes.[78]

Finally, according to Betz, "All Christian believers, and not just leaders, have a delegated authority, founded on the reign of Christ as Lord and his disarming of the powers of evil, which entails a vocation of both freedom and service."[79] Yet because Christians can be addicted to authority, Betz gives this word of caution: "There is only one Lord, Jesus Christ, and those who 'lord it' over Christian congregations or agencies are usurping his authority, just as the heavenly and earthly powers of evil have done throughout history."[80] As leaders, we must remember that our delegated authority is only valid when under the authority of Christ, the chief Shepherd—and it is given for the flourishing of the community and the wider commonwealth.[81] Therefore, although we may be tempted to usurp God's authority, we are accountable to God for the proper use of our authority.[82] "They dare not mimic the work of the devil and dominate God's dear ones, but rather must follow Christ's example of servant-leadership."[83] Houston validates the claim that if we hope to properly diagnose the problem of domineering leadership in the church, it is essential to develop a theology of the Powers. Before examining Wink's view of the Powers, I will summarize what I have explored so far.

SUMMARY OF SECTION ONE

In chapter one, I argued that although current assessments of the problem of domineering leadership provide great help, in order to develop a deeper understanding, we need to analyze the problem from a mythical (cosmic) view point by developing a theology of the Powers.[84] Although *mythology* is a complex word with many meanings, even within this book, here I am referring to it as "the real state of affairs."[85] But developing a theology of the Powers poses a hermeneutical challenge. To chart this challenge, I examined "the principalities and powers" from a traditional viewpoint (Arnold), a reductionistic model (Bultmann), and a dual-reference option (Berkhof). I then developed a dynamic typology of the Powers with the Ford/Frei scale, where I placed Arnold, Bultmann, and Berkhof. Their placement was based on their hermeneutical strategy and willingness to hold a theology that engages various academic disciplines while also seeking to appreciate the meaning of the text in the context of production. On this five-point scale, Arnold is a traditionalist (1), Bultmann a reinterpreter (4), and Berkhof a correlator (3), where he seeks to do justice to the text of production while simultaneously interpreting the principalities and powers for our current context (the context of reception).

In chapter two, I examined the need for missional leadership, primarily engaging the work of Van Gelder and Roxburgh. Van Gelder offers an excellent history of the development of missional theology from the early nineteenth century to today, and Roxburgh helps us understand how our approach to leadership in the church needs to correspond to this theological development. Although Van Gelder and Zscheile critique elements of the seminal work *Missional Church*, edited by Darrell Guder (and to which both Van Gelder and Roxburgh contributed), there is an unintentional minimization of missional spirituality, which I argued ought to be placed as the soil of the missional tree instead of located in one of the branches.

Regarding missional leadership and imitation, it seems that Van Gelder and Zscheile minimize imitation, with a desire to lead people to participate in the life of God and give greater credence to how the Spirit is at work in the world. In contrast, David Fitch—with more neo-Anabaptist leanings—proposes a Trinitarian view, where the Spirit extends the work of the incarnation and reign of the Son. This recognizes that Christ is not stuck in the past but lives on through the Spirit and his body, the church. Fitch proposes a more helpful solution to the problems of Christocentrism and ecclesiocentrism by recommending an "Incarnation-centered Trinitarian theology," reemphasizing how imitation of the incarnate Christ does not lead to triumphalism, because the logic of the incarnation is humility, vulnerability, and submission to the Father's work in the world.[86] In other words, if leaders and the church truly imitate Christ as the uncoercive Lamb who reigns, we are compelled to follow the way of Jesus in leadership. Roxburgh wisely reminds us that the missional leader needs to be a model and that leadership formation should take place as new leaders are apprenticed by experienced leaders. He inherently understands the popular aphorism that more is caught than taught. This point is accented by Houston in his aptly titled *Leading by Example*.

In their desire to help the church hold a more positive view of culture/ world, Van Gelder and Zscheile fail to distinguish between the anthropologically generated concept of *culture* and the theologically developed concept of *world*. Because they fail to define their terms, they emphasize the positive references and minimize the negative applications of the word *world* in Scripture. The near absence of a theology of the Powers is evident, and I seek to address that in this book. Conversely, in *The Gospel in a Pluralist Society*, Newbigin dedicates an entire chapter to the Powers, seeking to help those in the missional conversation understand the prominence of this theme in Scripture. Because Newbigin cites his dependence on Wink, it is also important to engage Wink's work on the topic.

Finally, in chapter two, there seems to be a consensus among Van Gelder, Zscheile, Roxburgh, and Romanuk that, because of how they shape the work of the church and leadership, identity and telos are important concepts to grasp. Although the plurality of leaders, the importance of apostolic leadership (the fivefold), and the priesthood of all believers are common themes, an imitation-based conceptual framework is missing from the conversation. This framework considers the work of the Powers and how imitation and desire link the missional leader to these Powers. If identity and a life worth imitating are key in missional leadership, then, for leaders, who we imitate is significant. It would be negligent to overlook how in Jesus' temptation in the desert, the devil was attacking Jesus' identity; on two separate occasions, the devil said, "If you are the Son of God . . . " (Matt. 4:3, 6). A well-developed missional theology is vital, but it is unhelpful if not accompanied by a missional spirituality informed by a robust understanding of the Powers. The imitation-based framework I will develop aims to enable missional leaders to live the kind of life that is worthy of imitation.

In chapter three, I examined Houston's study of 1 Peter, with the problem of domineering leadership as his focal point. Through Houston's work, key elements of the imitation-based framework emerged: leadership, imitation of desire, and imitation of Christ or the Powers, suggesting that a deep understanding of these elements is needed if we are going to get to the root of the problem.

Regarding leadership and imitation, Houston established the three applications of imitation. The leader has two options of who to imitate: they can unknowingly imitate the Powers by uncritically mimicking what they see in the world, or as Houston encourages, they can imitate Christ. The third application of imitation relates to the role of the leader and the necessity of a leader living as a Christlike example because of the influence on those who look to him or her. The analysis confirmed that imitation is significant in relation to missional leadership. Who the leader chooses to imitate can mean life or death for the leader's own soul. Imitating a leader who loves to be first is not only dangerous but is also evil. The dangers of mimicking the latest cultural trend can unknowingly change the telos and identity of missional leaders, thus misshaping their praxis.

The priority of imitating Christ was established as Houston corroborates Fitch's thought that one ought not decenter Christ but instead follow him. This was reinforced by looking at the life of Peter, who understood the highs and lows of his own grace-filled journey with Jesus. Peter not only guided leaders to follow Christ but also followed Christ to his own cross. A short review looking at key moments in the history of the church and the lives of leaders such as Thomas à Kempis, Kierkegaard, and Bonhoeffer bolstered this need to imitate and follow Christ. In addition, although the influence the leader has on their followers was highlighted as significant, this area needs to be developed. Girard's mimetic theory has the potential to motivate leaders to discover that the only way to escape the grip of the Powers is by imitating Christ; subsequently, leaders' desires will be imitated by those who look to them as models.

Houston's acknowledgment of the importance of desire in relation to leadership was strengthened but needs to be developed. Smith, in the footsteps of Augustine, demonstrates the centrality of desire through developing a philosophical anthropology of people-as-lovers, whose ultimate desires shape the core of their identity. Smith makes the case that information is not enough for transformation and that transformation requires formation. This solidifies the assertion that missional theology without a deep spirituality is insufficient to deal with the problem of domineering leadership. A comprehensive approach to the formation of the leader is required—through a missional spirituality that arrests the imagination of the leader and reshapes the leader's desires.

In addition, I confirmed and developed the contours of leadership, adding to the argument of the importance of identity and telos in the development of missional theology and missional leadership. This demonstrated (and will continue to demonstrate) how desires form the identity of the leader, and the supreme telos of the leader's desires profoundly shape the leader's identity and praxis.

I affirmed that Girard would be the ideal dialogue partner to explore both imitation and desire, as he uniquely combines the two into what he calls *mimetic desire*. His research has reshaped many fields of study, including theology. I explore mimetic desire and the mimetic cycle in subsequent chapters. Stringfellow provides a unique angle on how the Powers manifest themselves to misshape the leader's desires, corresponding with their identity, praxis, and telos. I explore this further in chapters eight and nine.

Houston's understanding of the Powers' unique work when it comes to leadership formation was insightful. Identifying Peter's warning about the Powers as central to Peter's overall message confirms the importance of this element as part of the conceptual framework. Houston's emphasis on the Powers was affirmed by the recent surge of scholarly interest in the Powers since the rise and fall of Hitler, which I noted in the first chapter. Wink and his trilogy on the Powers continue to significantly shape the conversation. His influence in the missional world, as evidenced by Newbigin, makes him an important dialogue partner.

Houston alerts us to the importance of understanding authority and power through an examination of the *exousia*. He speaks of the proper use and misuse of authority and how this relates to the Powers, which continually seek to usurp God's authority. In the final chapters of this book, the importance of the power of the Spirit will be made clear. The Spirit led Jesus into an encounter with the devil, and after having shown his faithfulness through the temptations, Jesus left the desert in the power of the Spirit.

The interlocutors I chose to develop this imitation-based framework bring specialties that will strengthen specific parts of the framework. Each has made the Powers central in their corpus of work. Houston demonstrates a link to domineering leadership and the Powers. The contributions of Wink, Girard, and Stringfellow provide theoretical and theological depth, as well as practical application.

SECTION TWO

MISSIONAL LEADERSHIP
AND THE POWERS

Walter Wink is the most cited and engaged author on the
Powers, and his trilogy relating to naming, unmasking,
and engaging the Powers is his seminal work. If we
are to translate the Powers to our context, it is vital to
critically engage Wink's work. In chapter four, I will
look at the life of Walter Wink, and I will also examine
the key themes in his trilogy. In chapter five, I engage the
life and work of Wink with critical openness, examining
issues pertinent to our understanding and diagnosis of
domineering leadership in the church.

4

COMPREHENDING THE POWERS

Shortly after moving to Los Angeles in 2002, I watched a local news story in which an investigative reporter was seeking to expose the dishonest tactics of a local car service store. The reporter and his undercover film crew took a fairly new car and gave it a full maintenance update, including installing a new air filter and topping up all fluids. They then took this vehicle for a simple oil change. The mechanic conducted a routine check of the air filters and fluids, and afterward he stated that the car required a change in transmission fluid. The reporter challenged this, so the mechanic brought in his manager to confirm his assessment.

The reporter and his crew then took this same vehicle to other stations that were part of this national chain. Every store tried to upsell them—often with the same upgrades that were just performed on the vehicle—sometimes to the tune of $200. The mechanic, and occasionally the manager, did everything they could to persuade this reporter to agree to the unnecessary services, and all the conversations were captured on film.

The reporter then returned with his film crew to each of the eight stores to tell them what they had done. Often the mechanic or manager would deny any wrongdoing. The reporter would then show them the recording of the conversation; at that point, the mechanic or manager had to eat their words and confess their misconduct.

The investigative story revealed that if employees failed to get a customer to spend, on average, at least $68 more than they had initially intended, they would eventually be terminated. Because they all had families to support, staff simply became accustomed to lying to customers.

This may be only a minor example, but all around the world, we have developed systems that oppress people. Some are forced to oppress others or face oppression themselves. Walter Wink gives examples of how these systems are at work in our lives:

> A contractor pays off a building inspector so he can violate code and put up a
> shoddy and possibly unsafe structure. A power plant exposes its employees

to radioactive poisoning; the employee who attempts to document these safety infractions is forced off the road by another car and dies. All her documents are missing.[1]

As I explore throughout this chapter, these are all examples of the Powers at work.

Walter Wink also writes:

> All of us deal with the Powers That Be. They staff our hospitals, run City Hall, sit around tables in corporate boardrooms, collect our taxes, and head our families. But the Powers That Be are more than just the people who run things. They are the systems themselves, the institutions and structures that weave society into an intricate fabric of power and relationships. These Powers surround us on every side. They are necessary. They are useful. We could do nothing without them. Who wants to do without timely mail delivery or well-maintained roads? But the Powers are also the source of unmitigated evils.[2]

These Powers are at work in our churches today, just as they were at work in the early church. Thus, if we, as missional leaders, are going to resist the Powers, we will need a robust and well-considered theology. To help form a greater understanding of the Powers, it is important to engage the work of Walter Wink, whose seminal work on the Powers has been cited by some of the most well-respected influencers in the missional conversation. As I mentioned in chapter two, Lesslie Newbigin devotes an entire chapter to this subject in his book *The Gospel in a Pluralist Society*. So who is Walter Wink, and why did the theme of the Powers capture his imagination?

INTRODUCING WALTER WINK

Walter Wink (1935–2012) was born in Dallas, Texas. Over the course of his career, he published sixteen books and hundreds of scholarly articles. He died at the age of seventy-six at his home in Sandisfield, Massachusetts, due to complications related to dementia.[3] Wink received his PhD in 1963 from Union Theological Seminary in New York City and taught New Testament at Union from 1967 to 1976. He was denied tenure due to the opening statement in his book *The Bible in Human Transformation* (1973): "Historical biblical criticism is bankrupt."[4] This did not sit well with his biblical studies colleagues, so they voted his tenure down.[5] In using the word *bankrupt*, Wink was not implying that historical biblical criticism is valueless. Rather, he considered it bankrupt "solely because it is incapable of achieving what most of its practitioners considered its purpose to be: so to interpret the Scriptures that the past becomes alive and illumines our present with new possibilities for personal and social transformation."[6]

In Wink's opinion, biblical scholars not only had quarantined themselves from the world of practitioners but also had given into an "ideology of objectivism," where unacknowledged interest and the illusion of "detached neutrality" had shaped their perspective.[7] He was also concerned about the "demystification" of the text, which resulted in the loss of the "numinous," or the loss of mystery.[8] Wink states that objectivism (or intellectualism) is "characterized by a complete separation of theory from practice, of intellect from emotion," forfeiting the goal of transformation.[9] For Wink, "The historical critical method has reduced the Bible to a dead letter. Our obeisance to technique has left the Bible sterile and ourselves empty."[10] His constructive task was therefore to address these particular critiques.

Wink's first two books detail his hermeneutical approach to Scripture.[11] This approach is both applied and amplified in his next five books, which cover the Powers.[12] His hermeneutic was to address the strong disconnect between the academy and communities of faith. In addition, he critiqued the current form of biblical criticism, which assumed an ideology of objectivism and tackled the text with detachment in such a way that the text became objectified and the subject unchanged. He writes, "Such detached neutrality in matters of faith is not neutrality at all, but already a decision against responding. At the outset, questions of truth and meaning have been excluded, since they can only be answered participatively, in terms of a lived response."[13] As he paid attention to his life and the text alike, he increasingly became a social justice activist.

If Christian leadership is primarily about being Christlike examples, it is imperative that we understand how the Powers seek to undermine us as leaders, as well as examine the lives and theology of our primary interlocutors. Wink proposes that part of the constructive task required to develop a new paradigm for hermeneutics is to understand that all scholarship is autobiographical and shaped by the history of the interpreter. In his own autobiographical reflection he writes, "My story may, at the very least, show why I theologically think the way that I do."[14]

EARLY LIFE

Wink's early life was shaped by a father who was a strong disciplinarian and a mother whose intellectual prowess pushed him to be a scholar.[15] These formative relationships profoundly shaped his self-perception and drove him to perfectionism. Reflecting on this, he writes, "My deep perfectionism did not arise from any form of indoctrination from fundamentalism. It came straight out of my desperate desire to win my parents'—and God's—love."[16] Intellectually, he comprehended God's love, but he had not internalized it. His early life experiences and subsequent wounds meant that perfectionism was a lifelong struggle for him.[17] Reflecting on his formative years, Wink not only recognized his longing to be loved and accepted but also that this desire, if not addressed in healthy ways, could become unhealthy. A desire to be loved and accepted can turn into the pursuit of accomplishment. To desire accomplishment or fruitfulness is not bad, but it becomes misshaped when carried out *for* love instead of *from* being loved. When Henri Nouwen describes the start of Jesus' ministry, he recalls that at Jesus' baptism, he heard a voice from heaven say, "This is my beloved Son, with whom I am well pleased" (Matt. 3:17 ESV). "These words revealed the true identity of Jesus as the beloved. Jesus truly heard that voice, and all of his thoughts, words, actions came forth from his deep knowledge that he was infinitely loved by God. Jesus lived his life from that inner place of love."[18] Identifying as the beloved is an integral concept for leaders to absorb and embody so that our lives and leadership flow from a secure identity found in Christ.

WINK'S PENTECOSTAL EXPERIENCE

Though Wink was raised Methodist, as a college student he went through an atheistic phase, until he heard a message preached on Matthew 6:25–34. He was struck by the promise made by Jesus, "But seek first his kingdom and his righteousness, and all these things will be given to you as well" (Matt. 6:33). When Wink heard this promise, he began to believe, and he wanted to see if God would deliver.[19] Wink's desire to test this promise opened him up to new experiences in Scripture and challenged his unconsciously held rationalist, materialist worldview. A charismatic encounter with the Holy Spirit would open him to a deeper understanding of God's presence and his own telos.

A liberal, rational Methodist, he found himself on one particular day in a room full of people enthusiastically singing with full hearts, raised hands, and an earnest desire to experience more of Jesus. Wink felt a burning sensation that eventually went through his entire body. When the service ended, those who wanted more prayer were asked to remain in the room. Wink decided to stay.[20]

Wink felt the power run through his body once again, starting at his feet and hands. He fell back and was caught by the ministers, who laid him down. He recalls that the power increased, touching specific parts of his body as he heard the preacher tell him, "Praise Him, open your mouth."[21] Wink writes, "Suddenly I found myself singing, stronger, stronger still, making up melodies in complete release, complete abandon, complete love. Then I spoke a little in tongues, but fear held me back. I didn't believe in it, you see. I sang, and sang, and praised God. Then I was swept with such joy that I began laughing where I lay."[22]

These experiences ultimately would shape his future approach to herme-neutics. In his years serving as a local pastor, at the ridicule of his ministerial colleagues, he regularly held healing services where he saw the Spirit physically heal people.[23] He shares one example of the healing of a woman who had a tumor the size of an orange in her uterus.[24] This experience of physical healing, and many after it, made it easy for Wink to believe that Jesus healed people of their illnesses—not just psychosomatic illnesses, but real medical diseases. Other scholars who have not seen God heal might easily dismiss the historicity of Jesus' healing, due in part to their hermeneutical approach being shaped by their materialist worldview. But for Wink, these experiences deeply shaped his developing approach to Scripture. Because he believed we all come to the text shaped by our autobiographical experiences, Wink thought that detached neutrality in approaching Scripture was pure fiction.

WINK'S PERSONAL ENCOUNTER WITH JUNGIAN THINKING

One of the profound experiences of Wink's adult life that deeply influenced his approach to Scripture, and therefore his understanding of the Powers, was his encounter with Elizabeth Boyden Howes, a Jungian analyst and founder of the Guild for Psychology Studies in San Francisco.

The first seminar Wink attended at the Guild was nothing short of transformational. The exercise for that day was to take the story of the healing of the paralytic in the Gospel of Mark and internalize it by creating a clay sculpture of one's own inner paralytic. Wink writes, "I had a PhD and a prestigious academic appointment; I 'had' no paralytic."[25] As far as Wink was concerned, his learning and role obviously spoke to his wholeness and maturity as a person. Playing along, however, he decided to engage in the exercise. He closed his eyes and let his hands do as they pleased. To his surprise, when he looked to see what his hands had created, he saw he had made a bird with a broken wing. Not being an artist, he was astonished that he had created this, and even more significant to him, "I suddenly knew precisely what that broken-winged bird was in me: an atrophied feeling function."[26] In response, for the next eight years, he carried a notebook around with him, jotting down feelings he had, in hope of recovering his capacity to feel.

This experience sparked his interest to engage in a Jungian analysis of Scripture, where he started to recognize and experience the power of archetypal images found in the Bible. One of the many places he demonstrates a Jungian analysis of Scripture is through his article on the life of Jacob, titled "Wresting with God: Psychological Insights in Bible Study."[27] Wink asserts that wrestling with the Spirit is common in various mythic traditions, and he views it as a "standard component in spiritual development."[28]

When drawing conclusions in this article, he states, "I have attempted to show that dialogue with and meditative reflection on the characters of biblical narrative can make concrete and evident what has been previously fugitive and subjective."[29] The goal in engaging Scripture, for Wink, is always the hope for both personal and social transformation. So, for example, if we are going to approach the epic story of Jacob wrestling with God, we need to live into the story and allow the story to provide mirrors to our own lives. We do not stop at internalizing the characters of the story, otherwise "we are guilty of mystifying the political and social relations implicit in the text and in our being as selves in the world."[30] Wink believed the social is always intertwined with the personal, and the aim of interacting with Scripture is the transformation of them both.

The depth of psychology that Wink discovered through Jung and others shaped his hermeneutical approach to Scripture. He believed we are not to read Scripture in a detached manner, and his intention in this approach was not to "reduce theology to psychology, or characters to categories, or biblical narrative to psychoanalysis case history, but rather to re-establish the ground of the narrative in psychic and historical experience."[31] In approaching the text in this way, his hope was to relate theological reflection to actual human experience; he did not seek to over-psychologize the procedure.[32]

Wink's desire for personal and social transformation was not just theoretical, and it was not just part of his academic writings. It was, indeed, deeply intertwined with his life.

WINK'S SOCIAL ACTIVISM

Wink's activism was shaped by an early experience of racism. At just six years old, while living in segregated Texas, Wink witnessed his Black friend unjustly accused of starting a dangerous fire. In fact, Wink had lit it. Despite Wink trying to convince the authorities that he was to blame, his young Black friend was punished. Wink writes, "That day I discovered something of what racism is. It just wasn't fair. How fortunate I was to have had this experience, so that when the Civil Rights Movement came along, I already had in my body a visceral reaction to the mistreatment of people of color."[33]

Wink's contexts and study helped him to name, unmask, and engage the Powers. As an adult participating in the civil rights movement, Wink met Martin Luther King Jr. and others who would inspire him toward more substantial activism in the future. This included him spending a season in Chile under the oppressive government of Pinochet and working with the South African Council of Churches in the fight against apartheid. In these different contexts, he "became increasingly convinced that nonviolence was the only way to overcome the domination of the Powers without creating new forms of domination."[34] Accordingly, he wanted to test his convictions and see if he could persuade both the Black and White clergy of South Africa to get involved in "nonviolent direct action against the apartheid regime."[35]

Having already written the first two books in his Powers trilogy, after his trip to South Africa, he ventured to write what was to become his sixth book on the Powers, now titled *Violence and Nonviolence in South Africa*

(1987).[36] As he attained funding to print this booklet, the small United Church of Christ congregation with which he was involved sent over three thousand copies of this book to both the White and Black clergy who understood English. The Catholic Church sent eight hundred copies to their clergy as well. The book angered those who were suffering unjustly, and it also angered those who were taking a violent approach. However, the third way of Jesus that he was proposing—neither violence nor passivity, but nonviolent direct actions—a year later, became the formal opinion and action of the South African Council of Churches.[37] Wink acknowledged that his book was just one factor that caused this reversal of approach.

As churches officially adopted this "third way of Jesus" approach to apartheid, in 1998, Wink and Richard Dears of the Fellowship of Reconciliation were invited to give workshops on active nonviolence in South Africa.[38] Dears was granted a visa, but Wink's visa application was denied. When Wink's host heard this, he encouraged Wink to enter the country illegally and suggested the best border crossing. With a desire to equip people for nonviolent resistance, Wink took his advice. As they came close to the border, Dears and Wink prayed that God would open a way for them to get through the border in a way similar to how he had opened the prison doors for Peter, Paul, and Silas.[39] Wink recounts that suddenly the sky turned black and rain started to pour down. When he encountered the border guard and heard him singing praises to God, Wink knew he would get through. In the darkness and rain, the guard simply asked Wink to read his passport to the other soldier. No one asked him if he had a visa, so they entered South Africa, drove to Johannesburg, and were miraculously able to teach their workshops.

Wink was inspired by the courage of those who attended the workshops, and he was moved by their willingness to take risks and suffer in the struggle against apartheid. After teaching workshops for one straight week, Wink turned himself in to the Ministry of Home Affairs, where he was asked to leave the country immediately.[40]

Wink's sixth book, which was originally titled *Jesus' Third Way*, helped give courage to the church in South Africa. This is indicated by the written response given by Peter Storey, the Methodist bishop of South Africa. Wink cherished this response dearly. The bishop first recounted how clever he thought it was that the book was wrapped in a plain brown wrapper, not denoting any marks from a publisher, for this likely helped the book get past the security police. More important for the bishop, however, was the content inside the book. Storey writes,

> Walter Wink's analysis of the prospects of violence and nonviolence in the anti-apartheid struggle were uncompromising; they left none of us off—proponents of violence and nonviolence alike. He chided us gently for our hypocrisy and impotence and showed us that the true realism lay,

as we should have known, not with "fight" or "flight," but with Jesus and his "Third way" of nonviolent direct action. Informed by the Gospels as well as by the hard math of struggle, Walter invited us to follow the tough advice and the example of Jesus in confronting the powers with a different kind of power. He reminded us of other struggles where the odds were stacked just as heavily against freedom, but where people trained in the Third Way of Jesus had overcome.[41]

Wink believed that if one did not know and imitate Jesus, it would be difficult to live humanly in a world dominated by the Powers. Thus Jesus increasingly became the key to his own identity.

WALTER WINK'S THEOLOGY OF THE POWERS

Wink's many life experiences meant that developing a theology of the Powers became an important calling for him. His trilogy is a seminal work in the field and has shaped the missional movement, likely because Lesslie Newbigin, the father of the missional movement, substantially drew upon Wink's work. Before engaging Wink, it is important for us to approach his work with critical openness, recognizing that, for Wink, this work was not only theoretical or theological but also biographical. Understanding Wink's approach to the Powers requires us first to understand his underlying assumptions regarding his adopted worldview.

UNDERSTANDING WORLDVIEWS

Wink's entire project of the theology of the Powers was built on the foundation of consciously adopting an *integral worldview*. As Wink says, "Our perception of the Powers is colored to a great extent by the way we view the world."[42] Wink contends there have only been a handful of worldviews in the history of the West.[43]

First, he names an *ancient worldview*, where heaven and earth mutually influence each other and are counterparts to each other. This view was shared not only by biblical writers but also by everyone who lived in the ancient world, including the Greeks, Romans, Babylonians, and Assyrians.[44]

Then Wink names the *spiritualist worldview*, which considers the material world to be evil and heaven and the spiritual to be good. This worldview was shared by the Gnostics and Manichaeans.[45]

Third, the *materialist worldview*, which became prominent during the Enlightenment, runs counter to the spiritualist worldview; it holds that reality can be detected by the five senses, through science. There is no heaven, no God, no soul, and the spiritual world is an illusion.[46] Wink discovered that he unconsciously held this view in his early life.

The fourth worldview Wink describes as the *theological worldview*, where "in reaction to materialism, Christian theologians invented the supernatural realm. . . . Acknowledging that this supersensible realm could not be known by the senses, they conceded earthly reality to modern science and preserved a privileged 'spiritual' realm immune to confirmation or refutation."[47]

Finally, there is the *integral worldview*. "This new worldview . . . is emerging from a confluence of sources: the reflections of Carl Jung, Teilhard de Chardin, Morton Kelsey, Thomas Berry, Matthew Fox, process philosophy, and the new physics. It sees everything as having an outer and an inner aspect."[48] It takes the ancient worldview seriously, in that both the ancient and integral worldview include a spatial element, but they combine them differently. In the ancient worldview, transcendence is considered upward, in heaven; while in an integral worldview, it is considered inward. In the integral worldview, spiritual reality is now the inner aspect of all social reality, "an inner realm every bit as rich and extensive as the outer realm" of the ancient worldview.[49] In order to make "the biblical data more intelligible for people today," Wink believes there is no worldview better to adopt than this one.[50] Though one's worldview shapes how one sees the world, Wink is clear in stating that worldviews are not the gospel, as evidenced by the fact that the ancient worldview was not unique to God's people.

Because he holds to the integral worldview, Wink considers spiritual reality to be the inner aspect of all social reality. Thus he proposes that the Powers be viewed "not as separate heavenly or ethereal entities, but as the *inner aspect of material or tangible manifestations of power*."[51] The Powers are not mere personifications. The demons that the ancients projected "onto the screen of the cosmos really are demonic, and play havoc with humanity; only they are not *up there* but *over there*, in the socio-political entities that make up the one-and-only real world."[52] Since Wink rejects a materialist worldview, he is not interested in engaging the Powers in the way of Bultmann's demythologizing project. Wink seeks to reinterpret the Powers within an integral worldview, writing, "the New Testament insists that demons can have no effect unless they are able to embody themselves in people (Mark 1:21–28 par.; Matt. 12:43–45/Luke 11:24–26), or pigs (Mark 5:1–20 par.), or political systems (Revelation 12–13)."[53]

NAMING THE POWERS

In his first book of the Powers trilogy, *Naming the Powers*, Wink recognizes that many modern readers are shaped by a materialist worldview. Therefore, when we read ancient accounts of people encountering the Powers, we quickly dismiss them, because our thinking is dictated by our worldview of materialism.[54] He writes, "It is as impossible for most of us to believe in the real existence of demonic or angelic powers as it is to believe in dragons, or elves, or a flat world."[55]

Acknowledging the enormous gap between those shaped by a materialist worldview and those shaped by an ancient worldview, he sees the importance of seeking to understand the Powers in their context of origin before transposing that understanding into an integral worldview. His best description of this task is articulated as follows:

> The ancients regarded the spiritual Powers as non-material, invisible, heavenly entities with specific characteristics or qualities. These Powers are good creations of a good God, but all of them have "fallen," becoming more or less evil in intent, and may even be set on the destruction of humanity. They were called angels, gods, spirits, demons, devils. This view was carried by the momentum of Jewish apocalyptic thought right into the New Testament, but Paul has already taken key steps toward "demythologizing" or at least depersonalizing it by means of the categories of sin, law, the flesh, and death. I suggest we follow Paul's lead in this, and attempt to reinterpret the mythic language of the Powers. By this I do not mean to abolish the New Testament myth but to transpose it into a new key. Or, put another way, the goal is not "demythologizing" if by that is meant removal of the mythic dimension, but rather juxtaposing the ancient myth with the emerging postmodern (mythic) worldview and asking how they might mutually illuminate each other.[56]

Here one can see Wink's dependence on Hendrik Berkhof. However, what Berkhof thought Paul was doing with the "principalities and powers," Wink seeks to do with every category of the Powers. Wink views myth as a way to describe "the atemporal, cosmic, supernatural aspect of the story," which he believes permeates "every statement made about the Powers."[57] The mythic "is the very framework of the entire notion of the Powers, the means by which they have been brought to language."[58]

Wink's first book is the most technical of the three books, as he seeks to approach his exegetical work by approaching power and the Powers synthetically, looking at all usage in the New Testament in context, as opposed to analytically, writer by writer. His goal is to understand how the writers of the New Testament experienced and described the Powers within the ancient worldview and the unconscious underlying assumptions they held.[59] He develops six basic rules from his initial exegetical work, and these become his interpretive lens:

1. "The language of power pervades the whole New Testament."
2. "The language of power in the New Testament is imprecise, liquid, interchangeable, and unsystematic."

3. "Despite all this imprecision and interchangeability, clear patterns of usage emerge."
4. "Because these terms are to a degree interchangeable, one or a pair or a series can be made to represent them all." (Wink mentions exceptions to this rule, when the context brings clarity.)
5. "These Powers are both heavenly and earthly, divine and human, spiritual and political, invisible and structural."
6. "These Powers are also both good and evil."[60]

Later in the book, Wink adds a seventh foundational rule, gained from his exegetical work, which produces the interpretive lens by which he engages the text:

7. "Unless the context further specifies (and some do), we are to take the terms for power in their most comprehensive sense, understanding them to mean both heavenly *and* earthly, divine *and* human, good *and* evil powers. No other conclusion would be consistent with the results of our word studies."[61]

One benefit of Wink painstakingly excavating the key words related to power and the Powers is that he did this in the context of when the text was written, prior to reinterpreting the Powers for an integral worldview. Reflecting on his word studies related to power and the Powers, he observes, "In biblical studies, word studies are the equivalent of field exploration and mineral classification in geology. Very little may seem to have been revealed in the field, yet when all the finds have been plotted, it is possible to view the whole map and predict where oil, or copper, or iron might be discovered."[62] Wink sets out to examine the identity of the "principalities and powers," considering the same passages that Berkhof examined and coming to similar conclusions.[63] I explore this further in chapter five.

UNMASKING THE POWERS

In his second book, *Unmasking the Powers*, Wink explores the invisible forces that determine human existence. While acknowledging that the modern materialist worldview has no place for Satan, demons, angels, and the gods, Wink believes that the reality to which this language pointed (in the ancient world) is real but resides in a cosmology and worldview predominant in that day. For Wink, cosmology is not the gospel; the ancient worldview simply determined how the message was spoken and understood. When the materialist worldview became the dominant myth of the West, some abandoned the faith, while others dismissed science. Instead, Wink interprets the Powers in a "new, postmaterialist cosmology."[64] In *Unmasking the Powers*, Wink examines Satan, demons, the angels of the church, the angels of nations, the gods, the elements of the universe, and the angels of nature—all of which a materialist worldview avoided. He translates this terminology into an integral worldview. The most relevant to examine are Satan, demons, and the angels of the church, as they more directly relate to understanding domineering leadership in the church.

Satan

Wink's analysis of Satan is unconventional. He speaks of Satan both as a servant of God with a potential path to redemption as well as the evil one. Wink does not hold that Satan was the snake in Genesis, based on Satan's later contextual appearances in the Old Testament. He writes, "We are not accustomed to thinking of Satan as God's servant. But when Satan makes his late appearance in the Old Testament, that is precisely what he is."[65] Wink notes that Satan only makes three appearances by name in the Old Testament: 1 Chronicles 21:1, where Satan enacts God's will "by visiting wrath on disobedient mortals";[66] Zechariah 3:1–5, in which Wink views Satan as an overzealous prosecuting attorney, not demonic;[67] and finally, in the prologue of Job, where Satan is in the company of the sons of God when they present themselves before the Lord. "Here again, Satan is not a fallen angel but a fully credentialed member of the heavenly court."[68] Although Wink concedes that Satan goes beyond prosecution to entrapment, saying, "excessive zeal for justice always becomes satanic," his diagnosis is that "Job's Satan, in short, while no friend of Job's, is in fact humanity's best friend, who lures God into a contest that will end by stripping *God* of the projections of the oppressors."[69]

Wink believes that Satan is misunderstood by most and that Satan acts as the shadow side of God. He states, "God alone is supreme; Satan is thoroughly integrated into the godhead in a wholly nondualistic fashion. Satan is not evil, or demonic, or fallen, or God's enemy. This adversary is merely a faithful, if overzealous, servant of God, entrusted with quality control and testing."[70] Although Wink's overall work is helpful, this understanding of Satan is problematic, and I will address it in the following chapter. I include it in this chapter merely to provide an overview of Wink's understanding.

Wink also sees redeeming qualities of Satan in the New Testament.[71] Referring to when Jesus says to Peter, "Get behind me, Satan" (Matt. 16:23), Wink writes, "Satan is God's sifter, the left hand of God, whose task it is to strain out the impurities in the disciples' commitment to God."[72] It is Wink's belief that Satan is the servant of the living God in this instance, doing things that Jesus himself was unable to do with Peter. He writes, "Satan is depicted here as able to accomplish something that Jesus had himself been unable to achieve during his ministry."[73]

In the Old and New Testaments, Wink sees Satan as both a servant of God and the evil one, and he views Satan's constellation to be determined by a person's "responses to the satanic occasion."[74] Wink holds that "Israelite religion originally had no place for Satan. God alone was the source of everything, good or ill. As Yahweh was ethicalized, good and evil were differentiated within the godhead, and Satan became the prosecuting attorney in the heavenly council."[75]

Demons

When it comes to demons, Wink seeks to "reconcile two contradictory views of the origin of the demonic."[76] One view—held by liberation theologians, Marxists, and other social theorists—is that "personal pathology, distress, and alienation are not due to a flawed personal psyche" but rather due "to oppressive structures of power."[77] The other view—held by many in the US—is that, though structures may contribute to "personal breakdown," it is ultimately "the consequence of personal developmental malfunctions."[78] Thus one view emphasizes the demonic as outer (oppressive systems), while the other views the demonic as inner (developmental malfunctions). Wink's integral worldview does not take an either/or approach but a both/and approach. Rather than seeing the demonic exclusively as a social (outer) problem, he also sees it as a personal (inner) issue. He states, "The notion that people are solely the victims of outer oppressive structures is materialistic, and denies human capacities for self-transcendence."[79] But at the same time, he says, "The view that psychopathology is rooted exclusively in the person is individualistic, and isolates people from the social matrix, without which human existence is impossible."[80] The individual and the social aspects of the demonic are both real, for the "individual can never be considered in isolation from the political, economic, and social conditions" in which we are all formed.[81]

But more than this, if we are to understand the outer demonic (social), dehumanizing aspects of the social systems, Wink believes we must understand this outer demonic as the "actual inner spirit of these suprahuman entities."[82] For social systems become demonic when the spirit of these social institutions defies its divine vocation to serve others and instead makes itself the ultimate end. Wink's integral worldview needs to be remembered here, as the Powers refers to the structured and invisible, the spiritual and political. It is important to remember that individuals have participated in building these social structures. Therefore, because individuals that live within these social structures are susceptible to their influence, the inner (individual) demonic feeds the outer (social) demonic, and the outer (social) feeds inner (individual).

While seeing the inner and outer as important manifestations of the demonic, in unmasking the demonic Wink makes some distinctions. There are three primary demonic manifestations:

- outer personal possession,
- collective possession, and
- the inner personal demonic.[83]

He describes the three this way:

> By outer personal possession I mean the possession of an individual by something that is alien and extrinsic to the self. By collective possession I mean the possession of groups or even nations by a god or demon capable of bending them as one into the service of death. And by the inner personal demonic I mean the struggle to integrate a split-off or repressed aspect that is intrinsic to the personality, an aspect that is only made evil by its rejection.[84]

Wink examines the various ways the demonic shows up in Scripture, taking seriously the effects it has on its victim(s). Below are some examples of each of these.

Outer Personal Possession. As a biblical example of outer personal demonic manifestation, Wink points to the Gerasene demoniac in Mark 5:1–20. Wink takes seven pages to explain this story. The social location—Decapolis—is significant for Wink. The fact that this demon says, "My name is Legion, for we are many" (Mark 5:9b) indicates that one person is bearing the brunt of the collective demonism. Wink writes, "Tradition rightly calls him the Gerasene demoniac, for that is precisely his function—to be the demoniac of the Gerasenes. That is why he pleads that his demons not be sent 'out of the country.' They 'belong' there. They are the spirit of the region, and the demonic is their incarnation."[85] Jesus casts the legion into two thousand pigs, which run off a cliff and are drowned in the lake below. When the town sees that the man is dressed and in his right mind, they plead for Jesus to leave. Wink makes the case that they beg Jesus to leave because they no longer had a person to carry their collective guilt.

Giving a more recent example, Wink shares a news story he heard when he was a pastor near Galveston, Texas, in the early 1960s. The story involved the pilot of the plane that dropped the atom bomb on Hiroshima: Major Claude Eatherly. Eatherly felt great remorse for what he had done and did not want to be seen as a war hero, so he committed some petty crimes and ended up in jail. Eventually, he was sent to a mental institution, based on the witness of a psychiatrist. In a letter to "the German philosopher Gunther Anders, Eatherly wrote, 'The truth is that society cannot accept the fact of my guilt without at the same time recognizing its own far deeper guilt.'"[86] Anders commends Major Eatherly's thoughts, saying, "Happy the times in which the insane speak out this way, wretched the times in which only the insane speak out this way."[87] Bertrand Russell also chimes in with some wisdom: "The world was prepared to honor him for his part in the massacre, but, when he repented, it turned against him, seeing in his act of repentance its own condemnation."[88] Wink concludes, "Outer personal possession thus reveals itself to be merely the personal pole of a collective malady afflicting an entire society. In outer personal possession one person bears the brunt of the collective demonism."[89]

With regard to outer personal possession, Wink gives helpful council in how to cast out demons by the power of the Spirit, but he cautions against unnecessary drama: "Jesus' exorcisms are . . . completely undramatic. He concedes the demons no power whatever. From his dimension of reality he sees them for what they are: the obsession of minds caught in darkness. So he simply dismisses them, and they flee."[90]

Collective Possession. The second manifestation of the demonic that Wink speaks of is collective demonization. He states, "In a highly individualistic society like ours it is rare to encounter single individuals who are possessed. Instead, the demonic has in our time taken the form of mass psychosis—what Rosen called 'socially shared psychopathology.'"[91] Not only did Søren Kierkegaard prophetically predict this, but the early church also understood that to some degree all people living in a world estranged by God are possessed and that "baptism was far more than a rite of passage; it was an exorcism."[92]

Wink points to the horrific examples in the past century of collective possession, naming Charles Manson, James Jones, and Adolf Hitler as examples. "Each tapped a deep longing in their followers to be cared for, to belong to a movement that gave their lives significance, to surrender themselves to the all-wise power of someone godlike."[93] He writes, "Collective demonism is the abdication of human answerability to God and the investment of final judgement in a divinized mortal."[94]

Collective demonization also manifests when people become captive to ideology. Wink writes, "Exorcism is radical. It answers to the problem of ideological blindness. Our involvement in evil goes far beyond our conscious, volitional participation in evil. To a much greater extent than we are aware, we are possessed by the values and powers of an unjust order."[95]

When it comes to exorcising collective possession, Wink writes, "The paradigmatic collective exorcism in the New Testament is Jesus' cleansing of the temple (Mark 11:11, 15–19 par.)."[96] This act takes place at the apex of Jesus' ministry, and is "the final provocation of his arrest and execution."[97] Wink writes, "Each account, even John's, uses the formulaic term for exorcism, *ekballo,* to describe his act of 'driving out' those who did commerce in the temple."[98] Wink mentions two more recent examples of exorcising collective possession: "The march across the Selma bridge by black civil rights advocates was an act of exorcism. It exposed the demon of racism, stripping away the screen of legality and custom for the entire world to see."[99] He also notes that "Caesar Chavez's struggles to organize farm workers in California was an exorcism. It unmasked the pitiless system of bracero labor and won both dignity and a living wage for some of America's worst-treated workers."[100]

Inner Personal Possession. The third manifestation Wink addresses is the inner personal demonic. Though the other forms of the demonic require exorcism, this form requires transformation. Quoting Mark 7:14–15, 21–23, where Jesus addresses the evil that originates in the human heart, Wink writes, "Jesus does not subscribe to the opinion that our emotions or habits should be cast out by exorcism. To attempt to cast out something essential to the self is like performing castration to deal with lust."[101] He mentions how he once took a depressed friend to a charismatic prayer meeting and the leader "cast out" her spirit of depression. Later, Wink learned that her depression was caused by repressed anger and frustration at her inability to express herself in a new faith community. "To 'cast it out' was merely to cast her depression's causes deeper into the unconscious, denying her the opportunity of gaining insight into her problem. And on top of everything else, it added an additional layer of guilt for not getting better."[102]

Table 4.1 summarizes the three ways Wink believes the demonic manifests itself and the appropriate response.[103]

Table 4.1. Wink's Responses to the Demonic

Manifestation	Description	Biblical Text	Remedy
Outer Personal	One person bears the brunt of the collective demonism	Mark 5:1–20	Exorcism, deliverance of a person or institution from its bondage to demonic evil
Collective	Diabolical possession *en masse*, divinizing some mortal above God	Ephesians 2:1–3	Symbolic acts of social protest through the ritual act of exorcism, unveiling ideological blindness
Inner Personal	The unintegrated aspect of the self, rendered grotesque from suppression or rejection	Mark 7:14–23	The shadow side must be owned and transformed

Wink believes that discernment is needed in dealing with the demonic. As this table illustrates, the remedy for the outer personal and collective differs from that for the inner personal.

Wink mentions that there is no room for abdicating personal responsibility for our own wrong choices by blaming Satan or the demons. For example, he says many in Germany during World War II allowed themselves to be possessed.[104] When speaking of the rise of Nazism, Wink writes, "They treat the demons as if they were disincarnate spiritual beings in the air, rather than the actual spirituality of Nazism. The demonic was inseparable from its political forms: the Hitler Youth, the SS, the Gestapo, the cooperation of the church, the ideology of Aryan racial purity, and the revival of Norse mythology."[105] For Wink, "The demonic was the interiority of the German state made into an idol. The demon was the Angel of Germany having turned its back on its vocation."[106]

Wink asserts that the Powers represent the mythic in Scripture—Satan, for example, is regarded as a snake and a dragon. Because they speak to the inner spiritual reality, these mythic characters hold significance far beyond Bultmann's demythologizing project. Wink follows what he believes to be Paul's methodology, demythologizing the Powers and ultimately identifying them with structures of human existence. Then with an integral worldview, he also seeks to *re*mythologize the Powers by recognizing that the Powers are the inner, invisible spiritual reality found in any organization or institution, whether that be a club, corporation, church, or nation. Therefore, if one seeks the transformation of an organization, it does not just happen by changing the people who hold different offices of power but by confronting the spirituality of the institution. This will be better understood as I examine Wink's understanding of the angels of churches.

Angels of Churches

Wink first discovered the angels of churches in 1964, when he was teaching the book of Revelation to some teens in the church he was serving in Hitchcock, Texas. He recognized that John addresses the churches differently than does Paul. Paul would typically write to the entire congregation. For example, "To the church in Corinth," while in the Apocalypse of John, John addressed his words to the angels of the churches.[107] It would be easy for Wink to agree with many in the 1960s that *angelos* simply means "messengers," as the word could be applied to humans as well as to heavenly agents. Recognizing these as human agents would have been more in line with his worldview at that time in his life. However, Wink writes, "I could not help but noticing that elsewhere in the book John never alludes to any such leaders. He himself seems to be the spiritual guide of these seven churches, and everywhere else that the term 'angel' appears in the Apocalypse, it unambiguously refers to heavenly messengers."[108] Beyond that, "John receives these letters in a heavenly vision which is itself mediated by an angel (Rev. 1:1)."[109]

Because Jewish and Christian literature of the time speaks of guardian angels over nations, nature, and individual people, and because early Christian theologians held to these being heavenly angels as opposed to human messengers, Wink felt compelled to interpret these messengers as angels. Of course, with his integral worldview—and because John addresses each angel as a single entity, "responsible for the church in its care"—it "would appear that the angel is not something separate from the congregation, but must somehow represent it as a totality."[110] The angel, for Wink, is the actual spirituality of the congregation: "As the corporate personality or felt sense of the whole, the angel of the church would have no separate existence apart from the people. But the converse would be equally true: the people would have no unity apart from the angel. Angel and people are the inner and outer aspects of one and the same reality."[111]

Wink then gives possible ways for one to discern the personality and vocation of the angel of a congregation. He starts with the visible, the outer, to discern the invisible or inner heart of the church. For instance, "all the values, prestige needs, aesthetics, and class status of a congregation will be projected into brick, board, and stone."[112] Some of the other outer manifestations Wink considers are the class, ethnic background, education, and age of the congregation; the structures of power; how the congregation handles conflict; high or low liturgies, as well as how inward or outward-facing the congregation is. These realities often continually shape the direction of the church or organization; though leaders change, *the personality of the organization* often remains the same. Wink asserts that the outer manifestations can shed light on the inner nature of the congregation, and he considers the angel of the church to incorporate both the visible and invisible realities of the church. He proposes that every collective entity, including the church, "that has continuity through time has an angel."[113] For example, there is an endurance that a school spirit has over generations. Churches also tend to display a continuity of their spirit: consider Notre Dame.

After understanding the personality of the church, Wink addresses how the vocation of the church determines how demonic or angelic the church happens to be. "The angel of a church becomes demonic when the congregation turns its back on the specific tasks set before it by God and makes some other goal its idol."[114] The goal of the Powers is idolatry, and only Christ, through his Spirit, can bring the necessary transformation in the church. Wink states,

> In the final analysis only Christ as the Spirit of the whole church can change a church, and only the renewed presence of that Spirit can bring the churches into line with their supreme vocation. Only as changes in personnel, programs, and relationships take place in congruence with that vocation will genuine transformation take place."[115]

In the remainder of *Unmasking the Powers*, Wink writes of the angels of nations, the gods, the elements of the universe, and the angels of nature. Wink believes that, as with the church, the angel of a nation is the "*inner spirituality of the social entity itself.*"[116] Though nations can help bond a diverse group of people, nationalism has an "irresistible tendency toward idolatry. In the name of this idol whole generations are maimed, slaughtered, exiled, and made idolaters. One hundred million lives have been offered on the altar of this Moloch thus far in the twentieth century."[117] Again, just as with the angels of churches, Wink believes that one needs to discern the personality and vocation of the angel of the nation, for angels tend to abandon their God-given vocations and lift themselves up as ultimate.

Throughout his trilogy, Wink recovers the importance of the Powers and how they shape reality. Though his project differs from Bultmann's, it also, by Wink's own admission, differs from the first-century understanding of the Powers. Wink states, "We cannot simply revive that ancient worldview without jettisoning much of what humanity has gained in the interval since. But we can reinterpret it. We can and must seek to recover in it the eternal truth revealed through its characteristic thought-forms, images, and presuppositions."[118] He believes the Powers are to be understood mythically: they are snakes, dragons, and four-headed creatures—the things of myth— so rather than embarking on a demythologizing journey (though he does this somewhat), he seeks to remythologize the Powers for those shaped by later worldviews. For Wink, the Powers are not just structures, as some liberation theologians might say, and they are not disincarnate spirits, as fundamentalists might believe—*rather, they are real spirituality embodied in concrete organizations, including the church and nations.*

ENGAGING THE POWERS

In the final book of the trilogy, *Engaging the Powers*, Wink addresses one of the most pressing questions facing the world today: "How can we oppose evil without creating new evils and being made evil ourselves?"[119] Wink believes that to engage evil in the world today, as well as to develop a social ethic from a New Testament perspective, requires a clear understanding of the Powers. He chooses the term *engage* as opposed to *confront, combat,* or *overcome,* because, for Wink, the Powers are created good; though fallen, they must be redeemed. He writes, "It is precisely because the Powers have been created in, through, and for the humanizing purposes of God in Christ that they must be honored, criticized, resisted, and redeemed."[120]

The Powers have an outer physical manifestation: the organization or institution, officers and offices. They also possess an inner spiritual reality: the heart and personality of an organization or church. "The Powers, properly speaking, are not just the spirituality of institutions, but their outer manifestations as well. The New Testament uses the language of power to refer now to the outer aspect, now to the inner aspect, now both together, as I have shown in *Naming the Powers*."[121]

The Powers are not a personification of the nature of the institution for Wink but the real spiritual ethos. Though he tends to think of the Powers as impersonal entities, Wink writes, "I have bracketed the question of the metaphysical status of the Powers, and have instead treated them phenomenologically—that is, I have attempted to describe the *experiences* that got called 'Satan,' 'demons,' 'powers,' 'angels,' and the like."[122] For him, demons are "the actual spirituality of systems and structures that have betrayed their divine vocations."[123] Wink calls this the "Domination System." The Domination System is when "an entire network of Powers become integrated around idolatrous values."[124] Wink refers to "'Satan' as the world-encompassing spirit of the Domination System."[125] So although Wink does not attempt to solve the metaphysical issue and prefers "to regard them as the impersonal spiritual realities at the center of institutional life," he nonetheless weighs in on the issue throughout his work.[126]

The Domination System

Wink first describes the Domination System when he demonstrates that the myth of redemptive violence is the spirituality of the modern world, grounded in the *Enuma Elish* myth, in which creation is an act of violence, where evil precedes good and order is established by disorder.[127] This myth goes by various names: "The Babylonian creation story, combat myth, the ideology of zealous nationalism."[128] Wink calls it the "myth of redemptive violence," the first articulation of "might makes right."[129] He states that this is the dominant myth in contemporary American culture, believed more than Judaism or Christianity.[130] In the myth of redemptive violence, "the survival and welfare of the nation are elevated as the highest earthly and heavenly good. There can be no gods before the nation. This myth not only establishes a patriotic religion at the heart of the state, but also gives that nation's imperialistic imperative divine sanction."[131] This myth is the spirituality of militarism and is religious in nature, for as Wink says, "One can only go to war religiously."[132] In other words, we make ultimate sacrifice for what we consider ultimate.

Defining the Terms: *Kosmos* (World), *Aiōn* (Age), *Sarx* (Flesh)

The Greek words *kosmos* (world), *aiōn* (age), and *sarx* (flesh) are the terms the writers of Scripture used to name the Domination System; they believed that by naming it, they could strip it "of its invisibility and legitimacy."[133] As I stated earlier, Wink mentions that when the word *world* is seen in the New Testament, it encompasses several meanings. It has positive connotations, as in "universe, the creation, humanity, the planet earth, the theater of history."[134] It is also used negatively, as when it "refers to *the human*

sociological realm that exists in estrangement from God."[135] This negative
view of the world contrasts with Craig Van Gelder and Dwight J. Zscheile's
attempts to view the world/culture more positively. As I demonstrate shortly,
the kingdom of this world is opposed to the kingdom of God. Since the term
world has so many different meanings, Wink finds it helpful to translate it
one way when referring to creation and people, whom God loves, and another
way to refer to that which is estranged from God. Wink suggests that if the
term *system* is used when referring to the *world* that is opposed to God, it
would bring some light to the naming and unmasking of the Powers.

For example, when the Pharisees challenge Jesus' authority to attack
their religious order, Jesus responds, "You are of this world; I am not of this
world" (John 8:23). Because Jesus is using the word *world* negatively here,
Wink asserts that using the word *system* might bring clarity and be less liable
to misinterpretation: "You are of this System; I am not of this System."[136]
If someone mistakes "this world" to mean that which God has created to
be good, it would make Jesus an otherworldly, nonhuman Gnostic when he
says, "I am not of this world." However, when *system* is used, it is obvious
that Jesus is not rejecting the good world that he has made. Instead, Jesus is
rejecting the Domination System that sees him as a threat because he testifies
against it, stating that its works are evil.[137]

When writing to the church in Ephesus, Paul speaks of the existing
system as a living death. The Phillips translation is written to "you, who
were spiritually dead all the time that you drifted along on the stream of this
world's ideas of living, and obeyed its unseen ruler" (Eph. 2:1 Phillips). Or
as Wink writes, using some of the key Greek terms in translating the second
part of the sentence: "'You walked according to the *aiōn* of this *kosmos*.'
This *kosmos* is the prevailing world-atmosphere that we breathe in like toxic
air, often without realizing it."[138] Wink believes that the Domination System
"penetrates everything, teaching us not only what to believe, but what we can
value and even what we can see."[139] And the presiding spirit of the Domination
System is Satan. Wink translates John 14:30–31 as follows: "I will no longer
talk much with you, for the ruler (*archōn*) of this System (*kosmos*) is coming.
He has no power over me; but I do as the Abba has commanded me, so that
the System may know that I love the Abba."[140]

If we, as leaders, are to learn how to name, unmask, and engage the
Powers, it is helpful for us to understand what *aiōn* means. It is often interchangeable with *kosmos* and translated as *world.* Instead of indicating the
structure of reality, it indicates the flow of time. "Any major time period in
the total temporal flow can be categorized as an *aiōn*."[141] Wink puts it this
way:

> The present world-period, however, is under the power of evil. Here
> again, as with *kosmos*, the term *aiōn* takes on a unique sense in some New

Testament passages. Thus the *kosmos* can be called "the present evil epoch (*aiōn*)" (Gal. 1:4), organized under Satan, "the god of this world-period (*aiōn*)" who "has blinded the minds of the unbelievers, to keep them from seeing the light of the gospel of the glory of Christ" (2 Cor. 4:4).[142]

In the same way that John uses *kosmos* to unmask the Domination System, uncovering the world system, Paul uses *aiōn* to speak of the Domination Epoch. Therefore, according to Wink, redeeming the time is not so much about being more efficient, but unmasking and engaging the oppression that has been taking place generation after generation under the current Domination Epoch. As Wink writes, "Evil in history was not always present; it had an origin in time. Likewise, evil will not always exist; it has an end in time, when 'this *aiōn*' is superseded by 'the *aiōn* to come' (Matt. 12:32). Thus, like 'world,' 'time' is good, fallen, and must itself be redeemed."[143]

The final term Wink seeks to clarify is *sarx*. Again, as with *kosmos* and *aiōn*, the term *sarx* (flesh) has both positive and negative connotations, depending on the context. Positively, it can refer to the physical body, the self, human beings, or humanity in general. Negatively, especially found in Paul, it is "in reference to the self in its alienated mode. Life lived 'according to the flesh' (*kata sarka*) denotes the self externalized and subjugated to the opinions of others."[144]

Wink continues to describe the alienated self: "It is the self socialized into a world of inauthentic values, values that lead it away from its own centeredness in God. It is the beachhead that the Domination System establishes in our beings. . . . it is pursuit of the values of the Domination System."[145] Wink describes *sarx* negatively as "a life lived according to the dictates of the Domination System."[146]

Each of these three terms is reflected as good in creation, though they become fallen and need redemption. God seeks to redeem bodies, time, and the world system, which, for Wink, speaks to the nature of the Domination System. In the remaining chapters of *Engaging the Powers*, Wink paints a picture of God's domination-free order (the kingdom of God). He speaks to how the victory of Christ helps us to engage the Powers and see the transformation for which we long. Wink believes that domination is more potent when we fail to perceive it, and that the victory of faith over the Powers is when we are "emancipated from their delusions."[147] Thus he not only gives us a vision of what God's domination-free order looks like, but he also gives concrete ways to engage the Powers in the way of Jesus, nonviolently. Discerning the spirits, being prayer warriors, lifting up God in praise, and living life in the Spirit hold promise to seeing the reign of God become more manifest on earth.

The Powers Are Good, Fallen, and Can Be Redeemed

Wink defines the good news as this: "God not only liberates us from the Powers, but liberates the Powers as well."[148] Looking to the hymn of the cosmic Christ in Colossians 1:16–20, where the Powers are described as having been created in, through, and for Christ, Wink suggests that the New Testament articulates that "evil is not intrinsic, but rather the result of idolatry."[149]

> For in him [Christ] all things were created; things in heaven and on earth, visible and invisible, whether thrones or powers or rulers or authorities; all things have been created through him and for him. He is before all things, and in him all things hold together. And he is the head of the body, the church; he is the beginning and the firstborn from among the dead, so that in everything he might have supremacy. For God was pleased to have all his fullness dwell in him, and through him to reconcile to himself all things, whether things on earth or things in heaven, by making peace through his blood, shed on the cross.
>
> COL. 1:16–20

We see here, in Wink's words, that the drama of Scripture is found in three simultaneous acts: the Powers are good, the Powers are fallen, and the Powers will be redeemed.[150]

The Powers are good in that, as the Colossians hymn indicates, they are God's creations, made to serve "the humanizing purposes of God in the world."[151] These powers are economic, political, and social structures required for human society. As Wink puts it, "They are not demonized as utterly evil; they are the good creations of a good God, and God, in the Genesis story of creation, creates no demons."[152] Although institutions are needed for human survival and it is appropriate for them to be concerned about their own survival, the danger comes when their survival becomes the ultimate goal. Here institutions become demonic.

Wink notes that while the Powers are good because they were created by God, it does not mean that God endorses any particular economic or political system. As Wink writes,

> The simultaneity of creation, fall, and redemption means that God at one and the same time *upholds* a given political or economic system, since some such system is required to support human life; *condemns* that system insofar as it is destructive of human actualization; and *presses for its transformation* into a more humane order. Conservatives stress the first, revolutionaries the second, reformers the third. The Christian is expected to hold together all three.[153]

Although the Powers are good, they are fallen and capable of radical evil. Wink has four significant points in regard to the doctrine of the fall. Here is the best summary of his understanding:

> I [Wink] submit (1) that the doctrine of the Fall provides an account of evil that acknowledges its brute reality while preserving the sovereignty and goodness of God and the creation; (2) that it is not just a temporal myth and thus did not simply happen "once upon a time," but is also a structural aspect of all personal and social existence; (3) that the doctrine of the Fall frees us from delusions about the perfectibility of ourselves and our institutions; and (4) that it reminds us that we cannot be saved from the Powers by anything within the Power System, but only by something that transcends it.[154]

The depth of the fall tempers expectations for Wink about what is possible on this side of the new heavens and new earth. For "the Powers are at one and the same time ordained by God and in the power of Satan."[155] Although the Powers can be made to positively serve human purposes, they are still fallen and in need of redemption. Fallenness is the fact that all live under the sway of the Domination System.[156] It is important to note that, for Wink, "there is in Scripture no account of the creation of the demons. Unlike the Powers, the demonic is not a constituent part of the universe. Its emergence is always an event in time, the consequence of wrong choices."[157] Institutions become demonic when they pursue idolatrous goals. "But what has become perverted in time can be redeemed in time."[158]

Wink asserts that the redemption of the Powers means taking seriously both the personal and social. The personal cannot be reduced to the social, as some liberationist theologians and philosophers believe, because "no structural change will, *of necessity*, produce good or transformed people."[159] Wink sympathizes with conversative groups within mainline American denominations who fault leaders who no longer see the need for personal evangelism, because he recognizes the problem is not just social but personal.[160] Wink believes that the reality of changed people who are reconciled with God and moving toward transformation is the very core of the gospel message.[161] And social change tends to happen when an individual or individuals stand up to unjust systems. Though human misery is caused by institutions, these institutions are maintained by people.

Wink thinks all evil cannot be wholly ascribed to social, political, or religious systems, because in the narrative of Genesis, the first fall is that of Adam and Eve. "Human sin is ontologically prior to all social systems and structures. Therefore, it cannot be reduced to social determinism, but is an act of willful rebellion against God (Genesis 3)."[162] The second fall that Wink notes is that of angels, saying "there is a rupture in the very spirituality of the universe (Gen. 6:1–4). Human sin cannot therefore account for all evil. There is a 'withinness' or spirituality in things that is capable of covetousness and insatiable greed."[163] The falls of humans and angels are then followed by the fall of nations (Genesis 11), where the systems and structures live their divine path through their idolatrous goals and hurt the people they were made to serve. For Wink, "Together, these three mythical tableaux from Genesis provide a vast panorama for contemplation. They prevent us from reducing people to society or society to people, the spiritual to the structural or the structural to the spiritual."[164]

Consequently, though the personal cannot be reduced to the social, it is also true that the social cannot be reduced to the personal, as some fundamentalist Christians might believe. Structures have their own laws, independent of individuals. And all companies, governments, and churches live in—and some *under*—the Domination System ruled and shaped by the evil one (Satan).

Jesus is not just Savior of souls but also of the systems and structures of the world. Therefore, Wink, throughout his writings, maintains that both evangelism and social justice go hand in hand; transformation and redemption must involve both personal and social aspects. Part of the church's evangelistic task, as Wink reminds us, is "proclaiming to the Principalities and Powers in the heavenly places the manifold wisdom of God (Eph. 3:10). And that means addressing the spirituality of actual institutions that have rebelled against their divine vocations and have made themselves gods."[165] The Powers are good, but the Powers are fallen; yet the hope is that because of the life, death, and resurrection of Christ, they will be redeemed, through personal and social transformation.

Wink has given us much to think about. His life warrants a close look at his theology. Because Wink's understanding of the Powers holds significant sway in the academic world, it is necessary to critically engage his theology of the Powers. But first I will consider his well-lived life through the lens of James William McClendon Jr.'s *Biography as Theology*, and with an understanding of Wink's life, I will consider his theology. For if we, as missional leaders, are unable to name, unmask, and engage the Powers, it will be difficult for us to overcome the problem of domineering leadership in the church.

5

INTERPRETING THE POWERS

Christians of nearly every stripe embrace Dietrich Bonhoeffer as a faithful servant of Christ, and he is also well-respected by many outside of the Christian faith. For different reasons, both the progressives and the conservatives claim him as their own. What is it about Bonhoeffer that is so compelling?

Bonhoeffer was a thoughtful writer on discipleship and ethics, but it is ultimately the life that he led—his lived-out ethics—that people find so inspiring. Both Bonhoeffer and Karl Barth guided the underground church by naming, unmasking, and engaging the Powers in the midst of a time when the majority of self-identified Christians failed to resist Hitler and his subversive ideology of Nazism. Other Christian theologians living in Germany at the time—such as Gerhard Kittel, Paul Althaus, and Walter Grundmann—aligned themselves with Hitler and his anti-Semitism.[1] History is the laboratory in which faith is tested, and as Glen Stassen writes, when we look in hindsight, "despite our different ethical perspectives," we widely agree about "who passed and who failed, who was faithful and who was unfaithful."[2]

A year before Hitler became chancellor, and a couple of years before Hitler became both president and chancellor, Bonhoeffer gave a lecture at an International Youth Conference, titled "The Church is Dead." He was calling the church to follow the Prince of Peace in the midst of a reality dominated by hatred, selfishness, division, fanaticism, fighting, mistrust, suspicions, and fears. At one point in his speech he said,

> How can one close one's eyes at the fact that demons themselves have taken over the rule of the world, that it is the powers of darkness who have here made an awful conspiracy and could break out at any moment? How could one think that these demons could be driven out, these powers annihilated with a bit of education in international understanding, with a bit of goodwill? . . .
>
> Christ must become present to us in preaching and in the sacraments just as in being the crucified one he has made peace with God and humanity. The

crucified Christ is our peace. He alone exorcizes the idols and the demons. The world trembles only before the cross, not before us.[3]

Bonhoeffer was able to clearly discern the Powers at work. When the majority of the church was captivated and lured to serve the Powers in their fallen state, Bonhoeffer resisted. While many Christians were looking to Hitler as the savior of Germany, Bonhoeffer recognized that Hitler was possessed by the Powers. If we hope to stand before Christ and have him say, "Well done, good and faithful servant" (Matt. 25:23), we, too, need to grow in our wisdom in how to name, unmask, and engage the Powers. The life and work of Walter Wink help us in this task.

UNDERSTANDING WINK THROUGH THE DOMINANT IMAGES THAT SHAPED HIS LIFE

To help us understand the life of Wink and the other dialogue partners in this book, I employ a methodology developed by James William McClendon Jr. in his book *Biography as Theology*. McClendon believes that "the hope of ethics, both secular and religious, lies in the recovery of what may be called an ethics of character."[4] He considers the prevailing understanding of the Western view of ethics (which is largely influenced by the Christian realism of Reinhold Niebuhr and the situation ethics of Joseph Fletcher) to be lacking.[5] While appreciating the valuable contribution these authors have made, he writes, "The shape of our times suggests that neither the one nor the other, nor both together, adequately express either the truly human or truly Christian ethical demand of the age waiting to be born."[6] He urges that a new approach to ethics is needed for today.

McClendon holds that a person's deepest beliefs shape their vision, which in turn shapes their character.[7] Character is forged in the context of communities of conviction. He defines conviction "as those tenacious beliefs that when held give definiteness to the character of a person or of a community, so that if they were surrendered, the person or community would be significantly changed."[8] McClendon notes that when leaders embody the convictions of the community in a compelling way, it gives fresh courage to the entire community to live more like Christ.[9]

Explementary leaders help the community better discern and form their own convictions regarding God, humanity, and creation.

These convictions, too, may be negated or enlarged, altered or reinforced, by the lives of such significant persons. Such lives, by their very attractiveness or beauty, may serve as data for a Christian thinker, enabling her more truly to reflect upon the tension between what is and what ought to be believed and lived by all.[10]

McClendon makes a case that we can develop better theological convictions by studying leaders who lived well, thus his title *Biography as Theology.*

> By recognizing that Christian beliefs are not so many "propositions" to be catalogued or juggled like truth-functions in a computer, but are living convictions which give shape to actual lives and actual communities, we open ourselves to the possibility that the only relevant critical examination of Christian beliefs may be one that begins by attending to lived lives.[11]

McClendon then studies the lives of Dag Hammarskjöld, Martin Luther King Jr., and Clarence Jordan—leaders he considers worthy of imitation—and attempts to "discover dominant images which unlock these biographies . . . [in order] to harvest some theology in the process."[12] McClendon does not attempt to construct a hagiography but instead shares both the strengths and weaknesses of these leaders, discerning the dominant images that shaped their lives.

If we were to study the life of the apostle Paul, for example, what might be the dominant image(s) that seemed to shape his life? Michael Gorman, in his study of the apostle Paul, argues that the guiding image shaping Paul's spirituality and life was *the cross of Christ*, hence the title of Gorman's book *Cruciformity: Paul's Narrative Spirituality of the Cross.*[13] Before examining the theology of Wink, I would like to consider the dominant images that seemed to shape his life.

WORD MADE FLESH

One of Wink's life-shaping metaphors was "Word made flesh." Wink married theory with practice and intellect with emotion for the sake of personal and social transformation, reflecting the concept of Word made flesh. The depth of his conviction was demonstrated in his willingness to risk and lose his tenure by challenging the normative approach to scriptural interpretation, which claimed objectivity and detached neutrality. He critiqued the tendency of academics to quarantine themselves from practitioners, and this shaped his desire to write for the community of faith as well as for the academy. Wink valued personal transformation and warned his students against "scholarship separated from the lived experience and from the engaged faith of readers."[14]

Wink's desire to empirically test God's promises opened him up to new opportunities where the Word became flesh in his life, and his unconsciously held rational, materialist worldview was challenged in the process. As I noted in the previous chapter, Wink conducted a weekly healing service at the church he was serving, risking the disapproval of his academic colleagues. As he began to see God physically heal people, it shaped his hermeneutical approach to the healing ministry of Jesus in the Gospels. Yet, because his colleagues were so skeptical, Wink found it difficult to share about his Pentecostal encounter. Wink therefore hid this experience until years later, when his spiritual director helped him to reclaim it. This may account for Wink's slightly underdeveloped pneumatology within his trilogy on the Powers.[15]

As I mentioned earlier, Wink's desire for personal transformation was evident in his first encounter with a Jungian approach to the text, which occurred in San Francisco, where, through an expression of art, he engaged in an eight-year project to rediscover his feelings. He would often warn his students to pay attention to the lives of scholars as well as to their work. Wink's commitment to his own spiritual development pushed him to immerse in Jungian thinking, which again reshaped his approach to the text. His pedagogical approach in the classroom was shaped by the communal experience of interpreting the text through a Jungian lens. As one student writes, "The participatory model of pedagogy itself has value beyond measure, both in the insights that evolve when a group labors together on a text, and in the empowerment of people as interpreters whose experience, ideas, and feelings are respected."[16] This student, now a professor herself, imitates many of the practices she learned from Wink. Summing up Wink's influence on many, Wayne Rollins writes,

> Wink's work to date is an extraordinary achievement . . . He has provided a paradigm for bringing together two sets of worlds formerly quarantined from one another. More than any other biblical scholar I know, Walter has bridged the gap between scholarship and life . . . between rationally objective and passionately subjective, between body and psyche, between book and being.[17]

Wink certainly left his mark on his fellow faculty and students, but he was also influential in other spheres.

KINGDOM ACTIVIST

The biblical promise that defined Wink's life was Matthew 6:33: "But seek first his kingdom and his righteousness, and all these things will be given to you as well." His telos was to see God's kingdom manifest itself more on this earth. Shaped by his boyhood experience of racism and by the influence of Martin Luther King Jr., Wink's praxis was just as important as his telos, for he understood that the end defines the means. His praxis was nonviolent direct action, and his work in South Africa helped to end apartheid. Though some might have theological disagreements with his vision of the kingdom, one would find it difficult to argue with his embodied practice. His willingness to put his life at risk in Selma, Chile, and South Africa demonstrate his commitment to see God's domination-free order (kingdom of God) actualized.

BEING HUMAN

The final telos in Wink's life was simply to be "human," through the imitation of Jesus. Wink makes a case that Jesus eschewed any pretentious titles and simply identified as the Son of Man.[18] In his work *The Human Being*, Wink undertakes a deep study of the term Son of Man, writing, "Idiomatically, the phrase simply means 'human being.'"[19] He believes we do not know what it means to be human and that "our society seems to be losing the battle for humanization. Violence, domination, killing, disrespect, terror, environmental degradation, and want have reached intolerable levels."[20] The Powers of domination have dehumanized us. Wink writes, "Humanity errs in believing that it is human. . . . We are only fragmentarily human, fleetingly human, brokenly human. We see glimpses of our humanness, we can dream of what a more humane existence and political order would be like, but we have not arrived at true humanness."[21] And it is Jesus who teaches us what it means to be human. "Jesus incarnated God in his own person in order to show all of us how to incarnate God. And to incarnate God is what it means to be fully human."[22]

All his life, Wink sought to increasingly know Jesus—the human one—recognizing Jesus as the key to his own identity. He writes, "I wanted to know who this Jesus really is. The church was my refuge; I learned about Jesus and, by his example, I saw how to live. His example of how to live opened up a new freedom that was felt, if not articulated."[23] For Wink, if one did not know and imitate Jesus, it would be difficult to live humanly in a world dominated by the Powers. Wink believes that if we are to imitate Jesus and seek God's domination-free order that Jesus was announcing, we would condemn all forms of domination, as Jesus did:

- patriarchy and the oppression of women and children;
- the economic exploitation and the impoverishment of entire classes of people;
- the family as chief instrument for socialization of children into oppressive roles and values;
- hierarchical power arrangements that disadvantage the weak while benefiting the strong;
- the subversion of the law by the defenders of privilege;
- rules of purity that keep people separated;
- racial superiority and ethnocentrism;
- the entire sacrificial system with its belief in sacral violence.[24]

Jesus exposed the Domination System, and Wink sought to do the same in his own life. But Wink recognized that this was a struggle for him, as it is for us. His desire was to become more real, more human.

Part of being human involves experiencing pain, weaknesses, and difficulties. Wink shares about the dark night of his soul in *Just Jesus*. This darkness caused him to write in his journal, "If I have a soul, it's silent. I don't know what the point of this book is anymore. If God won't heal me, God can go hang."[25] The dark night of his soul related to his continual health issues: "twenty years of restless leg syndrome (RLS), then prostate cancer (in remission), then pneumonia (healed), then dementia (fatal)," which he felt stripped him from his purpose on earth.[26] When health issues forced him to cancel his workshops and talks, he became depressed and felt as if a huge part of him had been amputated "without anesthesia."[27] In *Just Jesus*, Wink seeks to share more of his humanness, and he largely achieves this. However, the book never mentions the divorce from his first wife, which was referred to in Wink's obituary in the *New York Times*.[28] Steven Berry, who assisted Wink in writing *Just Jesus* because of Wink's dementia, confirmed that the full work on Wink's life is yet to be published.[29] But even with this omission, Wink exceeds most scholars in sharing his struggle to be human. And the many testimonies to Wink's life and work confirm that the mark he left on others was one of deep appreciation for a life well lived.[30] Because of this, it is worth examining his theology of the Powers.

WINK'S THEOLOGY OF THE POWERS AND MISSIONAL LEADERSHIP

Wink served the church by giving us the most comprehensive understanding of the Powers to date, one commendable to the Western academic milieu and experientially relevant in the face of evil today. His account of the Powers brings some apprehension to Van Gelder and Zscheile's positive view of the culture/world.[31] The goal of this analysis is to gain a better understanding of the nature and work of the Powers and to consider how that might inform our approach to missional leadership. Wink gives us much to digest. In this section, I will explore his worldview and ground rules, which are foundational to his project. I will then examine themes relevant to this book.

ANALYZING WINK'S WORLDVIEW AND GROUND RULES

First, Wink exegetes the text in context in order to understand what the Powers meant to the original recipients. He then transposes this understanding into what he considers to be the prevailing worldview of today, an integrated worldview. He wanted to make the Powers palatable to those unconsciously steeped in a materialist worldview and demonstrate the need for all to recognize the spiritual dimension of reality. For if we are going to join God in the renewal of all things, living into the telos of new creation, engaging the Powers is unavoidable. I believe Wink was successful in demonstrating the need to recognize the spiritual dimension of reality.

Wink would be a reinterpreter on the Ford/Frei scale (mentioned in chapter one), someone who sees "integration with modernity [or postmodernity] as more important and even essential to a modern theology."[32] He sought to do the hard work of contextualizing the message in today's Western context. Wink continually points out that worldviews are not the gospel but that "worldviews determine what we are allowed to believe about the world."[33] This rule also applies to the worldview Wink himself held. Translating the Powers to an integrated worldview was his primary theological task, yet he failed to give all the presuppositions he was working with when describing this worldview.

When *The Powers That Be*—the popular version of his trilogy—was published, he formally named the integrated worldview *panentheism* in contrast to *pantheism*. He writes, "In this worldview, soul permeates the universe. God is not just within me, but within everything. The universe is suffused with the divine. This is not pantheism, where everything is God, but pan*en*theism (*pan*, everything; *en*: in *theos*, God), where everything is in God and God in everything."[34] Some might dismiss Wink for this, but John W. Cooper (a classical theist who has done a major work in this area) describes the history, complexity, and variations of panentheism today.[35] He finds shades and varieties of panentheism in Jonathan Edwards, Paul Tillich, Jürgen Moltmann, and Wolfhart Pannenberg. Today, some—such as Moltmann and Wink—explicitly identify with panentheism, while others, in Cooper's opinion, are implicit, such as Pannenberg.[36]

Roger E. Olson writes about the complexity of defining panentheism today: "'Panentheism' is a somewhat flexible and evolving concept. When someone says 'panentheism' or 'panentheist' I ask what they mean. The term has no definite, universally agreed on definition. I no longer take it for granted."[37] For Olson, the affirmation of *creation ex nihilo* is "minimally necessary for a robust biblically and theologically sound doctrine."[38] Olson makes note that the classic text for the panentheist is Paul's quotation of the Greek poet: "'For in him we live and move and have our being'" (Acts 17:28). Yet Olson points out that this is directly preceded by "The God who made the world and everything in it is the Lord of heaven and earth and does not live in temples built by human hands. And he is not served by human hands, as if he needed anything. Rather, he himself gives everyone life and breath and everything else" (Acts 17:24–25). It is important to consider this in the analysis of Wink's work, for as Wink says, worldviews limit what one can believe.

One of the ways Wink's worldview seems limiting is in his understanding of the angels of churches. When Wink describes the angel of a church, it is not an external reality but the internal spirituality of the church. However, the

Scriptures seem to indicate that angels have appeared in exterior manifestations. The writer of Hebrews encourages hospitality, saying, "Do not forget to show hospitality to strangers, for by doing so some people have shown hospitality to angels without knowing it" (Heb. 13:2). Wink gives some helpful wisdom on the spirituality of the church, which can be discerned by looking at the outer (building, class) and inner (heart, vision) realities. Even so, to internalize angels to the soul of the church flattens the storyline of Scripture and seems to favor a disenchanted view of the world.[39] What would the story look like without the angel speaking to Mary, without angels singing at Jesus' birth? What would the narrative look like without the angels that ministered to Jesus in the wilderness, without the angel at Jesus' gravesite? What would the throne of God be like without the seraphim and cherubim and the myriad angels singing praises?

One should question not only certain aspects of this worldview but also Wink's fourth rule of interpretation, which states that the terms relating to the Powers are, to a degree, interchangeable.[40] This does not seem evident, though he does note there are exceptions where the context warrants it. Marva Dawn writes,

> Though the terms *arche, dunamis, exousia, thrones,* and *kuriotes* occur interchangeably on lists in the Scriptures, it seems that there are some differences between them and words for angels (*angelos*) and demons (*diamonia*)—names that often seem specifically to signify supernatural beings. Wink's mixing together of all the terms confuses the meanings of these two sets, though the biblical usage suggests some precision in its choices from the two kinds of terms. Thus, Wink's proposition 4—that all terms are interchangeable and that one or more can represent them all— seems to be in error.[41]

Although there are possible cracks in the foundation of his argument, Wink still brings much value to the Powers conversation. As this analysis proceeds, it is helpful to be alert to Wink's worldview and the exceptions to his fourth rule.

UNDERSTANDING THE "PRINCIPALITIES AND POWERS" IN PAUL

With regard to discerning the nature of the principalities and powers in Paul, New Testament scholar Andrew Lincoln poses two important questions. His first question is concerned with the exegetical task: how the first-century writers and readers would have understood the language about the Powers. His second question addresses the hermeneutical task: appropriating the Powers language for our time and setting.[42]

Wink separates exegetical work in discerning the text's meaning in the context of production from the hermeneutical work of appropriating the text in the context of reception. His exegetical work holds great value, as does his hermeneutical work. Though Lincoln commends people such as Clinton Arnold and their approach to exegesis, he finds fault with their approach to hermeneutics. He says, "While their concern for accurate exegesis is to be applauded, their own confusion about the relation of exegesis and contemporary appropriation may be as great as those they criticize."[43] Lincoln sees much value in appropriating the Powers as structures and ideologies, because Christians have always sought to reapply the text for their time and place.[44] Although he picks up on some flaws in the exegesis of Berkhof and Wink, he considers their interpretations and reapplication of the Powers to be more of a gift to the church than a concern.[45]

Lincoln, along with others, recognizes that understanding the nature and work of the Powers is part of the larger problem of "human life in the face of evil"; he also believes that the authors of Scripture are more interested in offering solutions to evil than explaining the mystery of its origin or becoming absorbed in debates about exousiology.[46]

Lincoln agrees with Arnold's exegesis, but he also gives three alternatives to appropriate the language of the principalities and powers today:

> (a) the relevant texts were referring to supernatural forces in their original communicative situation and this worldview is to be accepted or reasserted now [this is essentially what Clinton Arnold seeks to do]. (b) The texts were referring to supernatural forces then but are best appropriated in terms of ideologies and societal structures now. (c) The texts were referring to both supernatural and human or earthly forces then and so can be appropriated in terms of the latter now in continuity with the original meaning of the texts.[47]

Lincoln considers the first option untenable in the face of fully engaging the Powers today; and at the time of his writing, he felt like proponents of the third option had failed to make their case strongly enough.[48] He personally held to a variation of option B:

> This simply involves seeing an analogy between the function of the powers then and of ideologies and institutions now. Analogy, of course stresses significant similarities but also allows for differences. It is certainly not claiming any one-to-one correspondence between the original and the appropriation. But making this analogy could also be seen in terms of remythologization. Those who wish to go further, however, by saying that what in their experience Paul and his followers called principalities and powers is the same as what in our experience we encounter as ideologies and social structures, are more clearly involved in demythologizing

and claiming some one-to-one correspondence in experience between the original and the appropriation.[49]

Lincoln's approach seeks to be faithful to the context of production and, by valuing the contribution of Berkhof and Wink, sees much value in having a broader approach to hermeneutics than does Arnold. Still, there is compelling recent exegetical scholarship that supports the third option—in particular, New Testament professor Chris Forbes's exegetical work on the principalities and powers, which refers to them as both spiritual agents as well as ideologies and social structures.[50] Forbes's both/and characterization makes a case that "Paul's description of the 'spiritual world' combines elements familiar from the rest of the New Testament (angels and demons, etc.) with his own less personal, more abstract concept of 'principalities and powers.'"[51] Forbes argues that although Paul never takes angels and demons off the radar, in terms of frequency and theological development, Paul takes more interest in the principalities and powers, which for Forbes, is more abstract, like "the 'Law, Sin and Death,' and the 'elements of this world.'"[52] Forbes argues that the distinct concept of "principalities and powers" expressed by Paul is best understood in the popular expressions of Middle Platonism, found in Philo and Plutarch. So rather than demythologizing the demonology of his apocalyptic heritage, Paul saw a continuum between pure abstractions ("height" and "depth," Rom. 8:39), personifiable abstractions ("principalities and powers"), literary personifications ("Law, Sin, and Death"), and "actual" personal spiritual beings.[53] Forbes believes this view goes back as far as the fifth century BCE in Greek thinking and is found in the time of Paul's writing. He writes, "In his understanding of 'principalities and powers', Paul is working creatively between the angelology and demonology of his Jewish heritage, and the world-view of the thoughtful Graeco-Roman philosophical amateur."[54]

This understanding of the principalities and powers gives credence to the work of Arnold, Berkhof, Wink, and Lincoln, while issuing a correction to each of them. Seeing the principalities and powers from a both/and perspective (both as spiritual agents and social structures), as opposed to an either/or perspective, brings a greater continuity between the exegetical and hermeneutical task. Although Arnold's view speaks to the majority world (the Global South), and Berkhof and Wink appeal to those living in the plausibility structure of the Western milieu, Forbes's exegetical work comprehensively demonstrates how Paul was inspired by the Holy Spirit to speak to the reality of how the Powers are encountered in different contexts.

Scholars need not hold a disenchanted worldview in which angels and demons are reinterpreted as structures or as the inner spirituality of an organization alone. In fact, holding this idea seems to give an incomplete view of the forces that work against the leader. Thomas R. Yoder Neufeld, in his commentary on Ephesians, helpfully points out that the many descriptions of spiritual realities in 6:12 "are intended to be shorthand for the myriad of powers, great and small, personal and impersonal, individual and systemic, that resist the saving activity of God among humanity."[55]

Neufeld gives a helpful reminder that this terminology speaks to how these Powers shape the atmosphere of the world today. Understanding that the Powers involve spiritual entities as well as ideologies and social structures, Neufeld stresses how Paul encourages God's people as a collective community to put on the full armor of God as a concrete communal practice to resist the Powers.

In my studies and experience, it seems that the primary way the Powers manifest in the Western world is through social realities such as image, ideology, and institution, which I will address later in the book. Still, in places such as Africa, Latin America, and some parts of Asia, demon manifestations of another kind seem more common. Though Wink does not discount this, some of his writing seems to poke fun at the ancient worldview. As missional leaders, we will likely fail to minister to these cultures adequately without a comprehensive understanding of the Powers, including Satan, demons, the flesh, and world systems.[56] Given the increasing diversity in Western cultures, a lack of solid contextualization may prohibit leaders from ministering to every people group living in the West. African scholar Robert Ewusie Moses points out that the New Testament writers have a message "that demands an epistemological transformation, and is, therefore, a scandal to all who have not experienced this epistemological transformation."[57] Thus we must be careful when we seek to reinterpret the Powers for our context.

ANALYZING WINK'S VIEW OF SATAN

Wink espouses an unconventional view of Satan. Although analysis will show that his view of Satan's telos is precarious, Wink is right to note that Satan is a developing character in the biblical story, with little attention given to him in the Hebrew text.[58] Following Bernhard W. Anderson's overview of *Sin and the Powers of Chaos*, Susan R. Garrett gives a brief overview of biblical perspectives on Satan and evil from Genesis to Revelation.[59] When it comes to our understanding of evil and suffering in the world, the beginning of the story emphasizes the fault being humans' misuse of their God-given freedom and their consequent guilt and punishment. In Revelation, by contrast, the focus is no longer merely on human sin but on the wider dimensions of the evil that corrupts the cosmos. In Revelation, the serpent has become "the archenemy of God, the leader of the hosts of chaos, who foments a rebellion that spreads through the whole creation."[60] Garrett mentions that at the heart of Mosaic covenant theology, evil and suffering were the consequence of human failure.[61] In Daniel's time, the apocalyptic writers "provided 'a new understanding of the radical power of evil.'"[62] "To symbolize this tyranny of evil in society and in history, the book of Daniel reaches back into the mythic heritage that ancient Israelites shared with their neighbors."[63] Then there was a shift to Satan. Garrett explains,

> The story of Satan's emergence in the late pre-Christian era as archfiend of God and God's people is intricate and difficult. Over the course of centuries, Jews had reflected on various adversary-figures known from ancient myths about combat by God (or the gods) with divine enemies. These myths circulated throughout the ancient Near East and were preserved both in independent narratives and in snippets scattered throughout the Hebrew Scriptures. Adversary-figures from these myths included the rebellious angels of Genesis 6:1–4 and of subsequent legendary retellings, the dragon Leviathan, the arrogant rulers of Isaiah 14 and Ezekiel 28–32, a character named Belial (from a Hebrew word meaning "worthless, useless, productive of disorder"), and the archfiend from Zoroastrian religion (known as Angra Mianyu or Ahriman). In the third or second century BCE, ideas about these adversary figures began to merge with and shape developing views on the character of *satan* (a Hebrew word meaning "accuser" or "adversary") as known from Job, Zechariah, and 1 Chronicles.[64]

Garrett mentions that at the time Genesis was written, "the archfiend Satan was not yet in view, but as centuries passed interpretations of Genesis 3 changed."[65] This is confirmed by biblical theologians John and J. Harvey Walton, and the historical development of Satan is confirmed by Lincoln.[66]

By New Testament times, Jesus describes Satan as the thief who "comes only to steal and kill and destroy" (John 10:10). Thus, when Wink characterizes Satan more positively in the New Testament, it seems inaccurate. For although God, in his sovereignty, can use the devil for his own purposes, this does not overturn the fact that Satan's sole mission is to kill, steal, and destroy. As Gregory Boyd writes, "It is one thing to say that God in his sovereign wisdom is able to put Satan's evil activity *to good use*, and quite another thing to say that Satan *carries out* God's good purposes by engaging in his evil activity."[67]

It seems that Wink's view of Satan leans more heavily on Carl Jung, as Jung believes that God would be better understood as Quaternity instead of Trinity. Les Oglesby, quoting Jung, says, "Christ and the devil appear as equal and opposite, thus conforming to the idea of the 'adversary'. This opposition means conflict to the last, and it is the task of humanity to endure this conflict until the time or turning-point is reached where good and evil begin to relativize themselves."[68] For Jung, the devil represents the shadow side of God; and humanity, along with the Holy Spirit, would help resolve the tension between the brothers—Christ and the antichrist (Satan).[69] This dependence on Jung is seen throughout Wink's writings, though Wink views Satan more darkly when considering Satan as the spirit of the Domination System. Wink seems to have hope for Satan's redemption when he writes, "Then perhaps, if we can live through that dark interval between Satan's death and resurrection, we may yet see Satan functioning again—as a servant of the living God!"[70] This seems contrary to the telos that Jesus gives to Satan and his demons (Matt. 25:41; Rom. 16:20; Rev. 20:10).

UNDERSTANDING THE DEMONIC

Wink's view of the demonic seems to better reflect Revelation, and his analysis of the different manifestations of the demonic and their remedies is helpful. Yet, although he provides some distinction between Satan, the demonic, and principalities, I do not think he is as clear as he could be. He does provide the following helpful distinction between the demonic and the principalities and powers:

> We, and the Powers, are the good creations of a good God. By contrast, there is in Scripture no account of the creation of the demons. Unlike the Powers, the demonic is not a constituent part of the universe. Its emergence is always an event in time, the consequence of wrong choices. An institution becomes demonic when it abandons its divine vocation for the pursuit of its own idolatrous goals. But what has become perverted in time can be redeemed in time.[71]

Pentecostal scholar Amos Yong, appreciative of Wink, gives a helpful emergent view of the demonic. He believes the Powers in their fallen state are "susceptible to demonic manifestations."[72] He clarifies this in three sub-theses:

First, "the demonic has no ontological reality of its own but is rather a perversion of the goodness of the orders of creation—or, put alternatively, since the demonic is not created by God, it does not possess its own being."[73] In this he agrees with Wink. Barth affirms this Augustinian claim regarding evil.[74]

Second, "the demonic is, nevertheless, objective as an emergent reality, parasitic and dependent upon certain configurations of the material, institutional, and organizational structures of powers, but yet irreducible to the sum of its constituent parts."[75] This seems stronger than Barth's idea of "nothingness." Yong's Pentecostal background and phenomenological studies testify to the reality of the demonic.[76]

Third, "once emergent, the demonic manifests as a force of destruction wielded in and through the fallen and disordered powers, appearing in ways to suggest the powers have become transcendental realities, 'larger' than what they are, certainly overreaching their authority, and seemingly personal and intentional in their destructive capacities."[77]

If we take these three statements collectively, we can see how institutions of various sorts, in their fallen state, are susceptible to the "emergence of demonic trajectories."[78] "If and when this happens, governments become tyrannical, nations become anarchic, economic systems become unjust, and social systems foster death instead of life."[79] An obvious example of this in our day would be Kim Jong-un in North Korea, but perhaps more subtle examples would be runaway capitalism, as depicted in the popular 2021 Netflix series *Squid Game*, or forced socialism, as demonstrated in the history of countries such as Russia or East Germany.[80] Marva Dawn makes the point that churches can also become fallen powers, making them susceptible to the demonic.[81]

THE IMPORTANCE OF STOICHEIA

In *Naming the Powers*, Wink examines the word *stoicheia* in the seven places it is found in the New Testament, noting that it is used in the following ways:

- The ABCs, the elementary or first principles of faith—Heb. 5:22, and Gal. 4:9 in part
- The constituent elements of the physical universe—2 Peter. 3:10, 12
- The basic constituents of religious existence common to Jews and Gentiles alike (rituals, festivals, laws, beliefs)—Gal. 4:3, 9; Col. 2:20
- The first elements or founding principles of the physical universe—Col. 2:8[82]

Wink asserts that the theological issue that emerges for Paul in relation to *stoicheia* "focuses on the problem of idolatry."[83] Paul warns the Colossians that if they are captivated by "hollow and deceptive philosophy, which depends on human traditions and elemental spiritual forces of this world rather than on Christ," they are in danger (Col. 2: 8). Wink writes,

> What is most basic to existence begins to be worshiped, either overtly or, as more than often happens, unconsciously, as people abandon themselves to religious practices or philosophical ideals or ideological principles. When that happens, the *stoicheia* become functional gods, and their devotees are alienated from the One in and through and for whom even these most basic things in existence were created.[84]

Note how Wink points out that Paul's concern is the problem of idolatry. As I will explore later, idolatry is a significant theme for William Stringfellow. Though many in the West consider idols a thing of the past, Stringfellow exposes this fallacy by naming the popular idols common to daily existence: "religion, work, money, status, sex, patriotism."[85] He describes idols as imposters of God. When human beings seek to justify themselves, offer themselves, and give tribute to their chosen idols, they end up in bondage to death. The result is that idolatry "defies God and dehumanizes men."[86] *Stoicheia* correlates with some of the ways William Stringfellow conceptualizes the Powers in today's vernacular: the ideas of image, ideology, and institution, as I will examine later, in chapter eight.

THE DOMINATION SYSTEM

This critical analysis of Wink has increased the awareness of the ubiquity of the Powers and unmasked how they subvert God's purposes and intentions. Wink writes,

> Surveying all the data covered, it is amazing that this has been so consistently overlooked. On every page of the New Testament one finds the terminology of power: those incumbents, offices, structures, roles, institutions, ideologies, rituals, rules, agents, and spiritual influences by which power is established and exercised. The language and reality of power pervade the New Testament because power is one of the primary ways the world is organized and runs. No human activity can be described without recourse to this language.[87]

When leaders of any institution or organization (including church leaders) rest their authority on false transcendence, they are susceptible to the demonic abuse of their authority and power. As I show later when I engage René Girard, false transcendence is when leaders live under the sway of Satan. When leaders knowingly or unknowingly rely on false transcendence, they fall to coercive worldly power as opposed to living in the power of the Spirit as evidenced by the fruit of the Spirit.

Wink refers to the Powers as being created good, and having fallen, they can be redeemed. However, if there is no distinction between Satan and the demonic (which seem unredeemable) and the principalities and powers (which are created good), then the redemption of the Powers that Paul writes about in Colossians 1:16 would be confusing. Stringfellow, Yong, Berkhof, and others believe that the subcategory of the principalities and powers is distinct from Satan and the demonic. As Yong writes, "The powers are creations of God ordained for his purposes. . . . But the powers are fallen, and in their fallen condition are susceptible to demonic manifestations. . . . But the powers can be redeemed."[88] This makes the most sense of the texts on the principalities and powers in Paul, especially when one considers the Greek words that are used in Colossians 1:16 in Wink's analysis of the verse, prior to his reinterpretation of the Powers.

There are a number of key words to explore in Colossians 1:16. The first word is *thrones*, which is more about the symbolic location of power, like the "county *seat*, the judge's *bench*, the *chair*person, the *oval office*," more than it is about the person inhabiting that place of power.[89] One way to understand this is that the authority of that office outlasts its current occupant.[90] Another key word is *dominions* (NKJV; *kyiotétes*), which refers to the sphere of influence over which the thrones hold sway. This sphere of influence could be "visible (the actual land or area ruled) or invisible (its capacity to influence other Powers by threat or persuasion)."[91] *Principalities* (NKJV; *arché*) specifies not so much the person themselves, but "the person-in-office, the agent-in-role."[92] In other words, it only applies to the person when they are in that office, like when a person is serving in Congress or the Senate. Finally, there are *authorities* (*exousiai*), which Wink says refer to the way in which authority is maintained. "These are the invisible and visible authorizations and enforcements that undergird the chair. Legitimations would include the laws, rules, taboos, mores, codes, and constitutions by which power is licensed, and all the customs, traditions, rituals, manners, etiquette, and ideologies by which is it rationalized, justified, and made habitual."[93] Thus his paraphrase of Colossians 1:16 is the following:

> For within his [the Cosmic Christ's] wisdom every power in the universe has been created, those in heaven and those on earth, those visible and those invisible—whether seats of powers or spheres of influence, whether incumbents-in-office or legitimations and sanctions that keep them there—all these social and spiritual structures of reality are sampled with his imprint and exist solely to serve his purposes.[94]

Wink, according to his fourth rule, suggests that the Powers are interchangeable. Thus, when Paul writes in the verses following this that "God was pleased to have all his fullness dwell in him [Jesus], and through him to reconcile to himself all things, whether things on earth or things in heaven" (Col. 1:19–20), Wink seems to imply that Satan can be redeemable. But as Dawn has already pointed out, angels and demons are of a different nature, and they are not listed in this passage; neither is Satan. This seems to confirm the idea that the principalities and powers are redeemable, but Satan and the demonic are not.

The elements of power and authority mentioned in Colossians 1:16 include not only corporations, governments, and institutions, but also the church. This holds hope for the church that has come under the domination of the Powers, for churches can be redeemed from coercive power.

IMITATING JESUS AMID THE POWERS OF DOMINATION

Wink rightly emphasizes that our new spiritual renaissance will focus on the human Jesus and his teachings, and that "the sayings on nonviolence and love of enemies will hold a central place."[95] The acid test if we are to follow Jesus in today's polarized world is the ability to love our enemies, real or perceived. Wink believes that false prophets have something in common: the inability to love their enemies as Jesus did.[96] Quoting James A. Sanders, Wink says, "No false prophet can ever conceive of God as being God also of the enemy."[97] Wink writes of how many have dismissed Jesus' teaching on enemy love as "impractical, idealistic, and out of touch with the need of nations and oppressed peoples to defend themselves."[98] But Wink questions why this same charge or irrelevancy has not been applied to the account of redemptive violence, "despite the fact that it fails at least half the time."[99] He writes,

> Its exaltation of the salvific powers of killing, and the privileged position is it accorded by intellectuals and politicians alike (to say nothing of theologians), make redemptive violence the preferred myth of Marxists and capitalists, fascists and leftists, atheists and churchgoers alike. Redemptive violence is the prevailing ideology of the Institute of Religion and Democracy and segments of the World Council of Churches, of *Christianity Today* and *Christianity in Crisis*, of much of liberation theology and much of conservative theology.[100]

For Wink, the predominant ideology that undergirds the Domination System is the myth of redemptive violence, which is only countered by imitating the human Jesus. Wink gives concrete ways to deal with oppression through nonviolent direct action in the way of Jesus. Though a greater exploration of this theme is beyond the scope of this book, it is well worth further reading on the matter.[101] For though Jesus was willing to die, he was never willing to kill. As we will see when I engage Girard, domineering leaders do not tend to love their enemies; they tend to demonize and scapegoat them.

SUMMARY OF SECTION TWO

As a scholar and activist, Wink sought to name, unmask, and engage the Powers. This was not just something he wrote about but also something he actively lived. His project is best understood as taking the text seriously in its context of production and seeking to transpose it to the context of reception. Thus, instead of articulating the Powers in an ancient worldview (in which transcendence is considered upward), he translates them into an integral worldview (in which transcendence is considered inward). Therefore, for Wink there is an inner and outer dimension to the Powers. The outer represents the visible aspects of an organization or institution, including the building, officers, offices, and people. The inner consists of the invisible part of the organization, the spirituality or soul of the institution.

Much understanding can be gained from Wink's work. But some ideas may need to be clarified, namely some elements of his panentheistic worldview, which seems to flatten the narrative regarding angels, as well as his heavy reliance on Carl Jung, which leads to a misunderstanding of Satan's destiny.

The primary contribution Wink makes to this book is that he alerts us, as missional leaders, to the pervasive work of the Powers—in particular, through the ways in which he unmasks the Powers and eschews worldly power. He elevates the awareness of the Powers and helps to bring this theme into discussion in the academy. As Newbigin writes, "Walter Wink in his series of volumes on the principalities and powers has helped us to see afresh the relevance to our situation of the Biblical language of the powers. It is not true, Wink reminds us, that the Church's message is addressed only to individual people."[102]

By defining key terms such as *world*, *epoch*, and *flesh*, Wink clears up the ambiguity found in the work of Van Gelder and Zscheile. Wink demonstrates how the Powers work at every level possible, from the personal to the social to the cosmic. This corresponds to Stringfellow's articulation of the Powers, which I examine in chapter eight. There is no escaping the influence of the Powers. They are at work through all the ideologies that unconsciously hold people captive. They are at work through the various institutions and organizations in which leaders participate, including the church. In this way, Satan earns his title of being the "god of this world," for his influence is cosmic in nature. Lincoln confirms how ideologies hold people in bondage, from which they need to be redeemed.[103]

An understanding of the Powers alerts missional leaders to the ubiquity of the fall and to the need to name, unmask, and engage the Powers that seek to subvert them. The all-pervasiveness of the Powers should stimulate us, as missional leaders, to be cognizant of all the forces at work against us, and it should motivate our need to develop a spirituality in Christ, through the power of the Spirit. As Lincoln writes, "The real value of Wink's work, and the same holds true of Ellul's, lies not in its basis in exegesis of the Pauline principalities and powers, but in its ability to provide a penetrating and profound phenomenology of present powers of evil in the light of the gospel and an inspiring vision of the spirituality needed to engage such powers."[104] Thus Wink has accomplished the work needed for this imitation-based conceptual framework: demonstrating the central importance of a missional spirituality robust enough to counter the subversive work of the Powers and to redeem the principalities and powers.

Regarding missional leadership and imitation, Wink's life and work demonstrates the need for us, as leaders, to imitate the praxis of Christ—the only alternative being to mimic the Powers. Wink points out how the Powers seem to have captured both the left and the right, as they tend to mimic the Powers by engaging those in power with the same means: the use of force. The focus on imitating Christ helps us to recognize that the way of Jesus is radically different from the way of the world. Wink's efforts in combating racism in South Africa and his willingness to put his life at risk in Selma demonstrate his commitment to follow Christ, even if it meant suffering.

Wink's work on the Powers and James K. A. Smith's thoughts on the preeminence of desire, combined with Fitch's on the power of imitation, bring support to the underlying premise of this book: fallenness is imitating the Powers in their submission to Satan, which is bondage to idolatry and leads to dishonoring God and dehumanization. Meanwhile, redemption is imitating Christ in his submission to the Father, which is freedom from idolatry and leads to honoring God and human flourishing. Wink devotes an entire chapter to René Girard, whom I will engage in the next chapter. Girard's work demonstrates how leaders are tied to the Powers through mimetic desire.

Regarding leadership and desire in Wink's life, his desire to achieve was based on his desire to be loved. As I emphasized, when leaders seek to accomplish *for* love instead of *from* being God's beloved, it leads to a malformation of desire. Henri Nouwen reminds us that prior to Jesus being led by the Spirit into the wilderness to confront the devil, the words of the Father at Jesus' baptism named him as his beloved. Jesus was grounded in a spirituality that enabled him to resist imitating the devil by not taking on his desires. Instead, Jesus sought to do the will of him who sent him. Thus Wink gives much strength to the imitation-based framework being developed in this book.

In conclusion, when leaders live under what Wink has properly labeled the Domination System and end up mimicking the Powers, they begin to reflect this domination in their leadership. As I explore Girard and Stringfellow, a clearer picture of how this happens will emerge. Through Wink, we learn that it is crucial for us, as missional leaders, to develop a theology of the Powers so that we are able to name, unmask, and engage them at personal, social, and cosmic levels. The temptations we face require a holistic response that deals with our identity, praxis, and telos.

James K. A. Smith makes the case that human beings are not simply people-as-thinkers, shaped by ideas; or people-as-believers, shaped by faith—ultimately, humans are people-as-lovers, shaped by desire. So how do the ideas of imitation and desire interact, and how can an understanding of mimetic desire help us understand the ways the Powers seek to subvert us? Girard offers profound understanding in this.

SECTION THREE

MISSIONAL LEADERSHIP
AND IMITATION

MISSIONAL LEADERSHIP

In articulating a theology of the Powers, Wink
communicates that when we live under the Domination
System, we inevitably become domineering in our
leadership by mimicking the Powers. René Girard furthers
that understanding by highlighting how we, as humans,
are creatures of imitation, and when we choose to imitate
the wrong models, we unwittingly end up mimicking the
Powers. I summarize Girard's mimetic theory in chapter
six, and in chapter seven I analyze and engage mimetic
theory in areas pertinent to this book. I will demonstrate
how understanding mimetic theory—the mimetic cycle
in particular—will give us motivation to imitate Christ
and become models worth imitating. Engagement
with Girard's work will strengthen the imitation-based
framework by linking imitation and desire (mimetic
desire) to a theology of the Powers.

6

MIMETIC THEORY

Each of us is a model to someone. If you are a parent of young children, you serve as a model to them. You also serve as a model to those in your workplace or ministry. Whether your influence is with a few or with many, your example matters.

As humans, we are imitative by nature. Aristotle wrote, "Imitation is natural to man from childhood, one of his advantages over the lower animals being this, that he is the most imitative creature in the world."[1] As leaders, we have all heard the axiom that more is caught than taught. We can tell those in our congregations to go out on mission, or we can model it and take others with us. Parents can lecture about the importance of not being glued to screens, but if they do not model that, it is unlikely their children will do what they are told.

As a missional leader seeking to pattern my life after Jesus, my underlying assumption is that people learn from a combination of instruction, immersion in mission, and imitation. Faith, hope, and love are essential for building rich community—the greatest being love. Similarly, instruction, immersion, and imitation are necessary in making missional disciples—the greatest being imitation.

René Girard's key discovery, which he confirms through theology and various academic disciplines, is that those who look to us as models will imitate our desires. Through the work of James K. A. Smith, I have already explored how what makes us most human is our desires. We become what we love, and ultimately, what we love is what we worship. Whether or not we are aware of it, those desires also shape the desires of those who look to us as models. Likewise, whether consciously or not, we all have models who influence our desires. This is what Girard calls *mimetic desire*. We imitate the desires of those we look up to, our models.

INTRODUCING RENÉ GIRARD

René Girard (1923–2015) was born in Avignon, France, on Christmas Day. His full conversion to the Christian faith took place on Easter of 1959. Over the course of his career, he wrote more than twenty books and many articles.

Girard died at the age of ninety-one. As an academic, Girard's research and work spread across many disciplines, including history, philosophy, sociology, psychology, anthropology, and theology. Not only did Girard engage the literary works of Dostoevsky and Shakespeare, but he also critically engaged Freud, Nietzsche, Darwin, Lévi-Strauss, and others.[2] Girard served on the faculties of Indiana University, Duke University, Bryn Mawr College, and the State University of New York before becoming the Andrew B. Hammond Professor of French Language, Literature, and Civilization at Stanford University (1981–1995). Besides having two earned doctorates, one in France and one in the United States, he received six honorary doctorates from universities in the Netherlands, Belgium, Italy, Austria, Canada, and the UK.[3]

Although he received many distinguishing awards, Girard's election in 2005 to the Académie of Française, known informally as *les immortals* (consisting of forty members, including Voltaire, Jean Racine, and Victor Hugo), was his greatest achievement.[4] Though he regularly identified as a cultural anthropologist, his theological relevance can be measured by the contemporary theologians who have critically engaged his corpus in their written work, including John Milbank, Rowan Williams, Miroslav Volf, Sarah Coakley, and Hans Urs von Balthasar.[5] His ongoing legacy is evident in the shaping of conversations among economists, literary critics, philosophers, political scientists, psychologists, theologians, and others in the Colloquium on Violence and Religion (COV&R), founded in 1990 by those shaped by Girard's theory.[6] The stated purpose of this annual symposium is "to explore, criticize, and develop the mimetic model of the relationship between violence and religion in the genesis and maintenance of culture."[7] Girard's influence continues to widen, even after his death.

MOVING TO THE UNITED STATES

In 1947, Girard relocated to America, a move which proved to be significant for him. Biographer Cynthia Haven writes, "That event in 1947, he said, made everything else possible. René is an American phenomenon, as much as a French one. Without America and the bigger vision it offered after the war, there would have been no books, no theories, and no academic career."[8] Girard met his wife, Martha, in the United States, and "the stability and contentment of that 64-year marriage cannot be underestimated in supporting his very long, very fruitful career."[9]

TWO-STEPPED CONVERSION

A defining moment for Girard occurred as he, a cynical skeptic in the "spirit of the atheistic intellectuals" of his time, experienced first an intellectual conversion, followed by a deeper conversion to Christ and the church.[10] As Girard studied the lives and works of Stendahl, Cervantes, Flaubert, Proust, and Dostoevsky, he realized that what characterized their ongoing influence was a type of conversion reflected in their writing.[11] These conversion experiences are not necessarily of a religious nature—though they are for some. Girard observes a broader understanding of conversion taking place for such authors, noting "Conversion is a form of intelligence, of understanding," and it is both a process and an event.[12] This is evident to Girard in Dostoevsky's *Notes from the Underground*. Girard asserts, "What Dostoevsky says to the laissez-faire philosophers is that, in a world as empty of transcendence as ours now is, if people are left to their own devices, many of them will choose the underground."[13] For Dostoevsky, the "underground" represents people who live as if God didn't exist. It is in this place that mimetic desire reigns. Divested of transcendence, people invest in an immanent framework where they look for experts to imitate and subsequently find themselves trapped in the mimetic cycle. For "the negation of God does not eliminate transcendency but diverts it from the above to the below."[14] Idolatrous imitation of the neighbor becomes the rule in the underground. Pride increases, and humility is resisted.[15] Girard puts it this way:

> The more our ego-centeredness increases, the more likely it is to turn into an underground "other-centeredness" that is not "altruistic" in the slightest, even though it often masquerades as altruism. Mimetic desire is failed selfishness, impotent pride that generates the worshipful imitation of idols unrecognized as such, because they are hated as much as they are revered. The modern world insidiously brings back forms of self-enslavement from which Western society had largely escaped during the Christian centuries.
>
> The more Dostoevsky explores the underground, the more aware he becomes of this dark "satanic" dimension of modern life. In *Demons* and *The Brothers Karamazov* he explicitly interprets the fascination for obstacle/models as demonic possession, and the psychology of the underground turns to demonology. This is no surrender to irrationality but a denunciation of it.[16]

The only way to escape or experience salvation from the underground is through Christ—imitating Christ as opposed to imitating Satan. Girard says, "If we do not imitate Jesus, our models become the living obstacles that we also become for them."[17] Dostoevsky's Christian symbolism was important for Girard's own conversion—from the deathbed conversion of Stepan Verkhovensky in *Demons* (where Verkhovensky discovers his own foolishness and turns to the gospel), to the concluding chapters of *Crime and Punishment* and *The Brothers Karamazov*. Reflecting on these texts, Girard says, "This is the existential conversion that is demanded by a great work of art."[18]

It was when Girard penned the final chapter of his book *Deceit, Desire, and the Novel* that he underwent his own conversion experience. Girard says,

> In autumn 1958, I was working on my book about the novel, on the twelfth and last chapter that's entitled "Conclusion." I was thinking about the analogies between religious experience and the experience of a novelist who discovers that he's been consistently lying, lying for the benefit of his Ego, which in fact is made up of nothing but a thousand lies that have accumulated over a long period, sometimes built up over an entire lifetime.
>
> I ended up understanding that I was going through an experience of the kind that I was describing. The religious symbolism was present in the novelist in embryonic form, but in my case it started to work all by itself and caught fire spontaneously. I could no longer have any illusions about what was happening to me, and I was thrown for a loop, because I was proud of being a skeptic. It was very hard for me to imagine myself going to church, praying and so on. I was all puffed up, full of what the old catechisms used to call "human respect." Intellectually I was converted.[19]

As I mentioned earlier, Girard describes his experience of conversion to Christ in two stages: an intellectual conversion of the mind, followed by a spiritual conversion of the heart. His second conversion experience took place after he was diagnosed with cancer. As Girard was preparing for Lent, his anxiety about the cancer increased to the point that he was unable to sleep; finally, on Ash Wednesday, his doctor revealed that he had been completely and miraculously healed. Ash Wednesday was a true celebration for Girard. There was no holiday that could be compared to that day of deliverance.[20] He was grateful that his intellectual conversion took place before this; otherwise, he would say, "If it would have occurred afterwards, I would have never truly believed. My natural skepticism would have convinced me that my faith was a result of the scare I had received."[21] This prepared him to reconcile with the church so that he and his entire family could truly celebrate Easter, in Christ.

Like any new convert, Girard wanted others to experience the reconciliation he had experienced. In an interview with scholar and professor James G. Williams, he was asked whether, in a pluralist society, he favored "converting all non-Christians to Christianity?" His response was, "Jesus said, 'I am the way, the truth, and the life,' and he told his disciples to go into the world and make converts. If we give that up, are we still Christians?"[22] An academic apologist, Girard was of the opinion that anyone who did not share their faith with others had not found the truth. In an interview, he said, "I think the Christians who do not want to share their faith do not really believe. The fear of religious tyranny is an anachronism, a false issue which puts political correctness ahead of the truth. I believe there is a truth, and the only way of telling it is by connecting with people."[23]

It is in his magnum opus, *Things Hidden Since the Foundation of the World*, that he first clearly expresses his Christian faith. Girard was careful not to offend unnecessarily those to whom he was seeking to reveal the truth. Haven writes, "His conversion would be a costly personal decision. It closed off an audience; it alienated potential readers and fans. Yet he never backed away from what he understood, in startling moments of clarity, to be the truth."[24] His conversion shaped the remainder of his life and writing.

CORRESPONDENCE WITH SCHWAGER

The other moments of clarity for Girard occurred in conversations he had with intellectuals and theologians. One key theologian who was an important dialogue partner for Girard was Jesuit priest Raymund Schwager. Girardian scholar Scott Cowdell considers Schwager to be "Girard's first major theological interlocutor."[25]

After discovering Girard's book *Violence and the Sacred* from reading the journal *Esprit*, Schwager initiated correspondence with Girard in a letter he sent on March 18, 1974. Schwager informed Girard he was greatly impressed and "very inclined" to accept Girard's theory.[26] It was not long before Schwager moved from being very inclined to being totally convinced of the primary aspects of mimetic theory. He writes, "I must say that the encounter with your thought has influenced in a decisive way my thinking, my work, and even my way of experiencing the world. I am more and more grateful to you."[27] This conviction led him to write *Must There Be Scapegoats?*, which explores the Old and New Testaments through a Girardian lens. He does this sympathetically but not uncritically.[28] This book was published in German the same year (1978) that Girard's book *Things Hidden Since the Foundation of the World* was published in French. This book would become Girard's first substantial entry into the field of theology as well as his most acclaimed work.

Although they addressed each other formally in their letters, it did not take long for them each to find a friend and advocate in the other.[29] Not only was Schwager greatly influenced by Girard and consistently posed theological questions to him, but Schwager was also a needed dialogue partner for Girard. In a letter dated January 14, 1978, Girard writes, "I would very much like to be able to speak to you more frequently, because around me the incomprehension concerning all religious matters is total. . . . Unfortunately I have no contacts in theological circles."[30] In his professional career at the university, Girard consistently remained in fields outside of theology in areligious environments, so he treasured his interactions with Schwager. Their correspondence was regular, respectful, robust, and redemptive. It was interspersed by visits in person, which first took place in Girard's hometown, Avignon, France, in July 1975, and after that, regularly until Schwager's death in 2004.[31]

Their correspondence is robust, in part due to their differing starting points. As a Jesuit priest, Schwager starts with theology and seeks to take Girard's mimetic theory into account, while Girard consistently positions himself as a cultural anthropologist and literary critic and engages the Scripture from this starting point.[32] They each come to Scripture with different underlying assumptions, and in their correspondence, they test these assumptions through their dialogue.

One point in which Schwager consistently and respectfully challenges Girard is in his understanding of sacrifice. In *Things Hidden Since the Foundation of the World*, Girard argues for a non-sacrificial [nonviolent God] reading of the Gospel texts, which Schwager fully agrees with. However, Schwager disagrees with Girard's belief that the word *sacrifice* cannot be used positively. Girard avoids the term because of his concern that readers would naturally fall back into the idea of a violent God who needed to sacrifice in order to appease his anger. In *Things Hidden*, Girard writes about the problems he has with the Epistle to the Hebrews. He dislikes the sacrificial language, especially anything that may possibly implicate God in violence. He argues that "the Epistle to the Hebrews re-enacts what is re-enacted in all earlier formations of sacrifice. It discharges human violence, but to a lesser degree. It restates God's responsibility for the death of the victim, it also leaves a place, though indeterminate, for human responsibilities."[33]

In their correspondence, Schwager consistently tries to help Girard see that although the word *sacrifice* can have overwhelmingly negative connotations, such as the scapegoat mechanism, it can also carry a positive meaning. Schwager believes that when understood from the viewpoint that Jesus was a *willing* sacrifice, *sacrifice* could still be in line with Girard's basic framework without depicting God as violent. Schwager also insists that Girard not only see the cross as a source of knowledge (revelation) but also as a source of life.[34] This is not to say Girard did not consider it a source of life, but he did not place emphasis on this.

In the letter Schwager wrote after reading *Things Hidden*, he compliments Girard on his non-sacrificial reading of the Gospel, but he also offers a strong criticism of Girard's interpretation of the Epistle to the Hebrews, noting,

> The only point that continues to worry me is your judgement on the
> Epistle to the Hebrews. Frankly, here I see a trace of sacrificial thinking.

To unify the NT, you throw out a text The Epistle to the Hebrews . . . your scapegoat?!? One could say that it is a minor point, but I attach great importance to it, with respect to the reception of your thought in the theological world and in the church.[35]

This is a theme Schwager consistently brings to Girard's attention.

Although Schwager offers deep appreciation of all that Girard contributes to anthropology and theology, he expresses concern that Christians, especially theologians, would use Girard's critique of the book of Hebrews to justify dismissing Girard's core concerns. He says, "I think we can and should avoid this difficulty. My interpretation of the epistle remains entirely in line with your thinking . . . and I could add further arguments."[36]

Schwager continues to press Girard on this, until finally Girard retracts his negative assessment of the Epistle to Hebrews in an interview with Rebecca Adams in November 1992.[37] He admits he was wrong to dismiss Hebrews too quickly:[38] "So I scapegoated Hebrews and I scapegoated the word 'sacrifice'—I assumed it should have some kind of constant meaning."[39]

Girard, in his appreciation of Schwager, later writes,

Some of the arguments I make in *Things Hidden Since the Foundation of the World* agree with what I have just said here [Jesus is the perfect sacrifice that puts an end to all the others], but others run contrary to it, particularly the critique of the Letter to the Hebrews, which now seems to me unfair. I now detect a hesitation, a flaw in my book that makes me appreciate Schwager's greater decisiveness.[40]

Girard and Schwager also dialogue about their understanding of Satan. Schwager's first words to Girard on this topic are in his letter from Innsbruck on May 28, 1978, which mentions how the Church Fathers said that Christ defeated the devil on the cross. The dialogue concerning Satan continued through the years and likely enriched Girard's understanding, which I will explore in this chapter and examine in the next.

UNDERSTANDING RENÉ GIRARD'S MIMETIC THEORY

Although Girard's mimetic theory stretches its reach from the origins of humanity to the apocalypse, I will focus on how Girard links imitation and desire (mimetic desire) to the Powers. This will help to clarify the imitation-based framework, which brings fresh perspective to leadership theory and practice. The imitation framework makes the case that we are captive to imitation.

THE SCANDAL OF MIMETIC DESIRE

Girard believes that the genius novelists reveal truths about human nature better than do present-day social and human scientists.[41] Through their works, he discovered that desire is central to what it means to be human—in particular, mimetic desire (we imitate the desire of our models). Girard deepened his conviction through his study of anthropology and mythology. In *I See Satan Fall Like Lightning*, he writes about how the power of desire is reflected in the tenth and longest of the Ten Commandments: "You shall not covet your neighbor's house. You shall not covet your neighbor's wife, or his male or female servant, his ox or donkey, or anything that belongs to your neighbor" (Exod. 20:17). The prohibition against desiring the objects of our neighbors reveals that "our neighbor is the model of our desires."[42]

Mimetic desire pushes against the romantic notion that we are isolated individuals uninfluenced by others. Instead, it teaches us that we borrow our desires from our models. Mimetic rivalry occurs when the desiring subject and model compete for the same object of desire. When there is significant difference between the desiring subject and model, Girard calls this *external mediation*, because it presents no danger. For example, if the model lives in a different time in history, this will avert any potential rivalry. A king and a pauper, because of their social distance, are also in no danger of rivalry. However, when there is less social distance between the model and the disciple, *internal mediation* is at work, and there is greater potential for mimetic rivalry. For example, mimetic rivalry can be seen when a worker looks up to a manager and desires that role. Internal mediation is much more likely to occur in the setting of the church, where the proximity of the disciple and missional leader is closer. I will explore this in the next chapter.

Girard develops many unique terms to distinguish between types of desires. *Acquisitive mimesis* takes place when the desire for *an object* is borrowed from the disciple's model. This dynamic can be observed in any kindergarten across the globe. There may be one hundred toys in the room, but because acquisitive mimesis is at work, every child wants to play with the same toy. What holds even greater danger is what Girard labels *metaphysical mimesis*, which takes place when "the desiring subject wants to become his mediator; he wants to steal from the mediator his very being."[43] The closer the distance between model and the desiring subject, the more the subject's desire is aimed at the model's very being. Girard observes that the best novelists put acquisitive mimesis in the background and metaphysical in the foreground. He states, "Dostoyevsky by a stroke of genius places the mediator in the foreground and regulates the object to the background. At last novelistic composition reflects the real hierarchy of desire."[44]

What Girard discovers in his first book, starting with Stendhal and reaching new heights with Proust and Dostoevsky, is that denial of God does not eliminate transcendency; it simply diverts it to one's neighbor.[45] Girard identifies this as *deviated transcendency,* "the false sacred," which is a highly contagious *ontological disease* because if we do not find our grounding in God, we will be forced to find it in the other.

In Girard's book *Resurrection from the Underground,* he illuminates the psychology and metaphysics of the underground as he explores the work of Dostoevsky.[46] Pride is the "primary psychological (and before long metaphysical) motor which governs all the individual and collective manifestations of the underground life."[47] Pride blinds us to how mimetic desire is working in our lives, and it even causes us to conceal our own mimetic desire from ourselves. Girard writes, "Either we are innocent of all metaphysical desire or else that desire possesses us so completely that we are entirely unaware of it."[48] In *The Possessed,* Girard points out that the characters are all enslaved in the mimetic trap of the underground because they depend on their model for their very sense of being.

Through envious imitation of the model, when the imitator desires what the model desires and it is something that cannot or will not be shared, the model becomes an obstacle or *scandal* (stumbling block) to the subject. For example, if the model is married and desires their spouse and gives this desire to their disciple by no fault of their own, they become an obstacle to their disciple, because the model cannot share their spouse. However, if a pastor desires to be the sole lead pastor, which is something he or she could choose to share, that person becomes an obstacle to the disciple getting what they desire and becomes a negative scandal (stumbling block).

Although there is initially a difference between the model and the imitator, such as the distinction between a disciple and their pastor, eventually these differences reach a vanishing point, where the progressive and mutually reinforcing mimesis between model and imitator starts to lack any differentiation, making them *doubles* of each other. They become like twins, similar to Romulus and Remus, the brothers whose story tells of the events that led to the founding of Rome and the Roman Empire. Model and imitator become so obsessed and possessed by each other that they begin to mirror each other's emotions and actions.

> If the model himself becomes more interested in the object that he designates to his imitator as a result of the latter's imitations, then he himself falls victim to his contagion. In fact, he imitates his own desire, through the intermediary of the disciple. The disciple thus becomes model to his own model, and the model, reciprocally, becomes disciple to his own disciple.[49]

Taking the earlier example of the disciple and pastor, when the pastor increases their desire to be the sole lead pastor, the desire to be a pastor is increased in the disciple to the point that the pastor starts to desire the role even more. When mimetic rivalry is in this *double* state, the model starts to imitate the disciple's desires—the very desires the model gave them.

When the disciple and model become *mimetic doubles*, desires intensify, and because they both see value in the object of desire, there is increasing reciprocity of desires. Eventually, they become *monstrous doubles*, where each becomes the other's rival, leading to an outbreak of violence. Mimetic rivalry can become so intense "that rivals denigrate each other, steal the other's possessions, seduce the other's spouse, and finally, they even go as far as murder."[50] In other words, if the tenth commandment ("You shall not covet") is observed, "the four commandments that precede it would be superfluous."[51]

It is important to note that for Girard, mimetic desire is the principal— but not the only—reason for violence. The fragility of human relationships is due to the fact that people are creatures of imitation. Girardian scholar Cowdell writes, "This escalation toward mimeticism's terminal phase [final stage] begins when status, prestige, or honor becomes the sole desired object."[52] Cowdell calls this *prestige rivalry*, which you can find among professors, as well as in other occupations. This kind of rivalry invariably leads to conflict.[53] I will apply this concept to ecclesial leadership in the next chapter.

Jesus speaks to mimetic rivalry when he talks about scandal. Girard notes that in the teachings of Christ, "the words that designate mimetic rivalry and its consequences are the noun *skandalon* and the verb *skandalizein*."[54] Since the foundation of the world, humanity has failed to notice the way mimetic desire leads to mimetic rivalry and eventually to mimetic crisis. Scandals multiply; and envy, jealousy, and hatred spread among communities like a contagious disease.[55] A model becomes a scandal to the disciple when he or she becomes a negative obstacle to the disciple's desire, which has been borrowed from the model. "Scandals are so formidable that to put us on guard against them, Jesus resorts to an uncharacteristic hyperbolic style: 'If your hand scandalizes you, cut it off; if your eye scandalizes you, pull it out' (Matt. 18:8–9)."[56] Girard interprets the word *stumble* in these texts as "scandalizes," because the Greek word is *skandalizei*.

When Jesus says, "[Scandal] must come" (Matt. 18:7), he is not being fatalistic but realistic, in that mimetic rivalry is unavoidable. Such rivalry is unavoidable because envy and jealousy still abound. However, Jesus also says, "Woe to the person through whom they come" (Matt. 18:8). Girard recognizes that Jesus understands the difficulty of his message, for he knows that most of us prefer glory that comes from people whom we see instead of glory from an unseen God. But when we seek the applause of people, we multiply scandals. For seeking glory from people creates "mimetic rivalries often organized by the powers of this world, rivalries that are political, economic, athletic, sexual, artistic, intellectual . . . and even religious."[57]

Girard wisely points out that there is no field in which mimetic rivalry is absent, including the religious domain. Though scandals must come, woe to the one by whom they come, for the scandal between individuals gives birth to more scandals. Thus *mimetic rivalry* gives way to *mimetic contagion*, and this leads to a *mimetic crisis*, which I will now explore.

RECOGNIZING THE MIMETIC CYCLE

To understand how Girard understands Satan and the Powers, we first need to understand the cycle of mimetic violence, or what Girard labels the *mimetic cycle*.[58] He talks about the mimetic cycle in three steps (see figure 6.1):

1. *A mimetic crisis*: Scandals within the community become contagious. They have a snowball effect and create a *mimetic crisis*, where there is a war of *all against all*. The community is now at risk of self-destruction if there is no relief to this mounting violence.
2. *The scapegoat mechanism (or single-victim mechanism)*: At the climax of the crisis, the *scapegoat mechanism* is enacted, where, unanimously, the community automatically, randomly, and unconsciously selects a victim. The war of all against all is resolved through the *all against one*, the scapegoat.
3. *Temporary tranquility*: The scapegoat is not only considered the sinner and the cause of the crisis but also the savior—their expulsion brings instant reversal of the crisis and with it a newfound tranquility, unity, and reconciliation of the community. This *temporary tranquility* is enjoyed by the community until the cycle begins again.

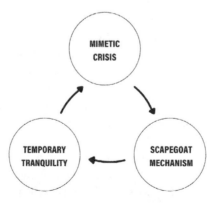

Figure 6.1 The Mimetic Cycle

Let us take a deeper look at this mimetic cycle. After exploring the literary giants in whose works Girard discovered mimetic desire and mimetic rivalry (his first primary discovery), he turned his attention to cultural anthropology (to discover the scapegoat mechanism—part two of the mimetic cycle). After ten years of reading and research, seeking to understand the dynamics of sacrifice and the origin of myth, rituals, and prohibitions, he released the groundbreaking works *Violence and the Sacred* and *The Scapegoat*. Within them, he expounds upon his fundamental discovery and explains the scapegoat mechanism.

When a mimetic crisis broke out in archaic (pre-state, nonlegal) societies, the scapegoat mechanism would be enacted as a way to establish and maintain social order. "When unappeased, violence seeks and always finds a surrogate victim. The creature that excited its fury is abruptly replaced by another, chosen only because it is vulnerable and close at hand."[59] Although philosopher Thomas Hobbes (someone Girard engaged regularly) and Girard hold many things in common, their point of departure is how each believes the mimetic crisis is resolved. Hobbes implies that the violence could be appeased by a "reasoned social contract between combatants."[60] However, Girard, through his study of anthropology, concludes that the mimetic crisis is more likely resolved through the sacrifice of the surrogate victim.[61] Girard writes that in the works of British anthropologists Godfrey Lienhardt and Victor Turner, they "portray sacrifice as practiced among the Dinka and the Ndembu as a deliberate act of collective substitution performed at the expense of the victim and absorbing all the internal tensions, feuds, and rivalries pent up within the community."[62]

The sacrifice of the scapegoat "serves to protect the entire community from its own violence; it prompts the entire community to choose victims outside itself."[63] The sacrificial victim in archaic societies had particular marks: it was typically the minority, the marginalized, or the weak who became victims. These were "prisoners of war, slaves, small children, unmarried adolescents, and the handicapped; it ranges from the very dregs of society, such as the Greek *pharmakos*, to the king himself."[64] However, as noted here, the victim could be the king, as the key to choosing the sacrificial victim is that the victim is someone who is both inside and outside—someone who is not fully integrated into the community.[65] So although the weak or handicapped are separated by their marginalization, the king is isolated by his position at the center of the community.[66] This is one of the reasons why a pastor can sometimes become the scapegoat in a church context. The essential characteristic of the victim is that there is an element of separation from the community. "Between these victims and the community a crucial link is missing, so they can be exposed to violence without fear of reprisal. Their death does not automatically entail an act of vengeance."[67] The sacrifice of the falsely accused victim, whether human or animal, serves to "quell violence within the community and to prevent conflicts from erupting."[68] The sacrifice leads to a return of tranquility within the community.

MIMETIC DESIRE IN THE PASSION NARRATIVE

The contagious power of mimetic desire is described in the Passion narrative with one crucial difference. Myths hide the insidious nature of the mimetic cycle "by suppressing or disguising collective murders and minimizing or eliminating the stereotypes of persecution in a hundred different ways."[69] But the Passion of Jesus reveals the scapegoat mechanism and thus disarms the work of the Powers by making public what was concealed from the foundation of the earth. Before the Bible and the life of Christ, humanity was imprisoned by the mimetic cycle, but the crucifixion and resurrection of Christ revealed what myths concealed.

Martin Kähler describes Mark's Gospel as a Passion narrative with an extended introduction, and Girard writes, "In the Gospels all themes lead to the Passion."[70] In other words, the reason the Gospels spend time on the Passion is because they are revealing a truth so central that they need the details and length to make their point. For much of Jesus' ministry, he enjoyed the favor of the crowds, even to the point of his entry into Jerusalem. But suddenly, the crowds turned against him, and their "hostility becomes so contagious that it spreads to the most diverse individuals."[71] This violent hostility against Jesus united all against him: Herod and Pilate (representing Rome) and the Jewish leaders, who, through a mockery of a trial, convicted Jesus. In so doing, they incited the people to the point that even the disciples could not withstand the mimetic contagion of the crowds. Though Pilate was warned by his wife through her dream, and though he desired to spare Jesus, his surrender to the wishes of the crowd demonstrates "the omnipotence of mimetic contagion. What motivates Pilate, as he hands Jesus over, is the fear of a riot."[72] This demonstrates Søren Kierkegaard's dictum "the crowd is untruth."[73]

The Roman and Jewish people were not the only ones who were caught in the mimetic contagion. The thieves on the cross and the disciples themselves became possessed by the mob mentality. Girard points out that when Peter, "the rock," was thrown into the crowd, he was unable to identify with Jesus anymore. He was not even able to affirm his commitment to Christ when a teenage girl questioned him. If this happened to Peter, how much more difficult would it be for the average person to resist this mimetic contagion?[74]

Although some commentators use psychology to suggest that Peter's impressionable and impulsive temperament gives the most explanatory power to Peter's threefold denial of Christ, Girard believes this minimizes the revelation in the Passion event. Girard believes that looking at the failure of Peter from an individualistic cause rather than through mimetic interpretation, we unconsciously think we would not have denied Jesus if we were in the same circumstances.[75] The Pharisees used a similar ploy when building tombs for the prophets their fathers killed, declaring they would not have done so themselves. However, Jesus admonishes their self-justifying actions. As Girard writes,

> The children repeat the crimes of their fathers precisely because they believe they are morally superior to them. This false difference is already the mimetic illusion of modern individualism, which represents the greatest resistance to the mimetic truth that is reenacted again and again in human relations. The paradox is that the resistance itself brings about the reenactment.[76]

In this, the mimetic cycle is in plain view, not just through literary giants and anthropological studies but in the Gospels themselves, though with a different twist. Since Jesus is declared innocent by the Father raising him from the dead, the mimetic cycle that has been in operation since the foundation of the world is revealed in the death and resurrection of Christ. Jesus becomes the *willing* scapegoat, exposing the scapegoat mechanism. Since Cain and Abel, mimetic desire has led to mimetic rivalry, which eventually becomes a mimetic crisis. A falsely accused victim is sacrificed, followed by temporary tranquility. This mimetic cycle, seen in the founding murder, reveals the one who was a murderer from the beginning—the devil, his Greek title; or Satan, which is his Hebrew name (John 8:44).[77]

THE DECONSTRUCTION OF SATAN

Unlike most modern theologians, who scarcely give this figure any attention, Girard does not shy away from writing about Satan and his surrogates. Through his use of mimetic theory, Girard seeks to demystify the devil. In his early works, he briefly speaks of the demonic; we read about it in *Deceit, Desire and the Novel* and even more in *Resurrection from the Underground: Feodor Dostoevsky*, as Dostoevsky's *Demons* speak of the demonic as well. During the middle of his career, Girard writes about Satan in *Job: The Victim of His People*. He covers the principalities and powers as well as the concept of "scandal" in *Things Hidden Since the Foundation of the World*, and he devotes entire chapters to Satan and demons in *The Scapegoat*. In his later work *I See Satan Fall Like Lightning*, Girard is entirely focused on this figure. Girard follows it up with an interview and a few chapters on the theme in *The One by Whom Scandal Comes*. Girard's understanding of Satan and Satan's relationship to the mimetic cycle is at the heart of mimetic theory; it could be said that the overarching theme of Girard's work is exousiology, albeit from a cultural-anthropological angle, which shapes his theology. This book, *The Scandal of Leadership*, is the first to explore this aspect of Girard with some depth while seeking to apply it to missional leadership.

According to Girard, the core decision each of us needs to make is this: *Who will I ultimately imitate?* He believes there are only two supreme "arch models": God and Satan.[78] As imitative beings, we will either imitate God or imitate Satan (the Powers). "If we listen to Satan, who may sound like a very progressive and likeable educator, we may feel initially that we are 'liberated,' but the impression does not last because Satan deprives us of everything that protects us from rivalistic imitation."[79] According to Girard, progressive educators eschew prohibitions as unnecessary, believing they can be transgressed without danger. However, as he demonstrates with the tenth commandment, prohibitions are designed to deter the mimetic cycle.

The devil seeks to seduce us, as leaders, to follow the wide road that leads to destruction. This is the route to mimetic rivalry and crisis, which leads to violence and scapegoating. If Christ is not our primary model, we will end up in the mimetic trap. Jesus recognized the importance of having a primary model, hence his dependence on the Father. This is one of the reasons why Jesus is unlike any guru. For, as Girard points out, most gurus are self-referential, claiming to have no model; whereas Jesus did and said what the Father did and said. Jesus understood that imitating his Father was the only way to escape the Powers.[80] Although godly models are good, when our primary model is someone other than Christ, we will start to borrow the desires of this model and become susceptible to mimetic rivalry.

If Jesus was tempted in every way, he must also have been tempted to take a person as his primary model instead of the Father. Who might he have been tempted to imitate? Maybe one of his closest disciples—Peter, James, or John? In their Gospels, Mark and Mathew say that after Jesus spoke of his Passion—his suffering, death, and resurrection—Peter rebuked Jesus for saying he would suffer and die. Jesus responded to his good friend Peter with a scathing rebuke of his own: "Get behind me, Satan! You are a stumbling block [*skandalon*] to me; you do not have in mind the concerns of God, but merely human concerns" (Matt. 16:23). Girard notes that he was not the first to relate Satan to scandal—Jesus was.[81]

What does Jesus indicate by calling Peter "Satan"? Is Peter possessed by Satan the way some Puritans thought the witches of Salem were?[82] The key to understanding this text is understanding how Satan is tied to Jesus' teaching on scandal through mimetic desire and mimetic rivalry. Girard summarizes it like this:

> Disappointed by what he takes to be the excessive resignation of Jesus, the disciple tries to breathe into him his own desire, his own worldly ambition [human concerns]. Peter invites Jesus, in short, to take Peter himself as the

model of his desire. If Jesus were to turn away from his Father to follow Peter, he and Peter both would quickly fall into mimetic rivalry, and the venture of the kingdom of God would melt away in insignificant quarrels.[83]

Girard identifies two types of texts in the Gospels relating to Satan. In one set of texts, Satan is "entirely deconstructed" by being equated to the mimetic principle, such as when Jesus is rebuking Peter, saying, "Get behind me, Satan." Peter was rebuked because his concerns were basic to humans— "merely human concerns." Girard writes, "Here Peter becomes the sower of scandals . . . and reaps the whirlwind of mimetic crises."[84] Girard also points out that Satan also appears in a supernatural role when Jesus meets him in the desert and gives a similar rebuke: "Get behind Me, Satan" (Luke 4:8 NKJV). Though Satan is personified in this text, Girard notes, "He still appears as the mimetic obstacle and model—the violent principle underlying all forms of earthly domination and all forms of idolatry, who tries to divert toward himself the adoration that is strictly due to God alone."[85] This is why Girard sees Satan as the "master of all mimetic tricks."[86]

One of the central texts for Girard's understanding of Satan is found in Jesus' question, "How can Satan cast out Satan?" (Mark 3:23 ESV). All three of the synoptic Gospels share this "parable," as Mark calls it. The parable has a double meaning. The first meaning seems obvious to all, including the scribes in Mark and the Pharisees in Matthew, who are engaging Jesus. But the second meaning, as Girard notes, is only comprehended by those who have ears to hear and eyes to see (Mark 4:1–13).[87]

One of the reasons Girard believes Jesus speaks in parables and metaphors is because "all human language, and other cultural institutions, in fact, originated in collective murder."[88] So if Jesus was going to communicate to people in his day—who only knew life in the mimetic cycle—he needed to be able to unveil truth to them creatively.

The question "How can Satan cast out Satan?" came just after Jesus had cast out a demon. Although the crowds were amazed, the scribes accused him of casting out demons by Beelzebub, the prince of the demons.

> And he called them to him, and said to them in parables, "How can Satan cast out Satan? If a kingdom is divided against itself, that kingdom cannot stand. And if a house is divided against itself, that house will not be able to stand. And if Satan has risen up against himself and is divided, he cannot stand, but is coming to an end."
>
> MARK 3:23–26 ESV

The first understanding Girard draws from the text is the truth that is understood by all: a kingdom—or a house—that is divided cannot stand. Simple enough. One can then draw the conclusion that if Satan is casting out Satan, he cannot stand. But the second, deeper understanding is the parabolic understanding. If, in fact, Jesus was casting out demons by the power of Beelzebub, why would the scribes and Pharisees have difficulty with this? For this would mean Satan's kingdom would be coming to an end (Mark 3:25). Of course, Scripture tells us that Jesus cast demons out by the Spirit of God, and thus the kingdom of God was upon them.

Girard sees in this parable the disclosure of the mimetic cycle, where Satan's ultimate power is his ability not only to create *disorder* (through the mimetic crisis) but also to create *order*, which is demonstrated in Satan's ability to cast out Satan (temporary tranquility through the scapegoat mechanism). In other words, Satan—the one who sows scandal through mimetic rivalry, creating a mimetic crisis—is the same one who uses mimetic contagion to have the crowd spontaneously and unanimously choose a scapegoat to cast out, thus creating temporary order again. Girard writes,

> Because of this extraordinary power [of creating disorder and order], Satan is the prince of this world. If he could not protect his domain from the violence that threatens to destroy it, even though it is essentially his own, he would not merit the title of prince, which the Gospels do not award him lightly. If he were purely a destroyer, Satan would have lost his domain long ago. To understand why he is the master of all the kingdoms of this world, we must take Jesus at his word: disorder expels disorder, or in other words Satan really expels Satan. By executing this extraordinary feat, he has been able to make himself indispensable, and so his power remains great.[89]

But Jesus sees an end to Satan's unique ability to sow disorder and temporary order. Thus he states in Luke, "I saw Satan fall like lightning from heaven" (Luke 10:18). Girard believes that this reference to Satan's fall corresponds with Jesus' death. Jesus' willingness to become the scapegoat exposes the mimetic cycle and the scapegoat mechanism, which has been hidden since the foundation of the world. After the Father declared Jesus to be innocent by raising him from the dead, Satan was disclosed as the "accuser" who falsely accuses innocent victims such as Job. The "violence of the cultural order is revealed in the Gospels," for humanity's complicity in the scapegoat mechanism has been revealed in Jesus. Thus "expulsion of violence by violence, is rendered useless by the revelation."[90] With the revealing of the scapegoat mechanism, all cultures that have been shaped by the Jesus story have gained the intelligence of the victim. In other words, we can now see how scapegoating works. Before Jesus, for the most part, there were no "victims," just "guilty" scapegoats. For when the community landed on a scapegoat, there was unanimity that this person or people were the true reason for the crisis the community was experiencing. But the Gospels reveal that Jesus was the innocent one. Therefore, cultures that have been penetrated with the gospel can no longer unanimously scapegoat people in the same way this has previously occurred throughout history. This does not mean scapegoating no longer takes place; it just does not tend to take place unanimously. Thus, as the parable says, ultimately Satan cannot continue to stand. His kingdom is coming to an end. Girard puts it this way:

> The kingdom of Satan corresponds to that part of human history . . . almost entirely governed by the single victim mechanism and the false religions it produces.
>
> The mimetic concept of Satan enables the New Testament to give evil its due without granting it any reality or ontological substance in its own right that would make of Satan a kind of god of evil. Satan does not "create" by his own means. Rather he sustains himself as a parasite on what God creates by imitating God in a manner that is jealous, grotesque, perverse, and as contrary as possible to the upright and obedient imitation of Jesus. To repeat, Satan is an imitator in the rival-istic sense of the word.[91]

Earlier, Girard writes of the mimetic cycle, "The devil, or Satan, signifies rivalistic contagion, up to and including the single victim mechanism. He may be located within the entire process or in one of its stages."[92] Girard demonstrates that the mimetic cycle and its connection to the devil is not just revealed in the synoptic Gospels but also in the Gospel of John. The following passage describes the consequences of mimetic rivalry in Jesus' dialogue with people who disputed Jesus' identity, people who claimed to have God as their Father:

> Jesus said to them, "If God were your Father, you would love me, for I have come here from God. I have not come on my own; God sent me. Why is my language not clear to you? Because you are unable to hear what I say. You belong to your father, *the devil*, and you want to carry out your father's *desires*. He was *a murderer from the beginning*, not holding to the truth, for there is no truth in him. When he lies, he speaks his native language, for he is a liar and the father of lies."
>
> JOHN 8:42–44, EMPHASES MINE

On what basis is Jesus saying to these descendants of Abraham that neither Abraham nor God is their father but rather that their real father is the devil? The devil is their father on the basis that they *mimic* the devil's *desires*. Again, our arch-models are either God or Satan. If we fail to imitate Christ, then our models can become obstacles to us, and us to them, where we descend into a mimetic crises of all against all, leading to the all against one.[93]

When we fall into the mimetic trap and become a scandal (obstacle), it not only demonstrates that we, like Peter, are imitating the desires of the devil, but it also becomes evident through the havoc that breaks out in a congregation. For example, when Mark Driscoll fell into the mimetic trap, it became evident through his scapegoating of other leaders. In the first episode of the podcast *The Rise and Fall of Mars Hill* titled "Who Killed Mars Hill?" we are told that "for years, conflict had been brewing inside of Mars Hill, largely centered on Mark and the culture of leadership around him. There were accusations of bullying, domineering, leveraging the church to build a personal brand, intimidation, and even violence."[94] At a church-planting boot camp, Driscoll, with pride as opposed to sadness, talked about the two fellow pastors he had just fired. Using the analogy of a bus, he told his listeners that this bus was not going to stop and that people who got in the way of the bus would get run over; if someone else wanted to drive, that person would be thrown off the bus.[95] We are told in the podcast that for "a long time, this was just accepted, but as the pile of dead bodies grew, tolerance lowered."[96] Here we see the Powers at work.

For Girard, the mimetic cycle is the devil deconstructed. He gives his most detailed understanding of Satan here:

> The devil's "quintessential being," the source from which he draws his lies, is the violent contagion that has no substance to it. The devil does not have a stable foundation; he has no *being* at all. To clothe himself in the semblance of being, he must act as a parasite on God's creatures. He is totally mimetic, which amounts to saying *nonexistent as an individual self*. The devil is also the father of lies; in certain manuscripts, he is the father of "liars" because his deceitful violence has repercussions for generation after generation in human cultures. These cultures remain dependent on their founding murders and the rituals that reproduce them.[97]

In response to whether he believes that Satan exists and is a real being, Girard says, "I follow traditional medieval theology on this point, which refuses to ascribe being to Satan. This is a logical and consistent position, but not an obligatory one."[98] Elsewhere, Girard states, "There is no article of the Creed that says, 'I believe in Satan and so forth.' We say, 'I believe in God.' I do not believe in Satan."[99] Ultimately, Girard is paradoxical when he talks about Satan, as is evident in this final statement: "So the greatest ruse of Satan is to convince us that he doesn't exist. But the next best ruse is to convince us that he exists."[100]

A FOUNDING MURDER AS THE FOUNDATION OF CULTURE

Girard notes how origin myths from around the world speak of how culture and institutions emerge from a founding murder, the scapegoat mechanism. Comparative mythologist Mircea Eliade, who does not tend to generalize and is more descriptive than explanatory in his approach, attests to this worldwide phenomenon. However, it is Girard who gives it explanatory power.[101] Through his study of anthropology, Girard makes the case that sacrificial ritual—the reenactment of the original founding murder—has been foundational in the development of human societies.[102] Girard reminds us that this concept of murder as the foundation for culture is not just found in origin myths but also in Scripture. Starting with Genesis and stretching to the Gospels, this reality is affirmed. We are told in Genesis 4:17 that Cain founded the first city. For Girard, the Genesis account of Cain's murder of his brother Abel is not just another founding myth but "the biblical interpretation of all founding myths. It recounts the bloody foundation of the beginnings of culture and the consequences of this foundation, which form the first mimetic cycle narrated in the Bible."[103]

Other founding myths hide human complicity in violence, deflecting responsibility to the gods and the false sacred, to which people must give sacrifices and engage rituals to maintain the peace of their communities. Meanwhile, the Hebrew Scriptures reveal some aspects of the mimetic cycle, starting with Cain, but the cycle is not fully revealed until the Passion narrative. Girard reminds us that, in Genesis, the concept of enemy brothers looms large: Cain and Abel, Jacob and Esau, Joseph and his brothers. Within this concept, mimetic desire leads to mimetic rivalry and mimetic crisis, where one becomes a scapegoat. This is the pattern of founding myths throughout human societies. Cain and Romulus, the murdering brothers, become the founders and fathers of cultures. Romulus murders his brother Remus, which leads to the foundation of Rome. And as I already mentioned, the death of Abel leads to Cain founding the first city in Scripture, one he names after his son Enoch.

The stories of Cain and Abel and Remus and Romulus have much in common, but the significant difference is that in the Roman myth, although Romulus regrets his action, he is ultimately justified in killing his brother. "His status is that of a sacrifice and High Priest; he incarnates Roman power under all its forms at one and the same time. The legislative, the judiciary, and the military forms cannot yet be distinguished from the religious; everything is already present within the last."[104] In contrast, Scripture paints Cain as a "vulgar murderer," even though he has similar powers granted him.[105] As Girard says, "The fact that the first murder precipitates the first cultural development of the human race does not in any way excuse the murderer [in] the biblical text."[106] Although the Hebrew Scriptures outshine the comparative myths of their day in revealing the murderer and the innocent victim, the mimetic cycle is not completely revealed until the Gospels. This is where Jesus reveals what has been hidden since the foundation of the world.

Jesus, in the Gospels of Matthew and Luke, refers to the murder of the prophets. Luke mentions "the blood of the prophets that has been shed since the beginning of the world, from the blood of Abel to the blood of Zechariah"

(Luke 11:50–1). Girard notes that the final link in this list of prophets is Jesus, as his crucifixion resembles the innocent victims that have gone before him.[107] This is confirmed in Girard's reading of the parable of the murderous vine-growers (Matt. 21:33–41). Each time the landowner sends his servants to collect his fruit, the tenants collectively gang up on them; beating one, killing another, and stoning a third. For Girard, each murder represents the completion of the mimetic cycle, and the Son becomes the last in a line of murdered messengers.[108] According to Girard, cultures are founded on murder, starting with Cain. This reality can be seen in the founding of America: indigenous Americans became the scapegoat. What the American myth conceals, Scripture reveals.

THE PRINCIPALITIES AND POWERS

Girard recognizes that early Christians had a distrust of sovereign states; thus, instead of calling the Roman Empire and Herodian tetrarchy by name, "the New Testament usually calls upon a specific vocabulary, that of 'principalities and powers.'"[109] In Girard's thinking, the principalities and powers are closely associated with Satan, yet distinct. He writes, "Though not identical with Satan, the powers are all his tributaries because they are all servants of the false gods that are the offspring of Satan, that is, the offspring of the founding murder."[110] Girard is struck by how many names the New Testament uses to designate these "ambiguous entities" and divides them into two groups. "Expressions like 'powers *of this world*,' 'kings *of the earth*,' 'principalities,' etc. assert the earthly character of the powers . . . on the other hand, expressions like 'princes of the kingdom of the air,' 'celestial powers,' etc. emphasize the extraterrestrial 'spiritual' nature of these entities."[111] These two groups of names represent the same entities in different but complementary ways. Girard believes the New Testament writers sought to clarify "the combination of material power and spiritual power that is the sovereign reality stemming from collective, founding murders."[112] The physical and spiritual realities point to the same entity, but they refer to differing dimensions; thus, human language cannot express this well. Language "does not command the necessary resources to express the power of bringing people together that false transcendence possesses in the real, material world, in spite of its falsity and imaginary nature."[113]

Along with Amos Yong, Wink, and others, Girard's understanding of the principalities and powers is that although they are based on the false transcendence of Satan, they are *not* categorically evil: "It is the transcendence on which they are based that is diabolical."[114] Remember the importance of making a distinction between Satan, the demonic, and the principalities and powers. Satan and the demonic have no future, but the principalities and powers, although fallen, were created good and can be redeemed. Girard would affirm this. He understands that the principalities and powers have "governed humanity since the world began."[115] They can appear as positive forces that help maintain order and prevent communities from destroying each other, or they can be obstacles revealing and concealing the fullness of revelation.[116] He sums up his understanding of the principalities and powers, saying,

> We can better understand the New Testament idea of the powers if we relate it to what is still, in my view, the best of the anthropological theories of social life, Émile Durkheims' concept of "social transcendence." The great sociologist found in primitive societies a fusion of the sacred and the social that comes quite close to the basic paradox of the powers and principalities.[117]

The principalities and powers are the "social phenomena that the founding murder created," expressed in physical reality through earthly rulers and expressed in spiritual reality through the social realities that typically seek to cover up human complicity to violence.[118]

DISARMING THE PRINCIPALITIES AND POWERS

According to Girard, since sovereign states like Rome were founded on murder and violence, and because some of the early Christians experienced the same fate as their Master, Christians found subversive ways to talk about the Roman Empire and the spirituality behind it, namely the principalities and powers. The dual reference that Girard gives to the principalities and powers as earthly and celestial has been widely adapted by theologians.[119]

The contribution Girard makes to this dual reference to the principalities and powers is his explanation of how they gain their transcendent spirituality from the false transcendency of the mimetic cycle, which for him is Satan. In the mimetic cycle, the scapegoat is first demonized, but after the community is reconciled and experiences temporary tranquility, the scapegoat is divinized. In fact, Girard believes that the development of monarchies occurred when there was a delay in the killing of the scapegoat. When the victim was chosen and "set aside" for sacrifice, there was already a "sacredness" about them. As their sacrifice was delayed, if the victim gathered enough followers, they began to be revered, looked up to, and given high status. In this way, the false sacred created a spirituality and power behind the human entity, all based on the false transcendency of the mimetic cycle. Girard believes that all human cultures and institutions are founded on this mimetic cycle. It is his way of describing the ubiquity of the fall.

The triumph of the cross is that Jesus becomes the willing scapegoat. In Jesus' death, as with every other scapegoat, the mimetic contagion of the crowds entrapped even Jesus' disciples, so that *all* came against the *one*. The work of Satan was happening again, just as it had since the foundation of the world. Thus all hope was lost on "Good" Friday.

Of course, that is not the end of the story. What makes this mimetic cycle different from all the rest in the history of the world is that Jesus is *shown* to be the innocent victim. When the Father raised Jesus from the dead, Satan and his work (the mimetic cycle) was exposed, which in turn disarmed the principalities and powers. It reveals the violence and false transcendency by which the principalities and powers gained their power and authority.

Girard reminds us that some would claim that the Passion narrative is mythology because, as in all mythology, the single-victim mechanism is the source of the divine; the one who was demonized becomes divinized. However, the Passion narrative is not like other myths. Girard explains, "If the transference that demonizes the victim is powerful enough, then the reconciliation is so sudden and complete that it appears to be miraculous and triggers a second transference superimposed on the first one, the transference of deification."[120]

Yet, in this Passion narrative, there is no guilt attributed to Jesus, "thus his divinity cannot rest on the same process as mythic deifications."[121] In addition, in mythology the victim is unanimously lifted to the level of divinity, but in the Gospel narrative, it is not the mob that recognizes Jesus as the Son of God but the rebellious minority, the disciples who witness his resurrection. "This dissident minority has no equivalent in the myths."[122] Jesus' death on the cross and his resurrection reveal what has been concealed from the foundation of the world: the mimetic cycle and "the founding murder and the origin of human culture."[123] The truth triumphs through the cross. For as Girard states, "Though ordinarily the accusation nails the victim to a cross, here by contrast the accusation itself is nailed and publicly exhibited and exposed as a lie."[124] Paul puts it this way in his letter to the Colossians:

> God made you alive with Christ. He forgave us all our sins, having cancelled the charge of our legal indebtedness, which stood against us and condemned us; he has taken it away, nailing it to the cross. And having disarmed the powers and authorities, he made a public spectacle of them, triumphing over them by the cross.
>
> COL. 2:13B-15

Girard links the leader to the Powers through mimetic desire, helping form our imitation-based framework. He also brings clarity to the necessity of the need to imitate Christ, especially regarding our desires. In addition, he demonstrates how the Powers have been disarmed through Christ. How does this understanding of mimetic theory help reshape how we lead in the church? As we critically engage Girard's life and mimetic theory, we will gain a better understanding of how to avoid mimicking the Powers, which always leads to fallen leadership incarnated through domineering leadership. And we will better learn what it means to imitate Christ, which leads to redeemed leadership and truly incarnate missional leadership.

7

THE POWER OF IMITATION

Understanding the power of imitation and how it works in and through our lives holds transformative value. It is one thing to be able to talk about how mimetic desire works. It is another thing to consider how mimetic desire is at work in our own lives.

Imagine you want to start a podcast. This desire means you have something you want to share with the world. If you want it to be a fruitful endeavor, what would be some of your first steps? Likely, you would consider other podcasts you find meaningful and learn what you can from them. You would discover how they began, how they decided on their primary themes, how they built their audience, and so forth. In other words, we search for models—people who are already doing the things we hope to do—in order to learn from them.

In the same way, Girard teaches us that our models form our desires. What we desire is something we imitate from our models. And because we are what we love, the power of imitation brings insight into the social nature of our very sense of being.

To get to the root of a thoughtful diagnosis of the problem of domineering leadership in the church requires not only a robust theology of the Powers but also a deep understanding of mimetic desire and the mimetic cycle as it relates to the Powers. The imitation-based framework brings these components together and helps us to form a deeper understanding.

Before moving forward, I must address some of the critiques of mimetic theory. However, in light of the importance of biography as theology, I will first consider some of the dominant images that have shaped the life of René Girard.

DOMINANT IMAGES THAT SHAPED THE LIFE OF RENÉ GIRARD

Unlike Walter Wink, whose activism was in the field, Girard's activism was primarily in the academy, and his preeminence in this sphere was demonstrated through his many honors and prominent academic roles. The dominant images that describe Girard's life are therefore reflective of his devotion to learning.

COLLABORATIVE TRUTH SEEKER

Girard's passion to seek and understand truth drove his voracious appetite to learn. He valued learning in community through collaboration. Many of his books were formed in conversation with other authors.

Trained as a historian, he was inclined to look for patterns. His first book, *Romantic Lie and Novelistic Truth*, indicates his search for truth.[1] By studying authors' lives and their work, he concluded that as the novelist experienced a conversion in their life, it would thus be reflected in their work. For example, Girard notes that early Dostoevsky would have been incapable of writing Dostoevsky's later work *Notes from the Underground* or his subsequent books.[2]

Although Girard appreciated novelists such as Dostoevsky and playwrights such as Shakespeare, his love for truth drove him to study history, philosophy, sociology, psychology, anthropology, and theology. Journalist Cynthia Haven, who wrote the first biography of Girard, remarks, "Girard's loyalty was not to a narrow academic discipline, but rather to a continuing human truth: 'Academic disciplines are more committed to methodology than truth.'"[3] Girard was not afraid to challenge some of the underlying assumptions in the various disciplines he studied. His journey to seek truth, wherever it may be found, was highlighted by neuropsychiatrist and psychologist Jean-Michel Oughourlian, who was greatly influenced by Girard. He writes,

> Intellectual matters aside, I think I share with all the authors of the present work the recognition that my desire as a thinker is mimetic and modeled on René's desire, which is to search unstintingly not for subjective truth, but for an objective reality and to recognize it as such whatever the price that has to be paid for this recognition.[4]

Girard's belief in the uniqueness of the Bible among all literature was unusual within the academic world. Jesuit priest Michael Kirwan writes, "Girard's theory is an explicit challenge to certain trends within postmodern thinking, not least because of his explicit allegiance to Christianity, which puts him at the margin of French and American academic establishments."[5] In Girard's pursuit of truth, he found in the Scriptures—especially the Gospels—something that required outside explanation. In his interview with UCLA doctoral student Thomas Bertonneau, Girard was asked, "Does one need to have faith, ultimately, to accept your theory?"[6] Girard's response was, "As I see it, my argument is quite logical. If you understand the old sacred as a closed system, and if you understand the Gospels as revelation of how that system works, then the Gospel cannot come from within the closure of violence."[7] Revelation of how the mimetic cycle works must come from an outside source. Girard's pursuit of truth, wherever he could find it, cultivated him to become an academic apologist.

ACADEMIC APOLOGIST

Theologian Grant Kaplan makes a convincing case that Girard brought many contributions to the field of what he calls *fundamental theology*, which includes apologetics but goes beyond it.[8] Speaking of the content and form of fundamental theology, Kaplan notes, "The conditions of modernity demand that theologians not only assist in the deepening and broadening of already existing faith, but that, in addition, theologians must address the unbeliever and engage the reasons and the framework in which unbelief and even hostility toward the Christian message have become viable alternatives to believing."[9] In this sense, for Kaplan, apologetics operates as a border discipline, "attempting to speak theologically, not so much as *faith seeking understanding* but rather *unbelief seeking belief.*"[10] For Kaplan, fundamental theology covers a similar terrain to apologetics but with a different orientation. To understand how fundamental theology relates to apologetics, he refers to Jesuit theologian Karl Rahner. "For Rahner, fundamental theology concerns itself both with providing a defense against those who deny Christianity's revelation and with 'clarifying *fundamental* questions for Christian theology's self-understanding.'"[11]

Wolfgang Palaver, a leading theological expositor of mimetic theory writes, "Girard's primary objective exists much more in an anthropological apologetics of biblical thought, or rather in displaying the plausibility of biblical revelation without having to revert to any rash theological presuppositions."[12] Girard's desire to appeal to those outside the faith sometimes left him vulnerable to those within the faith. When Palaver compares Girard's mimetic theory to Kant's project (*Religion within the Boundaries of Mere Reason*), he notes the similarities as well as the significant differences. Both emphasize the "presence of evil in humanity" and offer "a kind of anthropological apologetics."[13] However, because Kant situates his apology within the realm of sociology apart from theology, it "contains only irreligious, indirectly theological analysis."[14] But Palaver observes that Girard, in opposition to Kant, gives room for the influence of grace, writing, "Only with the help of the grace of God, thus, can humanity free itself from the dungeon of scapegoat logic. Grace is the boundary of Girard's anthropological apologetics, in particular where he demonstrates that it is essential for overcoming the scapegoat mechanism."[15]

Professor and Anglican theologian Scott Cowdell recognizes Girard's missionary instincts. He notes how in Girard's correspondence with Schwager, "He feels obligated to stay within the critical enterprise [cultural anthropology] so that his work can connect with a whole modern audience that is cut off from the Judeo-Christian tradition."[16] Cowdell insightfully makes the point that rather than avoiding the theological, Girard uses his cultural anthropology to clarify the gospel apologetically for the sake of mission.[17] Cowdell goes on to examine Girard's method, "in which the scientific and the theological are combined via the incarnational to yield the apologetic."[18]

If doubt remains of Girard being a Christian apologist to the academy and beyond, one need only to attend to his own words:

> Since the beginning of the "novelistic conversion" in *Deceit, Desire, and the Novel*, all of my books have been more or less explicit apologies of Christianity. I would like this one [*Battling to the End*] to be even more explicit. What we are saying will become more understandable with time because, unquestionably, we are accelerating swiftly towards the destruction of the world.[19]

Girard goes on to say that the good news of Christ—his willingness to be the victim and to sacrifice himself—was effectuated for the reconciliation of the world. It is Girard's belief that because Christ came to reveal that his kingdom was not of this world, once we admit to our complicity of violence (through the mimetic cycle), we can better participate in the kingdom of God.[20] Near the end of Girard's life he became concerned that if we fail to accept the revelation of Christ, we will experience the apocalypse at our own hands. He writes,

> Christianity is the only religion that has foreseen its own failure. This prescience is known as the apocalypse. Indeed, it is in the apocalyptic text that the word of God is most forceful, repudiating mistakes that are entirely the fault of humans, who are less and less inclined to acknowledge the mechanisms of their violence.[21]

Girard was passionate in his final days, sounding the trumpet of our need to convert to Christ or face the apocalypse.

GIRARD'S MIMETIC THEORY AND MISSIONAL LEADERSHIP

Having looked at the dominant images that guided Girard's life, I will now engage his mimetic theory and explore how it has the potential to reshape missional leadership. While Wink helps us begin to develop a more robust theology of the Powers, Girard allows us to understand the significant threat that the Powers pose to us, as missional leaders, *through* mimetic desire. First, it is important to respond to those who dismiss Girard as insignificant in this conversation.

IN DEFENSE OF GIRARD

Richard Whitehouse, a British regional network tutor, levels against Girard the critique that "he does not address the classical spiritual warfare texts," and that "in Girard's case a theory is brought to the text rather than being read out of that text."[22] Additionally, Whitehouse writes, "Girard's assumptions are derived principally from his analysis of medieval and modern French literature, both of which carry their own cultural assumptions; it is kind of a literary-cultural 'double whammy'!"[23] Thus he dismisses Girard from the conversation.

Answering the Critique Regarding Classical Warfare Texts

Regarding Whitehouse's first critique—that Girard does not address the classical warfare texts—it should be noted that Girard was not a theologian by training or vocation. Instead, he dialogued with and contributed to the theological field as a cultural anthropologist.[24] His anthropological work gave him unique insights into theology. Unlike many contemporaries, Girard wrote consistently about Satan, engaged in exegetical work on the demonic, and defined the principalities and powers in a way that agrees with the work of theologians such as Wink and Yong. Girard's ability to marry anthropology and theology provides a robust approach to leadership and the Powers, which, if ignored, leaves this field of study more barren. In addition, Wink (the most cited person on the Powers and one to whom Newbigin and other missional leaders show their indebtedness) believes that Girard's mimetic cycle and understanding of Jesus as the willing scapegoat, which reveal the mimetic cycle that has been in operation since the foundation of the earth, "are among the most profound intellectual discoveries of our time."[25]

Answering the Critique That Mimetic Theory Was Derived from French Literature

Another of Whitehouse's critiques was his belief that Girard's mimetic theory primarily hangs on a limited number of French novelists with similar backgrounds and cultural assumptions. It should be noted that although the five authors Girard cites in his first book (which Whitehouse alludes to here) include French novelists—Proust, Stendhal, and Flaubert—he also includes a Russian and a Spaniard—Dostoevsky and Cervantes. In addition, because Girard's first publication focused on mimetic desire, it is often assumed that in his early work Girard was not operating with any knowledge of the scapegoat mechanism or the revelation that Scripture brings. However, Cowdell rightly remarks, "I have come to realize that all three elements [mimetic desire, the scapegoat mechanism, and the uniqueness of Scripture] are to some extent present from the beginning for Girard, so that these discoveries should not be strictly linked to the order of their appearance in a series of major publications." It ought to be evident that Girard was attuned to the revelation of Scripture prior to the publication of his first book, *Deceit, Desire, and the Novel* (the English translation of *Romantic Lie and Novelistic Truth*, published in 1961), because his two-stepped conversion took place by Easter of 1959. Girard was intrigued by the novelists' use of Scripture, often in their conclusions, and he believed that the best genius novelists are those who not only identify the problem but also come to a proper conclusion:[26] "Truth is active throughout the great novel but its primary location is in the conclusion. The conclusion is the temple of truth. The conclusion is the site of the presence of truth, and therefore a place avoided by error."[27] Girard ends his first book with the conclusion from *The Brothers Karamazov*, where the words "*memory, death, love*, and *resurrection* are found in the mouths of the children."[28] Here, the hope of the gospel is addressed.

Girard's mimetic theory did not just hang on a limited number of French authors; it was developed and confirmed throughout his writing career and his study in various disciplines that span time from ancient civilizations to our present day. He started his pursuit by accident, through literature; but the scapegoat mechanism took ten years of research in anthropology, ethnology, and mythology (which spans many cultures and time periods). And like most, all of Girard's learning informed his understanding and experiences, including his first two earned PhDs.

Answering the Critique That Girard Reads into the Text

Whitehouse's final critique is more common: "In Girard's case a theory is brought to the text rather than being read out of that text."[29] Although there are several books that address this issue, Cowdell's contribution merits attention.[30] Cowdell approaches this critique head-on, with considerable honesty. First, he acknowledges Girard's methodological paradox, "in which theological claims appear to be both primary and secondary in his project."[31] He also notes that "Girard regards his thesis as being 'in line with all the great dogmas, while it endows them with an anthropological underpinning that has gone unnoticed.'"[32] Cowdell writes, "In an unusual juxtaposition—and one that eludes many of Girard's critics—social science and scriptural revelation are linked in mimetic theory."[33] Note that Girard does indeed read Scripture with a mimetic heuristic, but as I will soon demonstrate, this heuristic can be found in Scripture itself.

In addition, this critique insinuates that Girard's mimetic theory is always read into the text but fails to recognize where Girard states how the text goes beyond his theory. For example, Girard mentions that there are some things in Scripture that cannot be explained in terms of "his social-scientific approach," such as the resurrection.[34] Girard writes, "The Resurrection is not only a miracle, a prodigious transgression of natural laws. It is the spectacular sign of the entrance into the world of a power superior to violent contagion."[35] Elsewhere, Girard writes, "There can be no mimetic theory of the Resurrection. The Resurrection is either an invention of religious propaganda or the source of truth. From both a structural and dynamic point of view, the anthropological and theological significance of the Resurrection is so coherent that it is very difficult to imagine that it could be an invention."[36]

Cowdell notes that Schwager "offered this sharp rejoinder to anyone accusing Girard of reducing Christian faith to mere knowledge of a social process."[37] Schwager states, "Since [Girard] expressly believes in the true divinity and humanity of Christ, the working of the Holy Spirit in history, and even the virgin birth, and since he attributes central importance to Christ's cross and salvific activity, such broad sweeping criticism rules itself out of court."[38] However, Cowdell understands there is still a tension in Girard's work, "introducing doubt into his reception by theologians."[39] So, in his book, he continues to make persuasive arguments on why Girard ought to be well received.

Cowdell makes the case that in Girard's efforts to widen the reception of the gospel, he never "surrenders his methodological paradox."[40] But he also reminds us that Girard did not uncritically adopt common thinking in anthropology or other social sciences. Girard thought that modern-day Christianity seemed to bow down to contemporary thought, failing to understand the supremacy of revelation. Quoting Girard, "Christians don't see that they have at their disposal an instrument that is completely superior to the whole mishmash of psychoanalysis and sociology that they conscientiously feed themselves. It's the old story of Esau sacrificing his inheritance for a plate of lentils."[41]

Girard's mimetic theory is revealed in Christ, and his interactions with others reveal his understanding of the uniqueness of Scripture. One such dialogue takes place in the book *When These Things Begin*, in which a recorded conversation between writer Michel Treguer and Girard was published. Girard acknowledges the power of Scripture when answering Treguer's skepticism, claiming, "What I am saying is that Christianity reveals its power by interrupting the world in all its ambiguity. It gives us an understanding of human cultures that is incomparably better than that offered by the social sciences."[42] For Girard, it is Scripture and Christ that bring this clarity. Although Girard consistently followed his calling as a cultural anthropologist with the goal of reaching those outside of the church, his third major discovery—the power found in the revelation of Scripture—took place before he penned his first book. So although he didn't explicitly reveal his Christian faith until his fifth book, *Things Hidden Before the Foundation of the World*, most who study Girard recognize that his three significant discoveries—mimetic desire, the scapegoat mechanism, and the uniqueness of Scripture—are rudimentarily evident in his first book. When Whitehouse claims we should be skeptical of Girard because he is simply reading mimetic theory into the text, it is important to remember that the text shaped Girard's understanding of mimetic theory, for without Christ and without Scripture, there is no mimetic theory.

So did Girard read his mimetic theory into Scripture? Girard's humility as a cultural anthropologist who didn't claim exegetical acumen is evident. However, when we stack up his ideas alongside those of New Testament scholars—namely Graham Houston and Scot McKnight—we see that mimetic theory was not a presupposition read into the text but rather a theological-anthropological reality demonstrated by New Testament authors. To continue with this argument, I will now explore McKnight's exegetical work on James.

LEADERSHIP, MIMETIC DESIRE, AND THE POWERS IN JAMES

First, it must be said that McKnight at no time refers to René Girard, nor is Girard in his bibliography. This is McKnight's work in conversation with other New Testament scholars who have studied James. James 3:1–4:12—in particular, James 3:13–4:9—reveals how mimetic desire and the Powers are connected, but it is worth considering the wider biblical text for context.

After reviewing ten outlines of James developed by other scholars, McKnight follows in the footsteps of Richard Bauckham, and outlines the passage this way:

> 6. General exhortation for teachers (3:1–4:12)
> 6.1 Teachers and the tongue (3:1–12)
> 6.2 Teachers and wisdom (3:13–18)
> 6.3 Teachers and dissensions (4:1–10)
> 6.4 Teachers, the community, and the tongue (4:11–12)[43]

McKnight's summary of 6.1, *teachers and the tongue,* is that "James is concerned about the teachers in the messianic community, and his concern is with their tongue—he advises them not to pursue teaching and to guard their tongues. Why? Because the tongue's impact is disproportionate to its size."[44] James is pleading with these teachers to "realize the incongruity of being one who blesses God and at the same time curses humans who are made in God's likeness."[45] It is highly likely that these teachers have a scapegoat whom they are cursing. James says this ought not to be so. As McKnight writes, "A better way is the way of wisdom, and the proper goal of the teacher is neither control nor curse but wisdom."[46]

In exploring 6.2, *teachers and wisdom,* McKnight writes, "The speech patterns that most concerned James—speech that like a spark sets the messianic community on fire with destructive forces—are about envy, ambition, and boasting (3:14–16)."[47] The problem that James was uncovering is described in the verses to which McKnight points. "But if you harbor bitter envy and selfish ambition in your hearts, do not boast about it or deny the truth. Such 'wisdom' does not come down from heaven but is earthly, unspiritual, demonic. For where you have envy and selfish ambition, there you find disorder and every evil practice" (3:14–16). Envy, which Christian tradition considers a deadly sin, is mimetic desire, as will become evident as the passage progresses.

McKnight notes James's question "Who is wise and understanding among you?" (3:13a). This rhetorical question was "not so much to *identify* who are such persons as to *describe* such persons," as James's answer reveals (emphases mine).[48] McKnight notes, "James's description will not permit the teacher to think his or her mastery of theology or exegesis is sufficient to pass muster. What passes muster for James is behavior shaped by humble wisdom."[49] James answers his question, saying, "Let them show it by their good life" (3:13b). In other words, a changed life is evidence of good theology.

McKnight, in exegeting James, then describes

- the problem;
- the source of false wisdom;
- the communal impact; and
- the potential for true wisdom.

The *problem* James addresses is the envy and selfish ambition in the leader's heart. "In two verses James will reveal that the leader marked by [selfish] 'ambition' creates disorder in the community (3:16). Theologian Sophie Laws has a notable definition of the term selfish *ambition*: 'Unscrupulous determination to gain one's own ends.'"[50] McKnight writes, "Zealous [envious], ambitious teachers, because they are concerned with their own reputation and the power that comes to those with cognitive skills, both boast (cf. Jer 9:23–24) and deny the truth."[51] James says proclamation requires performance in one's life.

James points to *the source of false wisdom*, in that it comes from below; it is "earthly, unspiritual, demonic" (3:15). James is now linking envious desires to the work of the Powers. The effects of a leader caught in the mimetic cycle are described by McKnight:

James . . . is neck-deep in a pastoral problem of immense proportions. Those who are designed to follow Jesus, to live a life of loving God and others, and to live out the will of God are being fractured into bits by teachers who abuse their authority, seek to establish their reputations, and frame everything so as to enlarge their own borders, and James knows that the messianic community is at a crossroads. Either it gets back on track or it will disintegrate into ineffective witness and missed opportunity. The options are two: either the teachers pursue a wisdom that comes from God (see 3:17–18), or they continue on their reckless, destructive path, which comes from Gehenna and the evil spirit-world. Such a spirit-world distorts human community and institutionalizes injustices.[52]

Although the *communal impact* of the problem of envy and selfish ambition is noted here, McKnight notes that the concrete manifestations of envy and selfish ambition are not named until 4:1: "What causes fights and quarrels among you? Don't they come from your desires that battle within you?" McKnight writes, "Zeal [envy] and [selfish] ambition break loose moral anchors, on the part of teachers, their followers, and their opponents, so that control and dominance become the guiding lights."[53]

McKnight reminds us of the *potential for true wisdom*, highlighting how James encourages the teacher or leader of the community to live from wisdom that comes from above, not below. "Wisdom transcends cognitive mastery of facts and information. It is skill in living according to God's moral order . . . The wise person lives in God's world in God's way with God's people and so enjoys the blessing of the only wise God."[54]

McKnight then moves to 6.3, *teachers and dissension*. He notes that the origin of the division is in the malformed desires of the leaders: "You desire but do not have, so you kill" (4:2). Although McKnight is not viewing this from a Girardian perspective, it is clear this is the scapegoat mechanism in action. When McKnight talks about this verse, he translates the "conflicts and disputes" as "warring and swording," an outright battle, and he explores whether James is talking about literal murder here.[55] McKnight ends up siding with theologian Ralph P. Martin, who writes, "Since James and his community were situated in a Zealot-invested society and since it is quite conceivable that (at least) some of the Jewish Christians were former Zealots (cf. Luke 6:15; Acts 1:13), the taking of another's life is not out of the realm of possibility for church members as a response to disagreement."[56] McKnight, after further arguments, writes, "There is very little to suggest that these texts speak of anything but actual murder."[57] McKnight notes the nature of the teacher's desire that James has concerns about. He names the teacher's desire "for power, control, and partisanship."[58] "James has teachers in mind, and their problem was loose tongues used to abuse individuals and divide the community."[59]

McKnight goes on to write that disputes and conflicts come from the desires of the teachers. "James pushes them to consider the origins of their behaviors in their own craving desires for power and control. He pushes further and says, evidently, that their craving desires lead to murder and to the disputes and conflicts in the messianic community."[60]

McKnight then addresses the issue that leaders do not have what they want because they do not ask, and even when they ask, they do so with wrong motives, for their own pleasure. He does not view this as hedonistic pleasures, because it is the same word used in 4.1: "Their zeal [envy], ambition, craving, and desires shaped everything they did. They wanted self-glory and power, not wisdom."[61] Instead of directing their prayers toward the accumulation of wisdom, their prayers were filled with envy and selfish ambition.[62]

James considered these teachers to be adulterers because, rather than befriending God by asking for his wisdom, they befriended the world through their envy and self-ambition. Thus James gives us this equation: "Friendship with God = enmity with the world, and friendship with the world = enmity with God."[63] McKnight suggests that what James is addressing here, in the immediate context, is that friendship with the world "would have to include the zeal [envy], ambition, craving, and desires for power and control in the messianic community. Perhaps murder is in mind as well (4:2)."[64] Then McKnight insightfully says, "The immediate context then would suggest a variation on what Jesus said to his disciples about wanting to lord it over others as the Gentiles do (Mark 10:35–45). . . . In context, then, James's focus is on accusations against the teachers and leaders for creating chaos in the community by yearning for lordship."[65] In expounding on how God opposes the proud but gives grace to the humble, McKnight says that what grace refers to "is the grace of his gift of forgiveness to those who repent."[66] For this is what James calls them to do in the final leg of the passage (4:7–10).

McKnight lists the ten imperatives mentioned in these verses:

1. *Submit* yourselves therefore to God.
2. *Resist* the devil, and he will flee from you.
3. *Draw near* to God, and he will draw near to you.
4. *Cleanse* your hands, you sinners,
5. and *purify* your hearts, you double-minded.
6. *Lament*
7. and *mourn*
8. and *weep*.
9. *Let* your laughter *be turned* into mourning and your joy into dejection.
10. *Humble* yourselves before the Lord, and he will exalt you. [NRSV][67]

When examining this passage, McKnight considers the similarities with 1 Peter 5:5–9 and the striking parallels they have, pointing to "(1) humility, (2) citation of Proverbs 3:34, (3) the need to be humble before God, and (4) a call to resist the devil."[68] He then offers an astonishing insight: "One parallel does not a catechetical pattern make, but it is at least worthy of consideration to wonder if this language did not emerge from the catechetical tradition of the early churches for leaders, teachers, and those aspiring to be such."[69] These two passages deal with domineering leadership, and in both, the leader is tied to the Powers through mimetic desire.

McKnight makes this observation in this passage of James, writing, "If the emphasis so far has led us to think in terms of anthropology, James now brings into the discussion a cosmic force at work in the divisiveness of the community leaders. The desires that yearn toward envy are animated, at least in part, by 'the devil.'"[70] The Girardian link becomes clear here, for Satan is the mimetic cycle. Although we may not always consider the devil when dealing with the problem of domineering leadership, it is clear the early church took the devil more seriously, as references to resisting him are found in early Christian catechesis.[71] Although James names the influence of the Powers, McKnight notes that he never deemphasizes human responsibility.[72] This should also be the case in our day when it comes to domineering leadership. "The devil made me do it" is not an option, even though it holds some truth.

Girard's writing as an academic apologist began with mimetic desire, which he discovered through the genius novelists. He then developed the concept of the scapegoat mechanism through his study of anthropology and mythology. Then he went to the Gospels to demonstrate how Jesus reveals this mimetic cycle. While he self-identified as a cultural anthropologist and sought to engage with theology from an anthropological position, he expected that theologians would engage his theory from their own exegetical perspective. McKnight, in his exegesis of James, justifies the linking of mimetic desire to the Powers. Therefore, we find more exegetical evidence of Girard's mimetic cycle. What James describes theologically, Girard supports anthropologically.

McKnight's study of James provides evidence of what Cowdell writes regarding the methodology of Girard. He mentions how Girard thought it was important that "the religion of the Incarnation should be an anthropology as well as a theology. Incarnation means man and God together."[73] Cowdell responds, "Hence, in an unusual juxtaposition—and one that eludes many of Girard's critics—social science and scriptural revelation are linked in mimetic theory."[74] This gives at least one response to Whitehouse's critique of Girard reading his theory into the text. Girard certainly does read the Bible with a mimetic heuristic, which in this case brings great value, for we can find this heuristic in Scripture. Being aware of others' presuppositions as well as one's own is important for the scholar, for, as I mentioned earlier, no one comes to the text with complete objectivity. Furthermore, there is another critique of Girard that must be addressed.

LEADERSHIP AND POSITIVE MIMESIS

One of the common critiques of Girard is that although he consistently and deeply develops the concept of mimetic desire in all of its horrific forms, which are clearly seen in our world, he does little to develop the positive aspect of mimetic desire. New Testament professor Willard M. Swartley writes, "Girard speaks of positive mimesis. But overall Girard says relatively little about this, although at numerous points he speaks of good mimesis and occasionally commends Jesus as the good model."[75] He goes on to say that Girard typically focuses on mimetic desire in the negative way, which tends to lead to rivalry.

Thus, on at least two occasions, conferences sought to address this lack: the conference on René Girard and Biblical Peace Theology, held at Associated Mennonites Biblical Seminary in June of 1994, and the Colloquium on Violence and Religion (COV&R), which took place at Saint Paul University in Ottawa, Canada, in 2006. The various contributions at these conferences have subsequently become books.[76] I will draw from both of these resources.

Theologian Petra Steinmair-Pösel's contribution to COV&R unfolds through the meta-narrative of creation (mimetic desire and creative grace), the fall (conflictual mimesis and original sin), and Christ (grace and positive mimesis). She sees mimetic desire as part of God's good creation. "It is mimetic desire that makes a person receptive to her/his fellow human beings as well as to the divine."[77] In the beginning, at creation, mimetic desire is good and aims at transcendence. But the serpent distorts God's word, and presents God as a rival.[78] Therefore instead of gratefully receiving, the human attitude "gives way to acquisitive and rivalrous desire."[79] She goes on to write, "This rivalrous imitation of God means that human beings try to be like God—but not in accordance to their creation and vocation, but by trying to be like God out of their own effort, without God and against God."[80] Following this, in Genesis we see that conflicts erupt, blame shifting takes place (Adam and Eve), and eventually the death of the first human being occurs (Cain and Abel). As the story develops, the mimetic cycle breeds more and more violence.

So how does humanity break free from conflictual mimesis?[81]

Although the prohibitions given in the Ten Commandments were a form of grace to detour conflictual mimesis, ultimately through Jesus' incarnation, we see the undistorted image of God.[82] Like Adam, the devil tempts Jesus.[83] Unlike Adam, the second Adam's "image of the Father is not that of a rivalrous God, who wants to withhold something from God's creatures but is that of a loving Father who wants to give Godself as a present."[84] In addition, Jesus as a concrete man is "not an autonomous subject imitating the Father by virtue of his own efforts but by virtue of the Holy Spirit given to him."[85] Jesus not only gives us an undistorted view of God but also a quality of imitation worth mirroring.[86] "By means of his life and death and the sending of the divine Spirit after his ascension, Jesus—the *homo perfectus*—the undistorted image of God, makes possible a new, undisguised experience of God and consequently also new inter-human relationships, relationships which don't follow the structure of antagonistic mimesis."[87]

By God's grace, "because of the new image or rather the *new experience of God*, which Jesus communicates by means of his own life and acting," a new form of relationship is possible: positive mimesis.[88] There is now available for all humanity a new "*quality of imitation*, a quality that does not lead into mimetic conflicts, because it doesn't arise from an attitude of scarcity but from the experience of gratuitous forgiveness and from newly bestowed possibilities for life."[89]

This new quality of imitation does not take aim at replacing God but instead focuses on participating in the divine life. For Steinmair-Pösel, the foundation of positive mimesis is the gratuitous reception of the gift of God's grace and the willingness to pass on what one has received. Steinmair-Pösel believes that when the Eucharist becomes the center of the community—a place of receiving and thanksgiving—positive mimesis can be realized in the community. But because the community lives within "the ambivalent context of human institutions, positive mimesis is realized there only in a very fragile and fragmentary way."[90]

Swartley, in his chapter on "Discipleship and Imitation of Jesus," which was presented at the René Girard and Biblical Peace Theology conference, seeks to show that major strands of New Testament teaching are directed specifically to "transformation of desire that enables a positive *non-acquisitive mimesis*."[91] In addition, it was to show "how foundational and ubiquitous this idea is in the New Testament."[92] Swartley sees in the New Testament a stream of exhortations that repudiate "mimetic desire that generates rivalry and in turn leads to violence,"[93] as well as a call to positive mimesis in the New Testament canon, which is grounded in the event of Jesus' cross, "an event that exposes and, from Jesus' side, manifests the freedom and power of new creation."[94] Swartley believes that if Girard's thesis is correct—that mimetic rivalry enacted the scapegoat mechanism leading to Jesus' violent death, and that the life, death, and resurrection break the spiral of violence empowered by mimetic rivalry—"then it should be possible to show exegetically that Jesus' teaching on discipleship and the early church's teaching of imitation (later called *imitatio Christi*) are an antidote to aspirations of rivalry."[95]

Following the long tradition of *imitatio Christi*, Swartley first examines Paul's use of imitation, then its wider use in the New Testament. It should be noted that Paul called the community to imitate him and others as they imitate Christ. Thus, as Girard mentions, they are not like many current gurus, who are only self-referential in their call to imitate. Then Swartley examines the Gospel narratives that emphasize the call to follow Christ. He ends by including an even wider set of language around identifying with Christ—participating in his life, death, and resurrection—as what it means to live "in Christ." Swartley also lists the vices of the flesh and emphasizes the virtues of walking in the Spirit. Although he examines the wider examples of imitation in the New Testament, Swartley cautions, "The atonement is the precondition theologically and practically for all imitation 'in Christ,' and identification or correspondence paraenesis [instruction]. The potential of a new mimesis rests on God's inauguration of a new creation reality through the cross and, most significantly, the resurrection of Jesus Christ."[96]

In his essay, Swartley emphasizes that many of the imitation passages relate to people leading a cruciform life: a non-retaliatory life where violence is met with love instead of evil. Such individuals willingly suffer instead of participating in the scapegoat mechanism. Often, Paul asks people to follow his entire leadership team: Paul, Silvanus, and Timothy. "You became imitators of us and of the Lord, for you welcomed the message in the midst of severe suffering with the joy given by the Holy Spirit. And so you became a model to all the believers in Macedonia and Achaia" (1 Thess. 1:6–7). What we see here is positive mimesis taking place. Good models lead to others becoming good models—the multiplication of disciples in a positive form. They followed the suffering servant by participating mysteriously in his death and resurrection. Instead of engaging in conflictive mimesis and scapegoating others, they were willing to enter into the sufferings of Christ. They took on the mind of Christ, doing nothing from selfish ambition or empty deceit, but rather considering others more important, demonstrated by the willingness to enter a self-emptying, *kenotic* life, like him (Phil. 2:4–8).

Jim Fodor makes a good case that mimesis and participation are not mutually exclusive:

> Rather discipleship means maintaining these two central ideas in motion, keeping both in elliptical orbit around one another. If Christian mimesis is unavoidably participatory, so too participation in God's life proves inescapably mimetic—for the simple reason that we only know what it means to participate in God's life by imitating the pattern set forth in the Son.[97]

In conclusion and summary, Swartley writes,

> A mimesis pattern lies at the heart of NT thought. Any theology or ethics of the NT should make this point foundational, but few do. Just as world culture generally manifests energy via mimetic desire, so life in the kingdom of God, the new creation, is animated and empowered by a mimetic model. The key difference is that the lead Model is the new Adam precisely because he was tempted with the acquisitive mimesis in all ways such as we are but did not yield to that mimetic pattern that generates rivalry and violence. Jesus as faithful Servant of the Lord has opened up for us a new world of hope and potential; we are saved by his transforming of our desire. We seek then to follow in his steps and be conformed to his image.[98]

It is worth returning here to the imitation-based framework, represented in figure 7.1 As leaders, we are captive to imitation. We will either imitate the Powers in their submission to Satan and therefore incarnate domineering leadership, or we will imitate Christ in submission to the Father and subsequently incarnate true missional leadership. There is no neutral ground. With the help of McKnight, we have seen this pattern in 1 Peter 5 and through our study of James.

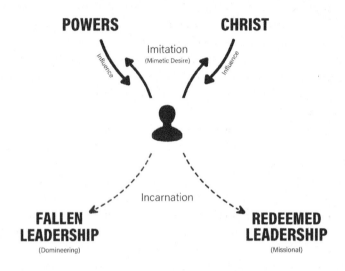

Figure 7.1 The Imitation-Based Framework

THE RECONSTRUCTION OF SATAN

Although it is vital to respond to some of the critiques leveled against Girard, it is also important to consider his understanding of Satan. Girard is always careful about how he talks of Satan (more careful than some Girardians), referring to the reality of Satan's work while also deconstructing him and naming his existence as the mimetic cycle. He is hesitant to give Satan any sense of being or personhood. Maria Stella Barberi, when interviewing Girard, stated, "If I understand you, then, you are saying there is no Satan, there are only satanic relations."[99] As I mentioned in the previous chapter, he follows traditional medieval theology in not ascribing being to Satan.[100]

Although Girard deconstructs Satan, to varying degrees, Walter Wink, William Stringfellow, and most others seem to avoid dealing with the onto-logical nature of the Powers. However, theologian Matthew Croasmun addresses the issue head-on in his book *The Emergence of Sin: The Cosmic Tyrant in Romans*.[101] It is important to examine Croasmun's work in order to better understand the ontological nature of Satan and thus develop a fuller understanding of the Powers. Girard deconstructs Satan in a helpful way, but Croasmun reconstructs Satan in a way that more fully equips us to understand his nature and work, which is essential if we are to develop a robust diagnosis for the problem of domineering leadership in the church.

The primary question Croasmun seeks to address is the following: *What are we to make of the word* ἁμαρτία *(sin) in Romans 5–8?*[102] "The noun ἁμαρτία is deployed in personal terms in these chapters. This is not disputed."[103] We see that ἁμαρτία "exercises dominion (5:21, 6:12)," "seizes opportunities to produce covetousness and kill (7:8,11)," and "is used as the subject of an active verb no fewer than eleven times."[104] Croasmun seeks to discover if Paul is using a literary personification or if he is engaged in person identification.

In order to answer this question, he first examines the historical argument between Bultmann (the demythologizer), Bultmann's doctoral student Ernst Käsemann (dualist), and current liberation theology.

REDUCTIONISM, DUALISM, AND EMERGENT PERSPECTIVES

As I have already demonstrated, Bultmann's demythologizing project sought to make sense of the Powers for modern readers. Bultmann was also seeking to resolve the apparent internal consistency regarding the contradiction "between the account of human beings living under these cosmic rulers, and the account of human agents responsible for their actions."[105] The most significant element that Bultmann seeks to guard in his project is human responsibility, often noting "that sin came into the world by sinning."[106] Although Croasmun can appreciate Bultmann's attention to human responsibility, he believes Bultmann is engaged in reductionism, because he assumes "that Sin as a cosmic power does not correspond to 'the actual state of affairs.'"[107]

Käsemann, on the other hand, argues, "Paul is describing the world as it actually is. To be human is to be the site of contestation for various powers. To be human is to be a node in a network, both social and cosmic."[108] For Käsemann, sin is a very literal demonic power, in the premodern sense.[109] Because Käsemann is seeking to refute Bultmann, who emphasizes personal responsibility, "Käsemann is largely content to describe Sin's cosmic dominion in the strongest terms possible."[110] The liberationist allows us to hold these two in tension but also introduces its own complications.[111]

Liberationists look at sin as manifest within social structures. The former archbishop of San Salvador Óscar Romero, for example, considered institutions sinful because they produce the fruit of sin, which in his context was expressed in the oppression and death of El Salvadorian people.[112] Sin does not only involve culpable people, but it also involves culpable systems, working at the social level, "constraining the moral freedom of human agents."[113] Leonardo Boff makes the case that the "fundamental nature of the social dimension of sin corresponds to an ontology of the human person that sees the social as primary, and the 'individual' appearing first of all within that web of relationships."[114] Boff and

Käsemann differ in that although Boff looks at sin fundamentally at the social level, Käsemann sees it as a cosmic level.[115] Both decenter the individual.

In partial critique of liberationists, who might not give the *cosmic* proper weight, Croasmun writes, "So, we have not two, but three different 'levels' of analysis competing for supremacy: the individual or psychological (Bultmann); the social (the liberationist); and the cosmic or mythological (Käsemann, et al.)."[116] In seeking to address the problem of causation and culpability within complex systems, Croasmun looks to Romans 5–8, with the goal of clarifying the ontologies of persons, including social and cosmic realities.[117] Looking at the body of sin (Rom. 6:6), he questions whether the social and cosmic are simply literary personifications or, in fact, person identification. He believes the problem of causation and culpability we see in Romans 5–8 can best be resolved with an "appropriate ontology."[118] He writes, "Sin in Romans is a matter of concrete action and also a matter of social structures, and *also* a cosmic tyrant."[119] Rather than take an either-or approach, he takes a comprehensive approach, using emergent science to bring a new perspective to our understanding of the text in an effort to solve this stalemate.

EMERGENTISM AS A TRANS-ORDINAL THEORY

Emergentism, as opposed to being a scientific theory in itself, seeks to understand the relationship between the sciences. In its full state, it operates as a trans-ordinal theory, integrating human knowledge.[120] It is a rival theory to reductionism and dualism.[121]

Dualism seeks to introduce *novel substances* as a way to best understand apparent discontinuities, such as the state between living and nonliving or conscious and unconscious.[122] But current scientific orthodoxy holds to the belief of "ontological monism—the universe consists of only one kind of substance," and therefore substance dualism is to be avoided.[123]

Reductionism, on the other hand, has similarities to emergentism, in that the domains of knowledge are stratified in the same way (see figure 7.2):[124]

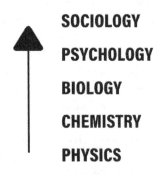

SOCIOLOGY

PSYCHOLOGY

BIOLOGY

CHEMISTRY

PHYSICS

Figure 7.2 Reductionism

Although both reductionism and emergentism hold to an ontological monism, the reductionist thinker would posit that the "lower level" (i.e., physics) is the most fundamental layer in giving explanation to the higher—in this case, chemistry, biology, psychology, and sociology. In regard to causation, the arrow always points up. In this way, all knowledge is unified.[125] Thus, if one wants to understand what is happening within psychology, it is reduced to neurology (biology), then the chemical process, and ultimately physics.

AN EMERGENT VIEW

Those who take an emergent view seek to avoid the pitfalls that come with dualism and reductionism, "while retaining the strengths of both."[126] For the emergent thinker, the world is made of "one stuff" and holds to the stratification of the sciences, as the reductionist would. But they would hold to a dialectic framework, where causation is bi-directional (up and down), as opposed to unidirectional (up). This bi-directional influence is established "by the two basic principles in emergentism: *supervenience* and *downward causation*."[127] (See figure 7.3.)

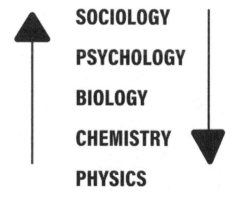

SOCIOLOGY

PSYCHOLOGY

BIOLOGY

CHEMISTRY

PHYSICS

Figure 7.3 Emergentism

Supervenience means that high-level entities are ontologically dependent on lower levels.[128] In other words, emergence is consistent with ontological monism.[129] Thus, if there is no brain, there is no mind, but the mind is not reducible to the brain.[130] Therefore, psychological behavior can never be fully explained through neuroscience.[131] In the same way, although the "social supervenes on the individual—that is, no individuals, no society," it is not reducible to the individual. This means that the social, although real and distinct from the individual, is not possible apart from the individual.[132] Essentially, supervenience appreciates the upward direction found in reductionism.

The second principle of emergentism is *downward causation*, in that what has emerged from the more foundational (for example, the social from the individual) also constrains what it emerged from. Croasmun writes, "Social groups exercise constraint on the individuals of which they are composed."[133] Consider this principle in relation to psychology and biology. While thoughts emerge from neurological processes (biology), the mind can also act upon the brain (psychology). This reflects the idea of downward causation.

Social theorists talk about both upward causation and downward constraint. "Social actors construct social systems that, in turn, constrain or even, on some accounts, construct those same social actors."[134] In other words, we create social structures, and they, in turn, recreate us. There is a dialectical relationship. This is likely why Wink emphasizes the need to engage the social and individual if transformation is to occur. By looking at downward causations in chemistry, biology, and sociology, Croasmun concludes that "downward causation is *possible* because it is *actual*."[135]

Although Croasmun demonstrates downward causation within these various disciplines, the beauty of emergence as a trans-ordinal theory is in its ability to conduct a multilevel analysis of a phenomenon. Croasmun's analysis of racism in the United States through an emergence lens, for example, is worth reading, as it demonstrates the principles of supervenience and downward causation.[136]

AN EMERGENT VIEW OF "SIN"

When applying this emergent lens toward "Sin," Bultmann would be in the reductionist camp, arguing that all agency is in the individual, "no matter how much it apparently emanates from social systems."[137] By contrast, Käsemann and those in his camp essentially propose a dualist position: "There are human sins, yes—but even more important is the reign of the cosmic power, Sin, which exists with so substantial freedom from the individual sins as to have an existence alongside the individual, as if the two were composed of two different substances."[138] Croasmun believes the more radical liberationists "seem to advance a distinct dualism of the social and the personal, as opposed to Käsemann's dualism of the cosmic and personal."[139] But, by and large, he regards the liberationist to be advocating an approach that is more in line with "some form of emergentism."[140] Thus Bultmann, with a modernist framework, tends to adopt a reductionist viewpoint; and Käsemann—with a more premodern view—adopts a dualistic view. And those less committed to either a modernist or premodern Western framework are more inclined to "something that looks more emergent."[141]

In examining emergentism and theology, Croasmun proposes to not only include the individual and social but also the cosmic, naming it a *mythological level* of emergence. In other words, just as the psychological emerges from the biological, the mythological emerges from the social. Thus he adds the new category of mythology (see figure 7.4):

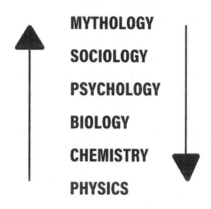

MYTHOLOGY

SOCIOLOGY

PSYCHOLOGY

BIOLOGY

CHEMISTRY

PHYSICS

Figure 7.4 Mythological Level of Emergence

Croasmun defines mythology as "the 'psychologies' of social 'bodies.'"[142] In conclusion, he writes, "So we might think of the cosmic power, Sin, itself supervening on a complex network of sinful social systems, which themselves supervene on the sinful exercise of individual human agency."[143]

But the question remains: in Romans 5–8, is the body of sin a personification or a person identification? Again, this is an important question, as it will help us to answer the ontological question regarding Satan.

THE EMERGENCE OF PEOPLE GREAT AND SMALL

In order to address this question, Croasmun believes "we need a trans-ordinal ontology that facilitates a multilevel account of ἁμαρτία [Sin]."[144] This leads him to ask two basic questions: First, what does it mean for an entity to be a person? And second, if the social is real and has agency, "how might complex social systems qualify as agents, or even persons?"[145]

Croasmun engages several social theorists—from Émile Durkheim, the late-nineteenth- and early twentieth-century father of sociology, to the present day—to discern these questions with an emergent lens. What he discovers is that "social realities can be described as personal on precisely the same grounds that individual persons are."[146] As Durkheim writes, "It is very true that society comprises no active forces other than those of individuals; but individuals, as they join together, form a psychological entity of a new species."[147] To demonstrate his point, Croasmun draws on the example of eusocial insects, such as bees. A colony of bees is made up of individual bees and the collective, the hive. The queen bee and her offspring, "the hive," are often called *superorganisms*. The workers are genetically identical and an extension of the queen's phenotype. There is only one queen for the reproduction of the hive. Croasmun questions which is the most critical—the bee or the hive, the individual or the superorganism? Moving from eusocial insects to the anatomy of group minds or group cognition, Croasmun writes, "The more we understand organisms as groups, the more reason we have to understand groups as organisms."[148]

Returning to his larger argument, Croasmun concludes, "Indeed, my contention is that Sin, as described by Paul in Romans 5–8, is precisely one of these social realities. The distinction between 'personification' and 'person identification' is demonstrated to have no basis."[149]

Croasmun considers these "superorganisms" social *bodies*, and he uses the category mythological to describe the social *minds* that emerge from these social *bodies*.[150] Just as we are a collection of cells, so social bodies are a collection of "selves." And this collection of selves entails a social body. And just like our mind emerges from our brain and has a downward effect on our brain, so social minds emerge from social bodies and have a downward effect. The social mind, or collective mind, is what Croasmun calls the "mythical."

Thus Croasmun substantiates Bultmann's slogan: "Sin came into the world by sinning." The individual is significant, but the individual is never an island. Therefore, Croasmun also verifies the liberationist, in that our individual sin takes place in the superorganism of the body of sin. It "emerges from the resultant complex interaction of sinning individuals and sinning institutions and exercises downward causation back upon institutions and individuals."[151] This also vindicates the "Käsemann school's instinct that Sin constrains the freedom of the human subject. Inasmuch as this downward causation 'trickles down' to the individual level via the social, it also vindicates the liberationist instinct that the freedom of the human subject is largely constrained by the power of sinful social structures."[152] With this hypothesis discovered in the realm of sociology, Croasmun then seeks to demonstrate this reality exegetically by going back to the Romans 5–8 text.

AN EMERGENT VIEW OF SIN IN ROMANS

As Croasmun goes back to the text, he seeks to give a multilevel account (individual, social, mythological) of the downward spiral we encounter in Romans 1–7, which is "a story of enslavement to s/Sin through law that results in death."[153] He moves from Adam sinning to the eventual emergence of the body of sin (Romans 6:6). He essentially gives an "account of the emergence of the person and cosmic power, Sin, from a supervenience base of human sinners and sinful social structures."[154] And he makes a strong point that those whom Paul is addressing "constitute a social body before they become the Body of Christ in baptism," because in Paul's time, there was already a strong understanding of social bodies. In fact, "the Stoics took the entire cosmos to be a living being."[155]

Social bodies in Paul's day came in various sizes, from the cosmic bodies of the stoics to the universal human body to body politic, represented in the Roman Empire.[156] The reality of social bodies was part of ancient culture. Croasmun agrees with Michelle Lee's argument that "the social body was not something that needed to be argued for; rather, it was the ontological basis from which ethical arguments could be constructed."[157] This would be why Paul in his letters uses the body of Christ as his flagship body. The body of Christ is a single body, a collection of "selves," with Christ as the head.

There are two key aspects to highlight from Croasmun's lengthier exploration: First, "the cosmic power, Sin, emerges from a supervenience base of human sins."[158] And second, we should understand "Sin as a super-organism with a group mind, emergent from a complex network of individual human persons and social institutions."[159]

THE BODY OF SIN AS PERSON IDENTIFICATION

Croasmun makes the case that that the body of sin is a "real" person, in the same way that you and I are "real" people. For just as the psychological (mind) emerges from the biological (brain) and has downward causation, so the mythical (body of sin) arises from the sociological (social body) and has downward causation through each category of reality. In this way, Croasmun, using emergent science, takes the strength of Bultmann, Käsemann, and liberationists, without holding to their weakness.

Summarizing his findings, Croasmun says, "The central interpretive proposal for Romans, then, is this: we can make sense of Paul's language about Sin as a cosmic power by understanding Sin as a mythological person emergent from a complex system of human transgressions."[160] In using the word *mythology*, Croasmun is not intending to use it in the way Girard uses *myth*. He understands that sin, *Roma* (goddess), and other mythological creatures are easily "dismissed by modern Westerners as 'merely mythological.' If such entities have been demythologized through reduction, I would seek to re-mythologize them, through providing an emergent ontology to describe their existence."[161] The question then becomes the following: Does this body of sin, with its collective mind that Croasmun describes in his book *The Emergence of Sin*, have a name?

NAMING THE BODY OF SIN

In his conclusion, Croasmun suggests this body of sin does have a name. But first, there are some important aspects of his conclusion that merit mentioning. One being that although sin demonstrates enormous power in our world, we need to remember that Scripture does not use the word *supernatural* when referring to aspects of creation. There is the Creator and creation. Thus Croasmun mentions that this post-Enlightenment construct of "natural" and "supernatural" "regularly deployed in post-Enlightenment Christian theology [is] usually a hindrance rather than a help."[162] For this gives sin too much power and can create dualistic thinking in the way of Käsemann. Instead, Croasmun makes a distinction between Creator and creation, placing the emergence of sin on the side of creation as an emergent reality.

So can we name this body of sin "Satan"? Croasmun writes,

> Understanding Satan as a real person, emergent from complex systems of human transgression, and tempting us to further transgression through the marginal control by setting the boundaries of our moral cognition, might allow us to locate Satan's power and authority in human freedom. Is it possible that Satan, in fact, is a person emergent from human evil?[163]

Although one might object based on "the synthetic, biblical, theological account of Satan as Edenic tempter," Croasmun suggests a solution: What if we "treat the story of any 'original' (in the temporal sense) sinful acts as heuristic[?] That is, we may want to suggest that the only account we can offer of sinning is one in which we are 'always already' under the thumb of a cosmic power that itself/himself/herself has emerged from our sinning."[164] If this is the case, then Croasmun's account of the emergence of sin—his description of this body of sin as a person who has cosmic dominion—would prove helpful. He suggests one could take this a step further, writing, "Satan and Sin share not just an ontology—a formal account of their being—but in fact might actually be the same entity."[165] And though equating Satan and Sin might flatten biblical and theological text, it is possible that, "constructively, one might want to say that they refer to the same personal entity who really does menace the human agent."[166]

REFLECTING ON THE USE OF SATAN IN THE NEW TESTAMENT

As I have reflected on Croasmun's work looking for a solid explanation to understand the ontology of Satan, I find his argument compelling. More than that, it seems to make sense of the New Testament's use of the word *Satan*. Although the scope of this book only permits a cursory glance at this, it is worth the reader undertaking further study. First, we are told that Satan is the "god of this world" (2 Cor. 4:4 ESV) and that "the whole world is under the control of the evil one" (1 John 5:19). If Satan is an emergent reality, there is no need to revert to dualism or to give him power equal to that of God. But these verses also confirm the cosmic nature of Satan, the body of sin, which works its mischief across all civilizations and people.

In addition, this view of Satan as an emergent reality makes sense in the life and teachings of Christ. For Satan is regarded as Christ's enemy who "comes only to steal and kill and destroy" (John 10:10). We see in the foundational teachings of Jesus in the Sermon on the Mount that we are called to love our enemies. But if we are to love our enemies, why doesn't Christ love Satan in order to model for us what this should look like? Why does Jesus say that hell was created for Satan and his angels? Why does the trajectory of Satan in the scriptural story move toward his demise? If he is a fallen angel, would not there be the possibility of his redemption, as Wink seems to indicate? By not distinguishing Satan, the demonic, and the principalities and powers—like the separation of bone and marrow—Wink's understanding that the Powers are good, fallen, and can be redeemed seems to push him to include Satan in this category. Yet while Wink speaks of Satan's resurrection, he is also careful to say that Satan and the demonic are not created by God, thus giving room for them to be emergent realities with a very different trajectory.

We are told in Ephesians 4:26–27 that if we go to bed angry, "we give the devil a foothold." Around the world, how many people will go to bed angry today? Is Satan therefore omnipresent? Orthodox Christianity would reserve this for God alone. But if we are to take this passage at face value, it would seem that omnipresence might be possible for the devil. However, an emergent view helps us to understand these verses by claiming that Satan is an emergent cosmic being who rules or "constrains" the world (downward causation). Therefore, in fact, the devil can get a foothold in every person who violates the command in Ephesians 4:26–27, while still being part of emergent creation, not equal to the Creator.

In the contentious passage in 1 Corinthians 5, in which Paul admonishes the Corinthians for putting up with a sexual immorality that even "pagans" could not tolerate, what did Paul suggest they do? He told them, "So when you are assembled and I am with you in spirit, and the power of our Lord Jesus is present, *hand this man over to Satan* for the destruction of the flesh, so that his spirit may be saved on the day of the Lord" (1 Cor. 5:4–5, emphasis mine). In this judgment, Paul's ultimate hope was redemption for the person. If Satan was an emergent reality (the only other cosmic entity apart from the body of Christ), then this passage would make sense—as this person was taken from the protection of the body of Christ and given over to Satan (the body of sin). Through this, perhaps he would come to his senses and repent.

As missional leaders, we have to be able to name and unmask the Powers if we hope to engage them well. Croasmun has given us a way to name the body of sin and understand the cosmic nature of Satan without reverting to dualistic thinking. He reminds us that there are essentially two cosmic bodies in the world: the body of sin (Satan) and the body of Christ. Before baptism, all of us were a part of a social body connected to the cosmic body of sin.[167] "This severity of the problem requires Paul to suggest a drastic solution: death through baptismal co-crucifixion with Christ (6:6). Sin's tyranny is, in a certain sense, inescapable."[168] Girard concurs with this: "The only feasible option, therefore is to die to that world and be raised to new life in a new world-body, the Body of Christ."[169] Yet, as Croasmun reminds us, "'dual membership' in these two world bodies seems to be possible."[170] Croasmun prescribes (apart from Girard's influence) mimetic obedience to Christ as the solution.[171] We are to be transformed by renewing our single "collective mind" so that we might have the mind of Christ (Rom. 12:1–2; Phil. 2:5).[172] This speaks of positive mimesis in a collective sense, which I will explore further in the final chapters.

So, is this body of sin Satan? In the final words of Croasmun's book, which primarily focuses on Romans 5–8, we find the body of sin is named later in the book of Romans in a way that speaks to the promise of Satan's ultimate destruction. After greeting many of his friends, Paul urges them "to watch out for those who cause divisions and put obstacles [scandals] in your way that are contrary to the teaching you have learned. Keep away from them. . . . The God of peace will soon crush Satan under your feet" (Romans 16:17, 20).

PRACTICAL IMPLICATIONS OF MIMETIC THEORY FOR LEADERSHIP

Girard's understanding of mimetic desire and its link to the Powers—in particular, Satan—provides a theoretical framework with practical implications. In the context of a congregation, if there are emerging leaders who look to the lead pastor as their model, and if the lead pastor desires to hold the *title* of the lead pastor (as opposed to the *work* of the lead pastor), this poses a threat. If the leader either develops or inherits a structure in which they choose not to share the leadership role, this leader becomes a scandal (obstacle, stumbling block) to any who look to them as their model. According to mimetic theory, disciples subconsciously capture the desires of their models. They then start to desire the title of lead pastor and the prestige that they feel comes with that title. In turn, the lead pastor senses that this person desires the title, which increases their own desire for the title, eventually leading to mimetic rivalry, often to the bewilderment of those caught in the mimetic trap. Mimetic desire creates antagonists out of the disciple and model, who previously were at peace with one another. As mimetic rivalry increases and scandals develop with other disciples, it can lead to a mimetic crisis, where everyone finds themselves against everyone, all against all, bewildered why this would be the case.

As tension builds in a congregation where there is much quarrelling and disputes (as James writes), to the point of a mimetic crisis, there is a need to release the tension. Unknowingly and somewhat haphazardly, a marginal individual or a marginalized group becomes the scapegoat. Alternatively, the scapegoat could also be the person at the top, the king, or in this case, the lead pastor. Applying Girard's mimetic leadership to the ecclesial leader has much potential to help leaders recognize the poison of envious desire. As Girard has said, "We can escape mimetism only by understanding the laws that govern it."[173]

SUMMARY OF SECTION THREE

Girard's primary contribution to the argument of this book is his linking of the leader to the Powers via mimetic desire, supplying the completion of the imitation-based framework for a new way of approaching leadership theory and practice. The mimetic cycle provides insight into how Satan uses the envious desires of leaders to create chaos and scapegoating in a community. The foundation of Girard's study is based on a broad number of disciplines, including the revelation of Scripture. As my exploration of McKnight's work on the book of James revealed, it is clear that James had already made the connection of leadership, envious desire, and the Powers. Both the book of James through the analysis provided by McKnight and the book of 1 Peter through Houston's engagement confirm these links. McKnight hints at the similarity of James and 1 Peter and suggests they may have acted as a catechism "for leaders, teachers and those aspiring to be as such."[174] McKnight's work, Cowdell's engagement with Girard, and my own defense of Girard suggest that Whitehouse's critique of Girard is unfounded.

Girard adds to the imitation-based framework by linking imitation and desire to the Powers via mimetic desire. By unveiling the mimetic cycle and tying it to Satan, the insidious nature of the Powers' work from the foundation of the world comes into view. Girard offers an explanation as to why Satan is the god of this world, as his cosmic influence through the founding murders is disclosed as the foundation of cultures as well as the institutions built from these cultures. Therefore, when leaders look uncritically to culture and the world for their approach to leadership, they can unknowingly open themselves up to demonic influence. Girard not only ties mimetic desire to the Powers but also gives the leader concrete ways to discern if the Powers are at work in their lives. For example, when we, as leaders, find ourselves concerned about status, prestige, and honor, it ought to alert us to the work of the Powers. When we are tempted to scapegoat someone made in the image of God, it ought to alert us to the work of the Powers. When we discern envious desires in our heart or selfish ambition, it ought to alert us to the work of the Powers in our lives. And we ought to be alert to the potential of dissension and chaos that might occur in the congregations we serve. Finally, Girard discloses how Satan uses pride to make us blind to our own envious desires, often concealing them by self-justification.

Though the concept of leadership and positive mimesis is underdeveloped in Girard, others who have been influenced by Girard have addressed this lack. The leader's awareness of the Powers working through mimetic desire (negative mimesis) is helpful to alert the leader to the Powers' work. However, positive mimesis holds promise for how imitation of Christ, through the power of the Holy Spirit, promotes a flourishing congregation. This was observed through the metanarrative provided by Steinmair-Pösel and the exegetical work of Swartley.

Finally, although Girard deconstructs Satan and prefers not to give Satan any sense of being, Croasmun reconstructs Satan as the emergent body of sin (Romans 6:6) and ultimately assigns him personhood. Girard was hesitant to give Satan any sense of personhood but didn't consider this to be an obligatory stance. If Girard were alive today and read Croasmun, it is possible that he might agree with the way in which Croasmun develops his argument, as Girard admired the work of Émile Durkheim, and Croasmun's understanding of Satan does not seem to contradict the primary components of mimetic theory.

Having developed a theology of the Powers through Wink and connecting imitation and desire to the Powers through Girard, I will seek to bring synthesis by looking at the contributions of William Stringfellow, who helps reveal how the principalities and powers can subvert us, as leaders, at the three contours of our leadership—identity, praxis, and telos.

SECTION FOUR

MISSIONAL LEADERSHIP
AND SUBVERSION

In an attempt to diagnose the problem of domineering leadership in the church, I have sought to develop an imitation-based framework. Fallen leadership occurs when leaders choose to imitate the Powers rather than Christ. Through critical engagement with Wink, I explored a theology of the Powers, and through engagement with Girard, I tied mimetic desire to the Powers. In this section, interaction with William Stringfellow will provide a way to concretely apply the imitation-based framework. In chapter eight, I will examine the work of the Powers by highlighting portions of Stringfellow's life as well as summarizing some of his work. I will uncover how the principalities of image, institution, and ideology seek to tempt us, as leaders, at the three contours of leadership—identity, praxis, and telos—in order to malform our desires. In chapter nine, I will engage Stringfellow by looking at how the Powers seek to subvert our leadership.

8

THE WORK OF THE POWERS

Have you ever felt tempted to build your own kingdom instead of God's kingdom? When is the last time you were drawn to unhealthy forms of power and control? Do egotistical thoughts tend to dominate your thinking, or do you think more about bringing glory to God?

The Powers seek to subvert us from fulfilling God's mission in the way of Christ. As Jesus began his ministry, the devil tried to distract him from fulfilling the mission of his Father by tempting him to bow down to the Powers (Matt. 4:1–11; Luke 4:1–13). Satan continued to tempt Jesus at other opportune times, but Jesus remained faithful to his calling and refused to use power for his own gain. His approach to leadership was counterintuitive. Rather than succumb to a worldly paradigm of leadership, he sought to subvert the political and cultural approach that had captivated those around him, even his own disciples. In fact, his ministry was to deliver and heal people who were possessed by the spirit of the age.

Jesus never bowed to the Powers. He resisted them, seeking to imitate and mirror the heart of his Father. But the Powers did not stand idly by and allow Jesus to break their spell on the world. The Powers crave ultimate devotion; and to capture our attention, so that we might fully give ourselves over to them, they have developed rules, systems, structures, and institutions that speak to the longings we each have. In time, they demand our ultimate allegiance to the point that we are willing to sacrifice anything and everything for them. Disguising themselves as light, they trick us into thinking we are living out our mission for God, when in reality, we have become captive to idols, which leads to death.

Death is a significant theological theme for Stringfellow. When he uses the term *death*, he is typically referring to the manifold applications used in Scripture.[1] When the Bible talks about death, it does not refer merely to physical death, but to "all forms of alienation of men from themselves and from one another and from God. Since idolatry of any kind demeans man, prevents him from becoming fully human, death is that which, under many disguises, idolaters really worship."[2] For Stringfellow, death is the devil incarnate, and thus he often uses the terms *death* and *devil* synonymously.[3]

As leaders, we are either servants of life or servants of death. When we carry a ladder rather than a cross, we become servants of death. When we climb for prestige, power, or money, we become servants of death. However, when we seek to imitate the crucified one, we become servants of life.

If we want to be servants of life who incarnate a missional rather than a domineering approach to leadership, we need to understand how the Powers seek to subvert our leadership. As I will demonstrate, Stringfellow's understanding of the principalities correlates with the contours of leadership: identity, praxis, and telos. This correlation, which I will explore in this chapter, will provide insight and understanding in how to resist the Powers.

The 2006 publication *Radical Christian and Exemplary Lawyer* reflects on Stringfellow and his life's work, with contributions from a number of scholars and writers who highly commend Stringfellow. Walter Wink, one of the contributors, writes the following:

> As I look back over that completed project [Wink's trilogy on the Powers] and having now read through most of his opus (a few of his books for the first time), I am able to see how very deeply I owe the strengths of my series on the powers to him and how its weaknesses reveal my failure to take him more seriously. (I also realize how much of his thought I had internalized without giving him sufficient credit.)[4]

In the foreword to Anthony Dancer's book on Stringfellow's life, Anglican bishop Rowan Williams writes,

> William Stringfellow is one of those people who is impossible to classify easily, and who is an equally unsettling figure for partisans of all complexions. A passionate radical, committed to the poor and a variety of "progressive" causes, he was a scathing critic of the reduction of Christianity to social service. A persistent proclaimer of the absolute authority of the Bible, he was perpetually in conflict with fundamentalists and deeply hostile to what he regarded as defensive, moralistic, or pietist readings. Identified by the greatest Protestant theologian of the twentieth century [Karl Barth] as the man that America should be listening to, he never held an academic post or indeed any significant public role.[5]

INTRODUCING WILLIAM STRINGFELLOW

Who was William Stringfellow, and what did he experience in his life that drew his attention to the theme of the Powers? It is fitting to share some of his significant life experiences, because Stringfellow sees biography as theology: "Any biography and every biography, is inherently theological in the sense that it contains already—literally by virtue of the Incarnation—the news of the gospel whether or not anyone discerns that. We are each one of us parables."[6] Agreeing with this, Anthony Dancer writes a biographical theology on Stringfellow, insisting that if we are to understand Stringfellow, his theology must be understood in light of his life and vice versa.

As I have already explored, biographical theology is crucial when applied to missional leadership, because missional theology is not simply conceptual but embodied theology, and the theme of imitation is central to incarnating missional leadership.

Stringfellow lived out his faith and developed his theology on the street and in the urban ghetto—he lived incarnationally before it became a popular term. Through his "self-induced poverty," he stood in solidarity with those he lived among, and it was in this context he consistently clashed with the Powers.[7] These clashes, as I will demonstrate, led him to make the principalities and powers a focal point of his theology and the area of study for which he became renowned.

Stringfellow's life spanned close to six decades (1928–1985), during which he wrote fifteen books and scores of theological articles.[8] His seminal work on the Powers was *Free in Obedience* (1964), and it was this book that seeded Wink's desire to write on the subject. Stringfellow's most comprehensive and influential work on the Powers is *An Ethic for Christians and Other Aliens in a Strange Land* (1973). In his formal education, he pursued his passion for the gospel and politics. He studied at Bates College, the London School of Economics, and received his law degree from Harvard Law School. As a lawyer, he represented prostitutes, the poor, and those on the margins of society.[9] Today, Stringfellow would be described as an early co-vocational missional practitioner who understood the importance of incarnational living. He knew that if he were to serve those in the ghetto, he needed to "experience the vulnerability of daily life," becoming poor in order to meaningfully connect with the poor.[10]

His involvement with the Episcopal Church in his youth shaped him deeply, especially his decision at the age of fourteen not to heed his priest's insistence that he become ordained. The clergyman seemed to give Stringfellow the impression that being ordained as a priest was "the seal of the Christian life and that the priesthood embodied a higher or better . . . disposition of one's life as a Christian."[11] But Stringfellow was already recognizing the importance of the incarnational life in the everyday world with everyday people, and how it was not about "religion" but about God's active presence in the world. Thus, his response: "I would be damned if I would be a priest."[12] He committed to spending his life refuting the idea that serious commitment to the Christian faith required ordination.[13] This may have been his first encounter of religion as a principality and power, but it certainly was not the last.

FROM HARVARD TO HARLEM

Stringfellow pursued law at Harvard, but unlike many of his fellow students, he was sufficiently aware of the Powers to view Harvard as a principality that sought to shape all who came within her reach. He was slightly older than the average student, having served in the Army and traveled to Europe and Asia before attending Harvard. While in London, he "died to the idea of career" and took up the vocation of simply being human by resisting the Powers and giving his allegiance to God.[14] Stringfellow considered the legal profession specifically, and occupations in general, as fallen principalities and powers engaged "in coercing, stifling, captivating, intimidating, and otherwise victimizing human beings. The demand for conformity in a profession commonly signifies the threat of death."[15] At Harvard, Stringfellow was learning to resist the Powers—according to his own account, he left Harvard "as someone virtually opposite" of the person Harvard sought to mold.[16]

Thus, while most of his fellow Harvard law school graduates went to work with the elite in Manhattan, serving the commercial principalities and powers, Stringfellow chose to call East Harlem his home for the next six years (1956–1962) to be an advocate for the outcasts in the slums.[17] It was while living in Harlem that Stringfellow came face-to-face with the principalities and powers, which were often the institutions that were supposed to be serving those living in East Harlem. He writes,

> In that urban ghetto my daily routine of cases and causes forced me to contend with death institutionalized in authorities, agencies, bureaucracies, and malfarious principalities and powers. Slowly I learned something that folk indigenous to the ghetto know: namely, that the power and purpose of death are incarnated in institutions and structures, procedures, and regimes—consolidated Edison or the Department of Welfare, the Mafia or the police, the Housing Authority or the social work bureaucracy, the hospital systems or the banks, liberal philanthropy or corporate real estate speculation. In the wisdom of the people of the East Harlem neighborhood, such principalities are identified as demonic powers because of the relentless and ruthless dehumanization that they cause.[18]

Context was everything for Stringfellow. He understood that our view of the world was affected by the point from which we view the world. What he had learned academically became empirically verified as he made the journey from Harvard to Harlem, discerning how the Word of God became manifest on the streets in the concrete realities of life in the ghetto.[19] Christ's incarnation informed how he lived his life.

It was the invitation of a friend in the East Harlem Protestant Parish (EHPP) that initially attracted Stringfellow to Harlem, a place forgotten by the rest of New York.[20] He took on the role of legal counsel for EHPP, but fifteen months later he resigned, feeling it necessary if he was to serve those in East Harlem more faithfully. His departure from EHPP was based on theological and tactical matters, which he made public in a seven-page letter.[21] "Essentially, his critique amounts to the fact that the GM [Group Ministry] and the EHPP were a fallen principality and would not recognize this fact and respond in faithfulness and obedience."[22] Others have commented that Stringfellow's resignation may also have been linked to his struggle with teamwork, a common issue for prophetic individuals.[23] Stringfellow believed the church has an essential role to play, but he thought that the GM misunderstood the place of the church in the world, as well as the place of the Word in the church. He felt they lacked an ecumenical spirit, that they had an imperialistic notion of mission, and "there was little being done and said in the EHPP which could not have been said, for example, by a social worker, psychologist, or anthropologist; it lacked the distinctive voice of a church rooted in the radical reality of the Word in the world."[24] He continued to practice law in Harlem for several more years, joining two fellow Harvard graduates to form the law firm Ellis, Patton, and Stringfellow.[25]

His life at Harvard and Harlem, in combination with discerning the Word of God active in the world, gave prominence and focus to his ability to name, unmask, and engage the principalities and powers at work, as well as their submission and service to death. As I mentioned earlier, for Stringfellow, "Death is a living power in this world, greater, apart from God himself, than any other reality in existence."[26] This prepared him for what most consider a watershed moment for Stringfellow's public life and theological focus: his public and private encounter with Karl Barth.[27]

THE ENDORSEMENT FROM KARL BARTH

In 1962, at the request of his son Markus, Karl Barth made his sole visit to the United States.[28] At the age of seventy-five, Barth traveled across the country for seven weeks to deliver lectures at a number of seminaries. The lecture at the University of Chicago, where Markus Barth was a professor, was significant for Stringfellow. Stringfellow was the only nonacademic theologian on the prestigious six-person panel for a question-and-answer session with Barth.[29] Stringfellow asked Barth two lengthy questions: one regarding the relationship of the churches to the state, and one on the principalities and powers.[30] The first question related to the church's prophetic role in America. Stringfellow thought that instead of appropriately challenging the nation, the church at large in America sanctified national self-interest. Before coming to the US, Barth agreed not to speak to issues related to America, as he wanted Americans to speak to these issues, so this question caused a stir in the gathering.[31] In Barth's response, he agreed with Stringfellow's preamble to his question. Then, after clarifying that he didn't come to America to criticize, Barth stood and pointed squarely at Stringfellow, saying, "Listen to this man."[32] Barth then insisted that the Christian life demands political action, and pointing to Romans 13, said, "Being subject to the state is an act of responsibility: we are responsible for the political order, responsible for seeking authentic politics. Our action is that of free obedience; an act born of the freedom of the resurrection, in obedience to God."[33] Barth's endorsement of Stringfellow at this prominent gathering was a significant encouragement for Stringfellow and helped confirm his sense of direction. In fact, Stringfellow's next book, *Free in Obedience*, was the first noteworthy articulation of the principalities and powers. It was chapter three of this book that inspired and seeded Wink's trilogy.

The second question Stringfellow asked Barth was on the principalities and powers, about which Stringfellow had been thinking deeply. He wanted Barth to affirm the importance of this topic, and he wanted to understand Barth's thoughts on the matter. Before asking his question, Stringfellow mentioned how most churches—both inside and outside of America—consider the Powers archaic and typically don't take them into account in understanding the narrative of God. He said to Barth,

> What there is of Protestant moral theology in America almost utterly ignores the attempt to account for, explicate, and relate one's self to the principalities and powers. Yet, empirically more and more, the principalities and powers seem to have an aggressive, indeed, possessive, ascendancy in American life—including, alas, the life of the American churches. Who are these principalities and powers? What is their significance in the creation and in the fall? What significance do they have with respect to merely human sin? What is their relation to the claim that Christ is the Lord of history? What is the relation of the power and presence of death in history to the principalities and powers, and therefore, practically speaking, what freedom does a Christian have from the domination of all these principalities and powers?[34]

Barth's response to Stringfellow clearly shaped and confirmed Stringfellow's understanding of the Powers, for Barth's response to these questions is practically quoted in Stringfellow's *Free in Obedience*.[35]

In *Free in Obedience*, Stringfellow writes about how the church can become a principality when the church seeks justification and freedom through the nation; when she becomes a handmaiden of the principalities of race, class, or commerce; or when "she becomes so preoccupied with the maintenance and preservation of its own institutional life."[36] Stringfellow expresses that the nation and the American way of life exerts pressure on the church to serve the national self-interest, in this way becoming a principality.[37] He believes that, just as Palm Sunday was a temptation for Jesus to heed to the temptation of the devil for worldly dominion, in the same way, the church today is tempted by the scandal of Palm Sunday. This happens when the church is "possessed with nostalgia for the parade, beguiled by the temptation to achieve or imitate worldly power and to build an earthly kingdom."[38] For Stringfellow, when the church uses the ends to justify the means, she becomes a principality. As an example, he notes that in the same way overseas missions in the past century required converts to become westernized before becoming believers, too often today the church expects people in the inner city to become middle class before becoming believers.[39] If we, as missional leaders, are to heed Stringfellow's insights, we will need to be able to name and unmask the Powers, or we will find ourselves imitating them, and we will become servants of death.

Barth not only connected with Stringfellow in this formal gathering, but he also accepted a personal invitation from Stringfellow for a guided tour of East Harlem and to share an informal meal with various people.[40] Barth seemed to enjoy his time with Stringfellow, for his endorsement of Stringfellow is also found in the introduction to Barth's book *Evangelical Theology.* When mentioning his trip to America and the various people he met, Barth said it was "the conscientious and thoughtful New York attorney William Stringfellow, who caught my attention more than any other person."[41] Barth's endorsement of Stringfellow not only brought him greater prominence but also, and more importantly, helped Stringfellow continue to focus on and expose the work of the Powers.

NATIONAL COUNCIL ON RACE AND RELIGION

One of the principalities Stringfellow consistently addressed was the principality of racism, and he also addressed the idolatry of race. This may have been why, in part, about a year after his encounter with Barth, he was invited to speak at the National Council on Race and Religion. Attending the event were more than 650 distinguished leaders, representing "nearly every religious body in America."[42] Key prominent speakers at this gathering included Abraham Heschel, Paul Tillich, and Martin Luther King Jr.[43] Stringfellow was to give a response to Rabbi Heschel. At least three of Stringfellow's comments stunned this gathering of leaders, and instead of getting to their feet with applause, as they did for Heschel, they responded with "boos, jeers and catcalls."[44] What was it that Stringfellow said that turned this nice group of "657 liberals bent on solving someone else's problems" hostile?[45]

First, he dismissed the conference as being "too little, too late, and too lily-white."[46] Having lived in Harlem, Stringfellow understood the Black community's contempt for the White church.[47] Stringfellow argued that the conference was too lily-white because only one Black person was asked to speak: Martin Luther King Jr.[48] Stringfellow believed it was too little because

White people, especially those in the northern states, failed to comprehend just how steeped they were in a culture of White supremacy. He noted how racism could be seen in every sphere of life, "in education, the law, politics, the economy, in religion."[49] Stringfellow went on to say that although the KKK is easy enough to recognize in the South, what is "much more typical, and much more important, is the less brutal, apparently more benign, but equally oppressive racism shown in the entrenched and practiced paternalism in the overwhelming multitudes of whites," which dehumanizes others, in particular Black people.[50] He stated, "The truth is that this conference represents a mentality . . . which thinks that the initiative in the racial crises resides with white folk. But the initiative has passed in the racial crisis in this country from white to black."[51]

Second, Stringfellow unmasked how many had adopted the ideology of humanism as a solution to racism. However, humanism assumes the problem is located only in the human heart and that the goal is equality. Note how Stringfellow's robust theology of the Powers gave him a more holistic approach to the issue of racism:

> This conference . . . represents a mentality which stupidly supposes that
> there is power and efficacy in individual action. From the point of view
> of either biblical religion, the monstrous American heresy is in thinking
> that the whole drama of history takes place between God and men. But
> the truth, biblically and theologically and empirically is quite otherwise:
> the drama of this history takes place amongst God and men and the prin-
> cipalities and powers, the greater institutions and ideologies active in the
> world.[52]

After his insistence that those at the conference take the Powers seriously, he began to unmask the principalities of humanism and racism. He proclaimed,

> It is the corruption and shallowness of humanism which beguiled Jew and
> Christian into believing that people are masters of institution or ideology.
> Or, to put it a bit differently, racism is not an evil in the hearts or minds of
> people; racism is a principality, a demonic power, a representative, image,
> and embodiment of death, over which men have little or no control, but
> which works its awful influence over the lives of men.[53]

At this conference, Stringfellow began to name and unmask the Powers in front of a crowd of intelligent people who seemed to have forgotten how the Powers work in the world. In regard to the Powers, for Stringfellow, there is just one solution—Jesus Christ—who at great and sufficient cost, overcame the Powers. When speaking of the principality of racism, Stringfellow proclaims that the issue is about "unity among men. The issue is not some common spiritual values, nor natural law, nor middle axioms. The issue is baptism. The issue is the unity of all mankind wrought in the life and work of Christ. Baptism is the sacrament of that unity of all men in God."[54]

This was met with hostility from this particular interfaith gathering. Stringfellow was no fundamentalist, but he also had not fallen captive to the ideology of liberalism or humanism, thinking that the evil we face can be managed and controlled through human initiative. Elsewhere, Stringfellow suggests that nobody has developed a substantial and coherent theological statement that deals with the heart of racism. "What can be found, usually, are recitations of the most elementary humanistic propositions about equality and liberty."[55]

Stringfellow believes that the gospel ultimately creates one new humanity: in Christ, there is no longer the divisions created by the Powers, which is why Stringfellow emphasizes baptism as the solution. Kellerman, an expert on Stringfellow, remarks, "Baptism always has about it an element of exorcism and for William Stringfellow it specifically celebrates and affirms freedom from the power of death and all its works—indeed from the principalities and powers of this world."[56] In other words, through baptism we are to die to racism and live to new humanity. Stringfellow believes that because the church in America simply imitated and repeated the slogans of humanism, it failed to be a witness to the world and allowed the principality of racism to dominate the church. About the church, he writes, "And they become by default—by silence, indifference, and irrelevance—handmaidens of the principality of racism, for the principality of racism is as well served by appeasement as by idolatry."[57]

Noting the church's tendency to mimic the world by holding to humanism, Stringfellow makes an important connection between imitation and the Powers. He therefore helps clarify the point I make in this book: when we fail to name and unmask the Powers, we end up imitating them in their submission to death, which is bondage to idolatry and leads to dishonoring God and dehumanization.

It is my opinion that the failure to develop a robust theology of the Powers allows racism to continue to manifest in the church today. The human heart must be changed by Jesus, but it doesn't end there. We need to resist the Powers so the church is not used as an agent in their demonic cause. Through his life, death, and resurrection, Christ "has destroyed the barrier, the dividing wall of hostility" (Eph. 2:14) between different people groups. Belief and baptism give us a new identity, which is socially constructed by the church through the Spirit, not current culture, and it is determined by new birth rather than by genealogy, geography, or ethnicity. The baptized swear allegiance to a different kind of King and a different kind of kingdom—one not characterized by racism, humanism, or nationalism, but by freedom and power to resist the Powers through imitation of Christ.

Stringfellow's practical advice to those assembled was to repent of their complicity to the problem with genuine tears of repentance. "If you want to do something, the most practical thing I can tell you is: weep. First of all, care enough to weep."[58]

Through this examination of some significant moments in the life of Stringfellow, it is clear how he became most well-known for his theological work on the principalities and powers. I will now summarize some of his thinking of how the Powers work.

THE WORK OF THE PRINCIPALITIES AND POWERS

Stringfellow complements the work of Wink and Girard, and he also offers concrete means by which one may apply their work. In addition, as I will demonstrate, his articulation of the principalities and powers corresponds with the three contours of leadership—identity (image), praxis (institution), and telos (ideology). Marva Dawn considers the most difficult work in interpreting the Powers to be appropriating the language of the first century into today's vernacular. In her research on Jacques Ellul's work on the Powers, she writes, "Probably the most thorough correspondence between the biblical concept of 'the principalities and powers' and its experience in contemporary life is articulated in the works of William Stringfellow."[59]

Stringfellow abbreviates the principalities and powers simply as "principalities." I employ this terminology in this chapter and the next. He asserts that although an understanding of the principalities has been lost to those inside the church, it is better understood by those outside. This was confirmed for him when he observed students from the Harvard Business school living "among the great corporate and commercial principalities . . . display an awareness, intelligence and insight between principalities and human beings, while the Harvard Divinity students considered the language and reality of such entities as archaic."[60] Within this context, Stringfellow declares, "Medieval demons are not dead, for demons are indeed the ministers of death. They were not exorcised in the building of the city. They still exist there."[61]

In his study of Scripture, Stringfellow believes that "the principalities are legion in species, number, variety, and name."[62] For him, they include all of reality, aside from God, people, and animals. In one list, he writes that the principalities include "powers, virtues, thrones, authorities, dominions, demons, princes, strongholds, lords, angels, gods, elements, spirits."[63] In addition, he alerts us to the fact that the Scriptures also give names to the principalities, such as "serpent, dragon, lion, beast." He also notes how the practice of naming principalities—such as naming nations and institutions as animals—continues today: "The bear is Russia, the tiger represents Princeton, the donkey the Democratic Party, the pig the police."[64]

Stringfellow realizes that some may consider the terms used for the principalities old-fashioned, peculiar, or unusual, so he transposes them in the hope that none would miss their significance. This is one of his most exhaustive lists of the principalities:

> They include all institutions, all ideologies, all images, all movements, all causes, all corporations, all bureaucracies, all traditions, all methods and routines, all conglomerates, all races, all nations, all idols. Thus, the Pentagon or the Ford Motor Company or Harvard University or the Diners Club or the Olympics or the Methodist Church or the Teamsters Union are all principalities. So are capitalism, Maoism, humanism, Mormonism, astrology, the Puritan work ethic, science and scientism, white supremacy, patriotism, plus many, many more—sports, sex, any profession or discipline, technology, money, the family—beyond any prospect of full enumeration. The principalities and powers *are* legion.[65]

It is clear from this list that churches are not exempt and can become principalities. In fact, in her book on the Powers, Marva Dawn includes an entire chapter on "Churches Being and Acting as Fallen Powers."[66] Wink also addresses this issue. For Stringfellow, an important characteristic of the principalities is that they are independent creatures, not instituted by people but in the original created order of God, and their vocation is to worship God and serve human beings.[67] However, in their fallen state, their purpose has been inverted, so now they seek to be gods and possess human beings.[68] Stringfellow believes that only through the power of the Spirit can we overcome the principalities. Trying to overcome them with human power is to live under an illusion, as they are too powerful. In their fallen state, they "claim autonomy from God, but in truth they are held captive to the power of death and seek to dehumanize people who are created to exercise dominion over them and all of creation."[69] In other words, they become idols.

People must contend with the conflicting claims of the principalities, for each one demands "loyalty, service and worship."[70] Each principality is in competition with the others, engaging in warfare with each other for the loyalty of the people.[71] People in their everyday lives are encircled "by a great constellation of principalities,"[72] be they the principalities of profession, family, or nation.[73] When principalities usurp the place of God and become idols, what was created to be good becomes demonic. Principalities work by making false promises that they can bring truth, meaning, and fulfillment.[74]

Reflecting on the vocational training that takes place in medical schools, engineering, and the military, and also reflecting on his own experience at Harvard Law School, Stringfellow observes the relentless indoctrination in such institutions. For example, at Harvard they sought to indoctrinate the students, him included, to conform "quickly and thoroughly to that prevailing stereotype deemed most beneficial to the profession and to its survival as an institution."[75] He was astonished to see how eagerly many of his peers completely surrendered to the process, "often squelching their own intelligent opinions or creative impulses in order to conform or to appear to be conforming."[76] Stringfellow respected the intellectual vigor at Harvard, but he was "appalled by the overwhelming subservience of legal education to the commercial powers and the principalities of property."[77] He also thought "that justice is a suitable topic for consideration in practically every course," but "it was seldom mentioned, and the term itself evoked ridicule, as if justice were a subject beneath the sophistication of lawyers."[78] Stringfellow observes that as people submit themselves to the principalities and imitate their ways, they become servants of death. He saw this firsthand in the lives of his fellow Harvard graduates.

Stringfellow believes that the most decisive clash with the principalities and powers was between Christ and the principalities, both Israel and Rome. "The ecclesiastical and civil rulers who accuse, try, condemn, and execute Christ act not essentially for themselves as individuals, but as representatives, indeed, as servants—of the principalities."[79]

PRINCIPALITIES AS IMAGE, INSTITUTION, AND IDEOLOGY

Stringfellow translates the principalities into today's current vernacular by using the key terms of *image*, *institution*, and *ideology*.

Image is a common principality because each person is accompanied by an image.[80] Stringfellow gives the example of Marilyn Monroe: there is Marilyn Monroe, the person; and Marilyn Monroe, the image—two distinct identities claiming the same name. Public image is a principality, in that although it bears a person's name, it exists independently of that person. For example, the person of Marilyn Monroe is long dead, but her image continues to exist, possibly more alive today than ever. As with any idol, our image desires full devotion, and it is in conflict with us until we fully give ourselves over.[81] The principality demands "that the person of the same name give up his life as a person to the service and homage of the image. And when that surrender is made, the person in fact dies, though not yet physically. For at that point he is literally possessed by his own image."[82] In other words, we either possess our image in God or become possessed by our image.

Institutions are the second principality Stringfellow names, because like any idol, they seek ultimate allegiance. Many people look for meaning in life through their work, which typically takes place in some kind of institution. According to Stringfellow, the guiding moral principle of any institution— be it university, corporation, church, or union—is its own survival, and in this way becomes demonic. He describes how institutions become ultimate, writing, "Everything else must finally be sacrificed to the cause of preserving the institution, and it is demanded by everyone who lives within the sphere of influence—officers, executives, employees, members, customers, and students—that they commit themselves to the service of that end, the survival of the institution."[83] Thus, when an institution exists as ultimate, like any idol, it seeks complete devotion of all the people in its domain so their ultimate sacrifice is given to the institution. But Stringfellow warns that although the institution promises benefits, fully giving ourselves over to any institution is an invitation to bondage.[84]

When it comes to churches, Dawn sees this dynamic in pastors, who often focus more on how many attend their meetings than they do seeking justice for the poor. She writes, "Both the concern for 'church growth' and the concern for survival (which sometimes are the same thing) lead to many of the tactics of fallen powers, such as competition, the overwhelming pressures on church leaders to be successful, reduction of the gospel for the sake of marketing and so forth."[85] Dawn illustrates that when the church seeks its own survival above that of the kingdom of God, it becomes a fallen principality.

Ideology, according to Stringfellow, is probably the most recognized principality today, although most of us do not realize how ideology enslaves us. He defines ideologies as the countless "isms" that seek to take people, especially leaders, captive. He mentions that while communism, fascism, racism, and nationalism are recognized by many as principalities that dehumanize people, it is less likely for us, as Americans, to recognize that humanism, capitalism, rationalism, and democracy are also fallen principalities.[86] All ideologies are principalities, for they have common characteristics: namely, they have absolutized themselves and demand unconditional loyalty from the individual and from society.

Ideologies have their own accounts of sin and redemption. For example, "Marxism asserts that it reveals and upholds the secret of history: that the destiny (literally, salvation) of all men and all nations is to be found and fulfilled in the ascendency and dominion of Marxism in the world."[87] The common element of every fallen principality is that they claim ultimate sovereignty, which is due only to God. They give a sense of meaning and significance to each person; for example, Marxism "requires of men, institutions and nation an unequivocal and militant obeisance, a sacrifice of all other supposedly lesser causes and rights to the idol of Marxism."[88]

In talking about the ideology of nationalism, Stringfellow mentions how Americans are persistently and perpetually assailed with the idea that their ultimate significance "depends upon the mere survival of the American nation and its 'way of life.'"[89] We see this when Christians chant "America first" instead of "kingdom first." When the survival of the nation becomes first and is made worthy of our ultimate devotion, service, loyalty, and—if need be—physical sacrifice, it becomes a fallen principality.[90] For when our ultimate service and devotion is given to a fallen principality, we become servants of death, resulting in bondage to idolatry, the dishonoring of God, and dehumanization.

Stringfellow believes that the principalities of image, institution, and ideology often share some characteristics with each other. For example, there is Hitler, the person and the image, but there are also aspects of ideology and institution bound up in his name. In the same way, nations as institutional powers tend to be combined with ideological principalities, such as America with capitalism and democracy, or Russia and China with communism. Thus, though these three principalities are distinct, they also overlap.

THE DEMONIC TACTICS OF THE PRINCIPALITIES AND POWERS

The first demonic tactic that Stringfellow attributes to the principalities is the denial of truth.[91] "A rudimentary claim with which the principalities confront and subvert persons is that truth in the sense of eventful and factual matter does not exist."[92] In other words, everything is "fake news." Stringfellow continues, "The truth is usurped and displaced by a self-serving version of events or fact, with whatever selectivity, diversion, falsehood, manipulation, exaggeration, evasion, concoction necessary to maintain the image, or enhance the survival . . . of the principality."[93] It is not just about "doctoring" the truth; the principalities seek to make the claim that truth *is* fiction.[94]

The tactics of the demonic powers tend to be verbal: babel, representing Babylon, seeking to reshape the mind and human consciousness.[95] (I discuss Stringfellow's understanding of Babylon later in this chapter.) The principalities seek to subvert the truth with propaganda via doublespeak and overtalk. Referring to doublespeak, Stringfellow writes, "These include heavy euphemism and coded phrases, the inversion of definitions, jargon, hyperbole, misnomer, slogan, argot, shibboleth, cliché."[96] "War is peace," the slogan used by the Party in Orwell's *1984*, is a classic example of such propaganda. "Fake news" is another example of this. Overtalk is when the "volume, speed, and redundancy" of doublespeak is communicated with such regularity that it incapacitates the hearers.[97] In other words, when doublespeak is repeated often and regularly at a fast pace, then what is untrue eventually is believed and accepted by those listening. When doublespeak is tied to overtalk, it strengthens this demonic tactic of the fallen principality.

THE UBIQUITY OF THE FALL

One of the common themes we find in Wink, Girard, and Stringfellow is the ubiquity of the fall. Stringfellow believes that "most Americans are

THE WORK OF THE POWERS | 179

grossly naïve or remarkably misinformed about the Fall."[98] For him, fallenness is a state of existence that is comprehensive in scope. Living in a state of fallenness means that all of creation—people and institutions, principalities and powers—live in estrangement from themselves and each other, having lost their true vocation of serving God. Stringfellow recounts how fallenness is a reversal of dominion, where the fallen principalities now rule us rather than us, under God, ruling them. In this condition, the principalities serve death by their idolatrous attempts to seek ultimate allegiance from people. Because we have been alienated from God, we often seek our identity, security and worth in the principalities of image, institution, and ideology, who disguise themselves as God, sovereign over history and life. Stringfellow states,

> The fall refers to the profound disorientation, affecting all relationships in the totality of creation, concerning identity, place, connection, purpose, vocation. The subject of the fall is not only the personal realm, in the sense of you and me, but the whole of creation and each and every item of created life. The fall means the reign of chaos throughout creation now, so that even that which is ordained by the ruling powers as "order" is in truth chaotic. The fall means a remarkable confusion which all beings—principalities as well as persons—suffer as to who they are and why they exist. The fall means the consignment of all created life and of the realm of time to the power of death.[99]

It is important to note here that, as missional leaders, when we seek validation in these areas through means other than God, we, too, can be confused about identity, security, and worth. As I will demonstrate, these areas represent a significant avenue in which the powers seek to undermine us as leaders. I will pursue this concept further in the following chapters.

Stringfellow addresses the ubiquity of the fall throughout his writing, because he believes that to minimize the fall is to live in an illusion without hope of true redemption. On the other hand, to recognize the pervasiveness and universality of the fall is to "view the world with unflinching, resilient realism."[100] For Stringfellow, when humanity blames all that is wrong with the world upon themselves, it is a form of arrogance, "just a perverse way of claiming that men can set things right and save themselves."[101] Stringfellow believes that when we recognize that the fall not only entails people but also principalities, as has been described, then we will recognize that redemption is only possible from a source outside of ourselves: God. Through Stringfellow's study of Revelation, he concludes that "any social concern of human beings which neglects or refuses to deal with the principalities . . . is doomed.[102] In the era of the fall, death reigns.

THE REIGN OF DEATH

As I mentioned earlier, Stringfellow believes that death pervades all of reality: "The whole of creation exists under the reign of death."[103] Stringfellow describes the many faces of death, empirically and theologically. Death is found in the ghettos as well as in places of affluence. Death presents itself in the ghettos in obvious ways: poverty, disease, unemployment, overcrowding, and the like. In places of affluence, the face of death tends to reveal itself through the search for status and prestige and is manifest through "social conformity, boredom, lust and ambition."[104] For Stringfellow, death is not simply the terminal end of one's life, but is defined by all that dehumanizes others, "all forms of diminution of human life and development and dignity."[105]

Death is a pervasive theme for Stringfellow, because in his theology of the powers, death is greater than all the principalities and powers. Because death is the devil incarnate, the fallen principalities are servants of death. Death is greater than the principalities because it outlasts all of them; it is the last enemy to be destroyed (1 Cor. 15:26). Stringfellow writes, "Institutions and ideologies, though they have immense survival capabilities, eventually die. The reality which survives them all is death itself."[106] Thus, when we idolize the principalities of image, institution, or ideology through worship, devotion, or imitation, we become enslaved to death. Apart from God's intervention, death reigns "in all things, at all times, whether recognized or not by men or nations; not just ultimately, but imminently; not just now and then, but all the time; not just in certain places, but everywhere; not just some day, but every day; not just for a few, but for all men; not just for human life, but for all of life."[107]

Death reigns in the city, in the country, and in the suburbs. The principalities—and the people who imitate and idolize them—are ultimately acolytes of death. Thus the principalities have no power to save themselves or people, for they are consigned to death.

Death is not merely a physical reality but a moral reality, which is why death and resurrection define Stringfellow's ethical approach more than do good and evil. He asserts that it is not possible for us to discern good and evil perfectly, because our understanding of good and evil is shaped contextually and culturally. Too often we end up being unknowingly and unavoidably complicit. This is not to say Stringfellow lacks conviction on moral issues but rather that God is the ultimate judge. Stringfellow prefers the concepts of death and resurrection to good and evil, saying, "Ethics concerns human action in relation to the principalities and powers in the Fall, where both human beings and principalities, as well as the rest of Creation, exist under the claim that death is morally sovereign in history."[108] Because death reigns in our post-Eden world, sin is now a symptom of death, as opposed to death being a symptom of sin. Stringfellow is elucidating an Eastern Orthodox and early church claim articulated by the author of Hebrews: the devil holds the power of death, and Jesus, through his death, frees us from the fear of death (Heb. 2:14–15). Professor and author Richard Beck writes, "It is this fear of death that creates the satanic influence, a fear that tempts us into sinful practices and lifestyles, a fear that keeps us demonically 'possessed' in our idolatrous service to the principalities and powers."[109]

Thus, for Stringfellow, ethics is about revealing and resisting the principalities in their submission to death, because when we submit to the principalities, it leads to dehumanization. By exposing and resisting the principalities, we can live humanly in the midst of death. Death is defeated in Christ, but the moral reality of death will prevail, unless we learn to comprehend death "sociologically and anthropologically, psychologically and psychically, economically and politically, societally and institutionally."[110] This is best understood through the lens of the nature and work of the Powers, which I examined earlier.

Finally, it is important to acknowledge that the devil is infrequently mentioned in Stringfellow's writing, but when he is, he is referred to as death incarnate.[111] Despite not developing this theme in his writing, Stringfellow nonetheless gives agency to the devil.[112] His preference for using *death* instead of *the devil* seems to be a contextual and missiological one. This can be inferred from the following statement:

> Not so very long ago, the presence and power of death were recognized and acknowledged by men as the *devil*. Nowadays people, both within and outside the churches, are hesitant to identify the reality and activity of death in terms of the descriptions and portraits of the *devil* regarded by their ancestors as significant and comprehensible. But that should not hinder modern folk from ascertaining the objective existence in this world of the power of death. One does not have to believe in an anthropomorphic idea of a *devil* with horns and a tail and a red complexion to admit, understand, and reconcile with any other realities of contemporary life the vitality of the power of death in history.[113] (Emphasis mine.)

Stringfellow considers it unwise to laugh or scoff at "the venerable images of the power of death named the 'Devil' or the 'Angel of Death,'" for these are the historical ways that people have "recognized that death is a living, active, decisive reality."[114] He believes these images of death are more realistic than those that treat death as only a destination or that seek to avoid facing death altogether. The militant vitality of death's reign is the only reality that all humanity shares. It is experienced both now, under the reign of death, and later, through the end of life. It causes the estrangement and alienation we experience "with everybody and everything, and . . . one's very own self.

Death means a total loss of identity."[115] Death is the one thing we cannot escape, apart from Christ. Death seeks to enslave people through the principalities and powers, who seek ultimate allegiance as imposters of God.

IMPOSTERS OF GOD (IDOLATRY)

Stringfellow believes that because we live in the epoch of the fall—where people and principalities are fallen—we seek to find our meaning, significance, and worth through the principalities of image, institution, and ideology. Because the principalities demand ultimate allegiance, we end up in bondage to idolatry. Although many of us in the West consider idols a thing of the past, Stringfellow exposes this fallacy by demonstrating that our favorite idols are those most common to our daily existence: "religion, work, money, status, sex, patriotism."[116] He describes idols as imposters of God. When we seek to justify ourselves, offer ourselves, and give tribute to our chosen idols, we end up in bondage to death. The result is that idolatry "defies God and dehumanizes men."[117] "When a principality claims moral pre-eminence in history over a man's life it represents an aspiration for salvation from death and a hope that service to the idol will give existence a meaning somehow transcending death."[118] One of the goals of this book is to expose these idols for what they are so that, instead of ruling over us, the principalities serve their intended purposes. For Stringfellow, idolatry is a form of demon possession that requires exorcism.[119] He mentions that this is why exorcism was consistently practiced at the baptism service in the early church.[120]

In describing the principality of and idolatry of nationalism, Stringfellow speaks of Babylon. In Revelation, Babylon is a city infested with demons and ruled by an ethic of death (Rev. 12:7–12; 13:1–8).[121] Babylon is a parable of every nation and principality, and it stands in stark contrast to Jerusalem, the parable of redemption.

> Babylon's futility is her idolatry—her boast of justifying significance or moral ultimacy in her destiny, her reputation, her capabilities, her authority, her glory as a nation. The moral pretenses of Imperial Rome, the millennial claims of Nazism, the arrogance of Marxist dogma, the anxious insistence that America be "number one" among nations are all versions of Babylon's idolatry. All share in this grandiose view of the nation by which the principality assumes the image of God.[122]

Revelation 17–21 presents the juxtaposition of Babylon and Jerusalem as a parable. Babylon represents every nation, some more than others. Jerusalem represents the church when she is living out her true vocation. Most nations pretend to be Jerusalem, the city on the hill, God's chosen nation. But Stringfellow warns, "As every nation incarnates Babylon and *imitates her idolatry*, so each nation strives, vainly to be or become Jerusalem" (emphasis mine).[123] In Revelation we are consistently called to come out of Babylon so that we might live humanly in the midst of the fall. "Jerusalem lives within and outside the nations, alongside and over against the nations, coincident with but set apart from the nations."[124] So, although every nation makes idolatrous claims, the church must be both for and against nations. The state is ordained by God, but nationalism is when the state has made itself God. Revelation indicates that nations are archetypal principalities, and "all other assorted, diverse, principalities resemble them, *imitate them*, and substitute for them (Rev. 13:8–17; 14:8,17)" (emphasis mine).[125] Thus nationalism is a present danger for missional leaders and the church, which is why we, as missional leaders, need to be able to name and unmask the powers. I will explore this later.

RESISTING THE POWERS

Stringfellow articulates that the larger parable all nations and principalities live out is the juxtaposition of Babylon and Jerusalem and of apocalypse and eschaton. "In history, in this time, Eden and the Fall, Jerusalem and Babylon, Eschaton and Apocalypse converge here and now."[126] Babylon represents apocalyptic reality, and Jerusalem represents the eschaton. Babylon represents fallenness, death, bondage to idolatry, dehumanization—the apocalypse; Jerusalem represents redemption, life, freedom from idolatry and human flourishing—the eschaton.[127]

Stringfellow encourages action through revealing and resisting the powers, and he articulates that God is building the city of salvation. God is doing this work in the midst of the principalities. The principalities are cultivating cities of death, and it seems as if they have successfully tempted the church to serve the principality of "image" instead of rooting her image in Christ. It seems the principality of ideology is often trusted over seeking the kingdom nonviolently, and institutional survival has become more important than trusting the way of Christ. Stringfellow believes the church, the people of God, must recognize that though we are helpless when it comes to defeating these suprahuman entities—the principalities—we are not hopeless. For Christ was crucified as a witness to the end of death's power over the world so that we might imitate him and experience resurrection freedom from the bondage of death and the powers. Confession of utter helplessness "is the first and free and most reckless acknowledgement of God's life and presence in the world."[128] Instead of submitting to the fallen principality of nationalism, the church exists to remind the nation of her proper vocation to serve God. Although Stringfellow holds on to resurrection hope, he also believes that a great deal of our work on this side of the new heavens and earth is to prophetically expose the principalities. He stresses the importance of learning to resist the principalities through the Holy Spirit, the active Word of God, and incarnational living. He believes that doing so will remind the principalities of their transience—that only God is sovereign over time and history.

RESURRECTION LIVING

Stringfellow writes, "Living in the freedom of the resurrection is, for the Christian and for the Church of Christ, the ethics of obedience."[129] The Holy Spirit is important in Stringfellow's theology. He writes, "Pentecost is the event marking the constitution of the Church in the world."[130] It is here that the church is authorized and empowered by God to live in the world for the sake of the world, free from idolatry and the bondage of death, free to imitate Christ, and free to expose the works of death and declare and honor the work of Christ.[131] We are to imitate Christ in the way that he overcame the fallen principalities through the power of the Spirit. For Stringfellow, resurrection living involves more than just having hope at the terminal point of our lives— it means that resurrection power over death is available in this life, in this world, right now.[132] In other words, "the Church lives now as the new society in the midst of the old, as the reconciled community when all else is broken and distorted, as the new creation during the era of the Fall, as the example and vindication of life transcending the power of death."[133]

Although Stringfellow articulates the continual need to resist the principalities on this side of the new heavens and the new earth, he—along with Wink, Yong, and others—believe in the redemption of the principalities. Stringfellow states, "Christ's resurrection is for men and for the whole of creation, including the principalities of this world."[134]

Stringfellow declares that in the resurrection, the principalities are exposed as "false lords over history" and that Christ is revealed to be the Lord of history. Thus he writes, "In Christ is both the end and fulfillment for all principalities, for all men, and for all things."[135] Resurrection living is resisting the fallen principalities right here and right now.

SACRAMENTAL ETHICS

Stringfellow privileges a sacramental approach to ethics, emphasizing the need to live humanly amid the fall. Living sacramentally is when the ordinary things of life—bread, wine, words, water, music, money, the table, marriage—are "rendered extraordinary, that which is merely worldly is transfigured, that which is most common becomes a means of worship, and each act or event of everyday life becomes sacramental—a sign and celebration of God's care for every act or event of everyday life in this world."[136]

According to Stringfellow, all of life is sacramental; for him, to live sacramentally is to live in a way that demonstrates signs of life in the midst of death. It is receiving our lives as a gift from God and then giving up our lives for the sake of others, in order to give the world new life.

For example, let's consider the ordinary nature of water and how the sacrament of baptism lends itself to living out the extraordinary life of reconciliation. Stringfellow writes,

> Baptism is the sacrament of the extraordinary unity among humanity wrought by God in overcoming the power and reign of death; in overcoming all that alienates, segregates, divides, and destroys human beings in their relationship to each other, within their own persons, and in the relationship with the rest of creation.[137]

Thus, according to Stringfellow, the vocation of those of us who are baptized is to live every day in the knowledge that death has no power over us and that resurrection living is to "live from day to day, whatever the day brings, in this extraordinary unity, in this reconciliation with all [people] and all things."[138] For Stringfellow, baptism and communion "are significant acts of resistance that are politically charged," as "both of these sacraments are to be contrasted with the social and political disunity engendered by racism. Thus, baptism is a symbol of unity, not merely ecclesial but also political and social."[139] As Stringfellow says, "Baptism is the assurance—accepted, enacted, verified, and represented by Christians—of the unity of *all humanity* in Christ."[140]

To illustrate what it means to live sacramentally, Stringfellow writes that if we hope to find freedom from the idolatry of money, we need to use it sacramentally—for the renewal of the world. He notes, "The sacramental use of money in the formal and gathered worship of the Church is authenticated—in the sacramental use of money in the common life of the world."[141] If we hope to have, use, and spend money without worshiping it, we must live into the confession that our money and our lives are not our own—they belong to the world that God loves.[142]

Even a jacket or coat can become a sacrament. Stringfellow writes about the time he visited a client a few blocks away from his house. On his way home, he noticed how much colder it had become. A few blocks away from his house, Stringfellow bumped into a boy on the street he had come to know. The boy asked him a question, and realizing that Stringfellow was shivering due to the cold, offered him his jacket. Because this boy was an addict and his coat was the only one he had, Stringfellow viewed the coat as a sacrament.[143] Living sacramentally is when the ordinary things in life—whether water, money, a jacket, or something else—become extraordinary because they are used in service of God's kingdom on earth.

WORD OF GOD

Stringfellow uses the term *Word of God* differently than most of us do today. Because so many political and religious leaders use the word idolatrously, Stringfellow eventually replaces *God* with the *Word of God*. He uses this term to refer to God's active presence in the world. For Stringfellow, the Word of God is not Scripture, as some might consider today, but *God's activity in the world*. Scripture helps us to discern God's active presence in the world, but Stringfellow does not consider it to be a synonymous term. Discerning the Word of God in the world comes through study of Scripture and looking for God's activity in our cities. Stringfellow considers it necessary to hold the newspaper in one hand and the Bible in the other in order to discern the active work of the Word of God in the world. According to Stringfellow, to equate the Word of God with Scripture is idolatrous. In describing how he uses Word of God, he writes,

> When, therefore, I use here this name of God [Word of God], it is delib-
> erately intended to invoke the scriptural saga of the Word of God active
> in common history from the first initiative of creation. Simultaneously I
> refer (as, so to say, both Isaiah and John insist), the selfsame Word of God
> incarnate in Jesus Christ. At the same time, I mean to recall the Word of
> God permeating the whole of creation and ready to be discerned in all
> things whatsoever in the fallenness of this world; at work contemporane-
> ously, incessantly agitating change in this world (as the event of Pentecost
> and the Acts of the Apostles each verify).[144]

The Word of God is a gift given to us in the midst of the fall to be able to reveal and resist the power of death in the world and help liberate people to live in the world for the sake of the world.

INCARNATIONAL WITNESS

Stringfellow advocates for a strong incarnational theology that understands God's work of salvation in time, history, and the everyday life of the Christian. He consistently warns against an escapist theology that imitates ideologies, religion, and various pagan philosophies that "construe rejection of this world as the premise of the gospel and departure from this world as the hope of the gospel."[145] For Stringfellow, anti-worldliness and other-worldliness is not only a misunderstanding of the gospel but "is actually conformity to the world with a vengeance. And, for professed Christians, it is the most igno-minious possible apostasy."[146] Incarnational witness for Stringfellow means that the real issues of faith have to do with everyday people, and witness to our faith means loving and serving people in the world.[147] Stringfellow asserts that when Jesus is not recognized as the Lord of this world, the Lord of time, and the Lord of history, we will end up imitating the principalities, thus serving death.

Stringfellow highlights the church's tendency to increasingly conform to the world whenever it seeks to become "established" in a given society. He points to the Constantine arrangement as an example of this. The temptation for the church when becoming "established" in a society is the failure to critique it, thus making it a servant to the principalities. He writes,

> The course of European and American Christendom since then [Constantine arrangement], has been scandalized by bizarre happenings: The Crusades, the Inquisition, the suppression of the Peasant's Revolt, the practice of genocide against North American Indians, the sanction of black chattel slavery in the United States, the opportune merger of white colonialism and the missionary enterprise in the nineteenth century, the seduction and surrender of the churches to Nazism—to name only a very few.[148]

When churches hold to an escapist theology, as opposed to an incarnational theology, they are likely to become seduced by the principalities of nationalism, racism, White supremacy, and other Powers. Churches will imitate the tactics of the principalities in the name of God, thinking that a good end justifies an evil means. If missional leaders are to reveal and resist the principalities, we must recognize that "the Bible deals with the sanctification of the actual history of nations and of human beings in this world as it is while that history is being lived."[149]

Advocating for an incarnational witness, Stringfellow was an early champion for the church to be a meaningful presence in the city. In 1964, at a time when churches were abandoning urban areas, he was writing about the importance of the church to be present in the city. He believes that if the gospel is to speak to our increasingly urbanized world, the church must have an incarnational presence in the city. He writes, "The rudiment of mission is knowledge of the city because the truth and grace of the Incarnation encompasses in God's care all that is the city."[150] And this knowledge of the city must have a rooted presence, "a radical intimacy with every corner and every echelon of the city's actual life in order to represent and honor God's concern for each fragment of the city."[151]

But because the church had an other-worldly orientation, Stringfellow claims it had "become theologically incapacitated," thus the churches "have pretty much forsaken the city both physically and psychologically. They do not know the city because they are stopped by a religion bearing only outer resemblance to the gospel; because they are not immersed in the common life of the city, their witness is peripheral, pietistic, self-serving, corny, and profane."[152] He pleads for the church to have an incarnational presence in the streets of the city. "First the Christians have to live a while in the streets before they can know how to minister to, how to *love*, the people of the streets and how to understand, to accept and enter into, the action on the streets."[153] Hearing and listening to the stories of real-life people was significant for Stringfellow.[154] He writes that if he were a bishop, after being present and listening, he would commission people to go into the city, "and just live on whatever means of survival prevailed in the block or neighborhood to which they were sent; they would have to live, in so far as possible, as those to whom they were sent."[155] He would have them knock on every door, recognizing most would not be open, and have them say, "'We have come to be with you because God cares for your life, we also care for you.' Period." There would be no programs, no invitations to a church service, no giveaways, "just the bare announcement of God's love and the freedom which that love gives to people to love each other."[156] He advocates a witness of mere presence.[157] Although presence is to be a consistent practice, it is not the only task for the church. He writes, "the essential and consistent task of Christians is to expose the transience of death's power in the world."[158]

Having taken a brief tour of Stringfellow's life and theology, I will now examine his life via biography as theology. I will then examine Stringfellow's theology of the Powers and consider missional leadership in light of the subversive nature of the Powers.

9

THE SUBVERSION AND RESISTANCE OF THE POWERS

There is power in naming things. We see this in Genesis, when God has Adam name all the wild beasts on the land and all the birds in the sky.[1] This seems to be tied to his ability to live out his role as a vice-regent under God and his gentle dominion over the rest of creation.[2] The power in naming is evident throughout the biblical narrative: God renames Abram ("exalted father") to Abraham ("father of many nations"), intertwining God's promise with Abraham's new name; God renames Jacob ("supplanter") to Israel ("he who struggles") because he wrestled with God and won; Jesus renamed Simon ("reed-like," "wavering") to Peter ("rock"), symbolizing Peter's transformation from one who was changeable by the wind to one who became solid and stable.[3]

But it is not only the naming of animals and people that holds power. Naming our emotions can also be powerful. Through a series of studies, Matthew D. Lieberman, UCLA associate professor of psychology and founder of social cognitive neuroscience, notes, "When you put feelings into words, you're activating this prefrontal region and seeing a reduced response in the amygdala. . . . In the same way you hit the brake when you're driving when you see a yellow light, when you put feelings into words you seem to be hitting the brakes on your emotional responses."[4] Naming our emotions thus helps us to tame them.

There is also power in naming the Powers, as I have already shown. It takes spiritual discernment to be able to identify, analyze, and articulate the Powers in order to unmask the ways they seek to subvert us. Walter Wink, René Girard, and William Stringfellow all play vital roles in helping us name the Powers. Stringfellow, in particular, translates the principalities and powers into current vernacular in a way that both honors the original meaning of the text and makes sense for us today. Such renaming is helpful. But naming and unmasking are only the first steps. As Wink puts it,

> The ultimate issue, however, is not whether we comprehend the Powers,
> but whether we confront them with their apostasy from their heavenly

calling. Understanding the Powers is but a step toward encountering them. We unmask them only in order to engage them, in the spirit and power of the One in whom and through whom and for whom they were created: the truly Human Being incarnated by Jesus.[5]

In addition to naming the Powers, it is also helpful to name the dominant images that shape our lives. I will now examine the dominant images that shaped Stringfellow.

DOMINANT IMAGES THAT SHAPED THE LIFE OF WILLIAM STRINGFELLOW

As I have already stated, Stringfellow views biography as theology. Utilizing James William McClendon's biography-as-theology process, what are the dominant images that shaped the life and character of William Stringfellow?

INCARNATIONAL PARABLE

The incarnation deeply shaped Stringfellow's life and theology, and he considered each of us to be "living parables." Thus the first dominant image for Stringfellow is *incarnational parable*. This seems logical, because context and vocation are central in Stringfellow's thinking. The Word of God encountering *us* in the world is significant for Stringfellow and is what makes each of us, as disciples of Jesus, good news people.

Following his graduation from Harvard Law School, Stringfellow's willingness to move to one of the roughest blocks in Harlem to live and serve among the poor and marginalized reflects his commitment to incarnational living. In the opening words of his book *My People Is the Enemy*, he candidly discloses the nature of his residence: "The stairway smelled of piss."[6] But it was not just the stairway that distinguished Harlem from the rest of Manhattan.

> Outside are air purifiers, private toilets, hi-fi, gourmet food, imported cars, and extra dry martini; inside Harlem are the smells of sweat and waste, bathtubs in the kitchens, antiquated direct current, predatory vermin, second-hand clothes, and a million empty beer cans in the gutters. Outside the ghetto are secure jobs, some chance for education, and even space to play; inside there is chronic unemployment, much illiteracy, and the numbers game.[7]

It was in this context that Stringfellow figured out his theology. For Stringfellow, "daily occurrences and ordinary people were the most profound source of theology. Biography and autobiography were, like parables, pregnant with meaning. This, he explained, was congruent with the incarnation."[8] Though Stringfellow entered Harlem as an alien in a strange land, when he left, he considered it home: "To outsiders it was hell on earth, to residents it was reality, but to Stringfellow, it was a sacrament of the Kingdom. He was home."[9] It was in Harlem that Stringfellow found the self-understanding and self-acceptance he was looking for, amid the "marginalized and dispossessed."[10] It was also significant for him because he "remembered that this is the sort of place in which most people live, in most of the world, for most of the time."[11] The incarnation, the embodiment of God, reflects, for Stringfellow, a "radical and preemptive concern for life in this world."[12] Because of God's concern for the "here and now," Stringfellow considers involvement in the affairs of this world to be nonnegotiable for the Christian. Thus Stringfellow sought to discern God's activity in the world, and being a living parable of God's Word was Stringfellow's way of doing so. This led to the second metaphor that shaped his life: being a *prophetic witness*.

PROPHETIC WITNESS

As I mentioned earlier, it was in Harlem that Stringfellow discovered the principalities and powers and the power of death, theological themes that became central in his work. This was not "a theoretical or academic discovery. It was a practical, empirical, and existential one that arose out of the coincidence of the Bible and his context."[13] And as with most prophets whose message is born through their life experiences, Stringfellow, like the prophets of old, recognizes that our faith in God is not just personal; it is political and social, and it should speak truth to the principalities and powers, which are servants of death.

William Coats, rector of St. Clement's Episcopal Church in Hawthorne, New Jersey, writes about the first time he encountered Stringfellow as a seminary student at General Theological Seminary in New York. He reflects,

> He spoke in quiet, direct tones. You often had to lean forward to pick up his words. The drama was mostly in content, but the tone added a subdued ferocity to the event. His speech was sarcastic, pained, searing but never loud or abrasive. At some point as he droned on about the hypocrisy of prejudice and the cruelty of oppression, about complicity and Christian evasion, about the corruption of the church and the need for radical political engagement, we sensed that the whole of our comfortable seminary education, with its complacent adhesion to Anglican pieties, was for naught. As the indictment mounted, the room became restless, the mood ascending toward open resentment.[14]

Coats then exclaims, "Here was a prophet!"[15] Though Coats had taken classes in Hebrew prophecy, after he experienced Stringfellow, prophecy took on a whole new meaning for him. He says, "Prophecy is not a thing, not a teaching, not simply shocking content. It is an occasion."[16] It was on this occasion— during his first encounter with Stringfellow—that Coats came to understand why God's people hated Jeremiah, killed the prophets, and ultimately killed Jesus. Reflecting on his encounter with Stringfellow, Coats names the task of the prophets: "They unveil the cruel contradiction on which all societies rest. They lay bare the lie on which all public life, so zealous to guard power and privilege, is based."[17] He continues, "Slowly, inexorably, our public life was being unmasked. We became frightened, because if Stringfellow was right, then the edifice of church life and political life was itself mendacious, distorted, and we were caught in a trap from which no amount of church or liberal pieties could extricate us."[18]

Stringfellow firmly believes that all judgment is ultimately God's. He also asserts that the church must live out her convictions and that she has a responsibility to be a prophetic witness in the world, for the sake of the world. According to Stringfellow, the church should not shrink from her prophetic calling.

> By the mercy of God, the inherent, invariable, unavoidable, intentional, unrelenting posture of the Church in the world is one of radical protest and profound dissent toward the prevailing status quo of secular society, whatever that may be at any given time, however much men boast that theirs is a great society.[19]

The church is to be actively involved in the world, as Jesus was, without being contaminated by the world. Reflecting on James 1:27, Stringfellow writes,

> Visit orphans, comfort widows, care for the unwanted, seek out the outcasts, love your enemy but *in a way* which leaves one free from the world, free from all worldly conformities, free from the secular ethics of success, free from the idols of security, riches, fame, property, popularity, free from self-indulgence and, what is in the end the same things, free from all attempts at self-justification, free from the wiles of the devil and free, at last, from the power of death at work in the world.
> Be in but not of the world. Be involved but unstained.[20]

Although the church's witness is political—in that the gospel speaks to all of life whether personal, social, cosmic, interpersonal—it should not be captive to worldly dogmas, as Marshall Johnston notes in his PhD on Stringfellow: "The political witness of the individual Christian and the corporate Church reflects a commitment to neither ideology nor institution." Thus, for Stringfellow, "the Church's witness, then, cannot be too closely identified with any particular movement, political theory, or utopian design."[21] Stringfellow states, "And though the Christian acts in this world and in particular circumstances in a society for this or that cause, he does so not as the servant of some race or class or political system or ideology but as an expression of his freedom from just such idols."[22]

Stringfellow lived out his prophetic witness by consistently addressing issues such as poverty, nationalism, and racism in America. He states that "the posture of the Christian is inherently and consistently radical."[23] For Stringfellow, this radicalism is not in the conventional political and economic sense. Instead, it involves Christians "perpetually [being] in the position of complaining about the status quo, whatever it happens to be. His insight and experience of reconciliation in Christ are such that no estate in secular history can possibly correspond to, or much approximate, the true society of which he is a citizen in Christ."[24] Stringfellow asserts that the church is always to have a prophetic stance and must live as a contrast society, practicing the politics of Jesus.

In the previous chapter, I explored how Stringfellow's prophetic witness is expressed in his address to the National Council on Race and Religion, in which he identifies racism as a principality. Because he views it this way, he believes racism cannot be overcome through ideologies such as humanism or liberalism, but only through baptism. For Stringfellow, our primary struggle is not between good and bad, but between death and resurrection. Only Christ has defeated death, and only when we truly live in Christ and imitate his ways can we participate in his work. Stringfellow says the battle involved "the power of death in this world and how death is overpowered in this life by the power of the Resurrection."[25]

Living in the power of the resurrection is to live in the reality that God, through Christ, has reconciled the world to himself. As Stringfellow writes, "Reconciliation is the event, as II Corinthians testifies, of a new order of corporate life of men and institutions inaugurated in the world in Christ."[26] When we understand and take in what Christ has done, it changes everything. "In view of this order, it is impossible to consider the reconciliation of one man outside of, or separately from, the estate of all other men and institutions, that is, *politically*."[27] And although people can resist, deny, or refuse this gift that God has given the world, "to be a Christian, to be already reconciled, means to love the world, all the world, just as it is—unconditionally."[28] Being a prophetic witness in the world for the sake of the world is to unconditionally love everyone in the world, be they friend or enemy. For when we love others unconditionally, we bear witness to the one new humanity Christ made possible.

Regarding the racial crisis of his day, Stringfellow writes, "Reconciliation means, among other things, that those Christians committed to direct action for equal rights for all citizens should nevertheless persevere in loving the humanity of the wide assortment of others assembled in political and social and religious opposition to integration in American public life."[29] It seems that Stringfellow might agitate anyone trapped by an ideology, for, on the one hand, he favored reparations as recommended by a Black council of believers, while at the same time he writes, "Those Christians who marched in Selma were called to affirm the essential humanity of Sheriff Clark, even though they have been beaten on his order."[30] It meant "forgiving the Ku Klux Klan, though they have not yet abandoned their violence and treachery."[31]

Stringfellow claims that as Christians live into the resurrection, they no longer need to fear death, as Christ has already conquered death. In regard to the racial crisis, he anticipated a time when the nonviolent tactics of the Black community—who in America have been persistently and consistently oppressed—might turn violent because their nonviolent tactics failed to work. He states that when this happens, such violence will be met by an overwhelming counterviolence "by the police—probably the Army—which the white establishment of America has at its command."[32] He asserts that when this "day of wrath" comes, if it ever does, that it will eventually lead to a police state. "In the day of wrath," the nation could be saved from such a calamity by White people recognizing that "this hostility or assault by the Black community against the white originates in the long terrible decades of exclusion and rejection" and that the violence they experience from the Black community would be "the offspring of white supremacy. The sins of the fathers are indeed visited upon their sons."[33]

If this day of wrath is to come, what does Stringfellow commend to White Christians living in America? "The witness of the white Christian, on such a day, must surely be the same as the witness already given by so many Negro [sic] Christians during those long years of anguish and protest: the witness of the Cross."[34] To be a prophetic witness to Christ, in the hope for one humanity, Stringfellow calls the White church to cruciform living, or perhaps more accurately, cruciform dying. He writes,

> The Cross means not only the consignment of Christ to death but His triumph over the power of death on behalf of the world. The Cross means the invincible power of God's love for the world, even though all the world betrays, denies, abhors, fears, or opposes the gift of his love for the world. The Cross means voluntary love which is undaunted by any hostility or hatred or violence or assaults. The Cross means voluntary love which is not threatened by death. The Cross means voluntary love which perseveres no matter what. The Cross means the gift of love even to one's own enemy— even to the one who would take one's life.[35]

According to Stringfellow, the principalities and powers are servants of death, thus the ultimate prophetic witness of Christ's victory over death is found in the one who is willing to imitate Christ, even in his death. For when

Christ was on the cross, he cried out to his Father, "Forgive them, for they do not know what they are doing" (Luke 23:34). Stringfellow continues, "Even if the knife is at the belly, let the white Christian not protest. Let him receive the assault recklessly, without precaution, without resistance, without rationalization, without extenuation, without murmur."[36] For the Christian who is free in Christ, death has been defeated in Christ. The empty cross reminds us that the One who willingly laid his life down was raised from the dead. And so Stringfellow concludes,

> This is why there is *no other* way that this enormous, desperate, growing accumulation of guilt, shame, estrangement, and terror can be absolved. There has never been—for any man, anywhere, at any time—any other way. In the work of God in our midst, reconciling black men, and white men, there is no escape from the Cross.[37]

AN EMERGENT VIEW OF RACISM

So how does the ideology of racism work through institutions? Because this was an issue in Stringfellow's day and continues to be an issue in ours, if we want to participate in the work of naming, unmasking, and engaging the Powers, it is helpful to take a deeper look at how the ideology of racism is at work in our world today. Croasmun's emergent view of racism complements and expounds on Stringfellow's, further demonstrating how an emergent view of the Powers is helpful.

For Stringfellow, racism is an ideology that has become embodied in our institutions and shapes every individual under its sphere. It is a principality that exerts great influence over human affairs. Humanism and liberalism or any human initiative are unable to defeat it. Writing in 1969, Stringfellow says,

> In truth, racism originated in America three and a half centuries ago—in 1619, when a Portuguese trader sold some black men into chattel slavery to some early white settlers in Virginia. From that time to the present day, white supremacy has been institutionalized as the dominant social ethic—and idol—of American society, permeating every facet and dimension of our culture. White supremacy has been so pervasive—and so seldom challenged—as the fundamental ethic of society that it has left to contemporary Americans, both white and black, an inheritance of racism often not readily recognized as such. It has become so deeply embedded in the basic institutions of society—in education, the law, politics, the economy, in religion—that it is taken for granted.[38]

Stringfellow considered racism to be a demonic power, and he asserts that the church has been complicit. He writes, "Everyone in the United States is now involved in the racial crisis. If there ever was an option on this subject, it has expired. The only issue that remains is *how* one is involved: obstinately, stupidly, irrationally—or with concern, intelligence, and compassion."[39]

Matthew Croasmun's view of racism sheds light on Stringfellow's understanding. He looks to Eduardo Bonilla-Silva, who states that there are at least three ways to conceive of how race "plays out in the social sciences."[40] First, there are those who believe that because race is socially constructed, "it is not 'real', and therefore is not a valid category of analysis" and must therefore be reduced to the individual level: "the socioeconomic status or educational background."[41] Croasmun compares this approach to the reductionist: "race supervenes on factors at the individual and social levels; therefore it is not 'real.'"[42] For the second group, who consider race as "an essential feature of humanity," Bonilla-Silva makes the case that "failing to pay attention to the social structures that give rise to racial differences themselves, largely functions to reinforce the racial order."[43] Croasmun classifies this group with the dualist, in that they believe that "race had some independent existence of its own outside or beyond the psychological or social."[44] The third perspective Bonilla-Silva mentions is those who acknowledge that "race, as other social categories such as class and gender, is constructed but insists it has a social reality. This means that after race—or class or gender—is created, it produces real effects on the actors racialized as 'Black' or 'white'."[45] Croasmun recognizes that this third way of understanding racism correlates with the emergent view. "He argues *both* that race is socially constructed— that is, it *supervenes* on the actions of social agents—but *also* that race acts back upon those individual agents."[46] Bonilla-Silva recognizes the downward causation of this emergent reality or entity called "race."[47] Thus racism cannot be fully dealt with at the individual or psychological level but needs to be evaluated at the social level, so "Bonilla-Silva's account of racism begins not with racists but with '*racialized social systems*.'"[48] Croasmun mentions places where Bonilla-Silva recognizes that "after a society becomes racialized, racialization develops a life of its own."[49] But he acknowledges that it is not completely "independent of the action of racialized actors."[50] Thus, according to Croasmun, this does not fall to dualism because there remains a relationship between the social and individual. Bonilla-Silva's understanding of racism fits the emergence view because, as Croasmun reflects,

> There is a bi-directional, causal relationship between racialized actors (racist or otherwise) and racialized social systems. These systems supervene on the individuals, and at the same time, the individuals are constrained by the systems, so much that they are said to be constituted as racialized actors precisely *because* of the constraint exerted by these same racialized structures.[51]

Thus not only does the individual racist create the social reality of racism, but the other part of the feedback loop understands "racialized systems give rise to racialized actors," to the point that Bonilla-Silvia argues that it is possible to have racism without racists.[52]

A trickle-down effect of racism can thus be seen in emergent theory. The downward causation in emergence theory speaks to more than just how the sociological constrains the psychological, so Croasmun looks at how this downward causation cascades into the relationship of the psychological to the neurological (biological).[53] Pointing to studies that have been conducted in neurology using functional MRI to study "amygdala response in the brains of subjects who identified as white (and, in one study, black) when presented with white and black faces previously unknown to subjects."[54] This "reptilian" part of the brain is related to fear conditioning and shows "increased amygdala activation when subjects were exposed to 'out-group' faces (whites confronted with black faces, and blacks confronted with white faces)."[55] It didn't matter if either considered themselves racist, "all subjects exhibited elevated amygdala activation when confronted with unfamiliar faces of the opposite race."[56] Croasmun points out that this is consistent with a reductionist account of race and racism, in that racial bias at the neurological level (biological) shapes the psychological level and eventually the sociological level.[57] In other words, it just moves upward.

However, two later studies suggest an emergent view. "Lieberman et al., in 2005, showed that blacks exhibited the same heightened amygdala response to black faces as did whites."[58] They concluded that "the amygdala activity typically associated with race-related processing may be a reflection of culturally learned negative associations regarding African American individuals."[59] A "unilateral association of fearful responses to black faces would require an explanation that involved causation from the social level."[60] Croasmun mentions another study that took place in 2008 with White Americans and Japanese, which demonstrated no elevated responses to out-group faces. This demonstrates that "previous findings of greater amygdala activity for outgroup neutral faces may reflect cultural knowledge of negative stereotypes specifically about African-Americans, rather than general negative stereotypes about other outgroup members."[61] The causal arrow pointing downward was so surprising that they have "launched an entirely new field: social neuroscience."[62] Thus Croasmun concludes, "Race as a category seems to be constituted and maintained through multiple feedback loops of supervenience and downward causation," which would be in support of an emergent view.[63]

OUR ROLE IN THE STORY OF RACISM

Undoubtedly, we all saw the video footage of the cruel murder of George Floyd, which took place on May 25, 2020, in Minneapolis by a police officer who was called to protect and serve the community. This demonstrated once again how racism, which has lived in the collective mind of the US since its conception, continues to degrade and destroy the Black, Indigenous, and people of color (BIPOC) community in this country, in particular, our African American brothers and sisters.

George Floyd's murder intensified the emotions of the US, in part because of the nation's long list of racist events, and in part because his murder is what cultural anthropologist Mary Douglas labels a "condensed symbol."[64] A condensed symbol is shorthand for an idea or set of practices that trigger and evoke an entire worldview though one image. In this case, George Floyd's murder represents the plight that African Americans have had to endure for far too long.

The enduring image is of a White officer pressing his knee with full force on the throat of a Black man for a total of eight minutes and forty-six seconds, a full minute after the paramedics arrived on the scene. This Black man, who was unarmed and did not resist arrest, pleaded for his life, telling the officer, "I can't breathe."

Though time has passed since this event took place, we still need to be present to this moment because of what it represents. We need to try and step into the shoes of our Black brothers and sisters, many who are suffocating physically, psychologically, sociologically, and economically. When an entire group is gasping for their very breath, it requires a response. A lack of response makes one complicit in the murder.

The White police officer was deaf to George Floyd's pleas. He was deaf to the bystanders who pleaded on behalf of George Floyd to let him up. Sadly, he was not the only deaf person on the scene; the Asian officer in the video was also deaf to the pleas of George Floyd and the bystanders. Furthermore, there were two more police officers behind the car who were both using their weight to hold George Floyd down on the ground.

As we contemplate this "condensed symbol," we must consider which person described in this event represents us the most.

As Stringfellow rightly points out, all of us are a part of this story, whether we are willing to acknowledge it or not. If you live in the US, you are part of this story. The question we each must ask of ourselves is the following: *Who am I in the story of racism in the US?*

The psalmist's prayer seems apt in light of this question: "Search me, O God, and know my heart; test me and know my thoughts. See if there is any wicked way in me, and lead me in the way everlasting" (Ps. 139:23–24 NRSV).

Even as I contemplate this condensed symbol once again, I find myself grieving, lamenting, and contemplating where my known and unknown, intentional and unintentional complicity adds to the demonic power of racism. And I ask what repentance, recompense, and renewal means for me in my local community and in our nation.

Although some must work at the national, state, and county policy level, if we are Christ-followers seeking to see the kingdom of God become more tangible where we live, we are all called to participate at the local grassroots level for a greater sense of justice and peace, especially for those whom the system has targeted unfairly. Posting some thoughts on Twitter, Facebook, or Instagram does not replace being locally rooted in our neighborhoods and finding active ways to join God at a grassroots level where we live.

Stringfellow knew what we often forget: until we recognize the nature and work of the Powers, there is no moving forward. Racism is not simply an injustice; it is idolatry. And the principalities and powers in their fallen state, as we know, seek ultimate allegiance. Thus we need to be immersed in Trinitarian living, in which we live into the reality of what Christ has accomplished.

When we fail to name and unmask the nature and work of the Powers, we end up imitating them in their submission to Satan (the body of sin), which is bondage to idolatry and leads to dishonoring God and dehumanization. The failure to have a robust understanding of the principalities and powers has allowed racism to continue to manifest itself in the church and in America today. The human heart must be changed by Jesus, but it doesn't end there. We need to know how to resist and redeem the Powers from turning the church into an agent of its demonic use.

According to Colossians 1:15–20, the principalities and powers were created good, are fallen, and need to be redeemed. The principalities have a visible and invisible reality, whether a nation, a city, a police force, or legal system. There is a visible reality—the institutions and organizations, the offices and officers. And there is an invisible aspect to the principalities—the soul of the organization, the spirituality of the organization, and the collective mind that shapes the organization. Principalities in their fallen state are susceptible to demonic influence.

Although Satan and the demonic don't seem to have a redemptive path, the principalities and powers do. But just like redeemed people, these organizations and principalities will discover that this redemptive process is often fragile and fragmentary on this side of the new heavens and new earth.

Regarding racism, we must realize that through his life, death, and resurrection, Christ "has destroyed the barrier, the dividing wall of hostility" (Eph. 2:14) between different people groups. Belief and baptism give us a new identity, which is socially constructed by the church through the Spirit, not by the current culture, and it is determined by new birth rather than geography, family origins, or skin color. The baptized swear allegiance to a different kind of King and a different kind of kingdom, one that is not characterized by racism, humanism, or nationalism. Instead, it chooses to imitate Christ, who was willing to die but never willing to kill.

The false gospel says that the good news is for another time and another place. It accepts the status quo. But the good news is that "the kingdom of God is at hand" (Mark 1:15 ESV). Thus we are to pray, "Your kingdom come, your will be done, on earth as it is in heaven" (Matt. 6:10). Then we are to act in such a way as to live into that prayer so that we become a sign, foretaste, and instrument of the kingdom in our local communities. Violence is not one of those actions.

The false tactics of the alt-right and alt-left promote violence and destruction.[65] They hold to the myth of redemptive violence, which claims that peace can come through violence. This false tactic needs to be discarded. We must remember that our battle is not against flesh and blood but against the Powers; and the weapons of our warfare are not of the flesh but have divine power to destroy strongholds (Eph. 6:12; 1 Cor. 10:4).

Peacemakers will be called children of God, and they will not use violence, because they realize that violence is never capable of bringing about peace. Jesus gives us another way. In his book *Engaging the Powers*, Wink poses this question: "How can we oppose evil without creating new evils and being made evil ourselves?"[66]

For Wink, transformation and redemption must involve both the personal and social together. Part of the church's evangelistic task, as Wink reminds us, is "proclaiming to the Principalities and Powers in the heavenly places the manifold wisdom of God (Eph. 3:10). And that means addressing the spirituality of actual institutions that have rebelled against their divine vocations and have made themselves gods."[67]

If we hope to make progress against racism, we must seek outside intervention. Persistent prayer is not optional; it is a prerequisite. Our societal systems need to be redeemed, as they repeatedly demonstrate the systemic power of racism.

The good news gives hope for the oppressor and the oppressed.[68] Living in the kingdom under the Lordship of Christ means that those of us in the place of privilege need to voluntarily lay down our rights and privileges in solidarity with the other (Phil. 2) because we value our relationship with the other as more important than our status. Those without privilege are called to live in mutuality with the formerly privileged, becoming one new family, one new humanity. If this is to happen, we must believe the gospel more than the myth of redemptive violence.

THE PRINCIPALITIES AND POWERS AND MISSIONAL LEADERSHIP

Stringfellow's life as an incarnational parable and prophetic witness is worthy of our imitation. So how might his theology of the Powers help shape our understanding of how the Powers seek to subvert us as missional leaders?

The principalities that Stringfellow articulates correlate with the three contours of leadership, as seen in table 9.1. The principality of *image* relates to *identity*; the principality of *institution* relates to our *praxis* as leaders; and the principality of *ideology* relates to our *telos*, all of which align with our ultimate desires. In the same way, Stringfellow mentions that the principalities are interconnected and shouldn't be sharply distinguished, so the identity, praxis, and telos of the leader also overlap and interconnect.

Table 9.1 The Contours of Leadership and the Principalities

Contours of Missional Leadership	The Principalities and Powers
Identity	Image
Praxis	Institution
Telos	Ideology

Stringfellow's theology helps us clarify precisely how the Powers seek to hold us captive. The principalities of image, institution, and ideology seek to subvert us at each of the contours of leadership, and as I will demonstrate in the next chapter, they align with how the devil sought to tempt Christ in the wilderness.

In brief, the principalities seek to have us become possessed by our image, instead of us possessing our image and holding fast to our identity in Christ. The principality of ideology seeks to subvert how we read the Scriptures, for when we are unaware of our captivity to an ideology, it misshapes the way we read the Scriptures, and subsequently our telos becomes misdirected. Finally, when we are possessed by our image and/ or misread the Scriptures, it inevitably misshapes our praxis, especially in regard to how we use power.

MARK DRISCOLL AND THE POWERS

To better understand how the Powers seek to subvert us, I will examine how they worked in the life and ministry of Mark Driscoll, whose leadership has been widely scrutinized through the podcast *The Rise and Fall of Mars Hill*.[69] I will explore his "fall" using William Stringfellow's articulation of the principalities and powers in today's vernacular: image, ideology, and institution. By taking the ideas presented in the last chapter and applying them to a current example, it will serve as a creative way to repeat important concepts so that we might be more vigilant in engaging the Powers.

Image. As we have learned from Stringfellow, an angel, or image, accompanies every person. So, in our example, there are two entities that claim and use the name of Mark Driscoll, former lead pastor of Mars Hill in Seattle and beyond: "one a principality, the other a person."[70] Each of us has an image that seeks to enslave, control, and destroy us.

In an article titled "Why Mark Driscoll's Fall and Mars Hill's Breakup Issues a Warning for Megastar Pastors," Sarah Pulliam Bailey, contributor to the *Religion News Service,* writes,

> For many megachurches, a pastor can become larger than the church itself—particularly for multisite churches where the pastor's sermon is the only thing binding disparate congregations connected by little more than a satellite feed. Before his resignation, the name "Mark Driscoll" was more widely known than "Mars Hill." The dueling brands sometimes clashed along the way; some say Driscoll once told staff "I am the brand."[71]

As I noted earlier, this "I am the brand" speech has been confirmed by Driscoll's staff in *The Rise and Fall of Mars Hill* podcast.[72] Joe Day, a worship leader who was on staff at Mars Hill for a decade, mentions how Driscoll stood up for an hour and preached on how he was the brand, and the staff's role was to bring people through the doors so that Mark could preach to them, because nobody could do it as well as Mark.[73] Driscoll's "I am the brand" speech encapsulates what Stringfellow refers to in regard to the principalities as *image.* One of the clearest indications of Driscoll falling to the principality of image was having Mars Hill pay $210,000 for the services of ResultSource, a book marketing company that helps authors buy their way onto bestseller lists. *Real Marriage,* which Driscoll coauthored with his wife, Grace, subsequently spent one week on the *New York Times* bestseller list.[74] Getting on this list is not simply about how many books are sold. If this was the case, millionaires could simply buy a huge stock of their own books in order to get on the list. In order to make it to the *New York Times* Best Seller list, books need to be sold from every region in the country, and ResultSource makes it appear as if all these books were spontaneously purchased by individuals. Eventually, Mars Hill made a statement that "while not uncommon or illegal, this unwise strategy is not one we have used before or since, and not one we will use again."[75]

ResultSource essentially expands an author's image. And indeed, the brand or image of Mark Driscoll potentially swallowed up the person of Mark Driscoll. Stringfellow's principality of image directly correlates with Wink's understanding of *sarx.* To recall Wink, when *sarx* is used negatively in Scripture, it is in "reference to the self in its alienated mode . . . subjugated to the opinion of others."[76] Being possessed by our image is falling to egotism. It is living in estrangement from God, the false self. In Wink's words, it is "a life lived according to the dictates of the Domination System."[77] And as Stringfellow has already made clear, public image is a principality, in that although it bears our name, it exists independently of us and lies beyond our control, and it is in conflict with us until we fully give ourselves over to the image. "And when that surrender is made, the person in fact dies, though not yet physically. For at that point he is literally possessed by his own image."[78]

If we seek to make a name for ourselves (our own glory), and if we seek first our reputation instead of seeking first the kingdom, not only do we fall to the principality of image, but we also open the door for Satan to work through the mimetic cycle. And as we saw with Girard, the mimetic cycle leads to "scandals," division, and scapegoating in the congregation. We see the evidence of this in Driscoll's ministry. The scapegoating of other leaders by Mark led to a pile of "dead bodies" thrown under the bus at his bidding. Life in the "underground," as Girard describes it, is ruled by pride. Pride conceals and blinds us to malformed desires, but those desires are revealed through dissension in the congregation. Dissension can take place through other rivalries as well. But the hoarding of recognition, the desire for titles and accolades produces the fruit of the underground: infighting, dissension, chaos, and scapegoating.

Ideology. Although image is typically the least powerful of the principalities, when combined with ideology and institution, it becomes difficult to resist. It seems that Mark Driscoll fell to the ideology of authoritarianism, transferring "worldly management methodology to [his] exercising of authority in the church" as a way to manufacture growth with great speed.[79] With this ideology, Mark Driscoll not only started a megachurch in Seattle, but he also planted fifteen satellite sites across five states. He was therefore able to project his image into each of these churches, week after week. Yet, as I previously mentioned, his methods included bullying, domineering leadership, intimidation, a hyper-macho reading of Scripture, and even violence.[80]

Institution. Finally, the principality in the form of institution also played a part in Driscoll's fall. Through some publicly posted letters and statements of former leaders, it is clear how the principality of institution worked alongside the ideology of authoritarianism. In the early years of Mars Hill, the church was led by a community of elders. Distributed authority was written into the bylaws of the church. So "even though Driscoll cultivated an authoritarian, tough-guy persona, the bylaws of the church didn't allow him to be an autocrat."[81] In those early days, the bylaws gave power to the twenty-four elders at the time, and Mark only had one vote. "Besides the council of elders, the bylaws also allowed for a five-member council of 'executive elders' who were elected for two-year terms to control day-to-day operations without consulting the rest," but if there were big decisions to be made, the elder council was invited to speak into those decisions.[82] But then in the summer of 2007, Driscoll "convinced the standing executive council to resign, replaced them with yes-men," and disregarded the council of elders.[83] He and his right-hand man, Jamie Munson, bought a building for four million dollars in Belltown, and the council of elders only learned about it by reading *The Seattle Times* and *The Stranger.*[84]

Then, in order to concentrate more power in Driscoll's hands, Driscoll and Munson made a proposal to rewrite the bylaws. Two of the elders, Paul Petry and Bent Meyer, thought this was a dangerous idea, and their dissent infuriated Mark. Following an ecclesial trial investigating Petry (who was not allowed to attend and was only able to respond to the charges), Petry was fired, and his family was publicly shunned at the command of Driscoll.[85] "The treatment of Petry produced such an outcry, according to ex-members, that Bent Meyer, the other elder who'd questioned Driscoll's rewrite of the bylaws, was given a gentler trial but still resigned in disgust."[86] This episode is what started to shake up the foundation of Mars Hill.

Rob Smith—who had served with Mars Hill for five years doing pastoral work at one of the campuses, as well as running Agathos, an independent organization serving orphans and widows in Zambia and South Africa— was asked to join the elder council a week before Petry's trial. Before Smith was allowed to join, he had to agree to shun Petry. Smith did not feel Petry received a fair trial and vehemently opposed this idea. When Driscoll discovered this, he turned his wrath on Smith. Driscoll wanted to take the other elders to confront him, but Smith insisted on meeting with Driscoll one-on-one. He recalls his time with Driscoll:

> It was the worst conversation I've ever had with any human being on earth . . . He was vile, he was vulgar, he threatened me with obscene language, said that he would destroy me, destroy my career, and make sure I never ministered again. I was shocked that a man of the cloth would speak that way to someone who worked with him for years. I went from a man of decent character to the worst troublemaker in Mars Hill history for simply asking someone else to have a fair trial.[87]

Driscoll kept his word to Smith. Agathos was heavily dependent on Mars Hill for funding. "Because of Smith's questioning of Driscoll's power grab, Smith says, Driscoll told his thousands of congregants to stop giving to the charity. As a result, 80 percent of Agathos's support evaporated."[88] Driscoll's desire to consolidate power by rewriting the bylaws led to these actions.

The morning after Petry and Meyer were fired, Driscoll had this to say to a team of pastors, a message that was recorded and can be listened to online:[89]

I am all about blessed subtraction. There is a pile of dead bodies behind the Mars Hill bus, and by God's grace it'll be a mountain by the time we're done. You either get on the bus or get run over by the bus. Those are the options, but the bus ain't going to stop. And um, I'm just a, I'm just a guy—we love you, but, this is what we are doing. There's a few kind of people—there's people who get in the way of the bus, they got to get run over. There are people who want to take turns driving the bus, they got to get thrown off, (chuckle), 'cause they want to go somewhere else. There are people who will be on the bus, leaders, and helpers and servants, they are awesome. There are also sometimes just nice people who sit on the bus and shut up, uh, they are not helping nor hurting, let them ride along . . . yesterday we fired two elders for the first time in the history of Mars Hill—last night. They're off the bus, under the bus. They were off mission, so now they are unemployed.[90]

In the early years of the church, Mars Hill was led by a community of elders. One of the sad realities of Mars Hill is that Mark created a structure that recreated him. As the revision of bylaws took place, "an oppressive heaviness began to overshadow everything. Saying that there was heavy coercion applied would be putting it mildly."[91]

Mark maneuvered the structure in such a way that he was fully in control, firing and scapegoating anyone who disagreed with him. Eventually, he believed he must be the sole one who wore "the ring" if the church was going to move forward in growth. Eventually, as I mentioned earlier, this led to his resignation. In his resignation letter, sent October 14, 2014, he writes, "I readily acknowledge I am an imperfect messenger of the gospel of Jesus Christ. There are many things I have confessed and repented of, privately and publicly, as you are well aware. Specifically, I have confessed to past pride, anger and a domineering spirit."[92]

Seven years later, after Driscoll's resignation, there were eighteen Mars Hill elders who issued a letter of confession to Bent Meyer and Paul Petry, where they publicly confessed their sin against them back in 2007, when they sided with Mark. At that time, they agreed not only to fire them, but also to shun Paul Petry and his entire family. They wrote, "We were wrong. We harmed you. You have lived with the pain of that for many years. As some of us have come to each of you privately, you have extended grace and forgiveness, and for that we thank you."[93]

When the principalities of image, institution, and ideology are in operation, not only do they subvert the leader, but they also often take captive the majority of the congregation. Through mimetic desire, they fall into the mimetic cycle, and the scapegoat mechanism kicks in. And although we don't tend to kill the scapegoat today, they are as good as dead to the

206 | SECTION FOUR: MISSIONAL LEADERSHIP AND SUBVERSION

congregation. Listen to how these eighteen elders in repentance recall their role in scapegoating:

> Paul, on December 5th, 2007 those of us who were elders at the time voted to instruct the members of Mars Hill to treat you as an unrepentant believer under church discipline after you had resigned your membership from the church. This treatment was to have included "rejection and disassociation" in the hope that you would "come to an acknowledgement of [your] sin and repent." This instruction was given with the weight of all twenty-seven elders at the time. This disciplinary rejection led to great loss to your family in extreme financial hardship, sudden loss of long standing friendships, spiritual and emotional trauma to your family, and the public shaming of your character. We share responsibility for those losses due to our participation in the vote.[94]

The public repentance of these eighteen elders demonstrates how Jesus' willingness to become the scapegoat has disarmed the principalities and powers. When Jesus was declared innocent by the Father raising him from the dead, it revealed the false transcendency by which the principalities gained their power and authority. The triumph of the cross is revealed among these eighteen elders: through this letter of confession, instead of Meyer and Petry nailed to the cross, the accusations against Meyer and Petry are nailed to the cross and are publicly exhibited and exposed as lies. In this way, the principalities and powers have been disarmed.

Stringfellow believes that it is only through the Spirit that we ultimately overcome the principalities, where we become free to imitate Christ, free to expose the works of death, and free to honor the work of Christ. In the same way, for Girard, the Paraclete takes the opposite role of Satan. While Satan is the accuser, the Spirit is the defender. Girard writes,

> Satan only reigns by virtue of the representations of persecution that held sway prior to the Gospels. Satan therefore is essentially the *accuser*, the one who deceives men by making them believe that innocent victims are guilty. But, who is the Paraclete?
>
> *Parakleitos*, in Greek, is the exact equivalent of advocate or the Latin *advocatus*. The Paraclete is called on behalf of the prisoner, the victim, to speak in his place and his name, to act in his defense. The Paraclete is the universal advocate, the chief defender of all innocent victims, *the destroyer of every representation of persecution*. He is truly the spirit of truth that dissipates the fog of mythology.[95]

We see in this situation that the Spirit of God started to possess these elders who previously were the accusers. Having seen the light, they have become the defenders, owning their own complicity of falling into the mimetic cycle—the work of the accuser.

THE CRITICAL NEED AMID THE LEADERSHIP CRISIS

As leaders in the church, we are called to be vision-casters, communicators, pastors, cultural architects, organizers, overseers, change agents, innovators, team builders, servants, pioneers, influencers, motivators, equippers, decision-makers . . . and the list goes on. There are books that teach us to be visionary leaders, inspiring leaders, adaptive leaders, relational leaders, intuitive leaders, strategic leaders, servant leaders, missional leaders, organic leaders, and more. But what is the critical leadership need in the midst of these leadership crises?

There are two ways to view leadership: *positionally* or *operationally*. In figure 9.1, the vertical axis represents positional leadership, and the horizontal axis represents operational leadership.[96] At the top of the vertical axis is a top-down approach to leadership. We are all familiar with this style of leadership. On the lower part of the vertical axis is a bottom-up form of leadership, which is democratic or revolutionary. On the horizontal axis are leaders who lead from behind, from the middle, and from the front.

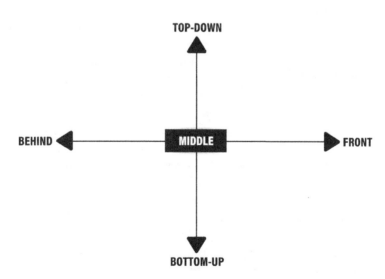

Figure 9.1 The Leadership Matrix

The most common approach for operational leadership tends to be leadership from the front, where a leader proclaims a vision and takes ownership for the success or failure of a mission. Leading from the middle involves coming alongside people, getting into the ditches with others. Leading from behind is about training others and sending them out on mission. It is about leading behind the scenes. Positional leadership can be from the bottom-up or the top-down.

We need people to lead from all these stances. Looking at the various approaches to leadership—the positional and operational as well as the different positions from which a leader must lead—is both helpful and problematic. It can be helpful in considering the different ways we are called to lead in various circumstances. But it can be problematic if our hearts are not right; if our desires are for prestige, power, or control, then whatever position of leadership we find ourselves in can be harmful and outright dangerous. The key to being fruitful when leading in any of these positions is to *lead by example*—not just with our actions but with our desires. For if Girard is right about mimetic desire, which I believe he is, then anyone who follows us will imitate our desires.

Consider the following illustration.[97] What is the right way to worship at a service? Some churches have contemporary music; others use the pipe organ. Some congregations don't use any musical instruments at all. Many churches meet in church buildings, some in houses, others under a tree. The style or place in which we worship is not the most important thing about our worship. What matters is that we worship in spirit and in truth.

When it comes to leading, sometimes we will find ourselves leading from the top; at other times we might find ourselves leading from the bottom. Sometimes our leadership will be from the front; other times from behind or the middle. Where we find ourselves leading from doesn't really matter; what matters is how we lead—not in a domineering manner, but in the way of Jesus. *We lead by example.*

On the Leadership Matrix diagram, it is clear that leaders need to occupy different stances, but this doesn't determine whether we exercise transformative, godly leadership. Position is not irrelevant; it is just not determinative. The desires of our heart are the determining factors, for that is what people will imitate. If we desire prestige, power, and control, we will cultivate mimetic rivalry, which could lead to mimetic contagion and to scapegoating. This was apparent in the life and ministry of Mark Driscoll at Mars Hill. On the other hand, if we desire God and his kingdom, we will make disciples who will seek God and his kingdom first, which will spark a kingdom movement.

One of the greatest challenges we face as leaders is being able to resist the Powers. One leader who I believe embodied this was Dallas Willard. Willard was a professor of philosophy at the University of Southern California. He also taught at Fuller Theological Seminary and many other places. He is known as a spiritual formation guru and authored many significant books, including *The Spirit of the Disciplines* and *The Divine Conspiracy*. Willard passed away in 2013, but I remember the meaningful times I was able to share with him.

Our network once invited him to speak at our conference. I happened to be the host of the particular session in which Dallas was to speak. It was my responsibility to lead a question-and-answer time after his talk. Just before I went up, I felt the Spirit leading me to say something I didn't want to say because I thought it might embarrass Dallas. So I rejected what I sensed to be the Spirit's prompting. Then I sensed the Spirit prompt me once more, just before I got up. So I stood beside Dallas and said what came to my mind.

"Dallas, I've noticed that you are not a good speaker," I said. "You're not a charismatic speaker. You speak with a monotone voice. You are just not an impressive speaker."

I could sense the uneasiness of the audience and noticed a few raised eyebrows. They must have been thinking, *What in the world is JR doing?*

Despite this, I continued. "But then I noticed something else. When you were speaking, everyone was on the edge of their seat, just waiting for the next word to drop from your mouth."

He patted me on my shoulder, as if to comfort me. He nodded his head during the entire time I was nervously talking; and in the midst of the awkward laughter of the crowd, he shared how he purposely chose not to use the common tactics that speakers use, because he wanted people to see God's power at work through him. Dallas did indeed have a presence about him, a power and authority that was not his own.

Willard wrote several books, many on discipleship, but never once did he write a book proposal. He never sought to put himself forward. He only responded to requests that publishers made of him. Dallas has been an example to me and many others, and he embodied what it means to be an example in the way of Christ. He was a kenotic leader who resisted the principalities of image, institution, and ideology.

SUMMARY OF SECTION FOUR

William Stringfellow was a man before his time. His incarnational presence in the grittiest part of New York City enabled him to see with different eyes and to hear with different ears. As a prophetic witness, Stringfellow reminds us (the church) of our prophetic calling in the world. His context in Harlem and his reading of Scripture helped him to articulate the principalities and powers in our current vernacular. His keen understanding of the principalities of image, institution, and ideology allowed him to name, unmask, and engage the principalities in his context. Because he understood that racism and nationalism were principalities, his remedy required him to go beyond the ideologies of his day—humanism and liberalism—which still linger today. Stringfellow viewed life through the lens of the power of death and the power of the resurrection. We have a choice in which reality we are going to live. Because of the life, death, and resurrection of Christ, and because of the availability and power of the Holy Spirit, we can live in the new world order now. Stringfellow celebrates the gospel of life as much as he lambasts the reign of death. He believes that we become the church, the good news people, when we live in the reality of the work that Christ has already accomplished and that the Spirit makes accessible.

Along with Wink and Girard, Stringfellow confirms the ubiquity of the fall and that there are larger creatures in the world that can only be resisted with a power that transcends our world. Through his emphasis on the Powers and idolatry, Stringfellow confirms the underlying premise of this book: fallen leadership occurs when we imitate the principalities and powers in submission to Satan, which is bondage to idolatry and leads to dishonoring God and dehumanization. Redeemed leadership, or missional leadership, is when we imitate Christ in submission to the Father, which is freedom from idolatry and leads to honoring God and human flourishing.

I looked at how the principalities of image, institution, and ideology correspond to the contours of leadership—identity, praxis, and telos. Stringfellow *naming* these realities in our current vernacular gives us *power* to engage the Powers with greater wisdom and discernment. An examination of how these principalities worked in the life of Mark Driscoll provides a clearer understanding of how they seek to subvert our leadership.

I also made the case for how an emergent view of racism helps us to better name, unmask, and engage the principality of racism in the US. I looked at how racism is a reality in the collective mind of the US, and therefore, the only hope to combat it is with the help of an outside source. Prayer is a necessity, prayer that allows us to be dependent on the Spirit so we might imitate Christ and love all. For it is when we live into the reality of resurrection life that we can experience freedom from the bondage of death and accept the grace to love others as we have been loved.

Now that I have explored an understanding of the subversion and resistance of the Powers, I will turn toward a theological remedy to domineering leadership.

SECTION FIVE

MISSIONAL LEADERSHIP WORTHY OF IMITATION

Having taken four sections to dive deep into diagnosing the problem of domineering leadership, in this final section, I will point toward the remedy. Utilizing the imitation-based framework, I will examine how the temptations of Jesus take place within the contours of leadership (identity, praxis, and telos). By looking at how Christ developed his identity, I will consider practical ways for us to develop a sense of identity, and I will also examine the importance of both local and distant models in our lives. In chapter eleven, I will take a broad look at the book of Philippians from a Girardian point of view. Finally, in chapter twelve, I will examine the kenotic journey of Christ and how it was practiced in Paul's life. Reflecting on this, I will consider the life of Óscar Romero as a kenotic leader for us to imitate, and I will examine how the Lord's Prayer can help us to develop a kenotic spirituality.

10

TOWARD A THEOLOGICAL REMEDY

The task of this book has been theological—a theology that shapes our understanding and practice. While etymologically, *theology* simply means "the study of God," theological studies have broadened to include biblical, systematic, historical, and practical theology.[1] A well-developed theology involves an approach to spirituality and ethics, and it requires an exploration of reality through the various sciences. All of reality is theological. All of life expresses our theology. "Jesus is Lord" is a theological statement declaring the reality that Jesus is the reconciler of all of creation (Col. 1: 19–20). It also speaks to the fact that theology is not limited to one segment of our lives. Rather, it is an integrative approach to all of reality; it shapes our self-understanding and how we live with others in the world.

An impoverished theology misshapes our desires, disorients our sense of self (identity), brings a sense of despair and anxiety regarding the future (telos), and ultimately lends itself toward behavior (praxis) that hurts others and dishonors God. A robust theology can reshape our desires in a positive way, orienting them toward God and the realization of his kingdom on earth. It enables us to ground our sense of being or identity in Christ. And it leads us toward a self-giving, others-centered praxis as we are immersed in the experience of an uncommon love, an unending stream of grace and forgiveness, and the promise of a future architected by Divine love, which is our telos.

The imitation-based framework I developed throughout this book is a theological step toward a greater sense of reality, shedding light and gaining a deeper understanding of the problem of domineering leadership. Defining the issue through the imitation-based framework is a vital element of developing a remedy.

REFLECTING ON THE IMITATION-BASED FRAMEWORK

In this final section of the book, I will move toward a solution to the problem of domineering leadership. But let us first reflect upon the imitation-based framework that I have developed throughout these pages, as its sets the foundation for the remedy. We have come to understand how the Powers play a significant role in shaping our daily reality. Though the Powers are a prevalent theme in Scripture, the task of contextualization is daunting. I examined the Ford/Frei Scale—with the fivefold typology ranging from the traditionalist to the reductionist—to help analyze various approaches to the Powers, particularly focusing on the work of Clinton E. Arnold, Rudolf Bultmann, and Hendrick Berkhof.

Through study of the missional conversation, it became evident that leadership theory and practice needs to be linked with missional leadership, mimetic desire, the Powers, and Christ. In developing an imitation-based framework, my aim is to address the problem of domineering leadership more robustly and to equip us in developing a spirituality that reshapes our desires toward God, his kingdom, and his righteousness. The central question of this book is the following: *How might a theology of the Powers help us, as missional leaders, to practice a spirituality that reshapes our desires for the sake of discipleship, community, and mission?*

As missional theology developed, it highlighted the need for missional leadership. Craig Van Gelder calls attention to the missionary nature of God and the church, speaking to the importance of *identity* and how the Scriptures and the reign of God illustrate the narrative arc of Scripture from creation to new creation—the telos. Alan Roxburgh speaks to the centrality of the identity of the leader and the importance of the telos of God and new creation in guiding the leaders' work, or praxis. From these authors, the contours of leadership emerged. The importance of plurality in both leadership and fivefold intelligence (APEST) continues to be an important development in missional leadership. This is significant because, as René Girard demonstrates, when a model desires something that either cannot or will not be shared, such as a particular leadership role, there is a greater chance of mimetic rivalry, which can devolve into the mimetic cycle.

As I reviewed Graham Houston's work on 1 Peter dealing with domineering leadership, the imitation-based conceptual framework emerged. Houston gives us the dimensions in which imitation can take place with the missional leader:

- Who the leader imitates (the world or Jesus)
- Who imitates the leader as their model

I noted that this aligns with Girard's mimetic theory, which states that, in the ultimate sense, there are two arch-models for us as leaders: Satan or Jesus. When we uncritically mimic the principalities (as estranged from God), or when we look to the wrong models, we can fall into the mimetic trap of Satan and come under what Walter Wink calls the Domination System, where our praxis inevitably becomes domineering, as we unknowingly mimic the Powers, leading to the scandal of leadership. The scandal of leadership takes place when we, as leaders, scandalize those who look to us as models. If an individual desires to be the lead pastor and that person's desires are malformed, those who look to that leader will find themselves with this desire as well. This leads to rivalry, where one becomes a scandal (obstacle) to one's disciple(s) getting what he or she desires, resulting in division, chaos, and scapegoating.

Following in the path of Augustine and the early Church Fathers, James K. A. Smith draws attention to the centrality of desire, making the case that our desires define us. The centrality of desire is not only prominent in Girard but is the foundation of his work and is tied to the theme of imitation. I looked at the importance of desire—and envious desire and selfish ambition as the source of disorder and every evil practice—in Scot McKnight's exegetical study of the letter of James. McKnight put forth a comparison of James and 1 Peter, as did Houston, demonstrating the tie of mimetic desire to the Powers.

Wink's desire to achieve in his early life was based on his desire to be loved and accepted. All leaders are susceptible to this desire when we seek to accomplish *for* love, instead of *from* being loved. Henri Nouwen, reflecting on Jesus' ability to successfully face the temptations of the devil in the desert, emphasized that Jesus' identity was grounded in his Father's words, that he was his beloved son. Wink demonstrates, through his life, the importance of knowing and imitating Jesus, showing how it would be difficult to live humanly in a world dominated by the Powers apart from following Jesus' example. He notes that people, in their desire to eliminate evil, are likely to mimic the very evil they seek to eliminate, unless their identity is grounded in God. Wink stresses the importance of imitating the practice of Christ in nonviolent direct action. His desire to seek first God, his kingdom, and his righteousness led him to be a kingdom activist. He fruitfully named and unmasked racism in South Africa, taking a peacemaking approach to engaging the Powers. Wink was inspired and motivated for his entire writing project by William Stringfellow, who in his corpus, named and unmasked racism and nationalism in America.

Through Girard, I explored the concept of mimetic desire, linking missional leadership to mimetic desire and the Powers. Our desire to imitate either the Powers or Christ shapes our praxis. Stringfellow points out that when a church or organization is in survival mode (a yellow flag for leaders), it is more likely to imitate the Powers. Although Girard develops the concept of mimetic desire, he leaves positive mimesis relatively undeveloped. But those who have been shaped by his life and his writings have made significant contributions to this area of study. Petra Steinmair-Pösel demonstrates the potential of positive mimesis from the narrative arc of creation, the fall, and Christ. On this trajectory, through the grace of Christ, an undistorted view of God is available, which makes possible a new experience of God and a new form of relationship, as people participate in the divine life. When the Eucharist is celebrated as a place of receiving and thanksgiving, positive mimesis is possible; however, because of the Powers manifest through human institutions, it is likely only to be realized provisionally. Willard M. Swartley highlights how major strands of the New Testament are directed at the transformation of desire through good models who were following Christ. This enabled positive mimesis to take place, as with the Thessalonians who followed Paul, Timothy, and Silvanus and then became positive models to believers in Macedonia and Achaia (1 Thess. 1:6–7). Swartley also demonstrates the transformational nature of Jesus' teaching on discipleship and the early church's development of *imitatio Christi*. He emphasizes that many imitation passages relate to leading a cruciform life; in these, believers participated in the suffering of Christ as they sought to overcome evil with good rather than mimicking the ways of the world. This aligns with Wink's overall project in *Engaging the Powers*, in which he outlines an approach to mission that engages evil without "creating new evils and being made evil ourselves."[2]

Regarding the Powers, Lesslie Newbigin illustrates the pervasiveness of the Powers in the New Testament, a theme also found in the work of Arnold and Berkhof. In critical engagement with Wink, I developed a theology of the Powers, showing how they work from personal, social, and cosmic perspectives. I established the necessity to name, unmask, and engage the invisible forces that determine human existence. I further developed this by examining Stringfellow's understanding of the principalities (image, institution, and ideology) and applying them to the three contours of leadership (identity, praxis, and telos).

Wink's explanation of the outer personal, collective, and inner personal demonic provides unique remedies. Wink, along with Amos Yong, makes the case that the demonic is an emergent reality.[3] Wink identifies the Domination System as "an entire network of Powers becoming integrated around idolatrous values," and he considers Satan to be the spirit of the Domination System.[4] Girard deconstructs Satan as the mimetic cycle, while Matthew Croasmun reconstructs Satan as the "body of sin," giving Satan cosmic personhood. Although Wink follows Jung and identifies Satan more psychologically as the inner spirituality of the domination system, Croasmun's emergent view locates Satan as a cosmic entity, the mythical that emerges from the social and acts back upon it. In both cases, Satan is an emergent reality.

For Wink, the most believed myth in contemporary American culture is the myth of redemptive violence, which he views as nationalism becoming absolute. Stringfellow also names, unmasks, and engages nationalism and racism, offering practical help through his understanding of how institutions and ideology work. Wink's definition of the *world* provides the nuance necessary to understand both its positive (relating to people and creation) and negative ("to the *human sociological realm that exists in estrangement from God*") dimensions in Scripture.[5] This includes the principalities and powers in their fallen state. Creatures large and small seek to misshape our desires as leaders. Thus, Stringfellow speaks of the ubiquity of the fall. Girard's understanding of culture also reflects the pervasiveness of the fall. For Girard, culture has been fully enveloped in the mimetic cycle until Christ, who referred to Satan as the god of this world. Satan was a murderer from the beginning—from Cain and Abel, through the prophets, until Jesus, who fully revealed what was hidden from the foundation of the world. Jesus' willingness to become the scapegoat—despite his innocence and his victory over death, as evidenced in the resurrection—signaled the fall of Satan. The mimetic cycle was revealed and Satan's work laid bare.

For Wink, this *aiōn* (present age) refers to the present Domination Epoch, and *sarx* (flesh) could be positive or negative depending on context. In its negative form, living life "according to the flesh" denotes those who are "self-externalized and subjugated to the opinion of others."[6] Girard identifies this as mimetic desire. The negative side of *sarx* can also be described as the alienated self, the self that is socialized within the Domination System and Age, the self that is not centered in God. This is consistent with Stringfellow's articulation of "image." It is therefore essential that we, as leaders, find our identity in God.

Wink, following Berkhof, characterizes the Powers as being created good, falling, and in need of redemption. In considering the Powers in relation to Satan and the demonic, I concluded that their telos is destruction; the God of peace will crush Satan (the cosmic body of sin) under the feet of the church. But the telos of the principalities and powers is redemption in new creation. Wink's word study in Colossians 1:16 suggests that although the principalities are in their fallen state and are susceptible to the demonic and under the cosmic power of Satan, it seems these social realities have a path to redemption (Col. 1:15–20). Girard distinguishes between Satan and the principalities and powers. For Girard, when the principalities and powers (which are redeemable) find their source of authority in false transcendence (the mimetic cycle), they become demonic. This would also be true for churches as institutions, or denominations as institutions. The fact that the church is founded on a different kind of murder—one that reveals the false transcendence of the mimetic cycle—should prove helpful to those who have ears to hear. But, like Israel, the church is susceptible to imitating the institutions around her instead of Christ. Thus personal and social transformation are critical for Wink, Girard, and Stringfellow.

In the context of Wink's and Girard's work, missional leaders rest their authority and power on false transcendence when they live under the sway of the Domination System and mimic its ways. In the context of the Epistle of James, this evil is called satanic and demonic; in the context of 1 Peter, it is revealed as satanic. The remedy for leaders and churches that have opened themselves up to the demonic is clarified by McKnight's study of James. As leaders we must humble ourselves, submit ourselves to God, and resist the devil. When dealing with the demonic, repentance is to be drastic and complete. Thus, as leaders, we are called to repentance and to cleanse our hands, purify our hearts, lament, mourn, weep, and ultimately humble ourselves. For "God opposes the proud but gives grace to the humble" (James 4:6 NLT). In James, God is also revealed as the God of grace, giving us, as leaders, the opportunity to humble ourselves by repenting of the wrong desires that wreak havoc in the church.

Through this imitation-based framework, we can see that missional leaders can either imitate the Powers or imitate Christ. The primary focus of this book has been to diagnose the problem of domineering leadership by establishing the link between missional leadership, mimetic desire, and a theology of the Powers. This is illustrated by following the left side of figure 10.1, for when we, as leaders, unintentionally imitate the Powers, we incarnate fallen leadership. The scandal of "fallen" leadership takes place when we get caught in the mimetic trap.

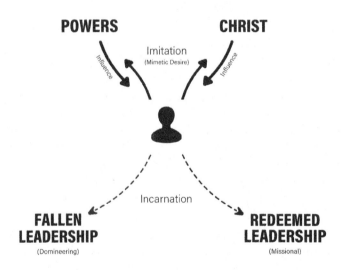

Figure 10.1 The Imitation-Based Framework

Although the Powers persistently seek to subvert us as missional leaders, the scandal of leadership can become positively "scandalous" when we opt to imitate Christ in the kenotic way of the cross instead of in the ways of the world (Phil. 2:1–8). I will define and explore the concept of kenotic leadership in the next two chapters.[7] This way of self-sacrificial, Jesus-centered leadership is scandalous to some and foolish to others—in the same way the cross was a scandal to the Jews and foolishness to the Greeks (1 Cor. 1:23).

In *The Day the Revolution Began*, British New Testament scholar N. T. Wright examines the significance of the cross, saying that through the cross of Christ, a new power entered the world, one that overcame the Powers: the power of *suffering love*. Wright makes the case that mission needs to take place in a cruciform manner: "The victory of the cross will be implemented through the means of the cross."[8] Yet this is the antithesis of those who only know how to lord it over others—theirs is the kind of leadership that "gets things done in the real world." The Powers persistently, forcefully, and sometimes violently target us, in the hope that we might imitate their ways instead of the way of Christ and the cross. However, the good news is that through the life, death, and resurrection of Christ, the Powers have been exposed, unmasked, and disarmed. They only have as much power as we choose to give them.

The "scandal" of leadership will be either negative or positive. The negative scandal occurs when we become obstacles to those who look to us as models. But it becomes a positive scandal when we imitate the way of Christ, which is often a scandal to the world in which we live because it always leads to a cross. If we choose not to imitate Christ, by default we are choosing to imitate the Powers. We are captive to imitation.

When we imitate the Powers, our desires become misshaped, and we incarnate our leadership in a domineering fashion. But when we imitate Christ, our desires become reshaped, and our leadership is incarnated missionally. Thus, as missional leaders, the ultimate battle we face is the spiritual battle for our hearts, souls, and desires.

The battle could be summarized by defining *fallen* and *redeemed* leadership. As a reminder, fallen leadership imitates the principalities in submission to Satan, which brings bondage to idolatry and leads to dishonoring God and dehumanization. Redeemed leadership imitates Jesus in submission to his Father, which brings freedom from idolatry and leads to honoring God and human flourishing.

Though I have demonstrated the contrast between imitating the Powers and imitating Christ throughout these pages, I have only alluded to the practice of positive mimesis and the impact this can have on a leader and congregation. In this final section of the book, I will look at some suggestions for life in the way of redeemed leadership.

It is important to realize that the mimetic cycle is a spiritual battle. The apostle James said that, because the problem lies not simply with abuse of power but with idolatry, to overcome this battle requires resistance and full repentance. If idolatry is the deeper issue, then the heart of the solution is the formation of identity grounded in a life in God. For when we choose God instead of falling to idolatry, and when we love God with all our heart, soul, strength, and mind, we are likely to love the other as ourselves. Then our praxis will reflect imitation of Christ in the power of the Spirit, leading to a suffering love rather than to a praxis that reflects imitation of the Powers and domineering leadership.

Historically, missional theology focused on equipping missional leaders theologically without fully addressing the identity and heart of the leader. As I explored earlier, this latter aspect is unintentionally minimized by Craig Van Gelder and Dwight J. Zscheile when they suggest that the spirituality of the leader is better located in one of the missional tree branches than in the soil for the missional tree.[9] When leaders are caught up with a holy love of God, they not only love God with their whole mind but with all of their being, which reflects a holistic theology. As James K. A. Smith explored, information without formation of desires does not address the heart of the problem.[10] When John the Seer wrote to the church in Ephesus, they were regarded as a church that worked hard, persevered in mission, and discerned between true and false apostles. However, the issue that threatened their witness was losing their first love. Not only did this endanger their witness, but it also meant the potential removal of their lampstand (i.e., witness) (Rev. 2:1–7). Thus if we want to be leaders worthy of imitation, we need to be willing to face the spiritual battle for our heart and soul, ground our identity as God's beloved, and imitate Christ instead of the Powers.

LEADERSHIP WORTHY OF IMITATION

What does it mean for us to become leaders worthy of imitation? McKnight notes the similarities between James 3–4 and 1 Peter 5 and suggests they may have served as an early catechism for the development of teachers and leaders. These passages speak to the spiritual battle with Satan. To be leaders worthy of imitation, we must engage with the path to maturity marked out by the apostle John:

- Understanding our sins are forgiven
- Secure in our identity in knowing God
- Understanding how to overcome the evil one

In his first letter, John says, "I am writing to you, dear children, because your sins have been forgiven on account of his name. I am writing to you, fathers, because you know him who is from the beginning. I am writing to you, young men, because you have overcome the evil one" (1 John 2:12–13). If those who are young in their faith need to understand how to overcome the evil one, how much more important is it for those who are in positions of leading and teaching? The need to understand the works of Satan is also noted by Paul. When he writes to Timothy, he advises him against new converts becoming leaders too quickly, cautioning that it could make them proud and cause them to fall into the condemnation of the devil (1 Tim. 3:6). Even deacons ought to be tested before holding this role (1 Tim. 3:10). This all speaks to why I have taken significant time to explore a theology of the Powers.

In the remainder of this chapter, I will speak to the contours of leadership—identity, praxis, and telos, exploring our lives as missional leaders. This will involve mimetic desire, thus emphasizing the imitation-based framework in the remedy. This framework helps us to understand the importance of being a leader worthy of imitation. Although all three concepts (identity, praxis and telos) interrelate, in this chapter, I will explore the work of identity formation through the lens of Christ's identity formation. I will look at this as illustrated in his baptism and subsequent temptations, for, as I previously mentioned, identity is foundational.

When reflecting upon fallen leaders at the start of this book, I observed the common characteristics of fallen leadership. This included seeking status, a sense of self-importance, using status to push an agenda, and pride—all of which lead to manipulation and the abuse of power and role. Church leaders who display such traits most assuredly have fallen to the principalities and powers. As missional leaders, we can be tempted to find our meaning, significance, and worth through the principalities and powers of image, institution, and ideology, each of which demands ultimate allegiance. However, as Stringfellow reminds us, when human beings seek to justify themselves and offer themselves up to their chosen idols, they end up in bondage to death.

THE TEMPTATIONS OF JESUS

The Scriptures and the creeds tell us that Jesus was fully God and fully human. As the writer of Hebrews says, "For we do not have a high priest who is unable to empathize with our weaknesses, but we have one who has been tempted in every way, just as we are—yet he did not sin" (Heb. 4:15). Dietrich Bonhoeffer considers the temptations of Jesus as a way to live into the line of the Lord's Prayer that reads, "Lead us not into temptation" (Matt. 6:13). Bonhoeffer writes, "He who taught the disciples to pray in this way was Jesus Christ, who alone must have known what temptation was. And because he knew he wanted his disciples to pray 'Lead us not into temptation.' From the point of view of the temptation of Jesus Christ alone can we understand the meaning of temptation for us."[11]

The temptations of Jesus are significant, and the nature of the temptations is particularly instructive. Each of the three synoptic Gospels mentions the temptations of Jesus in the wilderness. It was after the Spirit descended on Jesus at his baptism and the voice from heaven said, "You are my beloved Son; with you I am well pleased" (Mark 1:11 ESV), that "the Spirit immediately drove him out into the wilderness" (Mark 1:12 ESV) to be tempted. Greek scholar Gerald Hawthorne mentions that the word *drove* "indicates at least that the Spirit of God directed Jesus to alter whatever plans he might otherwise have had and to go to this particular place."[12] It is unclear how the Spirit led him to the wilderness: "Whether [Jesus was led by] some ecstatic experience . . . or by a quiet, but strong, inner conviction is not stated. But what is stated is that when the Spirit indicated to Jesus that the acceptance of his Servant vocation must lead him into the wilderness, he surrendered his own plans and followed the Spirit's promptings."[13] Note that not only was he led into the wilderness by the Spirit but also that "Jesus returned to Galilee in the power of the Spirit" (Luke 4:14). Before Jesus embarked on his mission, he faced Satan and his temptations with the help of the Spirit. He did not attempt his ministry apart from the power of the Spirit. Hawthorne writes, after reflecting on each of the synoptic Gospels,

> It is impossible to escape the conclusion that these Gospel writers want their readers to understand that Jesus met and conquered the usurping enemy of God not by his own power alone but aided in his victory by the power of the Holy Spirit. He was fortified in his determination to obey the Father by the strengthening force of the Spirit within him. And it is in this same strength that Jesus was able to go forth into Galilee "and to commence a task which include[d] the release of the devil's captives ([Luke] 4:18; cf. 13:6). Thus, at the outset of his ministry Jesus is depicted as over-coming the evil one who stands in opposition to the work of the Kingdom of God ([Luke] 11:19,20)" through the all-sufficient energizing power of the Spirit of God.[14]

Hawthorne reminds us that after Jesus successfully faced the temptations of the devil, he moved forward in his ministry by the power of the Spirit, with his identity firmly based in the Father's love. The fact that the devil starts with the question "If you are the Son of God" and in the account in Luke ends with "If you are the Son of God" indicates for both Jacques Ellul and Henri Nouwen, that at the core of these temptations is the issue of *identity*. The significance of grounding our identity in God is seen here and correlates with Roxburgh's earlier thoughts regarding how identity is foundational to our leadership.

Reflecting on the story of Jesus' baptism and temptation is important for our own identity formation, which may be why each of the synoptic Gospels mention this event in the life of Jesus. These are temptations that we can all expect to experience. In the conclusion of her study of Mark, Susan Garrett writes, "Mark emphasizes that followers of Jesus must expect to undergo times of testing. Moreover, for us, as for Christ, the tests will be *real*: the spirit will lead us into the wilderness, into solitude, into abandonment."[15] Thus I will explore the temptations of Jesus as archetypal for followers of Jesus, especially those who are about to engage in some form of leadership in the church.

Although there are many ways to understand the temptations of Jesus, I will primarily draw from Stringfellow, Ellul, and Nouwen. Stringfellow's work on the principalities of image, institution, and ideology can be linked to these three temptations, and therefore it is pertinent to our understanding. Ellul was a contemporary of Stringfellow, and his influential work on the Powers makes him an additionally helpful interlocutor for our remedy to domineering leadership. I include Nouwen because of his ability to help us understand the temptations of Jesus from a spiritual formation perspective. I will address the temptations of Jesus in the order that Luke gives us.

THE ECONOMIC TEMPTATION (IMAGE)

The first temptation Jesus faced was to turn the stone into bread. Ellul labels this an *economic temptation*.[16] Because this temptation begins with "If you are the Son of God," we are reminded that this temptation relates to Jesus' sense of identity. As leaders, we too often allow our self-worth to be dependent on our net worth. Nouwen writes, "This temptation touches us at the center of our identity. In a variety of ways, we are made to believe that we are what we produce. This leads to a preoccupation with products, visible results, tangible goods, and progress."[17] When we produce, we are often rewarded economically. However, when we get our sense of worth and status from money and what money can buy, it is building our identity by mimicking the ways of the world. In this way, the principality of *image* seeks to undermine us by having us base our sense of identity on something other than Christ.

If we build our sense of identity by imitating the principalities, we will become anxious leaders who get caught up in comparing ourselves with others. For Nouwen, when our identity is not established as God's beloved son or daughter, we are left to find our identity in what *we have* or what *we can produce*. Nouwen reminds us that the only way to find true selfhood is to be fed by the Word of God. He writes, "We are not the bread we offer, but people who are fed by the Word of God and thereby find true selfhood."[18] Ellul notes, "Nourishment through the word of God is as fundamental for a person's whole being as bread is for the body. This nourishment for the being can only come from being itself, only from the one who can say, 'I am,' for only he is without limits in time or space."[19] The word that Jesus held tightly was the word given him before he performed any miracles, conducted any ministry, or taught any sermons: "This is my beloved Son, with whom I am well pleased" (Matt. 3:17b ESV). Nouwen writes,

> You are *not* what others, or even you, think about yourself. You are *not* what you do. You are *not* what you have. You are a full member of the human family, having been known before you were conceived and molded in your mother's womb. In times when you feel bad about yourself, try to choose to remain true to the truth of who you really are. Look in the mirror each day and claim your true identity. . . . Choose now and continue to choose this incredible truth. As a spiritual practice claim and reclaim your primal identity as beloved daughter or son of a personal Creator.[20]

Nouwen and Ellul remind us, as leaders, to live into our true selves. We are to be bearers of *God's* image, not *our* image. When we are possessed by the principality of image, we will become slaves to image management and lead anxious lives. Jesus was determined not to establish his identity based on how status is attained in our world. He understood that if he was going to faithfully do the will of his Father, through the power of the Spirit, his identity must find its foundation from the word given by his Father. He refused to gain his sense of self from the god of this world's dictates, which require unending validation. Instead, he nourished his relationship with the Father and Spirit and relied on them for his sense of significance. If we are going to overcome this temptation, we need to determine that the only way to gain a true sense of self is to establish it in God. Our true selves are discovered and nourished by participating in the divine life of God. When our identity is not grounded in the life of God, we will fall to the temptation to imitate false models of "success" and inevitably end up in the mimetic cycle of those who live "underground."

A leader's hunger for glory is not all wrong. The hunger for greatness indicates the destiny we have as believers; as co-heirs with Christ, we were made to reflect the glory of God. Paul reminds his readers, "It is that very Spirit bearing witness with our spirit that we are children of God, and if children, then heirs, heirs of God and joint heirs with Christ—if, in fact we suffer with him so that we may also be glorified with him" (Rom. 8:16–17 NRSV). God does not hoard his glory but distributes it. As Nouwen writes,

> When we start living according to this truth, our lives will be radically transformed. We will not only come to know the full freedom of the children of God but also the full rejection of the world. It is understandable that we hesitate to claim the honor so as to avoid the pain. But provided we are willing to share in Christ's suffering, we also will share in his glory.[21]

When we choose to find our identity in God instead of the world, we must be willing to descend into greatness. After all, Jesus says that the way to become great is to become a servant, and the way to become the greatest is to become the slave. If we seek to find our status by the ways of the world, we will be focused on ourselves, but when we find our sense of identity in God, we are free to serve in an others-centered way. Nouwen writes, "This experience of God's acceptance frees us from our needy self and thus creates new space where we can pay selfless attention to others."[22] The path to glory is through being willing to suffer with Christ. Resurrection always follows the cross.

THE POLITICAL TEMPTATION (INSTITUTION)

Following Luke's narrative, the temptation of being offered all the kingdoms is, for Ellul, a *political temptation*, the *temptation for power*. Nouwen also views it in relation to power. This temptation has rough correspondence to the principality of institution, the *praxis* of the leader. For Nouwen, this temptation speaks to the desire for security and control. Ellul writes, "The devil suggests that Jesus simply accomplish what God sent him to do! Yet, Jesus refuses. He refuses his own temptation to wield universal power rapidly, to wield it himself by taking it."[23] Too often our leadership training has been built upon the ways of this world. Too often we are taught to take control instead of surrender to the Spirit. The desire for control often leads to pragmatism: "If it works, do it!" The problem with pragmatism is that when it becomes the highest goal, we are tempted to accomplish the work of the kingdom by submitting to the god of this world. When we surrender to the Spirit and determine not to find our identity through our accomplishments, we are free to experience the power of God in our lives.

As leaders we can be drawn to imitate the world's idea of leadership by imitating others who "seem" to be accomplishing much for the kingdom. But as we have discovered, many leaders today who have fallen to domineering forms of leadership have used a "command and control" approach, an approach that is ultimately built on sand. When we lead in such a way, we essentially give our soul to the devil. This confirms Girard's and Wink's theories about the principalities: when any institution or organization—church or otherwise—base their authority and power on false transcendency, they inevitably mimic the Domination System, which ends up producing domineering leaders.

Jesus responds to this temptation by saying, "It is written, 'Worship the Lord your God and serve him only'" (Luke 4:8). Nouwen makes the point that the way of Christ is undivided allegiance to his Father. He writes, "As long as we divide our time and energy between God and others, we forget that service outside of God becomes self-seeking, and self-seeking service leads to manipulation, and manipulation to power games, and power games to violence, and violence to destruction—even when it falls under the name of ministry."[24] Nouwen reminds us that the ends never justify the means, that the mission of God can only move forward by *the ways of God*. After all, Jesus is not just the truth and the life but also *the way*. Nouwen writes, "The true challenge is to make service to our neighbor the manifestation and celebration of our total and undivided service to God. Only when all of our service finds its source and goal in God can we be free from the desire for power and proceed to serve our neighbors for their sake and not our own."[25]

When it comes to how power is exercised in community, the good news is that the tower of Babel was reversed at Pentecost. As Stringfellow writes, "Pentecost is the event marking the constitution of the Church in the world," where the church is authorized and empowered by God to live in the world for the sake of the world, free from idolatry and the bondage of death, free to imitate Christ.[26] For Stringfellow,

> The charismatic gifts of the Spirit furnish the only powers to which humans have access against the aggressions of the principalities. These gifts dispel idolatry and free human beings to celebrate Creation, which is, biblically speaking, integral to the worship of God. The gifts equip persons to live humanly in the midst of the Fall. The *exercise of these gifts constitutes the essential tactics of resistance to the power of death.*[27]

We imitate the way of Jesus by operating in the power of the Spirit as under-shepherds of Christ.

THE RELIGIOUS TEMPTATION (IDEOLOGY)

Ellul labels the final temptation an *ideological-religious temptation*. The devil tried to turn the table on Jesus, quoting the Bible, "If you are the Son of God . . . throw yourself down from here. For it is written, 'He will command his angels concerning you to guard you carefully'" (Luke 4:9b–10). Ellul's justification for this label is that this temptation happens at the top of the temple, in the religious setting of Jerusalem. In addition, this is the only temptation where the devil directly quotes from Scripture. This illustrates how ideology can shape a leader's reading and interpretation of Scripture. The Scriptures have been used to justify extreme activities, including slavery and violence of many kinds, but too often there is a lack of awareness of how an ideology can take us captive as leaders in more subtle ways. The very text that was designed to release leaders to love and liberate others, to join God in redeeming all things, is too often used to dominate others. Jesus had to rescue the Scriptures from the hands of the Pharisees and Sadducees, who often used the text as a weapon of oppression instead of an instrument of liberation.

We can see how ideology has misshaped mission, especially in relation to the founding of the United States of America. In his insightful book

Rescuing the Gospel from the Cowboys, author and leader Richard Twiss gives a devasting account of colonization in the past and the present. As a First Nation man, he seeks to lead Native Americans in the work of decolonizing the gospel: "We must progress beyond the narrative of Euro-American imperialism, conquest and assimilation via Christian missions—and move forward as prophetic advocates seeking guidance from our very present Creator made known among us in Jesus, who is the Christ."[28] Reading and interpreting Scripture through the lens of an ideology can misshape us and our mission as we twist Scripture for our own purposes.

Professor and author David Koyzis, in his book *Political Visions and Illusions*, makes the case that ideology is idolatry because ideologies tend to have their own accounts of sin and redemption. As Christian economist and Dutch politician Bob Goudzwaard puts it, "The mature ideology is a false revelation of creation, fall and redemption."[29] Not only do such ideologies have their own soteriology, but they have their own eschatology—their own telos, be it capitalism, liberalism, nationalism, or communism.[30] Like any idol, every ideology seeks ultimate allegiance and promises to save people from some real or perceived evil. The cosmic body of sin (Satan), represented by the world estranged from God, does not simply seek to infect people with ideologies one by one, but instead works at a cosmic level, where the collective mind of nations and complete people groups is taken captive.

One of the ways Girard helps us to recognize if we are unknowingly taken captive by an ideology is by recognizing that every ideology has a scapegoat—someone who can be blamed and cast out of the collective whole in order to regain equilibrium. For Freud, it was the father and the law. For Marx, the bourgeoisie and the capitalist. For Nietzsche, it was slave morality.[31] Ideology scapegoats and demonizes others, creating polarization, cutting off communication and the possibility of reconciliation. The founding murder of America was intertwined with the principality of racism, which is an ideology influencing the collective mind of the nation by the cosmic body of sin. It manifests structurally in many principalities, to the point that, as Eduardo Bonilla-Silva reminds us, "Racism now exists without racists."[32] In this, he is not claiming there are no racists but rather emphasizing the systematic power of racism on all.

If we are captivated by ideologies, it can create divisions in the church. If others look to us as models, they will tend to imitate our malformed desires, to the point that churches start to scapegoat "the other" and segregate by ideology instead of being the one new humanity made possible by Christ's death. While some Christians in America seem captivated by nationalism and conservatism, progressive liberalism mirrors these actions and in turn scapegoats those who are captive to conservatism. If churches become captive to ideologies, the church simply starts to mimic the world and thus no longer remains a faithful witness to God's kingdom. But when life in God and the kingdom of God is the telos of the church, there is room for everyone at the table: Jew and Greek, slave and free, male and female, *conservative* and *progressive*.[33] The antidote to ideology is a proper understanding of the kingdom of God and Jesus' approach to bringing it about. Reflecting on the temptations I reviewed gives insight to this antidote.

The Middle-Eastern Jesus clung to his Father and rightly appropriated the Word of God, which helped him stay faithful to his calling, trusting God even through his death. The Word of God gives the leader discernment in facing the Powers. As Stringfellow writes,

> In the face of death, live humanly. In the middle of chaos, celebrate the Word. Amidst Babel, speak the truth. Confront the noise and verbiage and falsehood of death with the truth and potency and efficacy of the Word of God. Know the Word, teach the Word, nurture the Word, do the Word, live the Word. And more than that, in the Word of God, expose death and all death's works and wiles, rebuke lies, cast out demons, exorcise, cleanse the possessed, raise those who are dead in mind and conscience.[34]

Table 10.1 sums up how the Powers seek to undermine our leadership through the archetypal temptations, suggesting a way to overcome these temptations.

Table 10.1 The Contours of Leadership, Temptations, and Remedy

Contour of Leadership	Temptation	Primary Question	Remedy
Identity	Economic (Image) - Temptation to find our significance in what we do and what we have	Where do we find our significance?	Discovering our identity through abiding in the life of God through the Word of God
Praxis	Political (Institution) - Temptation for security by having a desire to "take control"	How do we use our power?	Surrendering to the Spirit by joining God in bringing the kingdom in the way of Christ
Telos	Religious (Ideology) - Temptation to read Scripture and understand God's mission through a misshaped ideology	How do we understand God's redemptive story?	Living in God and having a healthy view of the kingdom of God

HOW JESUS DEVELOPED HIS SENSE OF SELF

In the temptations of Jesus, we see how the principalities of image, institution, and ideology work to subvert us in the areas of our identity, praxis, and telos. We have seen how the temptations in the wilderness spoke to the source of Jesus' identity. This demonstrates that the battle is for the heart and identity of the leader. So how are we to develop our sense of identity? What does Jesus teach us about this?

It seems that Jesus, in his humanity, needed to develop a sense of self like every other human being. According to mimetic theory, our sense of self is developed through "the other." For Jesus, the other was an undistorted view of his Father. In responding to healing on the Sabbath, Jesus says, "Very truly I tell you, the Son can do nothing by himself; he can do only what he sees his Father doing, because whatever the Father does the Son also does" (John 5:19). In our naivety, the modern self objects, thinking, *Where is Jesus' creativity? He seems so robotic.* The self-made person wonders, *Why simply mimic the Father?* Such thoughts reveal the contemporary false belief that we are not shaped by others.

However, if mimetic desire is true, our desires are indeed borrowed from our models. And this would be true for Jesus in his humanity as well. Girard uses the term *interdividuality* to explain the idea that we find ourselves in the other. Jesus describes this when he says, "Believe me when I say that I am in the Father and the Father is in me" (John 14:11). It seems that the key to defeating the Powers for Jesus was mimicking the Father with dependence on the Spirit. As Jesus desired the Father and received full love and acceptance from him, it created in Jesus a desire to respond in love and loyalty to his Father. As he lived in the Word and the Word lived in him, his desire for the Father and his ways enabled him to resist Satan in the wilderness. Jesus' relationship with the Spirit was clearly evident throughout; as Jesus moved forward in ministry, he did so with the Spirit's power.

The human journey depicted at the fall can be described as trying to find our identity in rivalrous imitation of God. This results in us seeking to find our identity through "the other" or groups of others who are caught in the mimetic trap of the false sacred. When we develop a false self, a self that is built on a sense of belonging through excluding or scapegoating the other, we are on shaky ground. But the new self, as Scott Cowdell reminds us, is a gift that emerges through a process "of conversion away from the desires of others toward the desire of Christ—the ultimate other—so the self is created by the influence of his self."[35] When we are apprehended and captivated by the love and acceptance of God, this new self is constituted by the loving, self-giving, divine one, who now lives within (Gal. 2:20). When we as leaders regularly commune with the Father, Son, and Spirit, our hearts and desires become captivated by this unending dance of mutual love and joy in the divine, which overflows into the lives of our communities. As we commune with God, we receive the mind of Christ and prioritize others above ourselves (Phil. 2:3–4). If those we are discipling look to us as their models, then we serve as mediators for our disciples' desires and sense of self. As our disciples' desires and sense of self come into being through that mediation, reflecting the interdividuality of humanity, our sense of self is subsequently shaped and built through this relationship. Then our sense of self and the desires are created in the disciples, and the sense of self and desires of the leader are shaped reciprocally. Therefore, the more we edify those we disciple, the more we edify ourselves. This positive mimesis is reflected in the gospel promise that whoever loses their life for Christ or others, will find it (Mark 8:35).[36] "Faith is the trust that puts the other first, and hope is the confidence that by doing so one will receive from the other one's true self."[37]

There is only one ultimate source of unending love and joy. Apart from abiding in this source, we can do nothing (John 15:5). For leaders, there is no other foundation that can endure the storms of ministry. When we, as leaders, are apprehended by God's love, we contribute this suffering power of love to the community. The apostle Paul describes this in the thirteenth chapter of his first letter to the Corinthians. It is a love that is patient and kind because there is a deep awareness of the patience and kindness of God. It is *not* a love that envies the other and gets caught in the mimetic cycle, for one's sense of self is found in God. It is not proud and cannot boast, because this radical new life and identity in Christ is received as a gift. This love is not self-seeking, because it has discovered the truth that self-seeking love comes back void, while prioritizing the love for the other has a rich return. Love is not easily angered, because we have a proper view of the patience and kindness of God. It keeps no record of wrongs, because we have confidence in our own forgiveness and are self-aware of our need for forgiveness. "Love does not delight in evil but rejoices with the truth. It always protects, always trusts, always hopes, always perseveres" (1 Cor. 13:6–7).

FORMATION OF DESIRE THROUGH LOCAL EXEMPLARY MODELS

As we seek to ground our identity in God, our selection of models is vital, for our models shape our desires. Mimesis empirically validates the truth that bad company corrupts good character; thus it is important that we, as leaders, not only model ourselves on Jesus but also find local models who seek to imitate Christ by their way of life (1 Cor. 15:33). Cowdell writes, "Abiding faith means drawing our being no longer from others who are living under the sway of the false sacred—chiefly under the power of the commodity form and the life agenda it imposes on the modern West—but, rather, from those who have come under the sway of Christ and his non-rivalistic desire."[38]

Paul's final charge to Timothy in the book of 2 Timothy is instructive here. Timothy is the disciple Paul lifted as an example of kenotic living (Phil. 2:19–22) in the context of leaders who seemed to have fallen into the mimetic cycle (Phil. 4:2). Paul's charge to Timothy in the context of dealing with those clearly under the sway of the false sacred (2 Tim. 3:1–9) is the following: "But as for you, continue in what you have learned and have become convinced of, because you know those from whom you learned it" (2 Tim. 3:14). Paul was being self-referential here. This concept of *knowing those* from whom we learn seems important in the current celebrity culture found in the US church. Podcasts of "famous" preachers sometimes replace local flesh and blood leaders on the ground. Congregants of the megachurch Willow Creek had little to no access to their former leader Bill Hybels. The independent investigation of Willow Creek indicated that Hybels's domineering leadership was felt most acutely and primarily recognized by those in his inner circle because other staff did not have sufficient proximity to him to be able to discern what was happening.

Incarnational leadership is important for today, and the missional conversation advanced the value of incarnational living, but there would also be great benefit in exploring the idea of incarnational discipleship for the development of emerging leaders. Incarnational discipleship—life-on-life learning—is integral to mission and movement in light of how mimetic desire works. Jesus understood the power of positive mimesis, which is why he was devoted to the Twelve.

Professor and author Phil Meadows speaks to this issue in his article "Making Disciples That Renew the Church."[39] Meadows contends that if, instead of trying to *do* church differently, leaders start with the commission to make disciples, this will lead to the renewal of the church. He observes four principles: First, making disciples leads to vital congregations. Second, authentic worship arises from and develops changed lives. Third, if discipleship with transformation of the disciple is foundational, then real fellowship takes place when people are equipped to live in God's presence and follow the lead of the Spirit. Fourth, mission takes place through transformative discipleship of multiplying disciples who are alive to God and who, by word and deed together, help others discover the source of all good things. With discipleship and life transformation prioritized, strategies can follow.

FORMATION OF DESIRES THROUGH DISTANT MODELS

Although it is important to continue to value contributions outside the life-on-life context, both geographically and historically, these must never replace our connection to local leadership. Theology developed in different historical or cultural contexts enables us as, missional leaders, to be more alert to prevailing ideologies that might captivate us in our own historical and geographical contexts. Considering this, it is important to reflect on how we can wisely engage with those who are beyond our immediate contexts. Although every leader is a fragile clay jar (2 Cor. 4:7), and even Paul had not yet become what he desired (Phil. 3:12), Paul did reach the point where he could, with a measure of confidence, call for others to imitate him as he had imitated Christ (1 Cor. 11:1; Phil. 4:9).

In considering the formation of our desires through distant models, it is helpful to return to biography as theology, as commended by James William McClendon.[40] All three of the interlocuters within this book consider biography to be vital. Girard not only studied the works of people such as Dostoevsky and other novelists, he also studied their lives. He discovered a correlation between the transformation of the novelists' lives and the depth of truth revealed in their writing. When I examined the theology of Wink, Girard, and Stringfellow, I also considered their lives. By looking at their biographies, I was able to develop some dominant images that shaped their lives.

Wink's dominant images include *Word made flesh*, *kingdom activist*, and *being human*. Through the life of Girard, we see that his dominant images are that of a *collaborative truth seeker* and *academic apologist*. Through examining Stringfellow, we learned the intensity of being an *incarnational parable* and a *prophetic witness*. Wink, Girard, and Stringfellow are just three examples of distant models. Each of us will develop other distant models that shape us.

It can be helpful to find distant models who exemplify the fivefold ministry (Ephesians 4:11) in different ways. For me in my role as *teacher*, some of my distant models include N. T. Wright, Walter Brueggemann, Sarah Coakley, Ellen Davis, and Willie James Jennings. Amos Yong is a less distant teaching model for me. When it comes to *pastors*, I look to Eugene Peterson, Ruth Haley Barton, Henri Nouwen, and Joan Chittister. Regarding *evangelists*, my models include Lesslie Newbigin, Richard Twiss, David Bosch, and Ruth Padilla DeBorst. For *prophets*, I look to Leonardo Boff, Marva Dawn, David Fitch, and Martin Luther King Jr. I initially had a difficult time finding a model in the category of *apostles*. Apostles often tend to be so active that they do not take the time to write. We probably would not have as many of the Epistles of Paul if he had not spent so much time in prison. But eventually I discovered that Roland Allen and John Wesley were good distant models in this area. Alan Hirsch is a not-so-distant apostolic mentor for me.

I am constantly reading and seeking to find more distant models from the majority world. H. Vinson Synan and Miguel Álvarez have been a great help in pointing me toward theologians in the majority world, along with Allen Yeh, Veli-Matti Kärkkäinen, Henning Wrogemann, and Graham Hill.[41]

SELFLESS LEADERSHIP IN THE PRAXIS OF MISSION

The agenda to develop a life worth imitating also involves the missional leader understanding that power is a gift and must be guided by love. Power can be distorted when used improperly, typically when we as leaders desire control instead of trusting in the power of the Spirit. To demonize power only pushes it underground where it eventually emerges in unhealthy ways. Power shaped by Christ's love brings life. As Andy Crouch writes, "Power is nothing—worse than nothing—without love. But love without power is less than it was meant to be. Love without the capacity to make something of the world, without the ability to respond to and make room for the beloved's flourishing, is frustrated love."[42] He continues, "Love transfigures power. Absolute love transfigures absolute power. And power transfigured by love is power that made and saves the world."[43]

It is important for us, as missional leaders, to develop a healthy view of power.[44] An agenda for developing missional leaders worthy of imitation involves a kenotic spirituality that leads them into mission by the power of love.[45] Having a holy love affair with God is not only the root solution to the problem of idolatry, but it is also what motivates us for mission. Paul writes, "For Christ's love compels us, because we are convinced that one died for all, and therefore all died. And he died for all, that those who live should no longer live for themselves but for him who died for them and was raised again" (2 Cor. 5:14–15). Reflecting on holistic mission in this evil age dominated by the Powers, N. T. Wright speaks of the role of suffering:

> Those who are eager for "bringing the kingdom," for social and cultural renewal in our day, can easily forget that the revolution that began on the cross only works through the cross. And those who are eager to "save souls for heaven" are likely to regard suffering simply as something through which most of us some of the time and some of us most of the time will have to pass, rather than as something by means of which the rescuing love of God is poured out into the world. The latter is closer to the mark. "The blood of the martyrs is the seed of the church." This well-known quotation from the African theologian Tertullian, writing around AD 200, reflects the early Christian perception that suffering and dying for the faith is not simply a necessary evil, the inevitable concomitant of following a way that the world sees as dangerously subversive. Suffering and dying is *the way by which the world is changed*. This is how the revolution continues.[46]

When we experience the love of Christ in our life, it leads us to be on mission with a sacrificial love. When the love of God is our motivation for mission, it will be reflected in our praxis.

One shining example of kenotic love in the history of the church is St. Francis, who lived in the medieval period of church history, when Christendom reigned. He demonstrates that there has always been a faithful remnant through the ages who have not bent their knee to Baal. In a post-Christendom era, where people are skeptical of power and truth, learning to genuinely embody the good news is imperative. St. Francis lived this kind of life. With the Gospels as his rule of life, he sought to follow in Jesus' footsteps. He was a peacemaker who loved his enemies, traveled light, welcomed strangers, loved the outcasts, loved the environment, and lived in *communitas*.[47] Francis understood the concepts of reciprocity and *communitas*, which is why he called his order *Little Brothers*. In naming his order this and never becoming a priest, he demonstrated his desire to have no father superior, as was common in religious orders of his time. To Francis, God alone was Father, and all others were brothers and sisters. Francis believed that the only privilege was in having no privilege. He felt that Jesus, being in his very nature God, became flesh and claimed no special rights. Therefore, if Jesus rejected the privileges of God, how much more should the Little Brothers live in kinship with all people? In his letter to all the faithful he writes,

> We should never desire to be above others, but ought rather to be servants and subject "to every human creature for God's sake." And the spirit of the Lord shall rest upon all those who do these things and who persevere to the end, and He shall make His abode and dwelling in them, and they shall be children of the Heavenly Father whose works they do, and they are the spouses, brothers and mothers of our Lord Jesus Christ.[48]

Francis would often put himself under the leadership of one of the other Little Brothers, thus he was not only influenced by his Little Brothers but he also influenced them by way of humble example.[49] Even now, eight hundred years after his death, he is memorialized by the three religious orders he inspired, which include at least a million members today, both Catholic and protestant.[50] What was it about this man that has prompted so many to commend him? Marina Warner says, "The Franciscan spirit continues to be considered, by agnostics and atheists as well as believers, as the most genuine expression of Christ's teaching ever approved by the Vatican."[51]

Many who study the life of St. Francis have a difficult time understanding him. As the publishers of G. K. Chesterton's biography of Francis say, "He [Francis] was a man who loved women but vowed himself to chastity; an artist who loved the pleasures of the natural world as few have loved them, but vowed to himself to the most austere poverty, stripping himself naked in the public square so all could see that he had renounced his worldly goods; a clown who stood on his head in order to see the world aright."[52] G. K. Chesterton suggests that there is only one way to explain a person like this:

And for the modern reader the clue to asceticism and all the rest can best be found in the stories of lovers when they seemed to be rather like lunatics. Tell his life as a tale of one of the Troubadours, and the wild things he would do for his lady, and the whole modern puzzle disappears. In such a romance there would be no contradiction between the poet gathering flowers in the sun and enduring a freezing vigil in the snow, between his praising all earthly and bodily beauty and then refusing to eat, between glorifying gold and purple and perversely going in rags, between his showing pathetically a hunger for a happy life and a thirst for a heroic death. All these riddles would easily be resolved in the simplicity of any noble love; only this was so noble a love that nine men out of ten have hardly ever heard of it . . . The reader cannot even begin to see the sense of a story that may well seem to him a very wild one, until he understands that to this great mystic his religion was not a thing like a theory but a thing like a love-affair.[53]

St. Francis lived a life worth imitating. His identity was *re*formed by the love of God, and his telos was life in God and the kingdom of God. His identity and telos shaped his kenotic use of power (praxis) as he lived on mission. Thus his legacy of discipleship continues to this day. The contemporary church has much to learn from faithful examples such as Saints Francis, Benedict, and Ignatius—each of whom dismissed the false narratives and ideologies of their age that sought to take people captive.

In the final chapters of this book, by examining the book of Philippians through a Girardian lens, I will explore what it means to be a kenotic leader. Finally, I will look at how the Lord's Prayer can shape each of us to become a kenotic leader like St. Francis. The scandal of leadership can be turned on its head by following the scandalous way of Jesus.

11

A NEW WAY OF BEING AND BELONGING

Author Larry Crabb writes,

> Community matters. Just as our lungs require air, so our souls require what only community provides. We are designed by our Trinitarian God to live in relationship with each other. Without it we die. It's that simple. Without a community where we know, explore, discover and touch one another, we experience isolation and despair that drives us in wrong directions, and corrupts our efforts to live meaningfully and to love well.[1]

As human beings, we are born with the need to belong, and our belonging is tied to our sense of being: who we are and who we become. We are not isolated selves; we were born dependent on our parents, and we mature by moving from dependence to independence and eventually to interdependence. The relationships we form with others have profound effects on our lives, and because of mimetic desire, we will ultimately become like the people closest to us. This is why Scripture tells us that if we walk with the wise, we will become wise (Prov. 13:20) and that bad company corrupts good character (1 Cor. 15:33).

In these last two chapters, I will explore the book of Philippians to help us understand how our sense of being is developed by the group in which we feel the strongest sense of belonging. In this chapter I will look at the letter of Philippians as a whole—considering the context in which it was written, our current day context, key themes, its purpose, and a proposed outline—with the goal of cultivating a kenotic spirituality through the Christ hymn (Phil. 2:5–11) so that we can learn what it means to be kenotic leaders. I will look in detail at this hymn—or what professor and author Nijay Gupta calls an "Ode to Christ"—in the final chapter of the book. Exploring Philippians as a whole will help us to understand this poem, hymn, or narrative in the context of Paul's letter. Although I have consulted a number of scholarly works and commentaries, this is not intended to be a verse-by-verse commentary, nor does it seek to engage all of the current scholarly debates. My goal is to draw out significant themes in the letter through a Girardian lens, appreciating these themes in their original context with the aim to bring them to life in ours.[2]

In these final chapters, I will also be addressing the contours of missional leadership—in particular, the formation of our identities in community. Because we are story-formed and story-sharing people, I will share some stories in these final chapters, some of them personal.[3] Stories open us up to new dimensions; they tap into our emotions, our imaginations, our senses, and experiences. If faith were merely a concept, then a focus on intellect alone would make sense, but because faith is lived, we need stories that show how faith is embodied. Stories help to reform our desires.

As we get to the end of these final chapters, my hope is that we will learn some new ways of thinking, imagining, being, and belonging in which God transports us from the domain of death to the domain of life, living as resident aliens in this world. The domain of death is ordinary consciousness, status anxiety, mimetic rivalry, fragmented self, living in shame and unworthiness, in fear of death. The domain of life—which we enter by the Spirit, through the portal of grace—is where we become intoxicated with God and experience an aroused consciousness as well as an integrated self, free from status anxiety. It is where we are others-oriented and self-giving, with no fear of death, and inhabiting life as citizens of heaven on earth (Phil. 3:20).

A LOOK AT PHILIPPIANS THROUGH THE LENS OF GIRARD

Before diving into the themes of this letter, I will first consider its author, context, flow, and potential purposes.

ABOUT THE AUTHOR

The letter to the Philippians is considered to be one of the undisputed letters of the apostle Paul. Although not many argue against his authorship, it is not uncommon for scholars, philosophers, theologians, playwrights, historians, filmmakers, feminists, and writers to "scapegoat" the apostle Paul for his ideas. Though many in history have sought to scapegoat him, the criticisms are often built upon their interpretation of his ideas rather than the authorial intent of his writings.[4] I certainly have been skeptical of his writings in different seasons of my life. But when I have tried to scapegoat Paul, it was often my misconception of his ideas and thoughts that I was scapegoating. Even the apostle Peter found some of his letters hard to understand (2 Pet. 3:15–16). Theologians such as N. T. Wright, Michael Gorman, Robert Hamerton-Kelly, and others have been instrumental dialogue partners regarding Paul.[5] Wright helped alleviate some of my own trepidation regarding Paul's writings with his counsel to interpret Paul through Jesus prior to interpreting Jesus through Paul.[6]

Whether we seek to scapegoat Paul or consider him a theological hero, most agree that Paul experienced radical transformation in his life. Saul (before his name was changed to Paul) experienced a conversion on the road to Damascus (Acts 9:1–22). He was made blind in order to see how his understanding of God through his interpretation of Scripture made him captive to sacred violence, which he used to justify his participation in profound violence against the early church (Phil. 3:6a). Paul believed he was on God's mission based on God's Word, but during his conversion, he discovered he was persecuting Christ. As I discussed in chapters six and seven, Girard makes the case that whenever we get caught in the mimetic cycle—justifying our violence against another group through the scapegoat mechanism— we can be confident that we have become captive to ideology and fallen to the schemes of the devil. Succumbing to an ideological reading of Scripture is a temptation we all face—and as I noted in chapter ten, an ideological reading of Scripture was the third temptation Jesus successfully overcame: the religious temptation.

Jesus' strongest rebukes came to religious leaders who claimed to speak for God and yet excluded people from God's universal love.[7] We learn from the life of Jesus that God is a nonviolent God who comes to save us from the historical cycle of violence, in which we scapegoat the other and justify ourselves through our own sense of righteousness.

As I stated in the introduction to this chapter, individuals form their identities through the groups in which they find their greatest sense of belonging. We have seen throughout history that groups, countries, and institutions establish their fragmented identities based upon making other groups the enemy. But whenever we establish our sense of identity over and against another group, we can be sure we have left the path of Jesus, who became the forgiving victim in order that we no longer need to scapegoat others and justify our use of violence against the other.[8] In his conversion, Paul came to understand this. He wrote the letter to the Philippians from prison and demonstrated his love to those who unjustly threw him in jail. Paul learned enemy love and was able to withstand an incredible amount of violence through his union with Christ. In fact, the suffering he experienced at the hands of others seemed to be redeemed through his ecstatic experiences with Christ (Phil. 3:10–11). After Paul's conversion, he started to live differently: he could no longer kill his enemy in the name of God. His three days of blindness helped him to recognize his complicity to violence as well as the universal complicity to violence that we all share.[9] As the founder of the church in Philippi, Paul wanted to help the church understand that if they were to fully take hold of their identities as citizen of heaven (Phil. 3:20), their sense of being and belonging could have no other foundation than the forgiving victim—Jesus Christ.

At the time of this writing, Russia is in the throes of invading Ukraine, and the world is watching the unfolding events with horror. I recently spoke to Ruslan, one of my many Ukrainian friends. Ruslan was forced to send his wife and two children to Poland for their safety, but he was unable to join them because Ukrainian men between the ages of eighteen and sixty are required by law to stay. Ruslan shared with me some of the evils he and his friends were facing, including the wild dogs that were beginning to eat the flesh of the faces of the dead left to rot in the street. They feared that those dogs could become accustomed to eating human flesh and in their hunger start to attack living people. Despite being a firsthand witness to such atrocities on his doorstop, after listening to what President Vladimir Putin was saying to the Russian people only a few times, Ruslan found himself trusting what Putin had to say. He was convinced that if he listened to this propaganda long enough, he would believe Putin 100 percent. This is the power of propaganda: it keeps us in a mimetic cycle in which we build our sense of identity around a common enemy.

Ruslan found himself with nowhere to belong, confused about what to do and confused about his identity. He did not want to enlist in the Ukrainian army because he believes that, according to Scripture and the life of Jesus, it is not right to kill. But to be accepted as one of his people during this time, killing is necessary. In fact, in our dominant Western culture, it would be considered the honorable thing to do.

Our place of belonging determines our identity and rationality.[10] In other words, we become a somebody through the group to which we belong, and our perception of what is real news and what is fake news is often determined by the group in which we find our sense of belonging. As adults, our strongest places of belonging are with the groups of our choosing. For some, this is a country, which often means our belonging and identity is developed over and against another nation (e.g., "America First"), which can make us prone to violence. For others, our identity is found in belonging to "the deplorables" or the "woke" community, over and against the other, becoming mimetic doubles and entering the mimetic trap.[11]

Yet Paul understood that through Jesus' life, death, and resurrection, he enacted a new way of belonging, bringing together a universal body of people with a politic that revolves around a forgiving victim instead of a common enemy (Eph. 2:11–22). This universal body, which is open to all, has only one entrance: repentance. At the heart of this repentance is a confession of our own complicity in building an identity through the exclusion of our neighbor. The one entrance into the universal body of Christ, this new humanity, is to receive forgiveness from the One who laid down his life for us, for *all* of our neighbors, for the whole world. When we see this, we realize that because of Jesus' willing sacrifice, we have a new way to establish our sense of being, because we have a new way of belonging. Yet because of the pathological ways of belonging we have inherited as human beings, these old ways of belonging come back to haunt us. Thus Paul wanted to remind those in Philippi of life-transforming truths that resonate with our sense of being and belonging. Although he would have loved to share his thoughts with them in person, he had to settle for a letter, because he was literally chained to a guard, with the threat of death hanging over him (Phil. 1:12–26).

THE CONTEXT IN PHILIPPI

Understanding the context in which Paul addressed the church in Philippi is critical to interpreting his letter well. "The ancient city of Krenides was renamed 'Philippi' in 358 BCE when Philip II of Macedonia (the father of Alexander the Great) took control of the city. About two centuries later, it came under Roman rule."[12] As a Roman colony in the first century, it not only had the privileges of low taxation but also adopted the culture of Rome. Approximately ten thousand people lived in Philippi, with another five thousand living in the suburbs.[13] Using a sophisticated model, theologian Peter Oakes estimates that the population of Philippi would have "something like 37 per cent service groups, 20 per cent slaves, 20 per cent colonist farmers (10 per cent owning all their land, 10 per cent renting), 20 per cent poor, 3 per cent élite. All these figures include any family members."[14] The poor ranged from beggars to those trying to sell wood or some other commodity for existence. Regardless of how they made money, their income was below subsistence level.[15]

One of the defining marks of a Roman colony was the priority placed on status. "Throughout the Greek East, the arrival of Rome reinforced the importance of status and made the hierarchy of status more rigid. The maintenance of status and the proper observation of distinctions of status were imperatives of society. At Philippi, they would be particularly seen as imperatives of the Roman social order in the town."[16] There was no middle class—simply the elite and non-elite.[17] "The elite class subdivided into three aristocratic orders: senators, equestrians, and local municipal decurions."[18] There were subdivisions within these orders, as well as many divisions in the non-elites, because the Roman world loved to clearly define where someone was on the social ladder. Public expression of rank was displayed through attire, occupation, seating at public events and at banquets, and the legal system.[19]

In Philippi, there was therefore a preoccupation with honor, prestige, and reputation. Rome's *cursus honorum* was a pathway to move up the social ladder in the hope of gaining a greater reputation. The senatorial *cursus* in Rome was not left to chance but was a well-defined ascent. Honor was a dominant value that gave one a sense of identity; it was the preeminent public commodity, determined by the "larger social group to which an individual belonged."[20] It started with a noble birth, then wealth, then someone's legal status. *The cursus honorum* was essentially a race for honor and glory. "Apparently no aspect of life—not even the interpretation of dreams—was immune to the effects of what [professor of history] Lendon has labeled 'the deep structure' of honor and hierarchy in the Roman world."[21] This competition for honor was ingrained in Philippi, both among the elite and non-elite. Scholar Joseph Hellerman writes, "Rome was the most status-oriented society in Mediterranean antiquity. And no city in the Greek East was more Roman—and thus more preoccupied with honorary titles, public recognition, and social status—than the veteran colony at Philippi."[22] And the "Christians in the colony would hardly have been immune to these social pressures."[23]

OUR CURRENT CONTEXT

Of course, we are not immune to these social pressures either. Alain de Botton identifies five causes for *status anxiety* in our time: lovelessness, expectation, meritocracy, snobbery, and dependence.[24] Botton defines status as one's value and importance in the world.[25] And in part, status anxiety is the following:

> A worry, so pernicious as to be capable of ruining extended stretches of our lives, that we are in danger of failing to conform to the ideals of success laid down by our society and that we may as a result be stripped of dignity and respect; a worry that we are currently occupying too modest a rung or are about to fall to a lower one.[26]

It is our *desire* for status that can bring sorrow and great anxiety.

The first cause of status anxiety, according to Botton, is our need for love and our desire for status. He notes that every life can be defined by two great love stories: the first is our quest for sexual love; the second is our quest "for love from the world," which is "a more secret and shameful tale."[27] He suggests that the predominant impulse behind our desire to climb in social hierarchy may be rooted more in our desires to be loved and valued by others than in the material goods we accrue or the power we wield.[28] He writes, "Our sense of identity is held by the judgements of those we live among."[29] He continues, "If they are amused by our jokes, we grow confident in our power to amuse. If they praise us, we develop an impression of high merit."[30] Conversely, the absence of such love or appreciation from others can cause us to feel self-doubt or worthlessness. Jesus describes our proneness to status anxiety when speaking of the Pharisees who did not believe in him: "For they loved human praise more than the praise from God" (John 12:43). Our desire for human praise and love adds to our status anxiety.

The second reason for status anxiety, according to Botton, is that we have higher expectations in life than our ancestors did. Although the West has seen enormous progress in wealth, food supply, the ability to stamp out diseases, scientific knowledge, life expectancy, security, and economic opportunity, there has been "a rise in the level of status anxiety among ordinary Western citizens, by which is meant a rise in levels of concern about importance, achievement and income."[31] According to Botton, the "War of Independence" forever changed the basis on which we build our sense of status. Instead of our status primarily being ascribed according to our birth and family lineage, it has become more dynamic, primarily determined in direct proportion to our achievements, largely in the financial realm.[32]

In ancient times, the chasm between the elite and non-elite was impossible to cross. In the past, inequality was viewed as fair and part of the natural order of the world. But the possibility of equality brought greater expectations for achievement. We are given unlimited expectations through self-help books, motivational speakers, self-made millionaires, and the mass media—all of which have increased our status anxiety. Botton highlights how William James makes the case that "the rise in our level of expectations entails a rise in the dangers of humiliation."[33] This rise in expectations creates a gap between "who we might be, and who we really are."[34] This disparity creates a sense that we are deprived, whereas in times gone by, people were satisfied as long as they had a roof over their head, food to eat, and some recreational time. In this culture of high expectations, we tend to attribute our worth in comparison to those in similar stations in life. We are more likely to feel envious of those who are our "equals" if they excel more than us. High expectations create a perpetual status anxiety because of the difference of who we are and who we think we should or can be.

The third reason for status anxiety today is a reversal of the moral status of both the rich and the poor. In the pre-Enlightenment era there existed a mutual dependence between the nobility and the peasantry, but then, through the influence of the Romantics and Marxist ideology, Western society opposed the rich who exploited the poor. However, by the eighteenth century, the powers of social Darwinism and meritocracy embedded a social imaginary in which to be poor was considered shameful and dishonorable.

The fourth reason for status anxiety in our day is snobbery. We do not want to be looked down on by snobs. A snob is "someone offended by the lack of high status in *others*, a person who believes in a flawless equation between social rank and human worth."[35] Snobs look down on us if we hold a lower rank in society. Botton writes, "If poverty is the customary material penalty for low status, then neglect and faraway looks are the emotional penalties that a snobbish world appears unable to stop imposing on those bereft of the symbols of importance."[36] We all know that classic high school scene in which the uppity popular group looks down on the rest. When someone of "lower rank" comes to sit at their table, the leader of the group leaves and all follow, leaving the one person to sit by themselves in utter shame. Unfortunately, snobbery does not end in high school. This is why the apostle Paul writes to the Romans, "Do not be proud, but be willing to associate with people of low position" (Rom. 12:16b). In other words, do not be a snob.

The fifth and final factor that creates status anxiety for us today is what Botton calls "dependence." In other words, our current status is fragile—there are many things that lie outside of our control. As we have seen, in traditional society, high status was inherited—determined by birth—and therefore difficult to lose. But in our current context, Botton reminds us that status is typically gained through achievement, most often our financial achievement. Because of this, our status becomes more precarious. The invisible hand of the economy creates a little more uncertainty. Botton writes, "Anxiety is the handmaiden of contemporary ambition, for our livelihoods and esteem rest on at least five unpredictable elements, offering us five good reasons never to count on either attaining or holding on to our desired position within the hierarchy."[37]

The five unpredictable elements we depend on are the following:

1. *Talent.* But our talent can be fickle and difficult to direct at will, and therefore, it does not always help us achieve as we want.
2. *Luck.* Being in the right place at the right time, or meeting the right people, is circumstantial and often comes down to luck.
3. *An employer.* We can never guarantee that our employer's priorities correspond with ours, and we can never be sure of how long we will be employed in a role or who else might compete against us for particular roles.
4. *The profitability of the employer.* In a fast-changing, highly competitive world, companies under financial stress may need to let people go, sometimes those with high rank. The impending revolution in artificial intelligence will likely only exacerbate this.[38]
5. *The global economy.* We live in a world where what happens on the other side of the globe can have huge economic ramifications. The coronavirus pandemic demonstrated the anxiety this creates. Geopolitical wars also add to the uncertainty of the economic future.

Although our context differs in many ways from the context of Philippi, we are still human. Our desire for status, prestige, and honor has been mimetically passed down to us. We still suffer from status anxiety. Too often our self-worth is connected to our net worth. And the church is not immune to this. The celebrity status evident in the North American church—and other parts of the world—verifies our hunger and struggle for honor and status. For example, when there is a special city-wide event, the selection of the speaker, the allocation of honorable seats, and the person asked to pray create mimetic rivalry among leaders. It is not unusual for churches in the same neighborhood and city to view each other competitively instead of cooperatively. Boasting of accomplishments is not just expected in publishing, academia, and other areas; it is ingrained in the system. We are not much different from our forbearers. The principality of *image* is still alive and well.

Hellerman writes, "Excavations at Philippi have produced the most detailed inscriptions found anywhere in the Roman empire outlining the various honors enjoyed by the residents of a local municipality."[39] And although this was expected among the elites, this influenced the whole population in Philippi, where anyone "who could scrape together the resources necessary to erect an inscription of some kind apparently felt the need to publicly proclaim his achievements."[40] What might those a thousand of years from now discover about us, as they uncover our archeological artifacts?

THE PURPOSE OF THE LETTER TO THE PHILIPPIANS

This letter has many purposes—including an update of how their friends and servants Paul, Timothy, and Epaphroditus were doing, in addition to thanking the congregation for their generous financial gifts. However, it seems that the heart of this letter was a reminder to the church at Philippi of the matters of *being and belonging* to this colony of heaven so they might shine like stars and their colony of heaven might become a greater reality on earth. The elements of *being and belonging* to this colony of heaven on earth are related, because our sense of being, our identity, is only discovered relationally through the social other. Paul understood the power of imitation, thus his entire discourse elevated good models and warned against poor ones, encouraging the congregation to imitate the models that would allow them to experience life, even amid suffering (Phil. 3:17). The ultimate model is, of course, Christ himself, who did not try to grasp his sense of identity for himself but received it from his self-giving Father.

In the midst of growing disunity in the community, where the mimetic rivalry of the leaders (4:2) was contributing to the rivalry in the community (2:1–4), Paul was reminding his friends in Philippi that they belonged to Christ, the non-rivalrous Other who makes possible another way of belonging with each other. We no longer need to strive to find significance and create a sense of self through rivalry, over and against the other, for this is to remain in the domain of death. But since Christ conquered death through self-giving love, we can receive our identity from him and live in the domain of life. Because we belong to Christ, we can actualize, by faith through hope, the possibility of finding ourselves through the self-giving way of Christ. For it is only when we, in self-giving love, honor the other more than ourselves that we end up receiving the honor that comes from God. We are transformed *within* ourselves through our relationship with God and other people. Thus Paul was encouraging them by faith to lift the other up, for it is in lifting the other up that God lifts us up.

OUTLINE OF PHILIPPIANS THROUGH A GIRARDIAN LENS

Although our goal is to cultivate a kenotic spirituality through the Christ hymn (Phil. 2:5–11) so that we can learn what it means to be kenotic leaders, having a sense of Paul's rhetorical approach will prove helpful. Epaphroditus, who was at the time ministering to Paul in prison, was to take the letter to the church and read it to the entire congregation. It seems that Paul may have been using a deliberative rhetoric to persuade the Philippians to make decisions about the course they would take in their lives.[41] Building on the insights of scholars Ben Witherington III, Corné J. Bekker, Michael Bird, and Nijay K. Gupta, along with others, my outline will mostly follow in their path, with an attempt to bring a Girardian perspective to the outline.[42]

In the outline below, the dotted lines are intended to indicate the heart of Paul's letter to the Philippians (the middle section constitutes the vast majority of the letter), the indentations are to highlight the flow of his argument, and the italicized words are to emphasize my Girardian approach. It is important to absorb this outline, as it not only shows the flow of Paul's thinking but it also helps put the themes we will address in perspective.

1:1–2   Greetings from Paul and Timothy as *Slaves* of Christ
1:3–11   Warm Joyful Prayers for Paul's Friends—the Philippians
1:12–26   The Unstoppable Gospel *Modeled* through a Chained Prisoner—Paul
- - - - - - - - - - - - - -

1:27–30   Being and Belonging as Kingdom Citizens in the Midst of Adversity
    2:1–4   Remember Whose and Whom You Are—A New Way of Being and Belonging
        2:5–11   The *Ultimate Kenotic Model*—Jesus Christ
        2:12–18   Live Out What God Is Working In
        2:19–24   Timothy as *Kenotic Model*
        2:25–30   Epaphroditus as *Kenotic Model*
    3:1–4a   *Anti-models* to Being and Belonging
        3:4a–16   Paul as *Kenotic Model*
        3:17–19   Your Choice of *Models* Determines Your Fate
3:20–4:1   Being and Belonging as Kingdom Citizens

PASSAGES THAT HAVE SHAPED HISTORY

Before diving into the themes of Philippians, it is worthwhile to consider what theologian Markus Bockmuehl labels the effective history of Philippians.[43] He proposes that instead of just fusing the two horizons of the text—the ancient and modern—and then considering our current application, we first examine how the text has been received and applied in the history of the church. In other words, to bridge the gap between the ancient text and what is speaks to us today, we could ask, "How has this piece of Scripture made a concrete difference in the history of the church, how has it shaped people's thoughts, convictions and actions, or how has it failed to shape the church?"[44]

Of course, the letter to the Philippians has held a special place in the church in that it became part of the canon of Scripture. But which parts of Philippians seemed to have shaped the church more significantly? Bockmuehl mentions three of the most influential passages in Philippians.

THE NON-IMPORTANCE OF DEATH

The first influential passage is in Philippians 1, where Paul is reflecting on the possibility of his own martyrdom. He writes,

> For to me, to live is Christ and to die is gain. If I am to go on living in this body, this will mean fruitful labor for me. Yet what shall I choose? I do not know! I am torn between the two: I desire to depart and be with Christ, which is better by far; but it is more necessary for you that I remain in the body.
>
> PHIL. 1:21-24

Bockmuehl considers this passage to be the most important in the New Testament in relation to the notion that the Christian passes "directly through death to the afterlife."[45] He writes, "Thus death as gain and as going to be with the Lord is a constant theme in the Church Fathers, beginning with Clement of Rome, Polycarp, and Ignatius's letter to Rome (6.1). Phil. 1.23 is repeatedly quoted and alluded to in Tertullian, Origen and the Cappadocian Fathers."[46] This theme of death as gain because it means presence with the Lord has become "almost universal commonplace."[47]

Bockmuehl notes how this theme is found in the *Imitation of Christ* by Thomas à Kempis, Milton's *Paradise Lost*, and Richard Baxter's *Dying Thoughts*, which Baxter wrote for his "own comfort in facing death."[48] It also became a popularly preached passage during the Puritan Revival in New England.[49] Its relevance to the theme of martyrdom "can readily be illustrated with examples from Ignatius of Antioch all the way to contexts of persecution in the twentieth century."[50]

Paul was able to overcome the fear of death by reflecting on the crucified and risen Christ. Jesus knew he was destined to die. It was a deliberate choice, one that was made in his deep understanding of and desire for his Father, who knew not death. Jesus' vision of the everlasting, loving God enabled him to go to the cross in the midst of our death-based culture. Jesus allowed us to kill him as a way to show us how to escape a culture based on death, "allowing us to come to be what God always wanted us to be, that is, utterly and absolutely alive with him."[51] If we fear death, we are likely still bound to the domain of death. Paul did not fear death but looked at death as the means to life. By passing through death, Jesus demonstrates for us that death does not define ultimate reality.

Philippians 1:21–24 has been a life passage for me. There have been at least two times where death was staring me in the face as a Christ-follower. One time was when I picked up a hitchhiker. We were discussing his beliefs, and he told me he was an Aryan, misusing some verses in 1 Peter 2 as justification. In an attempt to correct his understanding, I pulled my car over in a half circle in Columbus, Ohio. As I was reaching into the back seat for my Bible, he put a gun to my head. I told him he did not have anything to fear; I was just getting my Bible. He put his gun back, and my heart started to beat again. God helped me to love this man, share with him, and even invite him to come with me to the hotel in which I was staying. God gave me the grace to not fear death. It led to this man's salvation later that week.

Another such occasion was when I was in Richmond, Virginia. I desired to share the gospel with at least one person a day, so I was spending time at the park at Virginia Commonwealth University (VCU), praying that God would provide the opportunity. There I encountered a student I was able to share the gospel with. He needed a place to stay, as he was traveling through Richmond, so I invited him to come with me. Because those I was staying with did not want to host a stranger, I decided to take him with me to my parents' home in northern Virginia. But it was getting late, and my finances were limited, so we decided to find a place to park and just sleep in the car for the night. As we were parking, he told me that he knew some people he thought needed to hear the gospel. But he warned me that they might want to kill me.

It was getting close to 1:00 a.m., and I was ruffled by his warning, so I told him we could go in the morning. Though I fully intended to share the gospel with these people, I still was disturbed by my hesitation. Feeling nervous, I told him I was going to take a walk, and as I was walking around town, the Philippians 1:21 passage came to my mind: "For to me, to live is Christ and to die is gain." Although I had recently preached on the passage, I was not fully believing it. I knew that to die would mean meeting Jesus face-to-face, which would be amazing, but at that moment, all I could think about were my earthly fears: *Nobody even knows where I am. And what about my ministry at Virginia Tech?* I sensed God saying in a gentle voice, "So do you like your ministry more than me?" I had to admit that at that moment I did. Somehow ministry had started to be my mistress, and I had lost my first love. Faced with this realization, I broke down in tears and repented. In the morning, I asked my new friend to take me to these people, but he had changed his mind.

These two different "brushes with death" taught me something about myself and my sense of identity. In the first instance, where I was given the grace to be bold in the face of death, my deepest sense of belonging was in Christ. Thus, even though my heart was racing, I was not moved by death and continued to minister to my new friend. In the second instance, where I was hesitant to share with those who might kill me, it seemed my desire to be "successful in ministry" was more important to me than Jesus. My sense of belonging was more dictated by others and how I was perceived. I had slipped into the mimetic trap, where my desire for the applause of people (status anxiety) had become greater than my desire for God. And although I was not able to share with those people, even though I had awakened willing to do so, God taught me an important lesson. Like Paul, I needed to learn how to "die daily" when it came to seeking approval from others and instead seek approval from God. The kenotic journey is not a one-and-done deal but a daily pilgrimage.

Jesus said, "My command is this: Love each other as I have loved you. Greater love has no one than this: to lay down one's life for one's friends. You are my friends if you do what I command (John 15:12–14). Reflecting on these verses, Girardian theologian James Alison writes,

> Jesus is saying something like this: "I am going to my death to make possible for you a model of creative practice which is not governed by death. From now on this is the only commandment which counts: that you should live your lives as a creative overcoming of death, showing that you are prepared to die because you are not moved by death, and you are doing this to make possible a similar living out for your friends. The measure in which they are your friends is the degree

in which, thanks to the perception which they have of your creative acting out of a life beyond the rule of death, they come to have their imagination expanded in the same way, and they too become capable of entering into this creative living out of a life that is not ruled by death."[52]

Alison helps us understand that, as Christ-followers, if we model a life in which we do not fear death, it can give courage to those who look up to us to imitate us and do the same.

ODE TO CHRIST

The second passage Bockmuehl notes as particularly significant in the history of the church is Philippians 2:5–11. Bockmuehl writes, "Perhaps no other Pauline pericope has been the subject of such sustained critical attention over the past thirty years of New Testament study; the bibliography of scholarly books and articles amounts to several hundred entries." There are multiple scholarly debates regarding this text. Is it Pauline or pre-Pauline? Is it a hymn, poem, or poetic narrative? Is the function of the passage ethical or kerygmatic—in other words, is Paul providing an ethical example for the Philippians to follow, or is he giving a summary statement of Christ's incarnation?

Although these remain hotly debated issues, Bockmuehl mentions the "far more wide-ranging formative importance which the passage has in fact had in the history of Christian doctrine, life and worship."[53] His research indicates that this is one of the "most influential passages in patristic literature, beginning with the Apostolic Fathers, Justin, Melito, Tertullian, Irenaeus and Clement of Alexandria."[54] This passage was key for the development of the two natures of Christ (divine and human). "The Fathers since Tertullian use this passage to stress the personal relevance of Christ's loving obedience at the cross for the individual Christian and for the Church."[55] And the example of the obedience of Christ "served repeatedly as an inspiration to martyrs."[56] The kenosis in this passage provided fertile theological soil through which Gregory of Nyssa and Cyril of Alexandria regularly ploughed. "There are also well over 30 significant choral arrangements based on Phil. 2:5–11, including many by famous composers such as Palestrina, Anton Bruckner, and Healey Willan."[57] The earliest reference to this passage was Polycarp's letter to the Philippians, and for "Irenaeus, the Christology of this verse was integral to the Rule of Faith, and defined the very purpose of the Parousia."[58] My hope, after looking at some other themes, is to look at this ode to Christ in order to cultivate a kenotic spirituality that allows us to become healthier missional leaders.

CITIZENS OF HEAVEN

The final passage Bockmuehl says has left a strong impression on the historical church is found in Philippians 3:20, where Paul reminds the saints in Philippi that "our citizenship is in heaven." Bockmuehl writes, "Beginning with the early patristic period, this passage (in practice inseparable from Phil. 1:27) has had an enormous influence on Christian attitudes to live in this world."[59] He mentions how Polycarp and Clement of Rome encouraged the Philippians and Corinthians to practice "the conduct of those who live without regrets as citizens in the city of God."[60] This passage was cited often in the patristic literature, especially in connection with passages that remind us that we are pilgrims and resident aliens.

The idea of "resident aliens" is a term used in Peter's first letter and is an important way for us to understand our identity (1 Pet. 2:11). It reminds us we are to pray for God's kingdom to become more real on earth (resident)—as it is in heaven—but also to remember that we are aliens, in the sense that we are not to live according to the ways of the world. Being a resident alien reminds us that although earth is our ultimate home (Rev. 21:1–5), we are to live in the world for the sake of the world in the way of Christ. As we learn the way of Christ (Phil. 2:5–11), it may seem scandalous, but we are to remember the words of Jesus, "Blessed is anyone who does not stumble on account of me" (Matt. 11:6), which, with our Girardian lens, means "Blessed is anyone who is not scandalized on account of me."

THEMES OF PHILIPPIANS

As I mentioned, there seems to be no singular purpose to Paul's letter. Paul was updating the Philippians on his imprisonment, thanking them for their generosity, letting them know how their friend Epaphroditus was doing, warning them of the enemies of the cross, as well as encouraging and consoling them in the midst of their suffering—inspiring them even to receive suffering as a gift. It is clear that Paul wanted the Philippians to know that the advancement of the gospel was what mattered most to him. His circumstances did not matter—whether he had little or much, or whether he lived or died. Even those who preached the gospel of rivalry, with the goal of aggravating him, did not matter to Paul.

What mattered to Paul was the gospel—the good news that Jesus is Lord and Caesar was not. Paul knew that this meant there is a whole new way to live that reverses the ways of the world. The gospel is nothing other than the reconciliation of the world to God through Christ, the reconciliation of us to one another, and the reconciliation of us to all of creation. Therefore, what mattered to Paul—what would make his joy complete—was for his friends in Philippi to understand that this good news meant that there was a whole new way of being and belonging. He wanted them to live into this new reality—mediated through Christ, by the Spirit—so that they could work out what God was working in them (Phil. 2:12–13).

THE PROBLEM OF MIMETIC RIVALRY

Disunity in the church was an area of critical concern for Paul because the unity of the church was inextricably linked with the good news for which Paul was giving his life. Jesus prayed that all believers would be "one," *through* and *in* the same way that Jesus and the Father are one. It is through such unity that the world will believe that Jesus was sent by the Father (John 17:21). Conversely, division and disunity hinder the world from being able to believe the gospel. When we compete with each other and with other churches or denominations (for example, with the Orthodox church or the Catholic church), we hinder people's ability to believe that the Father sent Jesus. Paul therefore methodically addresses this issue throughout his letter.

No commentator would deny that disunity is an issue Paul is seeking to address, and some believe it to be the primary purpose for Paul writing the letter.[61] Many link Paul's pleas for influential leaders in the church (Euodia and Syntyche) to be of the same mind (Phil. 4:2) with the general issue of disunity in the church addressed earlier in the letter (Phil. 1:27–30; 2:1–4).[62] Theologian Gordon Fee writes, "Paul now entreats these two leaders 'to have the same mindset,' [which] is precisely the language of 2:2."[63] Speaking of Philippians 4:2–3, N. T. Wright notes, "Verses 2–3 are a 'special appeal' to two women in Philippi who are in conflict. Apparently, the situation has been going on for some time, since Paul must have heard about it from Epaphroditus. No doubt he had this in mind when he wrote 2:1–4."[64] Scholar G. Walter Hansen writes, "Several recent scholars have argued that when the apostle had earlier called upon the congregation to take a united stand against opponents (1:27–30) and to demonstrate unity through humility (2:1–4), he had this concrete dispute between Euodia and Syntyche before his eyes."[65]

Some go even further, such as scholar Nils A. Dahl, who makes the case that Philippians is to be read "with the assumption that the disagreement between Euodia and Syntyche is the chief problem Paul faces and the main reason why his joy is incomplete."[66] Although scholars dispute the weight that one should give to this conflict with Euodia and Syntyche, many would agree that it was of such importance to Paul that he called them out by name, a practice that Paul tended to avoid when speaking of friends, except for in greetings.

Whatever weight one chooses to give to this conflict, Hansen's question and response are helpful here:

Why would Paul speak to these two women so urgently if their conflict did not have any impact on the church? But if their conflict seriously threatened the unity of the church, then this reference to them by name in a letter to be read to the whole church appropriately and understandably identifies a major cause of the problem of disunity addressed in numerous ways throughout the entire letter.[67]

Having twenty-five years of personal experience in leading churches, the empirical evidence I've gathered in that time substantiates Hansen's claim.

What was the nature of their conflict? This is a matter of speculation, because Paul does not tell us. Nevertheless, this has not stopped scholars debating this issue. It is beyond the scope of this book to discuss here, but whatever the issue may have been, it seems clear that these leaders had fallen into the mimetic trap and were engaging in mimetic rivalry. The issues that Paul was addressing in Philippians 2:1–4 dealt with selfish ambition and vain conceit. Gupta, among others, notes a better translation of "selfish ambition" is *rivalry*, and some Bible translations use this word.[68] Referring to Euodia and Syntyche, Hansen writes, "Whatever the specific issues may have been, the conflict was basically caused by pride, self-ambition and rivalry."[69]

It is important to remember that Euodia and Syntyche were leaders in the church for a reason. Paul was fond of them—these were women who labored beside him: fellow workers, whose names were in the book of life. They may have cofounded the church with Paul. But in a status-oriented society—in which the most valued and limited commodity was honor—it was easy to become susceptible to rivalry and competition without being fully aware of the fact.

As we learned from Girard and others, desire is at the heart of what it means to be human. And desire by its nature is mimetic, acquisitive, and rivalrous. Because desire is mimetic, it always has the potential to become competitive, as we desire the desires of others. Let me just create a possible scenario and say that Euodia wanted to be the *best* leader in the church. There is seemingly nothing wrong with this desire, but imagine Syntyche subconsciously imitated this idea of wanting to be the *best* leader. Such desires often happen without our awareness, so Syntyche denies her imitation of Euodia. As I have already demonstrated, mimetic desire means that whoever is the model will, by imitation, desire the very desire they gave to the other. In this scenario, Euodia's desire to be the best leader is increased, and in imitation of Euodia, Syntyche's desire is also increased in a snowball-like effect. Because there can only be one "best," they enter into mimetic rivalry with each other through their mutual imitation, each one believing their desire to be unique. The interesting paradox that starts to occur when two people become rivals is that the object of their desire (in the case of Euodia and Syntyche, to be the best leader) disappears and they become mimetic doubles, both repelled by each other the more they are attracted to each other. Maybe one reason why Paul does not point out the details of their conflict is because when individuals enter into mimetic rivalry, the object of their rivalry disappears and their focus becomes the *being* of the other person. In other words, they desire to be the other person.

Jean-Michel Oughourlian, a mimetic psychotherapist who has been studying Girard for more than thirty years, works with couples experiencing marital difficulties. He writes, "These [couples] often find themselves victims of a paradox that the very desire that originally drew them to each other and brought them into union has mysteriously transformed into a force that separates them as violently as it once united them."[70] Later, he writes, "I still feel surprised to see how many troubled couples are really prisoners of that mimetic mechanism working in them without their awareness."[71]

Oughourlian, speaking of the mimetic nature of desire, says,

> The true nature of desire, its *mimetic* character, along with our denial of that truth, leads us ceaselessly to copy within ourselves the desires of everyone we encounter, subjecting ourselves to their influence, and by the very act of imitation, making them into rivals and indeed obstacles to the fulfillment of what we think are our own desires.[72]

Speaking further on the rivalrous nature of desire, he writes,

> The other essential truth about desire is therefore that *rivalry* is always *connected with it*: because I desire the same thing as the other and deny his claim to be the origin of that desire, I make him my rival, and as this rivalry takes shape, I am led to desire all the more what he desires and to try to take it away from him. In this manner desire and conflict escalate.[73]

By nature, we are all caught up in mimetic desire; it is what makes us human. Mimesis is universal, like gravity; none of us can extricate ourselves from it. We are unceasingly under the influence of others. Imitation is the fashioner of desire.[74] If this is the case, how do we escape this mimetic trap? Oughourlian writes, "The purpose of mimetic psychotherapy is to release people who are bound up in those types of endless rivalry, to gradually unmask and unravel their illusory attachments and make them *free to choose other models*. Once our tendency to imitate is recognized as such and accepted, it can itself liberate us and protect us instead of enslaving us" (emphasis mine).[75] Paul may have addressed Euodia and Syntyche separately because they had become mimetic doubles, and he knew it was important for them to take their eyes off each other and imitate other models. Maybe that is why Paul arranges his entire letter around models he wanted them to imitate, as well as anti-models to avoid.

THE UNIVERSAL LAW OF MIMESIS

With this in mind, let us look once again at the outline of what commentators agree to be the heart of Paul's letter.

1:27–30 Being and Belonging as Kingdom Citizens in the Midst of Adversity
    2:1–4 Remember Whose and Whom You Are—A New Way of Being and Belonging
    2:5–11 The *Ultimate Kenotic Model*—Jesus Christ
    2:12–18 Live Out What God Is Working In
    2:19–24 Timothy as *Kenotic Model*
    2:25–30 Epaphroditus as *Kenotic Model*
3:1–4a *Anti-models* to Being and Belonging
    3:4a–16 Paul as *Kenotic Model*
    3:17–19 Your Choice of *Models* Determines Your Fate
3:20–4:1 Being and Belonging as Kingdom Citizens
    4:2–3 Mimetic Rivalry within Church Leadership Creates Disunity

Paul is essentially seeking to give Euodia, Syntyche, and the entire community models to imitate. As Paul writes, "Join together in following my example, brothers and sisters, and just as you have us as a model, keep your eyes on those who live as we do" (Phil. 3:17). In chapter twelve I will examine how Paul modeled kenotic leadership, but it is important to see how the remedy that Paul provided for this community that had fallen into mimetic rivalry was to propose models who are imitating the ultimate model: Jesus Christ.

Paul commends Timothy as a kenotic model: "I have no one else like him, who will show genuine concern for your welfare. For everyone looks out for their own interests, not those of Jesus Christ" (Phil. 2:20–21). Timothy had learned a new way of being and belonging. Because he belonged to Christ and had the mindset of Christ, he lived for others. Because he imitated the non-rivalrous way of Christ, he found a new sense of being. He was able to escape the mimetic trap.

Epaphroditus is also given as an example and model. Paul calls him his "brother, co-worker and fellow soldier" (Phil. 2:25). He shares how he risked his life and almost died for the work of Christ (Phil. 2:30). So not only was Paul commending Epaphroditus as his representative, but he was also lifting him up as a model to be emulated.

Paul then mentions some anti-models, which he calls "dogs," "evildoers," "mutilators of the flesh," and later broadly the "enemies of the cross." Regarding the enemies of the cross, he mentions that their mind is set on earthly things. The word "earthly" is the Greek word *epigeia*. It is the same

Greek word James uses when he says, "But if you harbor bitter envy and selfish ambition in your hearts, do not boast about it or deny the truth. Such 'wisdom' does not come down from heaven but is *earthly*, unspiritual, demonic" (James 3:14–15, emphasis mine). In other words, earthly is the "wisdom" of the world; it is envious rivalry. Those who Paul describes as "enemies of the cross" were still part of the old order of being and belonging.[76] They formed their sect over and against the way of the cross and the universality of Christ's message. By wanting people to become circumcised, they were finding a way to exclude others, thereby creating a greater status for themselves.

Thus Paul spoke harshly to groups who found their sense of belonging and being over and against others—in the same way Jesus did with religious groups of the time. Such groups were exclusive—the antithesis of the gospel, which is for everyone. This reminds us that there are only two ultimate models: Satan and Jesus. And as I mentioned earlier, the only way to escape the Powers is through the imitation of Christ, who lived his life in imitation of the Father.

Within the third chapter of Philippians, Paul offered himself as a model, which I will explore in the following chapter of this book. I believe Paul modeled for us how he understands the self-emptying love of Jesus in his own life. Scholar William Kurz writes on the *kenotic* imitation of Paul and of Christ in Philippians 2 and 3, demonstrating how Paul was applying his own imitation to Christ's *kenotic* journey.[77] Then, just after admonishing Euodia and Syntyche, Paul writes, "Whatever you have learned or received or heard from me, or seen in me—put it into practice. And the God of peace will be with you" (Phil. 4:9).

With this in mind, I will look at Philippians 2:5–11, the passage I have been building toward, which will show us what it means to have a kenotic spirituality. What exactly is the new way of being and belonging? What enables us to escape the mimetic rivalry that was so prevalent in both Paul's day and ours? It is important to note that just because mimesis is a universal mechanism, one that none of us can escape, does not mean it is deterministic.[78] Each of us has the opportunity to choose who we imitate. Because our choice of model will determine our desires, who we choose to imitate will either lead to freedom or destruction—the domain of life or the domain of death.

12

THE SCANDAL OF IMITATING CHRIST

The scandal of leadership can go in one of two directions: by falling to the Powers via the mimetic cycle, we can scandalize those who look to us as leaders, or we can scandalously imitate Christ. In other words, we can avoid becoming a negative scandal by following the scandalous way of Jesus in our approach to leadership. But what does it mean to be a missional leader in the way of Christ? And why is it scandalous?

To answer these questions, I will take a deeper look at Philippians 2:5–11, followed by examining a more recent example of a leader who imitated the way of Christ and practiced kenotic spirituality and leadership.

KENOTIC SPIRITUALITY

The romantic lie Girard warned us against is that our desires are self-generated and that we become somebody by ourselves. However, as I have previously explored, we do not discover our identities individually but through inter-dividuality. It is our relationship with others that creates our inner selves. In his letter to the Philippians, Paul was reminding the church that who they are is determined by to whom they belong: "Therefore if you have any encouragement from being united with Christ, if any comfort from his love, if any common sharing in the Spirit, if any tenderness and compassion, then make my joy by being like-minded, having the same love, being one in spirit and of one mind" (Phil. 2:1–2). Paul was reminding the Philippians that they were who they were because they belonged to Christ through the Spirit. Our identity is not something we construct but something we receive from Christ and one another. He wants them to be "of the same mind," because their sense of being is wrapped up in the community to which they belong. When we become Christians, our identity is not only as a son or daughter of God but also as a brother or sister to other believers. Our identity is therefore inextricably linked with other Christ-followers.

Paul then set forth Jesus as the supreme model—if they chose to imitate him, it would reshape how they related to one another (Phil. 2:5–11). Jesus has a non-rivalrous relationship with the Father. Everything he said and did reflected the Father (John 5:19). Jesus' own identity was shaped by his relationship with his self-giving, life-giving Father. As Christians, we are invited into this same relationship with our heavenly Father. Because our identity is received from Christ and others, how we view and treat others shapes how others view and treat us. This is why Paul is encouraging them as a whole community to have the mind of Christ. This corresponds to mimetic theory, in that to be human is to be an imitator.

If we want to move from the domain of death to the domain of life, we must adopt a new mindset, which will require us first realizing that if we try to construct our identity in competition with others, we will lose it. We will live as fragmented, anxious people. However, if we die to this way of constructing a sense of self and give ourselves to God and others, we will find that our sense of self becomes integrated—we can become our true selves in God.

Paul writes, "Do nothing out of selfish ambition or vain conceit. Rather, in humility value others above yourselves, not looking to your own interests but each of you to the interests of the others" (Phil. 2:3–4). Gupta translates these verses, "Reject any temptation to live according to point-scoring rivalry or self-glorification empty of substance; instead, let humility guide you, each of you treating the other as if they were your superior (and vice versa). Each one should not be preoccupied only with their own concerns, but with the concerns of others."[1] In other words, we will either build our sense of self according to dominant culture, or we will receive our sense of self from God through our interactions with others. Paul was certainly aware that in Philippi, status was everything. The whole city was entrenched in seeking their own honor over and above the honor of others. Bird and Gupta write, "To be 'humble' for Paul meant (1) that one did not dwell on their own high status, and (2) one did not judge or favor others based on *their* status. If *everyone* treated the other as superior in status (and vice versa), then this subverts the entire system."[2]

In the hinge verse (Phil. 2:5) between Philippians 2:1–4 and the Christ hymn in Philippians 2:6–11, Paul urges the saints in Philippi to relate to one another with the mind, orientation, attitude, and way of thinking of Christ: "In your relationships with one another, have the same mindset as Christ Jesus" (Phil. 2:5). This mindset sets the backdrop for this poetic narrative, or what many call the Christ hymn, which describes in detail what it means to practice kenotic spirituality.

Because Christ perfectly imitates the Father, what we learn through this poetic narrative or hymn is not only the way of Christ, but also of God the Father. N. T. Wright puts it this way: "The real theological emphasis of the hymn, therefore, is not simply a new view of Jesus. It is a new understanding of God. Against the age-old attempts of human beings to make God in their own (arrogant, self-glorifying) image, Calvary reveals the truth about what it meant to be God."[3]

THE CHRIST HYMN

Let us take a look at this Ode to Christ in order to see what we can learn about what it means to imitate him on this kenotic journey:

> Who, though he was in the form of God,
>> did not regard equality with God
>> as something to be exploited,
> but emptied himself,
>> taking the form of a slave,
>> being born in human likeness.
> And being found in human form,
>> he humbled himself
>> and became obedient to the point of death –
>> even death on a cross.
>
> Therefore God also highly exalted him
>> and gave him the name
>> that is above every name,
> so that at the name of Jesus
>> every knee should bend,
>> in heaven and on earth and under the earth,
> and every tongue should confess
>> that Jesus Christ is Lord,
>> to the glory of the Father.

PHIL. 2:6–11 NRSV

I have already explored the context of this passage. Though many use this Christ hymn to reflect deeply on the ontological nature of Christ (which has served the church in understanding the two natures of Christ), I agree with Joseph H. Hellerman that "what we have in Phil. 2:6–11 is Christology in the service of an overarching ecclesiological agenda."[4] Paul shared this poem to help the Philippians live into a new way of being and belonging that was in contrast to the dominant, status-driven culture in which they found themselves—a context not too different from our own.

Scholar David Black reminds us, "The various parts of the letter are not a random accumulation of general precepts but are relevant to a situation in which differences between key leaders in the Philippians situation have provoked animosities and contempt."[5] This kenotic pathway becomes a portal for us, as leaders, to move from a culture bound by death and move more fully into the domain of life, as we not only imitate the crucified and risen victim but participate in the life of our triune God. As we do this, we create positive mimesis in our congregations instead of mimetic rivalry.

Based on David Black's work, scholar Corné J. Bekker holds that "the entire hymn may be regarded as a chiasm that further serves to sharpen the rhetorical function of the hymn."[6] The chiasm functions to demonstrate our active part in the first section and God's active part in the second. Following his work, but with a different summary, here is the chiastic structure of the hymn, which helps us to start to consider what it means to take this kenotic pathway:

A1   Jesus does not selfishly exploit his *status* as God.
    B1   Instead, he *empties himself*, becoming a *nobody, a servant*.
        C   He *humbles* himself and is *obedient*, even unto a shameful death on a cross.
    B2   God exalts him and gives him the name above all names.
A2   Jesus is Lord of all, to the glory of the Father.

This hymn is typically divided into two primary parts: Jesus' active voluntary way of life (A1, B1, C) and the Father's exaltation of him (B2, A2). Paul's message, Hellerman suggests, is that, for citizens of heaven, there is an inverted approach to the pathway to honor. "Paul, in his presentation of Christ at the apex of his *cursus* in Philippians 2:6, begins to radically deconstruct Roman social values for persons who desire to live life according to the model of Jesus, as citizens of God's alternative community."[7] What does this inverted pathway look like? By following the way of Jesus, our status anxiety is removed as we no longer play by the rules of dominant culture. Jesus, who successfully overcame the temptations of the devil through the Spirit, engaged in concrete practices that enabled him to stay faithful to his Father. Jesus says, "By myself I can do nothing; I judge only as I hear, and my judgement is just, for I seek not to please myself but him who sent me" (John 5:30). Jesus desired to please his Father, and he therefore modeled his entire life around him—for as a human being, he, too, was tempted by mimetic rivalry, for he was tempted in every way that we are tempted (Heb. 4:15).

Kenotic spirituality is about having the same attitude and mind of Christ. Just as the Father was Jesus' ultimate model who shaped his desires and gave him his identity, so our ultimate model ought to be Christ, who reshapes our desires and gives us our identity. This enables us to respond to his call to this kenotic pathway of inverted honor. Jesus not only reshapes our desires but he also reshapes our practices, as we follow him who is *the way*, the truth, and the life (John 14:6). The kenotic pathway for us, if we are to follow the way of Jesus, involves

- refusing to exploit our status;
- regularly emptying ourselves; and
- revolutionary humble obedience.

REFUSING TO EXPLOIT OUR STATUS

The Roman rulers claimed divine status "and utilized their divine status to further enhance their own glory and honor," and Philippi's local elite imitated Rome's values "in their own social world."[8] However, Christ, who genuinely possessed divine status, took a different route, "and ultimately [received] the highest of honors for approaching his status and power in a radically countercultural way."[9] How was Jesus, in his humanity, able to do this? It was because his deep sense of being came from the fact that he belonged to the Father and Spirit. Jesus was dependent on the Father for his sense of being, his identity: "This is my son, whom I love; with him I am well pleased" (Matt. 3:17). Having received his identity from his Father, he was able to spurn the temptations of the devil and avoid falling into acquisitive mimesis. Because Christ experienced the love of the Father, there was no need for him to find status in the conventional world, in the ways of the world. And in contrast to the Roman elite, he refused to use his status as God in exploitative ways.

Paul understood what it meant to put full confidence in his inherited and achieved status. As author and professor Timothy Gombis writes, "Paul had formerly placed full confidence in his inherited credentials and in his lifetime pursuit of a constructed social identity based on the central elements of his Jewish heritage."[10] Paul contrasted himself with those he was highlighting as anti-models, who thought their practices of circumcision made them superior:

> If someone else thinks they have reasons to put confidence in the flesh, I have more: circumcised on the eighth day, of the people of Israel, of the tribe of Benjamin, a Hebrew of Hebrews; in regard to the law, a Pharisee; as for zeal, persecuting the church; as for righteousness based on the law, faultless.
>
> PHIL. 3:4B-6

Hellerman makes an astute point, saying that Paul's short autobiography was similar to the many inscriptions found across the city designed to honor people and households. Such inscriptions tended to follow a particular formula, starting with *ascribed* or inherited honors (which were considered more important) and then moving to *achieved* honors.[11] Paul's autobiography would therefore be an instantly recognizable style to the Philippians. And this "desire to pursue a social status determined by cultural expectations affects contemporary practitioners, as well."[12]

It is helpful at this point to recall Wink's definition of flesh in the negative sense. It is the self that is "subjugated to the opinion of others, socialized in the values of the domination system or domain of death."[13] Gombis writes, "The social approval Paul received based on this life of conformity to cultural expectations shaped his identity. He was an approved, exalted, and respected person. He was faithful to Torah, and he was certain that this is how the God of Israel would have seen him."[14]

Our sense of identity is misplaced when we try to construct it by our ascribed or achieved sense of status. When we find our sense of worth or value in the titles we possess or our achievements, it becomes selfish ambition. Titles are a reality we must live with, but finding our sense of value and worth in them creates mimetic rivalry.

Many commentators point out that although Paul was an apostle, he does not use this title in his letter to the Philippians. Instead, he deliberately chooses the label "slave" (Phil. 1:1 NLT). If we want to follow Christ, we, too, will refuse to exploit our status. The question each of us must ask ourselves is the following: *Have I become possessed by my image instead of fully possessing the identity I receive from my triune God?*

REGULARLY EMPTYING OURSELVES

The opposite of emptying ourselves is being full of ourselves. Being full of ourselves is having a sense of self-importance where we *exalt* ourselves above others, often based on our ascribed or achieved status. This attitude always ends in mimetic rivalry and disunity in the church. It does not appear that Jesus emptied himself of his power, for John tells us that he had all power (John 13:3), but he clearly did not wield it in a worldly or coercive way. Sarah Coakley thoughtfully defines *kenosis* as "choosing never to have certain (false and worldly) forms of power—forms sometimes wrongly construed as 'divine.'"[15] If Coakley is right, this means that in Jesus' kenosis, he demonstrates a lucid, true image of divine power, and we see a reflection of the Father's self-emptying way.

Because Jesus received his identity through his belonging to the Father, he was able to "let go" of trying to construct his own identity through titles or other means. While the disciples continued to fight about who was the greatest, Jesus showed them true greatness by becoming their slave and washing their feet (John 13:1–17). Through his actions, he was helping them to find the pathway to the domain of life, but their arguing suggests that they were content to remain in the domain of death, where mimetic rivalry prevails.

Paul, in his imitation of Christ, not only gave himself the title of a slave, but he "lets go," or empties himself of all his ascribed and achieved honor. After giving us his brief autobiography, he writes, "But whatever were gains to me I now consider loss for the sake of Christ. What is more, I consider everything a loss because of the surpassing worth of knowing Christ Jesus my Lord, for whose sake I have lost all things. I consider them garbage" (Phil 3:7–8a). Paul admits that all his previous attempts to construct a sense of identity were "garbage." They mean absolutely nothing. Gombis writes,

> Paul realizes that the only credential that matters is having his personal value and identity shaped by the cross. And because of that, his having a collection of socially and culturally impressive credentials becomes an obstacle, since they still appeal to him to establish his personal value in those terms—his value before others and before God.[16]

To travel down the kenotic pathway, we must empty ourselves of all the previous ways we sought to form our sense of identity. In terms of the world's perception of value, worth, and honor, we are to become nobodys so that God might make us somebodys.[17]

This requires a different mindset—it means we must live in this world with a different attitude, viewing reality in the same way Christ did. The promise of an integrated self—free from the approval of others, free from status anxiety, free from the fear of death—is available to all of us if we choose to imitate Christ through kenotic spirituality in the power of the Spirit.

THE PRACTICE OF EMPTYING OURSELVES

Kenotic spirituality has a concrete pathway; it is defined by our ultimate desires. And if we imitate Paul, as he asks us to, then our ultimate desire is to experientially know Christ. As Paul writes, "I want to know Christ—yes, to know the power of his resurrection and participation in his sufferings" (Phil. 3:10). Paul tells us that this pathway not only involves experiencing the power of the resurrection but also fellowship with his sufferings. "For it has been granted to you on behalf of Christ not only to believe in him, but also to suffer for him, since you are going through the same struggle you saw I had, and now hear that I still have" (Phil. 1:29–30). The kenotic pathway involves suffering, but in the end, all of our suffering is redeemed. There are some aspects of Christ that we will never know apart from suffering, and suffering often enables us to experience his love in new ways.

For example, when we seek to love someone and they stab us in the back, our human response is to imitate the Powers and take revenge. But when we look to Christ, we are shown a different way. He lived a perfect life of love yet still had people who turned on him, and even in his shameful death on the cross, he was able to cry out, "Father, forgive them, for they do not know what they are doing" (Luke 23:34). When we suffer for doing what is right, and we look to see where Jesus experienced the same, we are better able to understand his love for us and even his love for our enemy. This, in turn, helps us to love and forgive those who hurt us, because it is in our pain that we can experience the suffering that Jesus went through, not only for each of us individually, but also for the entire hurting world.

As we desire to know Christ, just like Paul desired to know Christ, we escape the dominion and fear of death because we are willing to die to the old ways of constructing our identity. Too often we have baptized the ways of the world in the church rather than following Christ. We must be willing to receive our sense of identity from Christ, and we must also acknowledge that our new sense of identity is to be found in the social other. We therefore need to be willing to take this kenotic journey with the whole community. When we view each other as competitors—whatever the competition might be—we need to turn our eyes to Jesus and his self-giving way in order that we can be self-giving toward one another. The kenotic journey involves falling out of obsession with those with whom we have fallen into mimetic rivalry and to instead become more obsessed with Christ.

This is not a one-and-done event. Paul said he had to "die daily" (1 Cor. 15:31 NKJV). Dying to our old way of constructing identity and sense of worth is a process. Swiss-American psychiatrist Elisabeth Kübler-Ross developed five helpful stages of acceptance of death that we can use as we choose to die to self:

The first stage is *denial*. We can take all we have learned in these pages and deny its reality, continuing to construct our sense of identity in the same way we always have. We can deny our complicity to violence and scape-goating. We can deny the reality that mimetic desire is a universal reality. We can deny the mimetic rivalries we get involved in through our desire to be the greatest. But, of course, this is to go against reality, if Jesus is the one who defines it.

The second stage is *anger*. If we take the kenotic pathway, we can feel upset that all our previous efforts to construct a sense of identity are lost. Every achievement through which we have gained a sense of self-importance is gone. We can feel angry that our whole life and all the energy we put into developing this image is dead.

This leads to *bargaining*, which is the third stage: *Well, God, I can see the truth of all of this, but is there not another path? You know my heart; I have tried to follow you in my life, but do I really have to give all of this up? Do I need to consider everything a loss? Can I not find a sense of security, value, and worth in this one achievement? Must I become a nobody? Do I really have to use my power for the sake of others?*

As we deeply contemplate these doubts and questions, we move to the fourth stage, which is *depression*. Here, we are in the wilderness, the desert. We are facing the realities of dying to this way of life—of giving up the "somebody" we have become through belonging to particular groups or exclusive communities. The strong sense of being we sought to develop has been exchanged for a seemingly weak sense of being through our belonging to Christ. It feels weak because everything around us—all the principalities and powers founded on murder—are seeking to keep us in their grasp.

But then we move into the final stage of *acceptance*. We become cognizant that our old ways of constructing identity were in vain. We are filled with a sense of calm and peace as we come to the realization that we no longer need to use our energy and effort to try and attain an honorable self. We can simply receive it from God. With acceptance comes contentment. As Paul writes,

> I have learned to be content whatever the circumstances. I know what it is to be in need, and I know what it is to have plenty. I have learned the secret of being content in any and every situation, whether well fed or hungry, whether living in plenty or in want. I can do all this through him who gives me strength.
>
> PHIL. 4:11-13

Rather than finding identity in ministry, we find our sense of worth, value, and identity in Christ and in a communal way of life in which we pursue humble obedience to God. We receive Jesus' invitation to "take my yoke upon you and learn from me, for I am gentle and humble in heart, and you will find rest for your souls. For my yoke is easy and my burden is light" (Matt. 11:28–30). This stage of acceptance involves taking his yoke and giving up our pursuit of constructing our identity in the domain of death in mimetic rivalry over and against the other(s) in our lives. Instead, we choose to rest in the non-rivalrous relation of our triune God.

REVOLUTIONARY HUMBLE OBEDIENCE

If we are to be missional leaders free of the mimetic trap within the Domination System and released to start a revolution of love, it will come through humble obedience to a non-rivalrous God. In contrast to the dominant culture in Philippi, Jesus took the pathway of humble obedience to his Father. Hellerman writes,

> Most countercultural vis-à-vis ancient social values is the fact that Christ humbled *himself. Being* humbled was common fare in the ancient world, where males sought to augment their own honor and social status at the expense of the honor and status of their peers. Humbling *oneself,* on the other hand, was not within the purview of the values of the dominant culture. The content of Christ's self-humiliation, moreover, resulted in his

utter degradation, as he underwent the most shameful public humiliation imaginable in the ancient world—death on a Roman cross.[18]

Paul was writing from prison, which in any culture and time, tends to be associated with shame. Yet even as he was misunderstood and facing death, Paul exuded joy, prayed passionate prayers on behalf of the Philippians, and was unfazed by those preaching the gospel with rivalrous intentions (Phil. 1:3–26). It appears that Paul shifted from the domain of death to the domain of life. His identity and sense of self was built on a solid foundation, and his approach to life and ministry emulated that of Christ. Gombis writes,

> Because Paul is the apostle of the crucified Lord, the measure of his faith-fulness is when his life and ministry resemble as closely as possible a dying corpse on a Roman cross, for that is the site on earth on which God poured out resurrection life. Paul ministered from a posture of vulnerability and with a heart opened wide, and if that resulted in social shame, he embraced it. If he attempted to minister from some other posture or approach, he would not be drawing upon God's resurrection power. Some other source of power would be at work, one that was infinitely inferior, with no power to transform the cosmos, lives, and communities. For Paul, any other form or mode of ministry diminishes and marginalizes the power of the cross and forfeits any access to the transforming power of God.[19]

As a crucified slave, Jesus soaked up all our shame. If we were religious people in Jesus' day watching him die upon the cross, we would have considered him cursed by God (Gal. 3:13). But with the advantage of hindsight, we are now able to look upon the cross differently: it can be something that moves us, that gives us courage. And although we would once have abhorred those who were revolutionary in their humble obedience, today we tend to honor those who display humble obedience—people such as Mother Teresa or St. Francis. Because of the example of Jesus, we are able to see the power of revolutionary obedience. Those with wisdom elevate those who elevate others above themselves.

When God exalted Jesus by raising him from the dead, reality shifted—humility was exalted! We see in the second part of the Christ hymn that God exalts the humble. Jesus was given the name above all names and is recognized for who he has always been: the Lord. Hellerman writes, "The exaltation of Christ (vv. 9–11) is, therefore, absolutely crucial to Paul's argument in the context of 2:5–11. Themes of *cursus*, honor, status, and power flow naturally throughout the text, from Jesus' humiliation to his exaltation, though in a decidedly countercultural way."[20] Because of Jesus' humble obedience to the Father and his willingness to dishonor "himself for the benefit of others, Jesus is exalted to the highest place by One whose position at the very apex of the pecking order of social reality assures Paul's readers that the status reversal of this crucified δοῦλος [slave] will ultimately be acknowledged by all."[21]

Although God exalts the humble, it might be a mistake to consider exaltation to be a prize or reward for humility. We do not become last in order to be first. The last is first in reality. Thus, to be humble is to be exalted. Jesus said, "And I, when I am lifted up from the earth, will draw all people to myself" (John 12:32). Theologian Richard Bauckham makes the case that we discover who God is in both the crucifixion and the resurrection. Bauckham writes, "Here God is seen to be God in his radical self-giving, descending to the most abject human condition, and in that human obedience, humiliation, suffering and death, being no less truly God than he is in his cosmic rule and glory on the heavenly throne."[22] In other words, kenosis becomes a permanent revelation of who God is: "The radical contrast of humiliation and exaltation is precisely the revelation of who God is in his radically self-giving love. He rules only as the one who serves. He is exalted above all only as the one who is with the lowest of the low."[23]

One might object that this kenotic journey is not for everyone. What about those who are already low in societal order or are oppressed? Hellerman reminds us that

> Paul, in his great Christological masterpiece, utilized the image of crucifixion not to elicit the reluctant submission of the powerless to their social superiors but, instead, to encourage those with some status in the community to regard their social capital not as "something to be exploited" but, rather, as something to utilize—even renounce, if necessary—in the service of others.[24]

In some ways, those whose status is already low will have shorter journeys to becoming "nobody." Maybe that is why James says that the poor are rich in faith (James 2:5).

A KENOTIC MODEL FOR OUR TIME—ÓSCAR ROMERO

Óscar Arnulfo Romero y Galdámez was born on August 15, 1917, in the town of Ciudad Barrios, located in the province of San Miguel in the northeastern part of El Salvador. I will briefly examine his life as an example of kenotic spirituality. Romero refused to exploit his status as archbishop, he regularly emptied himself, and he lived in revolutionary humble obedience to God in the way of Christ. He died as a martyr of the faith from an assassin's bullet on March 24, 1980, in San Salvador, while performing the Eucharist in a small chapel at Hospital de la Divina Providencia, a hospital that cared for the terminally ill. This was the "reward" for one who stood in solidarity with the poor and oppressed, who gave his last three years to naming, unmasking, and engaging the principalities and powers in his beloved country of El Salvador.

Romero's legacy is worldwide and goes beyond the Roman Catholic Church. Westminster Abbey in London honored Romero by placing a statue made after his likeness at the abbey's Great West Door, alongside statues of nine others martyred for their faith in the past century. He was placed between Martin Luther King Jr. and Dietrich Bonhoeffer. In 1979, Romero was nominated for the Nobel Peace Prize, the same year that Mother Teresa was the award recipient for her peacemaking work in Calcutta. He was given honorary doctorates from Georgetown University in Washington, DC, in 1978, and from the Belgian Catholic University in Louvain in 1980.[25] The "United Nations recognized Romero when they designated March 24, the anniversary of his assassination, as the 'International Day for the Right to the Truth concerning Gross Human Rights Violations for the Dignity of Victims.'"[26]

Scholar Michael Lee writes, "Like Bonhoeffer and King, Romero's lived example was rooted in a vision of the Christian gospel, of the reign of God preached by Jesus Christ that is manifest in peace and justice among human beings."[27] Let us take a brief look at his early years, his ministry years and context, and how he modeled a kenotic spirituality, which ultimately led to his death.

EARLY YEARS

Romero grew up in a humble village where the main industry was coffee production. His parents were small landowners, and his father was the village telegrapher and postmaster, which meant that the Romeros were better off than many. However, they had very little money, and Óscar and his brothers and sisters had no beds and all slept together on the floor.[28] The actions of greedy rich landowners and corrupt politicians eventually led to the impoverishment of his family.[29] Due to a childhood illness that prevented him from engaging in sports and rough play with other boys, Romero became isolated from other children in the village, which contributed to him developing a reclusive personality.[30] At the age of thirteen, Romero sensed a call to the priesthood, so he started minor seminary, which was essentially high school with religious instruction and discipline.[31] Romero's cultured father taught Óscar at a young age to play the flute and read music.[32] Later in his life, Romero learned to play the harmonium and piano, which provided him with a form of relaxation after he became archbishop.[33] He grew up in the midst of a country that experienced harsh dictators, peasant revolts, and extreme violence, including the revolt in 1932, during which hungry peasants rose up in arms for their land and were brutally crushed "by a psychopathic dictator, General Maximiliano Hernandez Martinez, who shot and hung over thirty thousand peasants in the first week of the conflict."[34] At the beginning of this revolt, Romero was fifteen years old and still in minor seminary.

Romero continued his studies for the priesthood, eventually moving to National Seminary, which was run by the Jesuits. He earned his master's degree at the Gregorian University in Rome. He stayed in Rome to start his doctoral degree, specializing in ascetical theology and studying the works of Luis de la Puente, a sixteenth-century Spanish Jesuit ascetical writer.[35] While working on his dissertation, he wrote in his diary, "In recent days, after reading some of Father la Puente at the curia, principally the life of Father Alvarez, the Lord has inspired in me a great desire for holiness. I've been thinking of how far a soul can ascend if it lets itself be possessed entirely by God."[36] But World War II interrupted his studies, and his bishop summoned him back to El Salvador.[37]

MINISTRY YEARS AND THEOLOGICAL AND POLITICAL CONTEXT

Within a few months after his return to El Salvador, where he was serving as a parish priest, Romero was called to be the secretary of the San Miguel diocese, a role he fulfilled for the next twenty-three years.[38] As an admirer of the Ignatian spirituality of the Jesuits, Romero would regularly go on month-long spiritual retreats to care for his soul. However, although he prioritized caring for his soul, it seems he did not place the same priority on caring for his emotional life.[39] According to biographer Father Delgado, Romero's unreasonable work load created anxiety and emotional stress that often led to him being overly strict with other priests.[40] Romero recounts the faults he observed in himself while in Mexico: he saw that he was "avoiding social relations with others, not getting to know people, concern about being criticized, perfectionism, disorder in [my] work, lack of austerity, lack of courage in speaking out and defining [my] opinions."[41] Although he was respected by many of his superiors, he experienced difficulties with his peers, sometimes displaying authoritarian tendencies.[42]

As the Roman Catholic Church entered a new era of Vatican II, between 1962 and 1965, Romero became known as the most powerful priest in San Miguel as well as a traditional conservative who preserved the established order; his supplemental role as editor of the diocesan newspaper was the chief means through which this power and persona were transmitted to the public.[43]

Vatican II was followed by a landmark conference in Medellín, Colombia, where the Catholic bishops of Latin American gathered to interpret Vatican II for their context. This document was essential for Romero's kenotic journey, as it became "a reflection on Vatican II in light of the conditions of poverty and structural injustice that characterized the Latin American continent."[44] The framers of this document utilized a theological method that started with the context in which people were living—their social, economic, and political lives—and in light of this, turned to Scripture with theological reflection. Essentially, the document recognized that we must join God in his work to bring about justice for the poor and oppressed.[45] These ideas challenged the current social order.

After having served as a priest for twenty-five years, Romero was named secretary general of the national bishop's conference and moved to San Salvador.[46] He worked hard in this role, and after a few years, the archbishop of San Salvador, Luis Chávez y González, who had known Romero since the 1940s, asked him to become an auxiliary bishop. According to Brockman, Romero hastily consulted two priest advisors and his doctor and then accepted the invitation.[47] But two years later, during his Ignatian practices at a retreat in Mexico City, he not only questioned his acceptance of being a priest, but also "felt similar qualms about his calling [as bishop] and also the motives of vanity mixed in with his desire to serve God and the church."[48] He "prayed for God's pardon for whatever was previously lacking in his motives and directed the effort of the retreat towards purifying them, saying that he wanted nothing else in his priestly life but God's glory, the church's service, and his own salvation."[49]

His ordination as auxiliary bishop took place on June 21, 1970, and about four years later he was appointed bishop of the Diocese of Santiago de María, a poor, rural region, similar to the one in which he was raised. It was here that he meaningfully reconnected with the poor, as he moved from his scribal roles to being bishop. By the mid 1970s, as the poor started standing up for their rights, the government army began killing them. When three peasants were massacred in his district, the people pleaded with Romero to take a public stance against the atrocities that were occurring. Instead, Romero decided to write a personal letter to the president. Brockman writes that Romero thought his "responsibility was to the church as an institution, and that he must avoid the embarrassment of speaking out on behalf of the victims who might be subversives or criminals."[50] However, when Romero became archbishop, this perspective changed.

The archbishop of San Salvador at the time, Luis Chávez, was supportive of the emerging liberation theology in Latin America, including that which was emerging in El Salvador.[51] He not only encouraged theological training that honored Vatican II and Medellín, but he also sponsored social initiatives aimed at relieving the plight of the poor and oppressed in El Salvador. One of the institutional changes taking place under his care was the emergence of base communities, which were started by priests for the poor, by the poor. Father Rutilio Grande, after becoming a pastor of a rural area, helped to start more than three dozen base communities that helped the people find their voice, understand the Bible, and become ambassadors of Christ to others.

THE SCANDAL OF IMITATING CHRIST | 273

Romero was suspicious of many of these groups and publicly critiqued them, but his relationship with Father Grande, which had begun when he was in seminary, helped him to understand that not all of these groups were the same. Although some were more influenced by Marxism and violence, others, like Father Grande, were disciples of Christ and were nonviolent; and, of course, there were also others who sat between these two views.

ROMERO'S TRANSFORMATION TO A PRIEST WITH THE POOR

While in Santiago de Maria, Romero not only observed the difficult life of the poor but also found ways to help them practically. Many would come during harvest time and work back-breaking hours harvesting the coffee for little pay. For most, this would be the only income they would make for the year. When Romero found a number of the laborers sleeping in the public square, he offered them accommodations in a building next to the cathedral, sheltering hundreds of these workers during the cooler weather. He also called on the ladies of charity to cook them meals at the end of the day, and at night he offered catechetical films in the open air for the workers.[52]

Romero's time in Santiago de Maria would in many ways prepare him for what was to come: Romero went from being a timid, indecisive leader who participated nicely within the elite power structures to a bold and daring one who loved both the oppressed and the oppressor. Romero stood with the oppressed and also lovingly called to conversion those who were being brutal to the peasants. This transformation came after what many refer to as Romero's conversion. This was not a conversion from no faith to faith, but a conversion from a reductionistic faith to a more robust faith, with the expectation that the kingdom of God would become more manifest on earth for everyone, especially the poor and oppressed. The late Anabaptist missiologist Wilbert R. Shenk said, "Conversion is needed whenever men and women do not acknowledge the reign of God."[53] In other words, we all need conversion.

Had Romero died at this stage of his life before becoming archbishop, there would have been no lasting legacy. What happened in his life that transformed him and his ministry? What was the nature of this "conversion" that Romero experienced, and how did it affect the way he led as archbishop of San Salvador, the most prestigious religious office in a country that was predominately Catholic? What changed in Romero's life that led to both his death and global honor?

APPOINTED AS ARCHBISHOP OF SAN SALVADOR

Romero was an unlikely candidate for the archbishop of San Salvador. Many thought that the natural successor to Chávez was his faithful auxiliary bishop, Arturo Rivera y Damas. "Certainly, within the progressive sectors of the church, Rivera was considered the only bishop who had a proven track record of supporting the pastoral approach influenced by Vatican II and Medellín."[54] Cardinal Sebastiano Baggio, whose job it was to scrutinize the candidates, at first thought Rivera to be the first choice. However, he was lobbied by various leaders representing the interest of the Salvadoran oligarchy, so the decision went to Romero. "Baggio later told Rivera that he nominated Romero because 'I would like for El Salvador a bishop less critical of the government than you.'"[55] Romero was considered "safe" by the oligarchy. His appointment was praised by conservatives, the oligarchy, and the government, but those who were oppressed and repressed by the current social structures feared the worst.

But it seems the Spirit of God had been slowly at work in Romero's life through his recent experiences as bishop of Santiago de Maria and his reflection on Vatican II and the Medellín documents. Romero was appointed archbishop of San Salvador on February 3, 1977, and installed on February 22, 1977. But a mere eighteen days after his installment, something took place that marked a dramatic change in the direction of his ministry as archbishop. The news arrived that Father Grande, Romero's close friend from seminary, along with seventy-two-year-old Manuel Solórzano and sixteen-year-old Nelson "Tilo" Lemus were assassinated just outside Grande's hometown. "Everyone suspected that the government and the clique of the oligarchs were responsible: Father Grande had been one of the most outspoken of those who were critical of the regime, defending the peasants, and had been active in helping to organize base communities. He had also been Archbishop Romero's friend."[56] On February 21, 2020, Pope Francis declared Father Grande a martyr of the church.

ÓSCAR ROMERO'S KENOTIC JOURNEY

Óscar Romero's conversion centered on his deep desire to imitate Christ and his engagement with a kenotic spirituality that led to him becoming a kenotic leader. In many ways, Romero's kenotic journey was deepened not by what he did *for* the poor but *by* the poor. Theologian Jon Sobrino writes,

> He found in the poor that which is scandalous in the mystery of God understood in a Christian sense: in those whom history crucifies is made present the crucified God. The kenotic dimension of God—God's emptying himself, in other words—goes on being foolishness, a scandal. It is the dividing line between authentic Christianity and other theistic beliefs. It is made manifest in the poor, in the oppressed and the repressed of his people. In their faces Romero saw the disfigured countenance of God.[57]

I will now examine Romero's life as archbishop through the lens of Philippians 2:6–11 in order to gain more insight into what the kenotic journey looks like—for Romero embodied it to the point of death by a bullet.

REFUSING TO EXPLOIT HIS STATUS AS ARCHBISHOP

Just as Jesus refused to exploit his status as God, Romero forsook the comfort, honor, and privileges that came with the office of the archbishop, the highest religious office in the country. In honor of his martyred friend, Father Grande, and his fellow travelers, Romero decided to hold one public mass for the entire archdiocese, to take a public stand against their assassination—quite a contrast to the earlier assassination that occurred when he was bishop, when his only action was to send a private letter to the president. At the public mass, Romero spoke of Grande's assassination, declaring, "We have asked the legal authorities to shed light on this criminal act, for they have in their hands the instruments of this nation's justice and they must clarify this situation."[58] Not knowing at the time who was responsible, he continued, "We are not accusing anyone nor are we making judgements before we have all the facts. We hope to hear the voice of an impartial justice since the cause of love cannot be separated from justice. There can be no true peace or love that is based on injustice or violence or intrigue."[59]

Around the time of Romero's appointment as archbishop, the country was nearing a presidential election. Traditionally, the archbishop would be visibly present at the inauguration, which in most countries would be a great honor. But Romero declared that "he would not attend any official governmental ceremonies until there was satisfactory evidence of a serious investigation into the murders."[60] These two decisions were "controversial, and were such a departure from what people expected that those who were happy about them began to speak about his 'conversion,' while those who were unhappy began to use the word 'betrayal.'"[61] Some of his fellow bishops benefited from a close relationship with the government, and they criticized Romero for "politicizing" the church by refusing to go to the inauguration. Romero responded by questioning when the archbishop being at the inauguration was ever *not* a political act.[62]

As Romero digested Vatican II and the Medellín documents, his embodied faith mirrored the developments occurring in missional theology, which emphasized the priority of the kingdom being manifest on earth. The developing theology of Romero is evident in his four annual pastoral letters.[63] He makes the case that the church is Christ in history. Romero did not stand with the right or the left, but he was also not centrist. He denounced the oligarchy (fourteen families and their allies), corrected the governing junta (if they failed to care for the people), and made a decisive stand with the poor and oppressed, which constituted the majority of the population. His politics were based on "what would lead to deeper truth, greater justice, stronger possibilities of peace."[64] As Lee writes, "Under the leadership of Oscar Romero, the Catholic Church in El Salvador went from legitimizing the government and protecting the status quo to denouncing injustice and defending human rights."[65]

Under Romero's leadership, the church was changing. As Lee puts it, "This church gave testimony to a faith that was no longer passive and fatalistic. Rather, it lived a faith that recognized the calling of discipleship to include changing society so that it more closely resembled God's will."[66] But, as Romero discovered, "it was a costly shift. Hundreds of religious and laypeople were arrested, tortured, or murdered. During his time as archbishop, Romero presided over the funerals of six priests. Others were deported."[67]

Romero did not blindly side with the poor and the base communities; he observed that some of the people's movement required critique. In one of his homilies he said,

> The church cannot agree with the forces that put their hope only in violence.
>
> The church does not want the liberation it preaches to be confused with liberations that are only political and temporal.
>
> The church does concern itself with earthly liberation—it feels pain for those who suffer, for the illiterate, for those without electricity, without a roof, without a home.[68]

In another homily he said,

> Let us not put our trust
> in earthly liberation movements.
> Yes, they are providential,
> But only if they do not forget
> That all the liberating force in the world
> comes from Christ.[69]

Although he gave preference to the poor, Romero always extended grace and love to all, even those who were killing and torturing his own people:

> For when Christ corrected those of his time,
> he did not hate them.
> He loved them
> because he wanted to snatch them
> from the claws of idolatry, of false positions,
> that they might seek the true way
> where they can find the mercy God offers.
> He wanted to forgive them and make them just.[70]

Romero, unlike some of his bishops, did not side with the wealthy for his benefit but accepted the persecution that came as he boldly stood with the poor. He refused the plush accommodation that came with the office of archbishop as well as an offer of a house and car from wealthy San Salvadorians. Instead, he chose to live in a simple room that the nuns created for him as an extension of the Hospital de la Divina Providencia, where he was eventually killed.

REGULARLY EMPTYING HIMSELF

Most of Romero's biographers point to the death of Father Grande as significant in Romero's "conversion." Maybe Father Grande became a model for Romero. For after Father Grande's assassination, Romero emptied himself of his timid self, his indecisiveness, and his mixed motives for high office by letting go of what others thought of him and being more concerned about what God thought of him. In emptying himself, he instead allowed himself to be filled by God. He became consumed with the stories of the poor—with those who were seeking justice for their missing loved ones, and with those who were tortured, kidnapped, and murdered. He became a bold defender of the poor and oppressed, willing to name, unmask, and engage the principalities and powers at work through the oligarchy and government.

Romero was also willing to "let go" of his links to those in power. Lee mentions that other commentators "have emphasized how the events surrounding Grande's death and funeral led Romero to rupture his links with those in power who previously supported him and to forge a new closeness with the people."[71] This was not an easy "letting go," as he felt pressure from the Catholic hierarchy to try and bring peace between the government and church. However, Romero was convinced that if peace were to come about, there must first be justice. On February 25, 1979, he preached,

> The church renews itself. We cannot preserve old traditions that no longer have any reason for being, much less those structures in which sin has enthroned itself and from which come abuses, injustices, and disorders.
>
> We cannot call a society, a government, or a situation Christian when our brothers and sisters suffer so much in those inveterate and unjust structures.[72]

Robert McDermott, speaking of Grande, put it this way: "For the new archbishop, the murder was a moment of truth. As he prayed over his dead friend, he was faced with conversion—a New Testament-style metanoia. He knew that he would have to choose sides."[73] Romero "let go" of his need to connect with those that had power and became a prophetic voice for the Salvadorian people. It was not that Romero disassociated from those in power. His hope was that they would be willing to fairly and thoroughly investigate the assassinations, but until they did, he needed to let them go and give them space to work out their salvation. Romero did not depend on power in the way this world understands power; he depended on power from on high. He writes in his homily on May 14, 1978:

> When the church ceases to let her strength
> Rest on the power from above—
> which Christ promised her
> and which he gave her on that day—
> and when the church leans rather on the weak forces
> of the power or wealth of this earth,
> then the church ceases to be newsworthy.
> The church will be fair to see,
> perennially young,
> attractive in every age,
> as long as she is faithful to the Spirit that floods her
> as she reflects that Spirit
> > through her communities,
> > through her pastors,
> > through her very life.[74]

Romero's regular Ignatian practices gave him a pattern by which he continually emptied himself so the Spirt of God could fill him. While in office, Romero chose not to cling to worldly power but the power of the Spirit. For Romero, poverty of spirit was a necessity, for only the hungry would be filled, and the full would go away empty. In his homily on December 12, 1977, he said,

> If at some time the church betrayed its spirit of poverty,
> then it was unfaithful to the gospel.
> which meant it to be distinct from the powers of the earth,
> not depending on money that makes humans happy,
> but depending on the power of Christ,
> on God's power.[75]

Sobrino, commenting on the institutional power of the church, noted that in Latin America, the church still had great social force, which could be harnessed in various ways. He writes, "At one extreme it would be possible to use politico-ecclesiastical means to influence society or to impose rules and regulations upon society from above."[76] At the other extreme "would be to reduce the world to its fate, or merely [try] to change the world by the subjective testimony of holiness."[77] From the perspective of his firsthand connection with Romero, Sobrino writes, "Archbishop Romero exercised an institutional power, but one different from both those extremes. He never wished to become one of the nation's important leaders, but he found himself a mediator, sometimes an arbiter, in a great variety of conflicts within society."[78] Sobrino notes how various groups came to Romero for mediation, and Romero put the full power of the institution in service to the poor. Romero could not make peace with the principalities and powers that were at work through the current government. Sobrino notes, "Romero broke with the model of church power as analogous to state power in a great number of ways. For example, he took part in no ceremony, political or ecclesiastical, that would have presented the two powers as being on the same footing and coexisting in supposed harmony."[79] Sobrino later writes, "He wanted to make it clear that one should not think of institutional authority of the church as power 'from above,' as similar to state power, as the natural dialogue partner of the state."[80]

But this did not mean the church had no power. Instead, Romero changed the whole notion of power. Sobrino makes the case that Romero used institutional power exercised through the proper means of the church, "especially through the word that creates a common awareness and not through politico-ecclesiastical means, always on the lookout for concessions from the state."[81] Sobrino saw that Romero exercised power for the good of the people, not the institution itself. As a result, the church found its home among the people. Sobrino writes that under Romero's leadership, "the church's institutional authority was not only *for* the people but *with* the people as well. It was no longer exercised from above but from within."[82] As Romero fully identified with the poor and oppressed, this transformed his use of power.

ROMERO'S REVOLUTIONARY HUMBLE OBEDIENCE

Finally, Romero is an example of revolutionary humble obedience. Often, when we think of a biblical example of humility and obedience, we think of Christ washing the disciples' feet. This was no doubt the work of someone secure in who they are. Jesus was not seeking to protect his image, and therefore, he was willing to take the role of the lowest-ranked slave and wash his disciples' feet. Too often, we believe that humble obedience must always be manifested this way. But humble obedience is also bold and prophetic. It is choosing to do the will of the Father, regardless of the consequences. Whenever disciples of Jesus engage in healthy prophetic ministry, there will be consequences. There will be a cost, as Romero understood only too well. However, this awareness did not deter Romero's humble obedience to Christ.

Sarah Coakley notes that, ultimately, the final test of understanding kenosis is through the lens of the fruit of the Spirit. She writes, "Love, joy, peace—yes, and all the other Pauline fruit and gifts." Under this larger framework of her understanding of Spirit and gifts, she mentions the need for "personal empowerment, prophetic resistance, courage in the face of oppression, and the destruction of false idolatry."[83] These elements were all represented in the life and ministry of Óscar Romero. He understood that to be faithful to Christ, he must proclaim the kingdom of God to all, the oppressed and oppressor alike. He was also aware that in Jesus' ministry he denounced all sin that would hinder the kingdom of God from becoming a reality. This included not just personal sin but structural sin as well. Romero realized—and helped others to realize—that as they stood against structural sin, they must be prepared to be persecuted and even martyred for their actions done by faith.

In his homily on April 12, 1979, he notes,

> The church celebrates its liturgy and preaches its message
> only for this:
> to save from sin,
> to save from slaveries,
> to overthrow idolatries,
> to proclaim the one God, who loves us.
> That will be the church's difficult mission,
> and it knows that in fulfilling that mission,
> which earned for Christ a cross and humiliations,
> it will have to be ready also not to betray that message
> and, if necessary, to suffer martyrdom like him—
> suffer the cross, humiliation, persecution.[84]

ROMERO'S NAMING, UNMASKING, AND ENGAGING OF THE POWERS

The church has the responsibility to name, unmask, and engage the powers by preaching to the people as well as the principalities and powers (Eph. 3:7–12). Under Romero, the church became the place where people would come and report the human rights abuses that were taking place all over the country. Using a team of lawyers to investigate every report, Romero would take time each week after his homily to name all the atrocities, murders, disappearances, kidnappings, torturing, and beatings that were taking place in his country. By doing so, he unmasked the powers that were at work in his country through the unjust social structures. This weekly naming of what was happening was broadcast by radio, with a listening audience larger than that of football (soccer) matches. It was said that you could walk through any town in El Salvador and not miss a word of his radio broadcast, as the broadcast was coming from almost every window and car throughout the town. Of course, this was a threat to the oligarchy and ruling government; to prevent this, at times, they would bomb the radio stations and create interference to the broadcasts. Romero boldly preached the kingdom of God, denounced sin, and prepared the people for the suffering that they would undoubtedly encounter as they sought to stay faithful to the gospel.

Romero was not under any illusion that the authorities would stand idle. He knew they would come for him, just like they came for his Master. He knew that his death was inevitable. Weeks before his assassination, he asked his driver to no longer chauffeur him, because he did not want his driver to die needlessly. In his homily on January 7, 1979, he was clearly aware of threats against his life:

> I was told this week that I should be careful,
> that something was being plotted against my life.
> I trust in the Lord.
> and know that the ways of providence
> protect one who tries to serve him.[85]

Like Paul, Romero knew that a death sentence was hanging over his head, and yet, like Paul, he continued his revolutionary humble obedience to Christ. It did not stop him from preaching the good news of the kingdom of God, the liberation of his people. Romero continued to broadcast and denounce the sin taking place in his country; and he continued to name and unmask the principalities and powers, as well as prepare people to be willing to die for their faith. The oligarchy controlled most of the media and falsely called Romero a communist, even though Romero named the ideology of Marxism as dangerous. However, Romero remained with the people and for the people—and the people listened to him with great joy.

Romero found his identity in God and therefore was not afraid to use the institution for the sake of the people or to use his platform to unmask the powers of ideology. In a homily given on April 10, 1978, which contained themes common to many of the homilies he preached, he said,

> Don't be led astray
> either by the allure of power and money
> or by following false ideologies.
> True hope is not found there either.
> True hope is not found
> in a revolution of violence and bloodshed,
> and hope is not found in money and power—
> neither on the left nor the right.
> The hope that we must account for
> and that makes us speak with valor
> is found in Christ, who reigns even after death,
> even after murderous death.
> And with him reign all who have preached
> his justice, his love, his hope, his peace.[86]

THE CONCLUSION OF ROMERO'S KENOTIC JOURNEY

Lee writes, "Romero's boldness in the face of threats came to a peak in his cathedral homily of March 23, [1980]." This was the day before his assassination. Toward the end of his homily, he was making clear that the archdiocese was "working for human liberation" and that this "was part of its transcendent calling." For Romero, the role of a Christian is not just to pray for God's kingdom to come and for his will to be done on earth as it is in heaven but also to join God in this work.[87] In this homily, he "addressed the members of the military and uttered his most famous last words":[88]

> Brothers, you are part of our people, and you will kill your very own poor brothers and sisters. Before the human command to kill, the divine command should prevail: Thou shalt not kill. No soldier is obliged to obey an order contrary to the law of God. No one has to follow an immoral law. It is time that you came to your senses and obey your consciences rather than sinful commands.
>
> The Church, the defender of the rights of God, the law of God, human rights, and the dignity of each person, cannot remain silent in the face of such abominations. We want the government to take seriously the fact that reforms stained with so much blood are worthless.
>
> In the name of God, and in the name of this suffering people who have suffered so much and whose laments cry out to heaven with greater intensity each day, I implore you, I beg you, I order you in the name of God: Stop the repression!"[89]

If the church is to be newsworthy today, we must take the kenotic pathway of Christ, refusing to use our status for our own benefit but rather for the benefit of the other. In that sense, Romero is a model for our time. We, too, must regularly empty ourselves to make room for God and the poor and oppressed. And we must be willing—like Romero, like Paul, like Peter, like St. Francis, and like so many who have gone before us—to exhibit a revolutionary humble obedience to Christ, trusting that those who die with him will rise again.

Just two weeks before his death, Romero was interviewed by one of the few newspapers that was not under the control of the oligarchy. Here are the words from that interview, as mentioned by Jon Sobrino:

> I have frequently been threatened with death. I must say that, as a Christian, I do not believe in death but in the resurrection. If they kill me, I will rise again in the people of El Salvador. I am not boasting; I say it with the greatest humility.
>
> As a pastor, I am bound by a divine command to give my life for those whom I love, and that includes all Salvadorians, even those who

are going to kill me. If they manage to carry out their threats, I shall be offering my blood for the redemption and resurrection of El Salvador.

Martyrdom is a grace from God that I do not believe I have earned. But if God accepts the sacrifice of my life, then may my blood be the seed of liberty, and a sign of the hope that will soon become a reality.

May my death, if it is accepted by God, be for the liberation of my people, and as a witness of hope in what is to come. You can tell them, if they succeed in killing me, that I pardon them, and I bless those who may carry out the killing.

But I wish that they could realize that they are wasting their time. A bishop will die, but the church of God—the people—will never die.[90]

PRACTICING THE KINGDOM PRAYER

How can we possibly imitate Christ and participate in the life of our triune God? The start of the answer is both simple yet difficult: through contextualized, communal prayer. When the disciples asked Jesus how they should pray, he gave them the kingdom prayer (also known as the Lord's Prayer). The kingdom prayer is reflective of the entire Sermon on the Mount, which is the kingdom manifesto of what it means to follow Christ concretely in this world. Thus this prayer can be used as a catechism that teaches us what it means to live under a different King and kingdom in our context. The prayer is in the plural (our), because healing and wholeness are always found in the context of communities seeking to live under the reign of God. In Jesus' kingdom prayer we discover five themes:

- Rooted identity
- Vocational faithfulness
- Contrast community
- Spiritual formation
- Kenotic leadership

ROOTED IDENTITY (OUR FATHER IN HEAVEN)

The prayer starts with "Our Father in heaven, hallowed be your name" (Matt. 6:9). We are reminded that we can only find wholeness in the context of community, for this is a communal prayer. As leaders, we need to be in deep community with other leaders, sharing our true selves with each other, praying for each other, helping each other to live into our identities in Christ together. We are also reminded that our central role in this journey of life is as his beloved children. We do not need to strive to create our identity, because Christ has already given us one—child, saint, forgiven, ambassador, priest. As leaders, our sense of identity deeply shapes who we are becoming as well as how we do ministry. Calling God "Father" reminds us of his closeness to us, as well as the fact that family has been redefined in the kingdom. True family is not determined by geography or genealogy but consists of people from all around the world who do the will of the Father (Matt. 12:50). In addition, we are reminded of the transcendent nature of God, who is able to give us perspective and energy, as one who surpasses our current situation. Jesus was able to exhibit a revolutionary, humble obedience because he grounded himself in the Father. As we, too, imitate Christ, we will ground ourselves in God and let the Father embrace us as his children. And as we understand our identity as children, we will live in greater dependence on what flows from the mouth of God and trust in his promise.

VOCATIONAL FAITHFULNESS (YOUR KINGDOM COME)

Jesus has called us out of this world (the ways of the world) and sent us back to live in the world, immersed in our triune God and seeking the good of our neighbors and neighborhood. We therefore pray, "Your kingdom come, your will be done, on earth as it is in heaven" (Matt. 6:10). The good news that we are called to proclaim is not a Gnostic gospel reserved for another time and place, but an incarnational gospel—the inbreaking kingdom of God that transforms the here and now in light of the renewal of all things (Rev. 21:1–5). Engaging in kingdom work requires reflection. Vocational faithfulness recognizes that we can be easily tempted to try and accomplish kingdom work in the ways of the world, instead of in the way of Christ. Too often the church seeks to bring about the kingdom of God by mimicking the methodology of the world and thus unwittingly imitating the powers in submission to the god of this age. But light does not come through darkness. The end never justifies the means, no matter how noble the ends. In fact, the means will always define the ends. Like Romero, we need to stay true to our calling, no matter what we might face.

CONTRAST COMMUNITY (OUR DAILY BREAD AND DEBTS)

We learn in the next section of this prayer that it is not intended to feed the illusion of our individualistic or consumerist tendencies, for this is a communal prayer: "Give us today our daily bread. And forgive us our debts, as we also have forgiven our debtors" (Matt. 6:11–12). Jesus proposes alternative social, economic, and political practices by which we are all invited to enjoy God's banquet in this age as we anticipate his banquet in the age to come. When we consider the life of Jesus, we are reminded to expand the table to include those whom religious leaders and society have dismissed and damned. The table is where we ask God to give us our daily bread—the place where we receive forgiveness and learn to forgive others in the same way that

Jesus, the forgiving victim, did on the cross. As we break bread together, we remember he was broken so that we might become one whole new humanity. As we drink from the cup, we remember his blood was spilled so that we do not need to spill more blood but instead seek the peace of our neighborhoods and the world. But often peace does not come without economic justice. Living as a contrast community is learning to embody forgiveness and seek reconciliation with friends and enemies. It is moving from acquisitive mimesis to imitating the self-giving Christ. It is displaying a sacrificial love through radical sharing and hospitality, recognizing that in Christ, there is one new humanity.

SPIRITUAL FORMATION (DELIVER US FROM EVIL)

As we seek to build contrast communities that are a sign, foretaste, and instrument of God's coming kingdom, we will inevitably face the counterattack of the powers, so we need to pray, "And lead us not into temptation, but deliver us from the evil one" (Matt. 6:13).[91] The evil one seeks to subvert our attempts to join God in seeing his kingdom become more visible in our neighborhoods through the way of Jesus. The principalities and powers desire us to imitate their ways to bring about the kingdom. The powers crave ultimate devotion. They have developed rules, systems, structures, and institutions that speak to the longings we each have, so we are tempted to give ourselves over to them. We need the Spirit and concrete spiritual disciplines to help us resist the temptation to try and make the kingdom of God visible. It can be easy to fall to the ideology of pragmatism: if it works, it must be good, and it must be true. Instead, we need to ask, *Do our ways demonstrate the fruit of the Spirit, or do they reveal the fruit of the flesh* (Gal. 5:19–6)? When we pray to be delivered from the evil one, we recognize that we are not capable of facing the onslaught of evil on our own. We must rely on the Holy Spirit, develop strong emotional support networks, and engage in practices that renew us physically, recharge us emotionally, and refresh us spiritually. Spiritual formation is the process by which we are being shaped into the image of Christ and are developing an inner life that is able to meet the internal and external demands we face.

KENOTIC LEADERSHIP (FOR YOURS IS THE KINGDOM)

The biggest temptation we face as leaders is to build our own kingdoms, by our own power, for our own glory. That is why tradition ends the kingdom prayer with, "For thine is the kingdom, and the power, and the glory, for ever. Amen" (Matt 6:13 KJV). Kenotic leadership takes place when we, as leaders, possess our image in God instead of becoming possessed by our image; it is when we can name, unmask, and engage various ideologies that seek to captivate and control us by having us rely on our own power for the sake of our egotistical desires of affirmation and attention. And when we, as leaders, understand that the ultimate telos of our lives is life in God and new creation, we will have a praxis in the scandalous, kenotic way of Jesus that is congruent with the reality of his kingdom.

SUMMARY OF SECTION FIVE

There is a battle for our hearts and souls. As leaders we can either become a scandal to those we disciple, or we can follow the scandalous way of Christ. This is the scandal of leadership, for we are all captive to imitation.

If we are going to overcome the evil one, we need to recognize that the temptations of Jesus are archetypal.

- *The economic temptation* is tied to how our *image* seeks to possess us (*identity*) instead of us possessing our image in God.
- *The political temptation* is reflective of *institution*, where we seek to find our security through controlling power, instead of living in the power of the Spirit. This speaks to our *praxis*.
- *The religious temptation* speaks to how *ideology* in our mind, or the collective mind of entities small and large, seeks to subvert how we read and understand the Scripture in a way that is incongruent with the kingdom of God. This speaks to our *telos*.

Leadership worthy of imitation takes place when we become leaders who are willing to face and overcome Satan, when we resist the devil and repent. Through positive mimesis, we then seek to form our identity in the love and acceptance of God. It is this love of God that reshapes our praxis as we live on mission. Shaped by God's love and looking to worthy models, we can model *kenotic* leadership. Suffering love and the positive use of power is reflected when our identity is formed by and compelled by God's love, and when we identify with the poor and oppressed. The key to a faithful praxis of power is when our lives are characterized by a love affair with God and when his kingdom becomes a reality, especially for those the current system oppresses.

By examining the book of Philippians with a Girardian lens, we learned a new way of being and belonging. Our sense of being is found through the group within which we most belong. As we first find our sense of belonging in Christ and those who are imitating him, we can move from the domain of death to the domain of life as we receive our identity from Christ and both imitate and participate in his death and resurrection. If we become embroiled in mimetic rivalry, we need to take our eyes off our rivals and turn toward Christ, as well as to other models whose desire is to know Christ, the power of his resurrection, and fellowship with his suffering, for all else is garbage!

With this in mind, I leave these final questions for you to ponder, as missional leaders of communities of faith:

1. Do I have a life worth imitating?
2. Do we have a community worth joining?
3. Do we have a mission worth dying for?

It all starts with the first question. As you ponder those questions, keep in mind the wisdom we received from Albert Schweitzer at the beginning of this book: "Example is not the *main* thing in influencing others. It is the *only* thing."[92]

CONCLUSION

This book began with the need to develop a robust diagnosis of the problem of domineering leadership in the church, as evidenced by the recent fall of several high-profile leaders, some of whom have deeply shaped the ethos of church leadership in North America and beyond. The underlying problem of the abuse of power goes deeper than conventional diagnosis allows. By linking missional leadership to a theology of the Powers via mimetic desire, I have argued for an imitation-based conceptual framework that can provide a more robust diagnosis of the problem and inspire a more faithful way forward. Beginning with the nature and work of the Powers made it possible to diagnose the root cause of fallen leadership as idolatry. Ultimately, the use or abuse of power is reflected in the spiritual battle between the fallen Powers of this world and the redemptive power of the Spirit for the heart, soul, and desires of the missional leader. Humans are captive to imitation, especially through mimetic desire, and there can be no neutrality: not to imitate Christ is to imitate the Powers, and when this happens, it leads to bondage, idolatry, and injustice, manifested by domineering leadership.

I have argued that talking about the mission of God without a robust theology of the Powers is incomplete and, in regard to leadership, is potentially harmful. In light of this, I have proposed that without a way to name, unmask, and engage the Powers, the missional leader remains vulnerable to patterns of domination. Instead of engaging in positive mimesis and imitating Christ and his ways, the leader falls into negative mimesis, mimicking the Powers instead. When the missional leader imitates the principalities of image, institution, and ideology, they are often slowly and imperceptibly led into idolatry and the abuse of power in the church.

In section one, after looking at a hermeneutical approach to the Powers, we explored the history and the development of the missional conversation through Craig Van Gelder. I argued that current missional theology is insufficient to diagnose the problem of fallen leadership. By unintentionally minimizing the spirituality of the leader, it gives the impression that solutions are found through information rather than through spiritual formation. Minimization of the imitation of Christ as well as the lack of definitions for the terms *world* and *culture* added to the problem. However, the contours of leadership given by Alan Roxburgh and others—identity, praxis, and telos—are extremely helpful.[1] Roxburgh names the true telos of the leader, and establishes the foundational importance of personal identity, which, in turn, shapes praxis. But by failing to significantly address the Powers, the missional leader is left vulnerable to their subtle influence.

Graham Houston's study of 1 Peter provides a biblical approach to addressing the problem of domineering leadership, from which an imitation-based framework for understanding missional leadership has emerged (see figure C.1). Although Houston's work highlights the concepts of imitation and the Powers, a more systematic approach was required to address the problem of fallen leadership in the church. To accomplish this, a more robust understanding of the Powers was needed, as well as a better comprehension of how imitation and desire work in relation to them. I sought a systematic integration of these concepts by bringing together the work of Walter Wink, René Girard, and William Stringfellow.

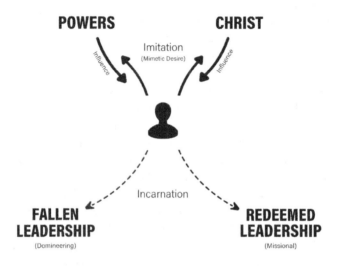

Figure C.1 The Imitation-Based Framework

Wink establishes a theology of the Powers for the imitation-based framework. In section two, I argued through Wink that the pervasiveness of the Powers in the New Testament demonstrates the need to understand how they subvert leadership in the church. Wink's argument alerts the leader to the ubiquity of the fall, the all-pervasive patterns of domination, and that confrontation with the Powers is inescapable for those who participate in God's mission. If missional leaders are to resist succumbing to patterns of domination and the Spirit of the domination system (Satan), they will need to name, unmask, and engage the Powers. Failure to be intentional about this leads to complicity with the Powers and ends in bondage to idolatry, dishonoring God, and dehumanization.

Girard establishes the link between a theology of the Powers and missional leadership in the imitation-based framework through the concept of mimetic desire. Wink provides a way to understand how the Powers work to subvert the missional leader from keeping the first commandment. Girard's work gets to the heart of the problem by exploring the tenth commandment ("You shall not covet") through the lens of anthropology.

Drawing on Girard in section three, I argued for imitation and desire as central to the problem of fallen leadership. The scandal of leadership occurs when the missional leader gets caught in the mimetic cycle through malformed desires. Malformed desires of the leader end in rivalry, as the disciple who looks to the leader as a model begins to desire what the model desires. As scandals (when the leader becomes an obstacle to their disciples) in the congregation increase, rivalry develops into a crisis, leading to the necessity of scapegoating, which allows the congregation temporary tranquility. Through an unveiling of the mimetic cycle that has taken place since the foundation of the world, the insidious work of the Powers was revealed. The way in which the Powers generate this crisis of leadership is evident in the book of James, where envy and self-ambition are called out as demonic and satanic. Leaders who engaged in this behavior were called adulterers. I argued that there are two ultimate models: Jesus and Satan. Failure to imitate Christ is to imitate Satan. The Powers conceal the mimetic cycle, but Jesus, through his willingness to become the scapegoat, revealed the mimetic cycle for what it is, and in doing so, proclaimed the fall of Satan. Missional leaders can escape the mimetic cycle by imitating the kenotic way of Christ and by understanding how the mimetic cycle works in their lives and the lives of their congregations. Jesus exposed the work of the Powers and saw the fall of Satan's ability to hold onto his kingdom. Yet pride continues to blind the minds of some leaders, preventing them from embracing the freedom Jesus achieved for humanity. Girard's work on mimetic desire supplies the link between missional leadership and the theology of the Powers, completing the imitation-based framework (figure C.1).

In section four, Stringfellow's work tied together Wink and Girard by applying the imitation-based framework to how the Powers seek to subvert the leader at the three contours of leadership—identity (image), praxis (institution), and telos (ideology). The insidious and crafty work of the Powers persistently acts upon the leader, often without the leader's understanding. Under the sway of Satan, these principalities subtly seek to possess those in leadership until they are fully enthralled. Submission to image, institution, or ideology devolves into idolatry. I argued that even potentially good things, such as the church as an institution, can become an idol when the church is in survival mode and when we, as leaders, desire to find security in things other than God. Idolatry always leads to injustice, the twin evils the Old Testament prophets continually railed against. When leaders give themselves over to the principalities, it results in an abuse of power. I argued that to deal with domineering leadership, we, as leaders, must understand that there is a spiritual battle for our hearts and desires. Although knowing the true telos of life in God is vital, without an understanding of how the Powers work, the leader remains vulnerable to their subtle influence.

In the final section of the book, I pointed toward a theological remedy, making the case that there is a need to develop a catechism that will promote leadership formation as the imitation of Christ through positive mimesis. An overview of the book of Philippians demonstrated how Paul understood the power of imitation through a new way of being and belonging. In seeking to resolve the mimetic rivalry that developed between two leaders in the church, Paul provided Jesus' kenotic journey as the supreme example. His letter was oriented around positive and negative models. I proposed that Epaphroditus, Timothy, and Paul were examples to imitate and the enemies of the cross as anti-models. I explored how Paul imitated Jesus' kenotic journey by refusing to exploit his status, regularly emptying himself, and engaging in revolutionary humble obedience. I looked at Óscar Romero as a contemporary example of someone who lived this out to the point of death. As we follow the scandalous way of Jesus, leaders form desires and patterns of life worth imitating. I offered a kenotic approach to help leaders ground their identity in God's love and consider ways to shape their desires in a manner that uses their power legitimately, as a gift. I suggested the Lord's Prayer as a solid practice to prevent us from building our own kingdoms, by our own power, for our own glory.

In summary, the imitation-based framework (see figure C.1) I developed in this book has linked missional leadership to the Powers via mimetic desire. This has shed light on the subtle ways the Powers seek to misshape the leader's desires and manipulate them to mimic their ways, providing a deep diagnosis of fallen leadership. Understanding the spiritual battle for the heart, soul, and desires of the missional leader equips us, as leaders, to be aware of how the Powers work, which helps us avoid fallen leadership and move toward redeemed leadership. Table C.1 helps to summarize the argument and connect the various terms used in this book, clarifying the findings of this study.

Table C.1 Dealing with a Domineering Praxis—Fallen and Redeemed Leadership

Contour of Missional Leadership	Expression of Principalities and Powers	Fallen Leadership		Redeemed Leadership	
		Desires	*Evidenced by*	*Desires*	*Evidenced by*
Identity	Image	Own glory For prestige For status	Egotism	For God and his glory	Others-centeredness
Praxis	Institution	Own power For security To control To survive	Domineering leadership	For the Spirit's power and righteousness	Kenosis
Telos	Ideology	Own kingdom To be right	Pride	For Christ's kingdom	Humility

SIGNIFICANCE OF THIS BOOK

I have sought to contribute to the field of missiology. The more the church becomes a credible sign and foretaste of God's kingdom through healthy leadership and communities, the more it can genuinely extend a new way of life, a life where we live by faith and are known for our love for others and for our concrete sense of hope for the fullness of new creation. This has shed light on the subtle ways the Powers seek to misshape the leader's desires and manipulate them to mimic their ways, providing a deep diagnosis of fallen leadership. I have demonstrated the need for us, as leaders, to be aware of how the Powers subvert our ministry by captivating our hearts in ways that lead to patterns of domination. Understanding the work of the Powers provides fresh motivation for us as missional leaders to consider our priorities. Having a solid missional theology without a deep spirituality becomes counterproductive if it contributes to neglecting the soul's relationship with God. The imitation-based framework developed here suggests that the first work of the missional leader is the formation of an identity in God. After developing a life worth imitating, we can develop a community worth joining, with a mission worth dying for.

I have argued for a more robust theology of the Powers in regard to missional leadership, which has been underdeveloped in the missional conversation. Though Newbigin spoke to its importance, there has been no work to date that has sought to combine Wink and Girard's understanding of the Powers with any depth. Intertwining Wink's voice as a theologian with Girard's voice as an anthropologist has yielded a substantial understanding of the Powers and the culture of church leadership. In addition, Stringfellow's approach to the principalities of image, institution, and ideology has been uniquely applied to the contours of leadership, with mimetic theory in mind. Providing an imitation-based framework has the potential to provide practical help to the missional leader regarding how the Powers subvert their leadership and how their leadership might grow through the imitation of Christ.

This book gives significant attention to the biblical narrative regarding the problem of domineering leadership. Although neither Houston nor McKnight seemed to draw on mimetic theory, their work implies a connection between desire and the Powers, which I systematized into the imitation-based framework by drawing on Wink and Girard. As far as I am aware, this book is the first work that significantly brings Girard into the Powers conversation and is the first time that his own synthesis of the Powers with mimetic theory has been applied to leadership in the church. The explanatory power that mimetic theory gives to the area of desire and its connection to the Powers is extraordinary.

Practically speaking, the imitation-based framework developed has the potential to shape disciplines of catechesis and spiritual formation, which alert missional leaders to how desire and the Powers might be at work in their lives and in the lives of the congregations they serve. Leaders can be equipped to see signs of negative mimesis, which will help in community formation. Positive mimesis helps us as leaders recognize potential in discipleship, emerging leadership development, mission, and movement.

Examining the book of Philippians through a Girardian lens provided a fresh look at Paul's letter and demonstrated the importance of where we find our sense of being and belonging. Taking a deep look at Philippians 2 allowed us to develop a kenotic spirituality that moves us from the domain of death to the domain of life.

Finally, the implications of this book not only justified the centrality of a leader's walk with God but also demonstrated the havoc, divisions, and scapegoating likely to occur when God does not hold first place in our lives. By observing the scandal of leadership and finding the root of the abuse of power in idolatry, fresh motivation is given to us as missional leaders to prioritize our relationship with the triune God. In addition, fresh light has been shed on how ideology misshapes the church and creates divisions in the church body, thus damaging the witness of the church. The concept of mimetic desire suggests a fresh approach to the imitation of Christ in the way of kenosis, as well as what it means to be and make disciples. The most significant way a person can imitate Christ is by imitating Jesus' desires for the Father and his dependence on the Spirit, which will lead to a kenotic spirituality. The implication for making disciples is that discipleship involves the leader's own desires, since those who look to the leader as a model will desire what the leader desires. The scandal of leadership is that we will either become scandals to those who look to us as models, or we will choose by the power of the Spirit to imitate the scandalous way of Jesus.

DIRECTIONS FOR FURTHER STUDY

In the development of this book, the imitation-based framework not only provided shape to the development of the argument but also helped to limit the scope of this book. Yet there are numerous areas that have been identified through the course of this book that could further strengthen the development and practical use of the framework for corollary developments in leadership theory.

First, there are avenues for further development of a theology of the Powers. Regarding Satan, comparing and contrasting different understandings of Satan could prove helpful from both an emergent and traditional view, using the work of Matthew Croasmun and Hans Urs von Balthasar. As I have demonstrated, in Croasmun's study of hamartiology, he examines Romans 5–8 and identifies the body of sin, the cosmic tyrant of Sin, as Satan.[2]

While Girard demystifies and deconstructs Satan, Croasmun reconstructs Satan as a cosmic body, as opposed to a fallen angel. Using the definition of personhood from emergent science, we recognized this body of Sin as a cosmic person with a collective mind. This cosmic body of Sin is comparable yet distinct from the cosmic body of Christ. Croasmun's understanding gives explanatory power to Satan as a figure in the New Testament, and why, although Satan is the archenemy of Christ, he does not need to engage in enemy love with him. This comparing and contrasting of an emergent and traditional view of Satan, provided by someone such as von Balthasar could be studied further in dialogue with the emergent view of the demonic, initially developed by Amos Yong and further developed by David Bradnick.[3] It could explore an intersection with the developing understanding of Satan across Jacque Ellul's early, middle, and late views. Both the emergent and traditional views of Satan coincide, in that the telos of Satan and the demonic are the same, which challenges Wink's view of Satan but corresponds with Girard's. Further study of my initial examination of this could prove helpful.

Second, through Wink's exegetical word study, it was discovered that the demonic and/or Satan were not to be understood as part of the cosmic reconciliation in Colossians 1:16. Because of Girard's and Yong's differentiation between the principalities and powers and Satan, I feel hope for the possibility that the principalities and powers may be redeemed. Considering that the reign of God (kingdom of God) widens the scope of mission to include social realities, further study of the extent to which institutions outside of the church could expect redemption this side of the eschaton would be beneficial, especially in light of an emergent or traditional view of Satan.

As such, a further elaboration of how ideology works in the collective mind of the cosmic body of Sin could be conducted in view of the potential of ideology to misshape leaders and congregations. Currently in the United States, there is a strong division between those unknowingly shaped by nationalism (and even White nationalism), progressivism, or liberalism.[4] Further research in this area could help missional leaders to deal with disunity. Lesslie Newbigin and others consider the unity of the church paramount. Jesus, too, speaks to unity and the love of one another in the body as an apologetic the church has to offer the world—his exhortation is prayed in the context of protecting believers from the evil one (John 17:13–23). In addition, the spiritual formation of leadership could be developed in light of the ideologies of capitalism and socialism.[5] An exploration of the liturgical power of the mall with an understanding of the market as god could be conducted, demonstrating how these practices misshape the desires of the leader, creating an identity of the leader as consumer, and highlighting the ideology of the American dream.[6] Counter-liturgies could be developed that reshape the desires of the leader for God and his kingdom and reorient the leader to the Christian calendar, the Scriptures, fellowship, and to silence and solitude.[7]

Recent books on missional spirituality could be read, considering the spiritual formation of leaders in light of the temptations of Christ and the spiritual battle for the heart of the leader.[8] This could be done in conjunction with James K. A. Smith's work on how thick liturgical practices reshape the desires of leaders and their identity and telos toward God and his kingdom.[9]

Examining the book of Philippians through a Girardian lens brought fresh contributions to the study of the book of Philippians. Studying other letters with a Girardian lens could prove insightful and helpful for missional leaders desiring to be an example worth imitating.

Although this study of Philippians is a good start, there could be a richer development of how positive mimesis works in the church regarding being and belonging, as well as mission and movement. Gossip and slander signal early stages of scapegoating, which may be why, after warning them twice, Paul gives the harsh recommendation to remove from fellowship those who stir up division (Titus 3:10–11). Understanding mimetic theory and the art of forgiveness in Christian community holds much promise. And looking further at how positive mimesis impacts discipleship and the multiplication of healthy leaders for mission and movement would be beneficial.

Finally, more work is needed to develop a holistic remedy, as this book has only started to point toward a solution. Women and people of color will need to address their unique challenges as to how this framework fleshes out in their context. For those of us who are White men, we will need to move toward a greater sense of accountability, community, and reciprocity with women, people of color, the marginalized, and the oppressed, allowing Acts 2 and Acts 6 to help shape the conversation and our actions.

FINAL REMARKS

The rich insights gained through the years of study that have produced this book have been a significant help for me personally and for the ministry God has given me. My hope is that after this academic book, God will give me the grace to publish some popular-level books highlighting the insights I have gained so that the church might have healthy leaders with flourishing churches for the sake of the world.

The greater hope is that my research would stimulate more writing in the field of missiology, which develops this imitation-based framework to help prevent fallen leadership and promote positive mimesis for discipleship, community, mission, and movement. As scholars take on the work regarding the suggested directions for further study, the church can become a greater sign, foretaste, and instrument of the kingdom.[10] As Newbigin writes:

> I have come to feel that the primary reality of which we have to take account in seeking for a Christian impact on public life is the Christian congregation. How is it possible that the gospel should be credible, that people should come to believe that the power which has the last word in human affairs is represented by a man hanging on a cross?
>
> I am suggesting that the only answer, the only hermeneutic of the gospel, is a congregation of men and women who believe it and live by it.[11]

Because redeemed leadership does not come about just by information, but by formation, it seems fitting to end this book with a prayer for us, as leaders, and for the congregations we serve.

Father,

We yearn to be the church you want us to become. Shape us into something beautiful. We recognize that you are the Potter and we are the clay. Please continue to mold us into the image of Christ.

We want to join in what you are already doing in the world. In our worship and life together, in our ministry and service to others, we want to give people a glimpse of your intentions for the whole world.

Help us to welcome the outcasts, love our enemies, and form a community that is visibly different from the culture around us as a sign of what you are doing in the world.

Help us experience your love and grace, grow in our relationship with Jesus, and experience the power of your Spirit as we offer your good news to others.

In Jesus' name, we pray, Amen.[12]

AFTERWORD
AMOS YONG

If you have read to this point, any sense of "What? Not another book on leadership!" that may have surfaced when you first encountered *The Scandal of Leadership* has now been overwhelmed by other more important—and urgent—questions. In this afterword, I will review three sets of these questions—the *who*, *how*, and *where*—of leadership.

The **who** *of leadership*: Leaders are, of course, human. *The Scandal of Leadership* not only recognizes this personal dimension of leadership but also adopts a biographically informed methodology that both acknowledges this aspect and invites leaders to honestly self-evaluate. If all theology is biographical, as James William McClendon teaches us, then so are any and all efforts at theorizing and theologizing leadership. JR Woodward brings his own biography as a long-time church planter and missional leader to this work. He also engages at the high levels of theoretical analysis by exploring the biographical details of his three primary interlocutors: Walter Wink, René Girard, and William Stringfellow. Even the exemplars—for example, Óscar Romero, the martyred archbishop of San Salvador—have, quite fittingly, been biographically presented for Woodward's triadic thesis involving Girard's mimetic theory.

The thread of mimesis running through *The Scandal of Leadership* also deserves further comment regarding the *who* of leadership. One significant thrust of Woodward's multi-pronged thesis is that leaders enact the performance scripts of those they admire, whether because of their impressive virtuosity or because of their noteworthy accomplishments, even if the means are questionable. This means that the reasons for our emulation are complicated, often driven less by aspirations toward Christlikeness and more by the sense of pain embedded in our pasts (which are soothed by high-achieving exemplars when measured by social conventions, even if the means fall short of biblical norms). In other words, *Why have we become leaders? What are we reacting to or even running from? Who are the models we are motivated to follow?* These and many other related questions will emerge for those readers who are willing to self-interrogate.

The **how** *of leadership*: We have now seen how Girardian mimesis invites us to assess how our visions of leadership—both the loci and its related purposes—are interrelated with the questions of leader identity and practice (the imitation of exemplars). Yet this identity-praxis-telos framing of leadership is embedded within a theology and cosmology of principalities and powers. Leaders are not mere individuals and persons, but they are also socially, cosmically, and spiritually shaped and constituted. Wink, among others, aids Woodward to help us understand this power dimension. This is not just in terms of how the Winkian notions are unfolded in what he calls the *Domination System*, amid which human lives are caught up, but also, for instance, in terms of the scriptural analyses of the apostolic navigation of Imperial Roman realities (the Domination System of the first-century messianic believers). Woodward's following in these Winkian pathways surely also resonates with the former's evangelical roots, not least the commitment to continually return to Scripture. This is manifested in *The Scandal of Leadership,* both in continued interaction with the work of biblical scholars and with the author's in-depth interpretations of New Testament texts, including a detailed (Winkian-Girardian) rereading of the book of Philippians for the purposes of reconstructing Christlikeness for twenty-first-century leaders.

Make no mistake, though: the *how* of leadership is the ongoing navigation of fallen principalities amid the divine redemption of the powers! The possibility of the latter is perhaps a controversial exegetical and theological issue. However, Christian leaders who are attuned to their organizational, institutional, and sociopolitical environments know both the opportunity and challenges of leadership. So, although *The Scandal of Leadership* is a serious book about the spiritual aspects of leadership, because the spiritual and the historical are never bifurcated (in part because of the Winkian-and-Girardian conceptualizations), it invites the reader to consider a spirituality of organizational management in relationship, in aspects such as finances, racism, or community development. As leaders, we are not merely individuals but are also situated thickly amid the forces of sinful human history as we traverse the powerful (and sometimes demonic or satanic, in all of their Winkian-Girardian and even biblical complexity) currents of political systems, social structures, and economic bottom-lines.

The **where** *of leadership*: At the early stages of the preceding pages, it quickly became apparent that this book is unlike many other volumes on leadership. Precisely because of the journey Woodward has led us through, I see this book resourcing and empowering Christian leaders in three ever-widening spheres of operation: the missional, the broadly Christian, and the public square. For those of us who know of Woodward's own background, we were expecting—and are not disappointed in receiving such—a work on missional leadership. The missiological, in this case, is not divorced from the principalities of society and powers of history. Missional leaders are now invited to consider, following Stringfellow, what it means to be subversive of or resistant to the powers of their missiological contexts. Missiological scholarship, so far, has not been attentive to the power dimension of Christian witness, and this is where *The Scandal of Leadership* fills the gap.

Yet the *missional* is irreducible to the *missiological*. More to the point, the *missional* in *The Scandal of Leadership* is synonymous with facilitating Christian witness and ministry in the footsteps of the kenotic Christ for the sake of the coming reign of God. Not only is the missiological expanded, but the work of Christian service and discipleship is also missionally infused, including the historic five offices (apostle, prophet, evangelist, pastor, and teacher) but also beyond these. All Christian life is hereby armed for resistance of and engagement with the Powers through the Spirit of the living Christ, for the sake of God's mission to save and redeem the world.

Thus, this volume also resources Christ-followers for service in and to the world at large. This is the public dimension of leadership in the footsteps of the suffering Christ. How might service, in emulation of the Lamb slain before the foundation of the world, unfold within the wider community, amid places such as the offices of city halls, along Wall Street, or across international and transnational spaces? The powers at work in each of these spheres are multilayered, but Woodward equips us to recognize their domineering character, to retrieve scriptural resources, and to respond in full awareness of our own entanglements while continuing to herald the divine rule.

Come, Holy Spirit—may you birth in each of us a fresh Pentecost that can enable redemptive intervention of this world in the name of Jesus!

ACKNOWLEDGMENTS

This book was birthed in me more than twenty years ago, due to circumstances I did not desire but wanted to understand. It has been nourished by friends and life experiences, as well as by close and distant mentors.

A book is much like a child, in that it takes a village to nurture. This book has been dependent on a community of people whose care, love, wisdom, and skills have allowed it to mature, and so I would like to thank the following people:

For those willing to experiment in shared polycentric leadership with me in the past and present—Joe Racek, Chris Backert, Jim Pace, Andy Bleyer, Dan White Jr., Eun Strawser, and more recently Jessie Cruickshank. You all have helped me to become a better leader.

For those who guided me on my PhD journey at the University of Manchester, including those at Cliff College and Nazarene Theological College. I particularly want to thank my primary supervisor, Phil Meadows, who encouraged me and prodded me to go down roads I didn't want to travel. In the end, this led to a much richer work, upon which this book was developed. The interaction with my PhD colleagues—especially Paul Hoffman, Tammie Grimm, and Gift Mtukwa—has been a true gift. Thank you for your encouragement and feedback.

For my friends at the V3 movement who prayed for me regularly, encouraged me often, and gave me the space to write—Mike Pumphrey, Lori Ruffin, Elice Kim, Matt Alexander, Josh Hayden, Justin Fung, Kyuboem Lee, Tial Chum, Muss, Cory Dorion, Ben Atkins, and Tonya White, and more recently Jeff Riggs and Emii Phillips-Kim. I want to give special thanks to Taeler Morgan for her help and encouragement, for without it, this book would have never come to fruition.

For my friends Won Choi, Vivek Jones, Silas Sham, Jeremy Chen, Guy Wasko, Luke and Lena Glover—I thank you for your prayers, conversations, and encouragement. A special thanks to Rudy Hermanto for your support. I deeply appreciate COR Church, including Bok and Hanna Oh, Kalvin and Susan Kim, James Hayes, and Sung Min Kim. Thank you, Vinay Goyal, for being such a gift and helping this book get off the ground. I am thankful for the friendship and support of Stephen Brown, Michael Putra, Wilhelmus Andrian, Aaron Monts, Jeffrey Choe, Tom and Lisa Hawkes, and Andrew Delinsky.

For those at the BGAV/Ascent who valued my learning, prayed for and encouraged me, and gave me space to pursue my research while working full-time—a special hat tip to Wayne Faison, John Upton, Julie Lukas, Leslie Straw, Laura McDaniel, Valerie Carter, Dean Miller, Susan McBride, Ken

Kessler, Glenn Akins, Gary Long, David Washburn, Paul Maconochie, Welford Orrock, John Chandler, and Marilee White.

For Pauline Dawkins-Cole and the international prayer team that prayed for me throughout my research and writing. The prayers of my Facebook community helped to sustain me in the times when I was unsure whether I could complete this task.

For my mentors Alan Hirsch, Amos Yong, and David Fitch, who provided me with support and example. Thank you for the valuable articles and writings you have sent me on this topic, for keeping me in prayer, and for giving your time for rich dialogue.

For those who have helped to bring this book to its current expression. Without the content editing and general help of Anna Robinson, this book would not have been published. She has been an amazing editor to work with and has helped to birth a much richer book than would have resulted if I had been left to myself. Thanks also to Jonathan King and Shu-Ling Lee for their editing help; it has been a gift. And much thanks to my fifteen readers—you know who you are. God will not forget your part in helping to bring this book to its current form. I had so much valuable feedback while writing this book that any weaknesses that remain are my own.

For my mom; my dad, who has passed on to be with the Lord; my brothers; and my extended family. Your support through the years has been invaluable.

For you, the reader. Thank you for your willingness to devote your time and energy in reading this book and engaging in dialogue with others. My prayer is that this book would become your good friend and would allow you to experience greater freedom in your life as you gain a clearer picture of the only One who makes freedom possible.

NOTES

PREFACE

1. C. S. Lewis, *The Screwtape Letters* (New York: HarperCollins, 1996), 187.
2. Ibid., 193–194.
3. JR Woodward, *Creating a Missional Culture: Equipping the Church for the Sake of the World* (Downers Grove, IL: InterVarsity Press, 2012).
4. Mike Cosper, *The Rise and Fall of Mars Hill*, June 21, 2021–July 1, 2022, produced by *Christianity Today*, podcast, https://www.christianitytoday.com/ct/podcasts/rise-and-fall-of-mars-hill/.

INTRODUCTION

1. Bobby Ross Jr., "Sex, Money . . . Pride? Why Pastors Are Stepping Down," *Christianity Today*, July 14, 2011, https://www.christianitytoday.com/ct/2011/julyweb-only/sexmoneypride.html.
2. Kate Shellnutt, "Acts 29 CEO Removed Amid 'Accusations of Abusive Leadership,'" *Christianity Today*, February 7, 2020, https://www.christianitytoday.com/news/2020/february/acts-29-ceo-steve-timmis-removed-spiritual-abuse-tch.html.
3. Sarah Pulliam Bailey, "Exclusive: Mark Driscoll's Resignation Letter to Mars Hill Church," *Religion News Service*, October 15, 2014, https://religionnews.com/2014/10/15/exclusive-mark-driscolls-resignation-letter-to-mars-hill-church/.
4. Ken Walker, "Is Buying Your Way Onto the Bestseller List Wrong?" *Christianity Today*, January 20, 2015, https://www.christianitytoday.com/ct/2015/januaryfebruary/buying-bestsellers-resultsource.html.
5. Karl Vaters, "Jesus and Crowds—An Unhappy Marriage," February 20, 2023, https://www.KarlVaters.com/jesus-unhappy.
6. Eugene Peterson, *The Pastor: A Memoir* (New York, HarperCollins, 2011), 156.
7. Ibid.
8. Ibid.
9. Soren Kierkegaard, *The Crowd is Untruth* (Pinkerton, OH: Beloved Publishing, 2015), 15.
10. Peterson, *The Pastor*, 156.
11. Ibid., 157–158.
12. Outreach 100, "2015 Largest Churches in America," accessed October 25, 2021, https://outreach100.com/largest-churches-in-america/2015.
13. Jo Anne Lyon et al., "Independent Advisory Group Report," 2019, https://www.willowcreek.org/-/media/images/7-0-about/elders2019/iagreport-022819.pdf?la=en.

14. Ibid., 4.

15. Ibid., 6.

16. Ibid.

17. Ibid.

18. Ibid., 13.

19. Mike Cosper, "The Brand," August 2, 2021, in *The Rise and Fall of Mars Hill*, produced by *Christianity Today*, podcast, 10:10, https://www.christianitytoday.com/ct/podcasts/rise-and-fall-of-mars-hill/rise-fall-mars-hill-podcast-mark-driscoll-brand.html.

20. Ibid., 20:32, 45:24, 48:04, 52:30, and 55:55.

21. Mike Cosper, "Who Killed Mars Hill?" June 21, 2021, in *The Rise and Fall of Mars Hill*, produced by *Christianity Today*, podcast, 17:38, https://www.christianitytoday.com/ct/podcasts/rise-and-fall-of-mars-hill/who-killed-mars-hill-church-mark-driscoll-rise-fall.html.

22. Roger E. Olson, "Evangelical Superstars and Why They Fall," *Patheos*, August 30, 2014, https://www.patheos.com/blogs/rogereolson/2014/08/evangelical-superstars-and-why-they-fall/; James Emery White, "The Pastoral Mess of 2016," *Crosswalk*, January 5, 2017, https://www.crosswalk.com/blogs/dr-james-emery-white/the-pastoral-mess-of-2016.html; Garrett Kell, "A Pattern among Fallen Pastors—Lessons for Us All," *All Things for Good* (blog), February 20, 2015, http://garrettkell.com/pattern-among-fallen-pastors-lessons-us/; Eddie Kaufholz, "The Mega-Problem Behind the 'Falls' of Megachurch Pastors," *Relevant*, November 6, 2020, https://relevantmagazine.com/current16/mega-problem-behind-falls-mega-church-pastors/; Scott Sauls, "On the Rise and Fall of Pastors," *Scott Sauls* (blog), May 15, 2020, https://scottsauls.com/blog/2020/05/15/pastors/.

23. Scott Sauls, "The Plight of the Falling Pastor," Interview by Daniel Darling, *Christianity Today*, June 24, 2016, https://www.christianitytoday.com/pastors/2016/june-web-exclusives/plight-of-falling-pastor.html.

24. H. B. London Jr. and Neil B. Wiseman, *Pastors at Greater Risk* (Grand Rapids, MI: Baker Books, 2003).

25. Michael Todd Wilson and Brad Hoffmann, *Preventing Ministry Failure: A ShepherdCare Guide for Pastors, Ministers and Other Caregivers* (Downers Grove, IL: InterVarsity Press, 2007).

26. Alan Roxburgh uses *identity* and *telos* and *work of the leader*. I chose to use *praxis* instead of *work*. These terms are affirmed by others addressing the dearth of literature in regards to theological reflection on leadership: Alan J. Roxburgh and Fred Romanuk, *The Missional Leader: Equipping Your Church to Reach a Changing World* (San Francisco, CA: Jossey-Bass, 2006); Michale Ayers, "Toward a Theology of Leadership," *Journal of Biblical Perspectives in Leadership* 1, no. 1 (Fall 2006): 3–27; Chloe Lynch, *Ecclesial Leadership as Friendship* (New York: Routledge, 2019).

27. Each contour of leadership has a corresponding temptation of image (identity), institution (praxis), and ideology (telos). William Stringfellow named these temptations, and in chapter 10 of this book, I will be linking them to these areas of leadership.

28. Wilson and Hoffmann, *Preventing Ministry Failure*, 16.

29. Ibid., 17.

30. Ibid., 18.

31. Ibid., 26.

32. Christopher J. H. Wright, *The Mission of God: Unlocking the Bible's Grand Narrative* (Downers Grove, IL: IVP Academic, 2006).

33. The following are some works on the Powers from a distinctly missional point of view. (Only the *Power and the Powers* has a chapter specifically on leadership and the Powers.) Thomas H. McAlpine, *Facing the Powers: What Are the Options?* (Eugene, OR: Wipf and Stock, 2003); Andrew Hardy, Dan Yarnell, and Richard Whitehouse, ed., *Power and the Powers: The Use and Abuse of Power in Its Missional Context* (Eugene, OR: Cascade Books, 2015); James V. Brownson et al., *StormFront: The Good News of God* (Grand Rapids, MI: William B. Eerdmans, 2003); A. Scott Moreau, ed., *Deliver Us from Evil: An Uneasy Frontier in Christian Mission* (Monrovia, CA: World Vision International, 2002); Loren L. Johns and James R. Krabill, eds., *Even the Demons Submit: Continuing Jesus' Ministry of Deliverance* (Scottdale, PA: Institute of Mennonite Studies, 2006).

34. N. T. Wright, *Jesus and the Victory of God* (Minneapolis, MN: Fortress, 1997); N. T. Wright, *Evil and the Justice of God*, (Downers Grove, IL: IVP, 2013); N. T. Wright, *The Day the Revolution Began: Reconsidering the Meaning of Jesus's Crucifixion* (New York: HarperOne, 2018); Walter Brueggemann, *Truth Speaks to Power: The Countercultural Nature of Scripture* (Louisville, KY: Westminster John Knox, 2013).

35. Lesslie Newbigin, *The Gospel in a Pluralist Society* (Grand Rapids, MI: William. B. Eerdmans, 1989); Lois Barrett, "Missional Witness: The Church as Apostle to the World," in *Missional Church: A Vision for the Sending of the Church in North America*, ed. Darrell L. Guder (Grand Rapids, MI: William B. Eerdmans, 1998).

36. I say reputedly, because it was not a part of his written corpus. Though it is popularly espoused, it cannot be confirmed.

37. Bruce Ashford and Scott Bridger, "Missiological Method," in *Missiology: An Introduction to the Foundations, History, and Strategies of World Missions*, rev. ed., ed. John Mark Terry (B and H Academic, 2015), 16.

38. *Euro-tribal* is a term developed by Roxburgh and Robinson. Alan J. Roxburgh and Martin Robinson, *Practices for the Refounding of God's People* (New York: Church Publishing Inc., 2018), 6.

39. Sharon M. Ravitch and Matthew Riggan, *Reason and Rigor: How Conceptual Frameworks Guide Research*, 2nd ed. (Los Angeles, CA: SAGE, 2016), 8.

40. Ibid., 9.

41. The meaning of *practical theology* I adopt here is defined by John Swinton and Harriet Mowat as "critical, theological reflection on the practices of the Church as they interact with the practices of the world, with a view to ensuring and enabling faithful participation in God's redemptive practices in, to, and for the world" (John Swinton and Harriet Mowatt, *Practical Theology and Qualitative Research*, [London: SCM, 2006], 7).

42. Jeanne Stevenson-Moessner, *Overture to Practical Theology: The Music of Religious Inquiry* (Eugene, OR: Cascade, 2016), 1–2.

43. *Empirical theology* is seeking to think theologically about current social realities.

44. Mandy Smith, *Unfettered: Imagining a Childlike Faith Beyond the Baggage of Western Culture* (Grand Rapids, MI: Brazos, 2021), 126.

1   A DEEPER DIAGNOSIS OF WHY LEADERS FALL

1. Gerard Kelly, *Retrofuture: Rediscovering Our Roots, Recharging Our Routes* (Downers Grove, IL: InterVarsity Press, 1999), 212.

2. I am using the word *mythologically* as Matthew Croasmun uses it in *The Emergence of Sin* (which I summarize in chapter seven of this book), meaning "the actual state of affairs," rather than the way René Girard views myth as hiding the truth that revelation reveals (see chapter six of this book).

3. *Mythological* will typically be used positively as a way to describe the unseen world that really does exist.

4. G. K. Chesterton, *The Scandal of Father Brown* (London: Cassell, 1935), 209.

5. Albert Einstein and Leopold Infeld, *The Evolution of Physics* (New York, Simon and Schuster, 1938), 95.

6. Lesslie Newbigin, *The Gospel in a Pluralist Society* (Grand Rapids, MI: William B. Eerdmans, 1989), 152

7. Ibid.

8. Ibid.

9. Ibid.

10. Marva J. Dawn, "The Concept of 'The Principalities and Powers' in the Works of Jacques Ellul" (PhD diss., University of Notre Dame, 1992), 5.

11. Marva J. Dawn, *Powers, Weakness, and the Tabernacling of God* (Grand Rapids, MI: William B. Eerdmans, 2001), 4; W. A. Visser 't Hooft, *The Kingship of Christ* (New York: Harper and Brothers, 1947), 15–31.

12. Bill Wylie-Kellermann, "Not Vice Versa. Reading the Powers Biblically: Stringfellow, Hermeneutics, and the Principalities," *Anglican Theological Review* 81, no. 4 (October 1, 1999): 665–682, https://www.proquest.com/docview/215274046.

13. Ibid, 665–682.

14. Walter Wink, *Naming the Powers: The Language of Power in the New Testament* (Philadelphia, PA: Fortress, 1984), 113.

15. Dawn, *Powers, Weakness, and the Tabernacling of God*, 1–34; Amos Yong, *In the Days of Caesar: Pentecostalism and Political Theology*, The Cadbury Lectures 2009 (Grand Rapids, MI: William B. Eerdmans, 2010), 134–150; Robert Ewusie Moses, "Powerful Practices: Paul's Principalities and Powers Revisited" (PhD diss., Duke Divinity School, 2012), 6–44.

16. Karl Barth, *Church and State*, trans. G. Ronald Howe, Church Classics (Greenville, S.C: Smyth and Helwys, 1991).

17. Vernon R. Mallow, *The Demonic: A Selected Theological Study: An Examination into the Theology of Edwin Lewis, Karl Barth, and Paul Tillich* (Lanham, MD: University Press of America, 1983), 102.

18. Paul Tillich, *The Eternal Now* (New York: Scribner, 1963), 51. In chapter seven of this book, with the help of Croasmun, I will explore this cosmic nature of Sin with a capital "S."

19. G. B. Caird, *Principalities and Powers: A Study in Pauline Theology: The Chancellor's Lectures for 1954 at Queen's University, Kingston Ontario* (Eugene, OR: Wipf and Stock, 2003).

20. Dawn, "The Concept of 'The Principalities and Powers,'" 54.

21. E. Gordon Rupp, *Principalities and Powers: Studies in the Christian Conflict in History* (London: The Epworth Press, 1952).

22. Dawn, "The Concept of 'The Principalities and Powers,'" 72.

23. Yong, *In the Days of Caesar*, 145.

24. Clinton E. Arnold, *Powers of Darkness: Principalities and Powers in Paul's Letters* (Downers Grove, IL: IVP Academic, 2009).

25. Ibid., 134.

26. James K. Beilby and Paul Rhodes Eddy, eds., *Understanding Spiritual Warfare: Four Views* (Grand Rapids, MI: Baker Academic, 2012), 32.

27. Arnold, *Powers of Darkness*, 183.

28. Ibid., 201.

29. Ibid.

30. Ibid.

31. Ibid., 205.

32. Moses, "Powerful Practices," 16.

33. Ibid., 19.

34. Hendrik Berkhof, *Christ and the Powers*, trans. John Howard Yoder, 2nd ed. (Scottdale, PA: Herald Press, 1977), 22.

35. Arnold, *Powers of Darkness*, 144.

36. Ibid., 164.

37. Ibid., 144.

38. Moses, "Powerful Practices," 19.

39. Ernst Käsemann, "The Eschatological Royal Reign of God," in *Your Kingdom Come: Mission Perspectives*, Report on the World Conference on Mission and Evangelism, Melbourne, Australia, 12–25 May (World Council of Churches, 1980); Marva J. Dawn, "The Concept of 'The Principalities and Powers'"; Dawn, *Powers, Weakness, and the Tabernacling of God*; Kabiro wa Gatumu, *The Pauline Concept of Supernatural Powers: A Reading from the African Worldview* (Eugene, OR: Wipf and Stock, 2008); Arnold, *Powers of Darkness*; Yong, *In the Days of Caesar*; James K. Beilby and Paul Rhodes Eddy, eds., *Understanding Spiritual Warfare*; Hardy, Whitehouse, and Yarnell, *Power and the Powers*; Esther Acolatse, *Powers, Principalities, and the Spirit: Biblical Realism in Africa and the West* (Grand Rapids, MI: William B. Eerdmans, 2018).

40. Moses, "Powerful Practices," 20.

41. Rudolf Bultmann, "New Testament and Mythology: The Problem of Demythologizing the New Testament Proclamation (1941)," in *New Testament and Mythology and Other Basic Writings*, trans. Schubert M. Ogden (Philadelphia, PA: Fortress Press, 1984), 1.

42. Ibid., 2.

43. Ibid., 3.

44. Ibid., 3–4.

45. Ibid., 4.

46. Ibid., 9.

47. Rudolf Bultmann, "On the Problem of Demythologizing (1952)," in *New Testament and Mythology and Other Basic Writings*, trans. Schubert M. Ogden (Philadelphia, PA: Fortress Press, 1984), 99.

48. *Kerygma* refers to the preaching of the apostles, or the basic teachings of the church.

49. Rudolf Bultmann, *Theology of the New Testament: Complete in One Volume* (New York: Prentice Hall, 1970), 259.

50. Gatumu, *The Pauline Concept of Natural Powers*, 194.

51. Ibid.

52. Moses, "Powerful Practices," 26.

53. Ibid., 27.

54. Karl Barth, *The Christian Life* (London; New York: T and T Clark, 2004), 218.

55. Moses, "Powerful Practices," 27.

56. Berkhof, *Christ and the Powers*.

57. John Howard Yoder, *The Politics of Jesus* (Grand Rapids, MI: William B. Eerdmans, 1994), 134–162.

58. Rom. 8:38; 1 Cor. 2:8; 1 Cor. 15:24–26; Eph. 1:20; Eph. 2:1–2; Eph. 6:12; Col. 1:16; Col. 2:15.

59. Berkhof, *Christ and the Powers*, 15.

60. Ibid., 17.

61. Ibid.

62. Ibid., 18.

63. Ibid., 19.

64. Ibid., 20.

65. Ibid., 21.

66. Ibid., 23.

67. Ibid., 25–26.

68. Ibid., 28.

69. Ibid., 29.

70. Ibid., 30.

71. Ibid., 32–33.

72. Ibid., 37.

73. Ibid., 43–67.

74. Rupp, *Principalities and Powers*; G. B. Caird, *The Language and Imagery of the Bible* (Philadelphia, PA: Westminster Press, 1980); Markus Barth, *The Broken Wall: A Study of the Epistle to the Ephesians* (Valley Forge, PA: Judson Press, 1959); William Stringfellow, *Free in Obedience* (Eugene, OR: Wipf and Stock, 2006); Robert E. Webber, *The Church in the World: Opposition, Tension, or Transformation* (Grand Rapids, MI: Zondervan, 1986); Newbigin, *The Gospel in a Pluralist Society*, 200–213.

75. Berkhof, *Christ and the Powers*, 24.

76. Hans W. Frei, *Types of Christian Theology*, eds. George Hunsinger and William Placher (New Haven: Yale University Press, 1992), 1–2.

77. Ibid., 2.

78. David Ford and Rachel Muers, eds., *The Modern Theologians: An Introduction to Christian Theology Since 1918*, 3rd ed. (Malden, MA: Wiley-Blackwell, 2005), 1–16.

79. Les Oglesby, C. G. *Jung and Hans Urs von Balthasar: God and Evil—A Critical Comparison* (London: Routledge, 2013).

80. Ford and Muers, *The Modern Theologians*, 2.

81. Oglesby, C. G. *Jung and Hans Urs von Balthasar*, 33.

82. Ford and Muers, *The Modern Theologians*, 5.

83. Ibid., 3.

2 THE NEED FOR MISSIONAL LEADERSHIP

1. Craig Van Gelder and Dwight J. Zscheile, *The Missional Church in Perspective: Mapping Trends and Shaping the Conversation* (Grand Rapids, MI: Baker Academic, 2011), 1.

2. David E. Fitch, "The Other Missional Conversation: Making Way for the Neo-Anabaptist Contribution to the Missional Movement in North America," *Missiology* 44, no. 4 (October 1, 2016): 467. Fitch considers Craig Van Gelder and Alan Roxburgh to be key representatives of The Missional Network, Alan Hirsch and Michael Frost to be key representatives on the missional evangelicals, and himself, Shane Claiborne and Jonathan Wilson-Hartgrove to fit within the neo-Anabaptist missional stream, working from the theology of Stuart Murray, Bryan Stone, Stanley Hauerwas, and John Howard Yoder.

3. Van Gelder and Zscheile, *The Missional Church in Perspective.*

4. Roxburgh and Romanuk, *The Missional Leader* (Minneapolis, MN, Fortress Press, 2006).

5. Fitch, "The Other Missional Conversation," 467.

6. Darrell L. Guder, ed., *Missional Church: A Vision for the Sending of the Church in North America* (Grand Rapids, MI: William B. Eerdmans, 1998), 6.

7. For faithful monastic orders see George G. Hunter III, *The Celtic Way of Evangelism: How Christianity Can Reach the West . . . AGAIN* (Nashville, TN: Abingdon Press, 2000); Joshua J. Mark, "Monastic Orders of the Middle Ages," *Ancient History Encyclopedia*, June 24, 2019, accessed July 29, 2020, https://www.ancient.eu/article/1407/monastic-orders-of-the-middle-ages/.

8. Van Gelder and Zscheile, *The Missional Church in Perspective*, 19.

9. Ibid., 22.

10. Michael W. Goheen, "Historical Perspectives on the Missional Church Movement: Probing Lesslie Newbigin's Formative Influence," *Trinity Journal for Theology and Ministry* Vol. 4, no. 2 (Fall 2010): 64.

11. Alan Roxburgh, "Missional Leadership: Equipping God's People for Mission," in *Missional Church: A Vision for the Sending of the Church in North America*, ed. Darrell L. Guder (Grand Rapids, MI: William B. Eerdmans, 1998), 190.

12. Ibid., 191.

13. Ibid.

14. Ibid.

15. Ibid., 192.

16. Ibid., 193.

17. Ibid.

18. Ibid., 194–198.

19. Ibid., 196.

20. Ibid., 196–198.

21. Ibid., 198.

22. Van Gelder and Zscheile, *The Missional Church in Perspective*, 11.

23. Ibid., 11–40.

24. Ibid., 27–29.

25. Ibid., 28.

26. Ibid., 33.

27. Roxburgh, "Missional Leadership," 199.

28. Ibid., 200.

29. Ibid., 204.

30. Ibid.

31. Ibid., 207.

32. Ibid., 208.

33. Ibid., 211.

34. Ibid.

35. Ibid., 219–220.

36. Ibid., 212.

37. Ibid.

38. Ephesians 4:11–13.

39. Roxburgh, "Missional Leadership," 199, 214.

40. Ibid., 199, 213.

41. Ibid.

42. Roxburgh and Romanuk, *The Missional Leader*, 115.

43. Ibid., 115.

44. Ibid., 118.

45. Van Gelder and Zscheile, *The Missional Church in Perspective*, 42.

46. Roger Helland and Leonard Hjalmarson, *Missional Spirituality: Embodying God's Love From Inside Out* (Downers Grove, IL: IVP, 2011).

47. Ibid., 64.

48. Ibid., 148–154. Part 2 of the book is titled "Perspectives That Extend the Missional Conversation."

49. Following the publication of *The Missional Church in Perspective*, here are some resources that were developed in this area of need: (note there is also a book edited

by Zscheile) Roger Helland and Leonard Hjalmarson, *Missional Spirituality: Embodying God's Love from the Inside Out* (Downers Grove, IL: IVP, 2011); Dwight Zscheile, ed., *Cultivating Sent Communities: Missional Spiritual Formation* (Grand Rapids, MI: William B. Eerdmans, 2012); David E. Fitch, *Faithful Presence: Seven Disciplines That Shape the Church for Mission* (Downers Grove, IL: IVP, 2016); Nathan A. Finn and Keith S. Whitfield, eds., *Spirituality for the Sent: Casting a New Vision for the Missional Church* (Downers Grove, IL: IVP Academic, 2017).

50. David E. Fitch, *The Great Giveaway: Reclaiming the Mission of the Church from Big Business, Parachurch Organizations, Psychotherapy, Consumer Capitalism, and Other Modern Maladies* (Grand Rapids, MI: Baker Books, 2005), 75.

51. John C. Maxwell, *The 21 Irrefutable Laws of Leadership: Follow Them and People Will Follow You*, 2nd ed. (Nashville, TN: Thomas Nelson, 2007), xx–xxi.

52. Fitch, *The Great Giveaway*, 75.

53. Ibid.

54. Roxburgh and Romanuk, *The Missional Leader*, 117.

55. Ibid., 117–118.

56. Roxburgh, "Missional Leadership," 185–186.

57. Ibid., 186.

58. Van Gelder and Zscheile, *The Missional Church in Perspective*, 60.

59. Ibid., 56.

60. Ibid.

61. Ibid., 57.

62. Ibid.

63. Michael Goheen, "'As the Father Has Sent me, I am Sending You': J.E. Lesslie Newbigin's Missionary Ecclesiology" (PhD diss; de Universiteit Utrecht, 2002), 313.

64. Van Gelder and Zscheile, *The Missional Church in Perspective*, 136.

65. Ibid., 60.

66. Ibid., 59.

67. Ibid., 133.

68. Ibid., 136.

69. William Stringfellow, *The Politics of Spirituality* (Eugene, OR: Wipf and Stock, 2006), 3.

70. Ibid.

71. Van Gelder and Zscheile, *The Missional Church in Perspective*, 125.

72. Scott Aniol, "Toward a Biblical Understanding of Culture," *Artistic Theologian*, October 31, 2012, http://artistictheologian.com/journal/at-volume-1-2012/toward-a-biblical-understanding-of-culture/.

73. Van Gelder and Zscheile, *The Missional Church in Perspective*, 136.

74. Walter Wink, *Engaging the Powers: Discernment and Resistance in a World of Domination*, The Powers, vol. 3 (Minneapolis, MN: Fortress, 1992), 51.

75. Van Gelder and Zscheile, *The Missional Church in Perspective*, 18; Michael W. Goheen, "Historical Perspectives on the Missional Church Movement: Probing Lesslie Newbigin's Formative Influence," *Trinity Journal for Theology and Ministry,* vol. 4, no. 2 (Fall 2010): 62–84.

76. Van Gelder and Zscheile, *The Missional Church in Perspective*, 59–60.

77. Newbigin, *The Gospel in a Pluralist Society*, 200.

78. Arthur C. Cochrane, *The Church's Confession under Hitler* (Philadelphia, PA: Westminster Press, 1962).

79. Newbigin, *The Gospel in a Pluralist Society*, x.

80. George Van Wyngaard, "The Public Role of the Christian Community in the Work of David Bosch," *Missionalia* 31 (April 1, 2011): 161.

81. Lesslie Newbigin, *Truth to Tell: The Gospel as Public Truth* (Grand Rapids, MI: William B. Eerdmans, 1991), 81.

82. Roxburgh and Romanuk, *The Missional Leader*, 210.

83. Alan Kreider, *The Change of Conversion and the Origin of Christendom*, reprint ed. (Eugene, OR: Wipf and Stock, 2007), 90.

84. Roxburgh and Romanuk, *The Missional Leader*, 120.

85. Van Gelder and Zscheile, *The Missional Church in Perspective*, 110.

86. Ibid., 119.

87. Ibid., 110–111.

88. Ibid., 111.

89. Ibid.

90. Mike Cosper, "The Things We Do to Women," July 26, 2021, in *The Rise and Fall of Mars Hill*, produced by *Christianity Today*, podcast, https://www.christianitytoday.com/ct/podcasts/rise-and-fall-of-mars-hill/mars-hill-mark-driscoll-podcast-things-we-do-women.html.

91. Fitch, "The Other Missional Conversation," 467.

92. Ibid., 468.

93. Ibid., 467–468.

94. Ibid., 467.

95. Ibid., 468.

96. Ibid., 467. Fitch identifies three missional streams. The Missional Network (TMN), represented by Van Gelder and Roxburgh, the missional evangelicals (ME) represented by Alan Hirsch and Michael Frost. And finally, the stream he identifies with, the neo-Anabaptist missional (NAM).

97. Ibid., 468.

98. Ibid., 469.

99. Van Gelder and Zscheile, *The Missional Church in Perspective*, 110–111.

100. Fitch, "The Other Missional Conversation," 469.

101. Ibid.

102. Ibid., 470.

103. Ibid.

104. Michael Frost and Alan Hirsch, *ReJesus: A Wild Messiah for a Missional Church* (Grand Rapids, MI: Baker, 2008), 42–43.

105. Alan Hirsch, *The Forgotten Ways: Reactivating Apostolic Movements*, 2nd ed. (Grand Rapids, MI: Brazos, 2016), 143.

106. Fitch, "The Other Missional Conversation," 471.

107. Ibid., 471–472.

108. Ibid., 472.

109. Ibid.

110. Ibid.

111. Ibid.

112. Ibid., 472–473.

113. Ibid.

114. Ibid.

115. Ibid., 474.

116. Ibid.

117. Ibid.

118. Ibid.

119. Roxburgh, "Missional Leadership," 212.

120. Ibid., 214.

121. Ibid., 214.

122. Ibid., 218.

123. JR Woodward, *Creating a Missional Culture: Equipping the Church for the Sake of the World* (Downers Grove: IL, InterVarsity Press, 2012), 63–109.

124. Ibid.

125. Hirsch, *The Forgotten Ways*, 152.

126. Michael Frost and Alan Hirsch, *The Shaping of Things to Come: Innovation and Mission for the 21st Century Church* (Peabody, MA: Hendrickson, 2003); Hirsch, *The Forgotten Ways*; Alan Hirsch and Tim Catchim, *The Permanent Revolution: Apostolic Imagination and Practice for the 21st Century Church* (San Francisco: Jossey-Bass, 2012); Alan Hirsch, *5Q: Reactivating the Original Intelligence and Capacity of the Body of Christ* (100 Movements, 2017); Fitch, *The Great Giveaway*; Fitch, *Faithful Presence*.

127. Woodward, *Creating a Missional Culture*, 113–167.

128. Ed Stetzer, "Laypeople and the Mission of God: Part II—Reclaiming the Priesthood of All Believers," *The Exchange | A Blog by Ed Stetzer*, accessed November 27, 2019, https://www.christianitytoday.com/edstetzer/2012/august/laypeople-and-mission-of-god-part-ii—reclaiming.html.

129. Ibid.

130. Ayers, "Toward a Theology of Leadership"; Lynch, *Ecclesial Leadership as Friendship*; Arthur Boers and Eugene Peterson, *Servants and Fools: A Biblical Theology of Leadership* (Nashville, TN: Abingdon, 2015); Christopher A. Beely and Joseph H. Britton, "Anglican Theological Review—a Quarterly Journal of Theological Reflection" vol. 91, no. 1, Introduction: Toward a Theology of Leadership (Winter 2009): 3–10.

131. Albert Schweitzer, *Albert Schweitzer Thoughts for Our Times*, ed. Erica Anderson (White Plains, NY: Peter Pauper, 1975), 51.

3 DOMINEERING LEADERSHIP IN THE FIRST-CENTURY CHURCH

1. Matt. 18:1; Mark 9:33–34; Luke 9:46; Luke 22:24.

2. Graham Houston, *Leading by Example: Peter's Way for the Church Today* (Colorado Springs, CO: Paternoster, 2008).

3. Houston was chosen as a primary source because he reads 1 Peter from the perspective of domineering leadership. Other resources include: Paul J. Achtemeier, *1 Peter*, ed. Eldon Jay Epp (Minneapolis, MN: Fortress Press, 1996); John H. Elliott, *A Home for the Homeless: A Social-Scientific Criticism of 1 Peter, Its Situation and Strategy* (Eugene, OR: Wipf and Stock Publishers, 2005); I. Howard Marshall, *1 Peter* (Downers Grove, IL: IVP Academic, 1991); Lauri Thurén, *Argument and Theology in 1 Peter* (Sheffield, England: Sheffield Academic Press, 1995); Dennis R. Edwards, *1 Peter*, ed. Tremper Longman III and Scot McKnight (Grand Rapids, MI: Zondervan Academic, 2017).

4. Graham points out that the term residential aliens fits both the social and religious rhetorical setting of those to whom Peter's letter would have circulated. Regarding the religious rhetorical setting, they were residents in the sense we have been created as earth creatures, and our ultimate home is new creation, the new heavens and new earth. We are aliens, in that the ways of the world ought to be foreign to us.

5. Houston, *Leading by Example*, 43.

6. Ibid., 51.

7. Ibid., 43.

8. Ibid., 15.

9. Ibid.

10. Ibid.

11. Ibid.

12. Ibid., 16.

13. Ibid., 18.

14. Ibid., 4.

15. Ibid., 10.

16. Ibid.

17. Ibid.

18. Ibid., 28–29.

19. Ibid., 29.

20. Ibid., 83.

21. Ibid., 84.

22. Ibid.

23. Ibid., 95.

24. Ibid., 85.

25. Ibid., 97.

26. Ibid., 85.

27. Ibid., 86.

28. Ibid.

29. Ibid., 16.

30. Ibid., 172.

31. Ibid., 18.

32. Ibid.

33. Ibid., 25–26.

34. Houston, *Leading by Example*, 99.

35. 1 Pet. 1:1; 2:21; 3:15, 17, 18; 4:1.

36. Soon-Gu Kwon, "Christ as Example: The *Imitatio Christi* Motive in Biblical and Christian Ethics," Acta Universitatis Upsaliensis 21 (Uppsala, Sweden: Uppsala University Library, 1998).

37. Ibid., 86.

38. Ibid., 99.

39. Dietrich Bonhoeffer, *Discipleship*, DBW, vol. 4 (Minneapolis, MN: Fortress, 2003), 59.

40. N. T. Wright, *Following Jesus: Biblical Reflections on Discipleship* (Grand Rapids, MI: William B. Eerdmans, 2014); Richard A. Burridge, *Imitating Jesus: An Inclusive Approach to New Testament Ethics* (Grand Rapids, MI: William B. Eerdmans, 2007); Jason B. Hood, *Imitating God in Christ: Recapturing a Biblical Pattern* (Downers Grove, IL: IVP Academic, 2013); Cornelis Bennema, *Mimesis in the Johannine Literature: A Study in Johannine Ethics* (London: T and T Clark, 2019); Peter James Hedderwick Adam, "The Practice of the Imitation of Christ with Special Reference to the Theology of Dietrich Bonhoeffer" (doctoral thesis, Durham University, 1981), http://etheses.dur.ac.uk/7559/.

41. James K. A. Smith, *Desiring the Kingdom: Worship, Worldview, and Cultural Formation* (Grand Rapids, MI: Baker Academic, 2009).

42. Ibid., 17–18.

43. Ibid., 46.

44. Ibid., 41–42.

45. Ibid., 42.

46. Ibid., 42–43.

47. Ibid., 43.

48. Ibid.

49. Ibid.

50. Ibid., 44.

51. Ibid., 45.

52. Ibid., 46.

53. Ibid., 47.

54. Ibid., 46.

55. Ibid., 52–53.

56. Ibid., 53.

57. Ibid.

58. Ibid., 26.

59. Ibid., 26–27.

60. Ibid., 51.

61. Ibid., 55–62.

62. Houston, *Leading by Example*, 80.

63. Ibid., 81.

64. Ibid.

65. Ibid., 84.

66. Ibid.

67. Ibid.

68. Ibid.

69. Ibid., 86.

70. Ibid.

71. Ibid., 89.

72. Ibid., 92.

73. Ibid.

74. Ibid.

75. Ibid., 92–93.

76. Ibid., 93.

77. Ibid.

78. Ibid., 93–94.

79. Ibid., 94.

80. Ibid., 95.

81. Ibid.

82. Ibid.

83. Ibid.

84. When I use the word *mythical* here, I am talking about a cosmic view and am employing the terminology used by Matthew Croasmun, whose work I engage in chapter seven of this book.

85. In chapter six of this book, I explore how Girard uses *myth* in a negative way, and in chapter seven, I describe how Croasmun uses it to explain the cosmic forces at hand or the "real state of affairs."

86. Fitch, "The Other Missional Conversation," 475.

4 COMPREHENDING THE POWERS

1. Walter Wink, *The Powers That Be: Theology for a New Millennium* (New York: Doubleday, 1998), 2.

2. Wink, *The Powers That Be*, 1.

3. Douglas Martin, "Walter Wink, Theologian and Author, Dies at 76," *The New York Times*, May 19, 2012, https://www.nytimes.com/2012/05/20/us/walter-wink-theologian-who-challenged-orthodoxy-dies-at-76.html.

4. Walter Wink, *The Bible in Human Transformation: Toward a New Paradigm in Bible Study*, 2nd ed. (Minneapolis, MN: Fortress, 2010), 1.

5. Walter Wink and Steven Berry, *Just Jesus: My Struggle to Become Human* (New York: Image, 2014), 115.

6. Wink, *The Bible in Human Transformation*, 1–2.

7. Wayne G. Rollins, "An Overview of the Work of Walter Wink," in *Enigmas and Powers: Engaging the Work of Walter Wink for Classroom, Church, and World*, ed. D. Seiple and Frederick W. Weidmann (Eugene, OR: Wipf and Stock, 2008), 4–5.

8. Ibid.

9. Wink, *The Bible in Human Transformation*, 4.

10. Ibid., 3.

11. Wink, *The Bible in Human Transformation*; Walter Wink, *Transforming Bible Study: A Leader's Guide* (Eugene, OR: Wipf and Stock, 2009).

12. Wink, *Naming the Powers*; Walter Wink, *Unmasking the Powers: The Invisible Forces That Determine Human Existence* (Minneapolis, MN: Fortress, 1993); Walter Wink, *Violence and Nonviolence in South Africa: Jesus' Third Way* (Philadelphia, PA: New Society, 1987); Wink, *Engaging the Powers*; Walter Wink, *Cracking the Gnostic Code: The Powers in Gnosticism* (Atlanta, GA: Scholars, 1994).

13. Wink, *The Bible in Human Transformation*, 2.

14. Walter Wink and Steven Berry, *Just Jesus: My Struggle to Become Human* (New York: Image, 2014), 14.

15. Wink and Berry, *Just Jesus*, 31.

16. Ibid., 28–29.

17. Ibid., 17–19.

18. Henri Nouwen, *You Are the Beloved: Daily Meditations for Spiritual Living* (New York: Convergent, 2017), 4.

19. Walter Wink, "Write What You See: An Odyssey by Walter Wink," *Westar Institute*, May 1994, https://www.westarinstitute.org/resources/the-fourth-r/write-what-you-see/.

20. Wink and Berry, *Just Jesus*, 46–48.

21. Ibid., 48.

22. Ibid., 48.

23. Ibid., 92.

24. Ibid., 92.

25. Wink and Berry, *Just Jesus*, 94.

26. Ibid., 94.

27. Walter Wink, "Wrestling with God: Psychological Insights in Bible Study," in *Psychology and the Bible: From Genesis to Apocalyptic Vision*, ed. J. Harold Ellens and Wayne G. Rollins (Westport, CT: Praeger, 2004), 9–22.

28. Ibid., 16.

29. Ibid., 16.

30. Ibid., 17.

31. Ibid., 18.

32. Ibid., 18.

33. Wink and Berry, *Just Jesus*, 36.

34. Ibid., 140.

35. Ibid., 141.

36. Walter Wink, *Violence and Nonviolence in South Africa: Jesus' Third Way* (Philadelphia, PN: New Society, 1987).

37. Wink and Berry, *Just Jesus*, 141.

38. Ibid., 141.

39. Ibid., 144.

40. Ibid., 144–45.

41. Ibid., 147.

42. Wink, *Engaging the Powers*, 3.

43. Wink, *The Powers That Be*, 14–15.

44. Wink, *Engaging the Powers*.

45. Ibid.

46. Ibid., 5.

47. Ibid., 5–6.

48. Wink, *Engaging the Powers*, 5.

49. Ibid., 6.

50. Ibid., 5.

51. Wink, *Naming the Powers*, 104.

52. Wink, *Engaging the Powers*, 8.

53. Ibid.

54. Wink, *Naming the Powers*, 4.

55. Ibid.

56. Ibid., 104.

57. Ibid., 103.

58. Ibid.

59. Ibid., 7.

60. Ibid., 7–12.

61. Ibid., 39.

62. Ibid., 99.

63. Rom. 13:1–3; Rom. 8:38–39; 1 Cor. 2:6–8; 1 Cor. 15:24–27a; Eph. 2:1–2; Eph. 3:10; Eph. 6:12; Col. 1:16; Col. 2:9–10; Col. 2:13–15; the seven references to *stoicheia* "elements."

64. Wink, *Unmasking the Powers*, 6.

65. Ibid., 12.

66. Ibid.

67. Ibid., 13.

68. Ibid.

69. Ibid., 13–14.

70. Ibid., 14.

71. Wink takes a redemptive view of Satan in the following passages: Matt. 4:1–11; Luke 4:1–13; 1 Cor. 5:1–5; 1 Cor. 7:5; 2 Cor. 12:1–10; Eph. 4:26–27; 1 Tim. 1:20; James 4:26–27; 2 Peter 2:10–11; and Jude 8–9.

72. Wink, *Unmasking the Powers*, 14.

73. Ibid., 15.

74. Ibid., 32.

75. Ibid., 31.

76. Ibid., 41.

77. Ibid.

78. Ibid.

79. Ibid., 42.

80. Ibid.

81. Ibid.

82. Ibid.

83. Ibid., 43.

84. Ibid.

85. Ibid., 46

86. Ibid., 48.

87. Ibid., 48, 49.

88. Ibid., 49.

89. Ibid., 50.

90. Ibid., 64.

91. Ibid., 50.

92. Ibid., 51.

93. Ibid.

94. Ibid.

95. Ibid., 67.

96. Ibid., 65.

97. Ibid.

98. Ibid.

99. Ibid., 64.

100. Ibid.

101. Ibid., 52.

102. Ibid., 53.

103. Ibid., 41–68.

104. Ibid., 54.

105. Ibid.
106. Ibid.
107. Ibid., 69.
108. Ibid., 70.
109. Ibid.
110. Ibid.
111. Ibid.
112. Ibid., 74.
113. Ibid., 79.
114. Ibid., 78.
115. Ibid., 81.
116. Ibid., 88.
117. Ibid., 87.
118. Wink, *Unmasking the Powers*, 172.
119. Wink, *Engaging the Powers*, 3.
120. Ibid., 10.
121. Ibid., 3.
122. Ibid., 8.
123. Ibid.
124. Ibid.
125. Ibid.
126. Ibid., 9.
127. Ibid., 14.
128. Ibid.
129. Ibid.
130. Ibid., 17.
131. Ibid., 26.
132. Ibid.
133. Ibid., 51.
134. Ibid.
135. Ibid.
136. Ibid., 52.
137. Ibid.
138. Ibid., 53.
139. Ibid.
140. Ibid., 57.
141. Ibid., 59.
142. Ibid.
143. Ibid., 59–60.

144. Ibid., 61–62.
145. Ibid.
146. Ibid., 62.
147. Ibid., 101, 103.
148. Ibid., 65.
149. Ibid.
150. Ibid.
151. Ibid., 66.
152. Ibid.
153. Ibid., 67.
154. Ibid., 69.
155. Ibid., 70.
156. Ibid., 72.
157. Ibid.
158. Ibid.
159. Ibid., 74.
160. Ibid.
161. Ibid.
162. Ibid., 77.
163. Ibid.
164. Ibid.
165. Ibid., 85.

5 INTERPRETING THE POWERS

1. Glen Harold Stassen, *A Thicker Jesus: Incarnational Discipleship in a Secular Age* (Louisville, KY: Westminster John Knox, 2012), 9.
2. Ibid., 9.
3. Dietrich Bonhoeffer, "The Church is Dead," lecture presented at the International Youth Conference of the Universal Christian Council on Life and Work and the World Alliance for Promoting International Friendship through the Churches, August 29, 1932, Gland, Switzerland.
4. James William McClendon Jr., *Biography as Theology: How Life Stories Can Remake Today's Theology*, reissue ed. (Eugene, OR: Wipf and Stock, 2002), 2.
5. Ibid., 1–23.
6. Ibid., 14.
7. Ibid., 17.
8. Ibid., 19.
9. Ibid., 22.
10. Ibid.

11. Ibid.

12. Ibid., 88.

13. Michael J. Gorman, *Cruciformity: Paul's Narrative Spirituality of the Cross* (Grand Rapids, MI: William B. Eerdmans, 2001).

14. Henry Mottu, "Walter Wink and Theology," in *Enigmas and Powers: Engaging the Work of Walter Wink for Classroom, Church, and World*, ed. D. Seiple and Frederick W. Weidmann (Eugene, OR: Wipf and Stock, 2008), 29.

15. The Holy Spirit is mentioned seven times in *Naming the Powers*, seven times in *Unmasking the Powers*, and twenty times in *Engaging the Powers*, primarily on pages 304–308.

16. Sharon H. Ringe, "Walter Wink and Pedagogy," in *Enigmas and Powers: Engaging the Work of Walter Wink for Classroom, Church, and World*, ed. D. Seiple and Frederick W. Weidmann (Eugene, OR: Wipf and Stock, 2008), 36.

17. Rollins, "An Overview of the Work of Walter Wink," 14.

18. Wink and Berry, *Just Jesus*, 25.

19. Walter Wink, *The Human Being: Jesus and the Enigma of the Son of the Man* (Minneapolis, MN: Fortress Press, 2002), 22–23.

20. Ibid., 1.

21. Ibid., 26.

22. Ibid., 30.

23. Wink and Berry, *Just Jesus*, 15.

24. Wink, *The Human Being*, 14.

25. Ibid., 17.

26. Ibid.

27. Ibid.

28. Martin, "Walter Wink, Theologian Who Challenged Orthodoxy, Dies at 76."

29. I discovered this through email interaction with Berry.

30. D. Seiple and Frederick W. Weidmann, eds., *Enigmas and Powers: Engaging the Work of Walter Wink for Classroom, Church, and World* (Eugene, OR: Wipf and Stock, 2008).

31. Van Gelder and Zscheile, as I mentioned previously, tended unhelpfully to meld these together.

32. Ford and Muers, *The Modern Theologians*, 5.

33. Wink, *The Powers That Be*, 22.

34. Ibid., 20.

35. John W. Cooper, *Panentheism: The Other God of the Philosophers: From Plato to the Present*, reprint ed. (Grand Rapids, MI: Baker Academic, 2013), 26–30.

36. Ibid.

37. Roger E. Olson, "What's Wrong with Panentheism?" *Roger E. Olson*, August 7, 2012, https://www.patheos.com/blogs/rogereolson/2012/08/whats-wrong-with-panentheism/.

38. Ibid.

39. Charles Taylor, *A Secular Age* (Cambridge, MA: The Belknap Press of Harvard University Press, 2007).

40. See page 102.

41. Dawn, *Powers, Weakness, and the Tabernacling of God*, 14.

42. Andrew T. Lincoln, "Liberation from the Powers: Supernatural or Societal Structures?" in *The Bible in Human Society: Essays in Honour of John Rogerson*, ed. M. Daniel Carroll R., David J.A. Clines, and Philip R. Davies (Sheffield, England: Sheiffield Academic Press, 1995), 337.

43. Ibid., 352.

44. Ibid.

45. Ibid.

46. Ibid., 352–353.

47. Ibid., 348.

48. Ibid., 349.

49. Ibid.

50. Chris Forbes, "Paul's Principalities and Powers: Demythologizing Apocalyptic?," *Journal for the Study of the New Testament* 23, no. 82 (July 1, 2001): 61–88.

51. Ibid.

52. Ibid., 88.

53. Chris Forbes, "Pauline Demonology and/or Cosmology? Principalities, Powers and the Elements of the World in Their Hellenistic Context," *Journal for the Study of the New Testament* 24, no. 3 (March 1, 2002): 51–73.

54. Ibid.

55. Thomas R. Yoder Neufeld, *Ephesians: Believers Church Bible Commentary* (Scottdale, PA: Herald Press, 2002), 296.

56. Moses, "Powerful Practices"; Kabiro wa Gatumu, *The Pauline Concept of Supernatural Powers*.

57. Moses, "Powerful Practices," 26.

58. Susan R. Garrett, *No Ordinary Angel: Celestial Spirits and Christian Claims about Jesus* (New Haven, CT: Yale University Press, 2008), 113.

59. Ibid., 103–138.

60. Ibid., 112.

61. Ibid., 113.

62. Ibid., 114.

63. Ibid., 115.

64. Ibid., 115–116.

65. Ibid., 117.

66. John H. Walton and J. Harvey Walton, eds., *Demons and Spirits in Biblical Theology: Reading the Biblical Text in Its Cultural and Literary Context* (Eugene, OR: Cascade, 2019), 128–147; Lincoln, "Liberation from the Powers," 349–352.

67. Gregory Boyd, "Response to Walter Wink," in *Understanding Spiritual Warfare*,

ed. James K. Beilby and Paul Rhodes Eddy (Grand Rapids, MI: Baker Academic, 2012), 80.

68. Oglesby, *C. G. Jung and Hans Urs von Balthasar*, 139–140.

69. Ibid., 127–143.

70. Wink, *Unmasking the Powers*, 11.

71. Wink, *Engaging the Powers*, 72.

72. Yong, *In the Days of Caesar*, 162.

73. Ibid.

74. Saint Augustine, *City of God*, edited and abridged by Vernon J. Bourke (New York: Random House, Inc, 1950), 207.

75. Yong, *In the Days of Caesar*, 162–163.

76. Amos Yong, *The Spirit of Creation: Modern Science and Divine Action in the Pentecostal-Charismatic Imagination* (Grand Rapids, MI: William B. Eerdmans, 2011), 173–225.

77. Yong, *In the Days of Caesar*, 163.

78. Ibid.

79. Ibid.

80. By "runaway capitalism," I mean a form a capitalism that is not human centered, where the wealth gap between the rich and poor increases due to corrupt systems. *Squid Game* is a series found on Netflix.

81. Dawn, *Powers, Weakness, and the Tabernacling of God*, 73–88.

82. Wink, *Naming the Powers*, 77.

83. Ibid.

84. Ibid.

85. William Stringfellow, *Imposters of God: Inquiries into Favorite Idols*, Reprint. (Eugene, OR: Wipf and Stock, 2006), 6.

86. Ibid., 9.

87. Wink, *Naming the Powers*, 99.

88. Yong, *In the Days of Caesar*, 162–163.

89. Wink, *Naming the Powers*, 65.

90. Ibid.

91. Ibid.

92. Ibid.

93. Ibid., 66.

94. Ibid.

95. Wink, *Engaging the Powers*, 263.

96. Ibid.

97. Ibid., 264.

98. Ibid.

99. Ibid.

100. Ibid.

101. Part three in *Engaging the Powers* focuses on "Engaging the Powers Nonviolently." In part four, he continues the theme with the title "The Powers and the Life of the Spirit."

102. Newbigin, *Truth to Tell*, 74.

103. Lincoln, "Liberation from the Powers," 351–352.

104. Ibid., 347.

6   MIMETIC THEORY

1. Aristotle, *The Complete Works of Aristotle: The Revised Oxford Translation*, vol. 2, ed. Jonathan Barnes (Princeton, NJ: Princeton University Press, 1984), 2318.

2. This is in direct contradiction to Richard Whitehouse's claim that "Girard's assumptions are derived principally from his analysis of medieval and modern French literature, both of which carry their own cultural assumptions." Some of Whitehouse's other critiques will be addressed later in this chapter. Richard Whitehouse, Andrew Hardy, and Dan Yarnell, "More Recent Approaches to Spiritual Conflict," in *Power and the Powers: The Use and Abuse of Power in Its Missional Context* (Eugene, OR: Cascade, 2015), 26.

3. Wolfgang Palaver, *René Girard's Mimetic Theory* (East Lansing, MI: Michigan State University Press, 2013), 309–312.

4. Ibid.

5. Grant Kaplan, *René Girard, Unlikely Apologist: Mimetic Theory and Fundamental Theology* (Notre Dame, IN: University of Notre Dame Press, 2016), 1.

6. René Girard, *The Girard Reader*, ed. James G Williams (New York: Crossroad, 1996), 5.

7. Ibid.

8. Cynthia L. Haven, "What Was the Most Important Moment in René Girard's Life? 'Coming to America,' He Said," *The Book Haven*, January 20, 2016, http://bookhaven.stanford.edu/2016/01/what-was-the-most-important-moment-in-rene-girards-life-coming-to-america-he-said/, accessed December 3, 2019. See also, Haven, *Evolution of Desire*, 47.

9. Ibid.

10. René Girard, "Epilogue: The Anthropology of the Cross," in *The Girard Reader*, ed. James G. Williams (New York: Crossroad, 1996), 283. Some call this second conversion experience sacramental, as he formally connected with the Catholic church.

11. Ibid., 284.

12. René Girard, Pierpaolo Antonello, and João Cezar de Castro Rocha, *Evolution and Conversion: Dialogues on the Origins of Culture* (London; New York: Bloomsbury Academic, 2017), 45.

13. René Girard, *Resurrection from the Underground: Feodor Dostoevsky*, ed. James G. Williams, trans. James G Williams (East Lansing, MI: Michigan State University Press, 2012), 82.

14. Robert Doran, "René Girard's Concept of Conversion and the 'Via Negativa': Revisiting 'Deceit, Desire, and the Novel,'" *Religion & Literature* 43, no. 3 (2011): 170–179.

15. Girard, *Resurrection from the Underground*, 84.

16. Ibid.

17. René Girard, *I See Satan Fall Like Lightning* (Maryknoll, NY: Orbis, 2001), 40.

18. Girard, "Epilogue: The Anthropology of the Cross," 284–285.

19. Girard, *When These Things Begin*, 129.

20. Ibid., 131.

21. Ibid.

22. Girard, "Epilogue: The Anthropology of the Cross," 286–287.

23. Ibid., 287.

24. Cynthia L. Haven, *Evolution of Desire: A Life of René Girard* (East Lansing, MI: Michigan State University Press, 2018), 119.

25. Scott Cowdell, *René Girard and the Nonviolent God* (Notre Dame, IN: University of Notre Dame Press, 2018), 57.

26. Scott Cowdell et al., eds., *René Girard and Raymund Schwager: Correspondence 1974–1991*, trans. Sheelah Treflé Hidden and Chris Fleming (New York: Bloomsbury Academic, 2016), 15.

27. Ibid., 36.

28. Raymund Schwager, *Must There Be Scapegoats? Violence and Redemption in the Bible* (New York: Crossroad, 2018), vii.

29. Their correspondence was in French, Girard's first language and Schwager's preferred foreign language. They used the formal *vous* (you) until 1984, when they started to use *tu* (Cowdell et al., *René Girard and Raymund Schwager*, 7).

30. Ibid., 47.

31. In 1990 the COV&R was initiated and became a place of regular contact.

32. Cowdell et al., *René Girard and Raymund Schwager*, 55, 77.

33. René Girard, Jean-Michel Oughourlian, and Guy Lefort, *Things Hidden Since the Foundation of the World* (Stanford, CA: Stanford University Press, 2002), 231.

34. Cowdell et al., *René Girard and Raymund Schwager*, 51.

35. Ibid., 59.

36. Ibid., 60.

37. Rebecca Adams and René Girard, "Violence, Difference, Sacrifice: A Conversation with René Girard," *Religion and Literature* 25, no. 2 (1993): 9–33.

38. Ibid., 28.

39. Ibid., 29.

40. René Girard, *The One by Whom Scandal Comes* (East Lansing, MI: Michigan State University Press, 2014), 44–45.

41 Michael Kirwan, *Discovering Girard* (Lanham, MD: Rowman and Littlefield, 2005), 40.

42. Girard, *I See Satan Fall Like Lightning*, 10.

43. René Girard, *Deceit, Desire, and the Novel: Self and Other in Literary Structure*, trans. Yvonne Freccero (Baltimore, MD: Johns Hopkins University Press, 1998), 54.

44. Girard, *Deceit, Desire, and the Novel*, 45.

45. Ibid., 59.

46. Girard, *Resurrection from the Underground.*

47. Ibid., 23.

48. Girard, *Deceit, Desire, and the Novel*, 258.

49. Girard, Oughourlian, and Lefort, *Things Hidden Since the Foundation of the World*, 299.

50. Girard, *I See Satan Fall Like Lightning*, 11.

51. Ibid.

52. Scott Cowdell, *René Girard and Secular Modernity Christ, Culture, and Crisis* (Notre Dame, IN: University of Notre Dame Press, 2013), 23.

53. Ibid.

54. Girard, *I See Satan Fall Like Lightning*, 16.

55. Ibid.

56. Ibid., 17.

57. Girard, *I See Satan Fall Like Lightening*, 17.

58. Ibid., 32.

59. Girard, *Violence and the Sacred*, 2.

60. Kirwan, *Discovering Girard*, 38.

61. Ibid. (Some of the anthropologists the Girard studies cite include Godfrey Lienhardt and Victor Turner.)

62. Girard, *Violence and the Sacred*, 7.

63. Ibid., 8.

64. Ibid., 12.

65. Ibid.

66. Ibid.

67. Ibid., 13.

68. Ibid., 14.

69. René Girard, *The Scapegoat* (Baltimore, MD: Johns Hopkins University Press, 1989), 165.

70. Ibid., 19.

71. Ibid.

72. Ibid., 20.

73. Søren Kierkegaard, *The Crowd Is Untruth* (Pickerton, OH: Beloved, 2015).

74. Girard, *The Scapegoat*, 19.

75. Girard, *I See Satan Fall Like Lightning*, 20.

76. Ibid.

77. Ibid., 32.

78. Girard, *I See Satan Fall Like Lightning*, 40.

79. Ibid., 32.

80. Ibid., 13.

81. Girard, *I See Satan Fall Like Lightning*, 33.

82. Girard, *The Scàpegoat*, 194.

83. Girard, *I See Satan Fall Like Lightning*, 33.

84. Ibid.

85. Girard, Oughourlian, and Lefort, *Things Hidden Since the Foundation of the World*, 419.

86. Ibid.

87. Girard, *The Scapegoat*, 193.

88. Ibid.

89. Girard, *I See Satan Fall Like Lightning*, 35.

90. Girard, *The Scapegoat*, 189.

91. Girard, *I See Satan Fall Like Lightning*, 44–45.

92. Ibid., 43.

93. Ibid., 40.

94. Mike Cosper, "Who Killed Mars Hill?" *The Rise and Fall of Mars Hill*, produced by Mike Cosper, podcast, June 21, 2021, 1:28, https://www.christianitytoday.com/ct/podcasts/rise-and-fall-of-mars-hill/who-killed-mars-hill-church-mark-driscoll-rise-fall.html.

95. Ibid. This is a paraphrase from the podcast: 18:00.

96. Ibid., 19:40.

97. Girard, *I See Satan Fall Like Lightning*, 42.

98. Girard, *The One by Whom Scandal Comes*, 53.

99. Steven E Berry and Michael Hardin, *Reading the Bible with René Girard: Conversations with Steven E. Berry* (Lancaster, PA: JDL, 2015), 75.

100. Ibid.

101. Girard, *I See Satan Fall Like Lightning*, 82–83.

102. Ibid., 95.

103. Ibid., 83.

104. Girard, Oughourlian, and Lefort, *Things Hidden Since the Foundation of the World*, 146–147.

105. Ibid., 147.

106. Ibid.

107. Girard, *I See Satan Fall Like Lightning*, 85.

108. Ibid., 43.

109. Ibid., 95.

110. Ibid., 96.

111. Ibid.

112. Ibid., 97.

113. Ibid., 97–98.

114. Ibid., 98.

115. Girard, Oughourlian, and Lefort, *Things Hidden Since the Foundation of the World*, 190.

116. Ibid., 191.

117. Girard, *I See Satan Fall Like Lightning*, 99–100.

118. Ibid., 95.

119. Yong, *In the Days of Caesar*, 148. (Yong lists some of theologians who have come to this conclusion.)

120. Girard, *I See Satan Fall Like Lightning*, 123.

121. Ibid.

122. Ibid.

123. Ibid., 125.

124. Ibid., 138.

7 THE POWER OF IMITATION

1. His first book, *Mensonge romantique et vérité romanesque,* was written in French; this is the translated French title. When it was published in English, the title became *Deceit, Desire, and the Novel: Self and Other in Literary Structure.*

2. Girard, *Resurrection from the Underground*, 16–17.

3. Cynthia L Haven, "The Evolution of René Girard," *America Magazine*, last modified November 16, 2018, https://www.americamagazine.org/arts-culture/2018/11/16/evolution-rene-girard.

4. Jean-Michel Oughourlian, "My Life with René," in *For René Girard: Essays in Friendship and in Truth*, ed. Sandor Goodhart et al. (Michigan State University Press, 2009), 54.

5. Kirwan, *Discovering Girard*, 90.

6. Thomas F. Bertonneau and René Girard, "The Logic of the Undecidable: An Interview with René Girard," *Paroles gelées* 5, no. 1 (1987): 16, https://escholarship.org/uc/item/7444f0z3.

7. Ibid., 16.

8. Grant Kaplan, *René Girard, Unlikely Apologist: Mimetic Theory and Fundamental Theology* (Notre Dame, IN: University of Notre Dame Press, 2016).

9. Kaplan, *René Girard, Unlikely Apologist*, 7.

10. Ibid.

11. Ibid., 8.

12. Wolfgang Palaver, *René Girard's Mimetic Theory* (Michigan State University Press, 2013), 228.

13. Ibid., 228–229.

14. Ibid., 229.

15. Ibid.

16. Cowdell, *René Girard and the Nonviolent God*, 85.

17. Ibid.

18. Ibid.

19. René Girard, *Battling to the End: Conversations with Benoît Chantre*, trans. Mary Baker (East Lansing, MI: Michigan State University Press, 2010), xv.

20. Ibid., xv–xvi.

21. Ibid., x.

22. Whitehouse, Hardy, and Yarnell, "More Recent Approaches to Spiritual Conflict," 26.

23. Ibid.

24. Scott Cowdell, *René Girard and the Nonviolent God* (Notre Dame, IN: University of Notre Dame Press, 2018), 85.

25. Wink, *Engaging the Powers*, 155.

26. Girard, *Deceit, Desire, and the Novel*, 309–314.

27. Ibid., 307.

28. Ibid., 314.

29. Whitehouse, Hardy, and Yarnell, "More Recent Approaches to Spiritual Conflict," 26.

30. Cowdell, *René Girard and the Nonviolent God*; Kaplan, *René Girard, Unlikely Apologist*; Palaver, *René Girard's Mimetic Theory*; Raymund Schwager, *Must There Be Scapegoats: Violence and Redemption in the Bible* (New York: The Crossroad Publishing Company, 2018).

31. Cowdell, *René Girard and the Nonviolent God*, 87.

32. Ibid., 86.

33. Ibid.

34. Ibid., 88.

35. Girard, *I See Satan Fall Like Lightning*, 189.

36. Girard, *The One by Whom Scandal Comes*, 67.

37. Cowdell, *René Girard and the Nonviolent God*, 86.

38. Raymund Schwager, "Christ's Death and the Prophetic Critique of Sacrifice," *Semeia; an Experimental Journal for Biblical Criticism* (December 1985): 110.

39. Cowdell, *René Girard and the Nonviolent God*, 87.

40. Ibid., 91.

41. Girard, *When These Things Begin*, 74.

42. Ibid., 120.

43. Scot McKnight, *The Letter of James* (Grand Rapids, MI: William B. Eerdmans, 2011), 55.

44. Ibid., 296–297.

45. Ibid., 297.

46. Ibid.

47. Ibid., 298.

48. Ibid., 299.

49. Ibid.

50. Sophie Laws, *The Epistle of James* (Black's New Testament Commentary) (Carol Stream, IL: Tyndale House Publishers, 1993), 160.

51. McKnight, *The Letter of James*, 305.

52. Ibid., 308.

53. Ibid., 309.

54. Ibid., 310.

55. McKnight, *The Letter of James*, 328.

56. Ralph P. Martin and John D. W. Watts, *James*, vol. 48, ed. David Allen Hubbard and Glenn W. Barker (Grand Rapids, MI: Zondervan Academic, 2015), 144.

57. McKnight, *The Letter of James*, 326.

58. Ibid., 323.

59. Ibid.

60. Ibid., 328.

61. Ibid., 330.

62. Ibid., 331.

63. Ibid., 333.

64. Ibid., 334.

65. Ibid., 334–335.

66. Ibid., 342.

67. Ibid., 345.

68. Ibid., 347.

69. Ibid.

70. Ibid., 348.

71. Ibid.

72. Ibid.

73. Cowdell, *René Girard and the Nonviolent God*, 86. (This quotation is from Kaplan's interview with Girard.)

74. Ibid.

75. Willard M. Swartley, "Discipleship and Imitation of Jesus/Suffering Servant: The Mimesis of New Creation," in *Violence Renounced: René Girard, Biblical Studies, and Peacemaking*, ed. Willard M. Swartley (Scottdale, PA: Herald, 2000), 218.

76. Willard M. Swartley, ed., *Violence Renounced* (Telford, PA: Pandora, 2000); Thomas Ryba and Vern Neufeld Redekop, eds., *René Girard and Creative Mimesis* (Lanham, MD: Lexington, 2013).

77. Petra Steinmair-Pösel, "Original Sin, Grace, and Positive Mimesis," in *René Girard and Creative Mimesis*, ed. Vern Neufeld Redekop and Thomas Ryba (Lanham, MD: Lexington, 2013), 224.

78. Ibid., 225.

79. Ibid., 226.

80. Ibid.

81. Ibid., 227.

82. Ibid.

83. Ibid., 227–228.

84. Ibid.

85. Ibid.

86. Ibid., 227.

87. Ibid., 228–229.

88. Ibid., 229.

89. Ibid.

90. Ibid.

91. William M. Swartley, "Discipleship and Imitation of Jesus/Suffering Servant: The Mimesis of New Creation," in *Violence Renounced: René Girard, Biblical Studies and Peacemaking* (Telford, PA: Pandora, 2000), 219.

92. Ibid.

93. Ibid.

94. Ibid.

95. Ibid., 220.

96. Ibid., 221.

97. Jim Fodor and Willard M. Swartley, "Christian Discipleship as Participative Imitation: Theological Reflections on Girardian Themes," in *Violence Renounces: René Girard, Biblical Studies and Peacemaking* (Scottdale, PA: Herald, 2000), 257.

98. Swartley, "Discipleship and Imitation of Jesus/Suffering Servant: The Mimesis of New Creation," 239.

99. René Girard, *The One by Whom the Scandal Comes*, translated by M. B. De Bevoirse (East Lansing, MI: Michigan University Press, 2014), 53.

100. Ibid.

101. Matthew Croasmun, *The Emergence of Sin: The Cosmic Tyrant in Romans* (Oxford: Oxford University Press, 2017).

102. Croasmun capitalizes the word *Sin* when speaking of the cosmic tyrant or the body of Sin that arises from "sin."

103. Ibid., 3.

104. Ibid.

105. Ibid., 4.

106. Ibid.

107. Ibid., 8

108. Ibid.

109. Ibid., 12.

110. Ibid., 13.

111. Ibid., 15.

112. Ibid.

113. Ibid., 16.

114. Ibid., 18.

115. Ibid.

116. Ibid., 20.

117. Ibid.
118. Ibid., 21.
119. Ibid., 21.
120. Ibid., 21.
121. Ibid.
122. Ibid., 26.
123. Ibid., 27.
124. Ibid., 27–28.
125. Ibid., 28.
126. Ibid.
127. Ibid.
128. Ibid., 33.
129. Ibid.
130. Ibid., 34–35.
131. Ibid., 35.
132. Ibid.
133. Ibid., 36.
134. Ibid. 45.
135. Ibid., 47.
136. Ibid., 47–52.
137. Ibid., 54.
138. Ibid.
139. Ibid.
140. Ibid.
141. Ibid., 55.
142. Ibid.
143. Ibid., 55–56.
144. Ibid., 58.
145. Ibid.
146. Ibid., 59.
147. Emile Kurkheim, *The Rules of Sociological Method and Selected Texts on Sociology and Its Method* (London: Macmillan, 1982), 251–52.
148. Croasmun, *The Emergence of Sin*, 80.
149. Ibid., 59.
150. Ibid.
151. Ibid., 99.
152. Ibid.
153. Ibid., 104.
154. Ibid.
155. Ibid., 113.

156. Ibid., 114.

157. Ibid., 116.

158. Ibid., 105.

159. Ibid.

160. Ibid., 177.

161. Ibid., 178.

162. Ibid., 188.

163. Ibid.

164. Ibid.

165. Ibid., 188–189.

166. Ibid., 189.

167. Ibid., 177.

168. Ibid., 186.

169. Ibid.

170. Ibid.

171. Ibid., 169. (Croasmun does not use or cite Girard.)

172. Ibid., 117.

173. René Girard, *Battling to the End*, x.

174. McKnight, *The Letter of James*, 347.

8 THE WORK OF THE POWERS

1. Stringfellow tends to approach his study of Scripture book by book rather than citing individual passages. Some of the Scripture he uses when speaking about death are 1 Corinthians 15:21–22 and Hebrews 2:14–15. He looks at how death outlasts other principalities, as described in 1 Corinthians 15:26. Stringfellow considers death to be the devil incarnate: Revelation 12:7–12; 13:1–8. He also draws on how St. Paul understood the reign of death: Romans 5:14, 17.

2. William Stringfellow, *Imposters of God*, 8.

3. William Stringfellow, *Free in Obedience*, 69. (Stringfellow prefers using the word *death* rather than *the devil*, because the medieval conceptions of the devil cause many not to take the devil as seriously as their ancestors did.)

4. Walter Wink, "Stringfellow on the Powers," in *Radical Christian and Exemplary Lawyer*, ed. Andrew W. McThenia Jr. (Eugene, OR: Wipf and Stock, 2006), 25–26.

5. Rowen Williams, foreword to *An Alien in a Strange Land: Theology in the Life of William Stringfellow*, by Anthony Dancer (Eugene, OR: Wipf and Stock, 2011), vii.

6. Anthony Dancer, *An Alien in a Strange Land: Theology in the Life of William Stringfellow* (Eugene, OR: Wipf and Stock, 2011), 8.

7. Ibid., 32.

8. William Stringfellow, *A Keeper of the Word: Selected Writings of William Stringfellow*, ed. Bill Wylie Kellerman (Grand Rapids, MI: William B. Eerdmans, 1996), 3.

9. William Stringfellow, *A Simplicity of Faith: My Experience in Mourning* (Eugene, OR: Wipf and Stock, 2005), 127.

10. William Stringfellow, *My People Is the Enemy: An Autobiographical Polemic* (New York: Holt, Rinehart and Winston, 1964), 53–54.

11. William Stringfellow, *A Second Birthday: A Personal Confrontation* (Eugene, OR: Wipf and Stock, 1970), 81, 82.

12. Ibid., 82.

13. Ibid.

14. Stringfellow, *Simplicity of Faith*, 125.

15. Ibid., 126.

16. Ibid.

17. Ibid., 126–128.

18. William Stringfellow, *Instead of Death,* expanded ed. (Eugene, OR: Wipf and Stock, 2004), 5.

19. Stringfellow likes to use the *Word of God* for God, Scripture, and the presence of God in the world, for he felt too many used the word *God* but gave their own definition of God apart from the Word.

20. Dancer, *An Alien in a Strange Land*, 79.

21. Ibid., 80.

22. Ibid., 81.

23. Kenneth Leech, "On Being a Prophet and a Theologian: Reflections on Stringfellow and the East Harlem Protestant Parish," in *William Stringfellow in Anglo-American Perspective,* ed. Anthony Dancer (Burlington, VT: Ashgate, 2005), 110.

24. Dancer, *An Alien in a Strange Land*, 83.

25. Marshall Johnston, "Bombast, Blasphemy and the Bastard Gospel: William Stringfellow and American Exceptionalism" PhD diss., Baylor University, 2007, 44–45.

26. Stringfellow, *My People is the Enemy*, 69.

27. Ibid., 49.

28. Center for Barth Studies, Princeton Theological Seminary, "Karl Barth: Biography," accessed 8/01/2021, http://barth.ptsem.edu/karl-barth/biography.

29. Other members of the panel were Professor Jarsolav Pelikan (moderator), Professor Edward Carnell (Fuller), Professor Hans Frei (Yale), Professor Jakob Peutuchowski (Hebrew Union College), Professor Bernard Cooke (Marquette University), Professor Schubert Ogden (Southern Methodist University), and William Stringfellow.

30. Dancer, *An Alien in a Strange Land*, 171.

31. Ibid., 173.

32. Ibid.

33. Ibid., 174.

34. University of Chicago Divinity School, "Introduction to Theology: Questions to and Discussions with Dr. Karl Barth," *Criterion* 2, no. 1 (1963): 3–24. (This statement and these questions are also found in chapter three of Stringfellow, *Free in Obedience*, 51–2.)

35. Anthony Dancer compares Barth's answer with Stringfellow's own writing, which in today's academic context would need to be footnoted, as the similarities are evident (Dancer, *An Alien in a Strange Land*, 176–179).

36. Stringfellow, *Free in Obedience*, 95.

37. Ibid., 84.

38. Ibid., 37.

39. Ibid., 38.

40. Dancer, *An Alien in a Strange Land*, 169.

41. Karl Barth, *Evangelical Theology: An Introduction* (Grand Rapids: William B. Eerdmans, 1963), ix.

42. Taylor Branch, *Pillar of Fire: America in the King Years 1963–1965* (New York: Simon and Shuster, 1998), 21.

43. Ibid.

44. Will Campbell, *Brother to a Dragonfly*, 25th anniversary ed. (London: Bloomsbury, 1977), 230.

45. Ibid.

46. Stringfellow, *My People Is the Enemy*, 136.

47. Ibid.

48. There were some Black leaders who introduced the speakers or prayed, but they were not given the opportunity to address the gathering as speakers.

49. Stringfellow, *Imposters of God*, 40.

50. Ibid.

51. William Stringfellow, "Care Enough to Weep," draft manuscript of address at the National Conference on Religion and Race in Chicago, January 14–17, 1963, 2. Box 7, William Stringfellow Papers, #4438, Department of Manuscripts and University Archives, Cornell University Library.

52. Ibid., 14–15.

53. Ibid., 14–15.

54. Ibid.

55. Stringfellow, *Free in Obedience,* 79.

56. Bill Wylie-Kellermann, "Not Vice Versa: Stringfellow, Hermeneutics, and the Principalities" in *William Stringfellow in Anglo-American Perspective*, ed. Anthony Dancer (Burlington, VT: Ashgate, 2005), 126.

57. Stringfellow, *Free in Obedience,* 79.

58. Stringfellow, *Care Enough to Weep*, 14–15.

59. Dawn, "The Concept of 'The Principalities and Powers,'" 74.

60. Stringfellow, *Free in Obedience*, 50–51.

61. Ibid., 26.

62. William Stringfellow, *An Ethic for Christians and Other Aliens in a Strange Land*, reprint ed. (Eugene, OR: Wipf and Stock, 2004), 77.

63. Ibid., 78.

64. Ibid.

65. Ibid.

66. Dawn, *Powers, Weakness, and the Tabernacling of God*, 73–122.

67. Stringfellow, *Free in Obedience*, 52.

68. Stringfellow, *An Ethic for Christians and Other Aliens in a Strange Land*, 82.

69. Ibid., 80.

70. Stringfellow, *Free in Obedience*, 60.

71. Ibid., 60–61.

72. Ibid., 61.

73. Ibid., 60.

74. Ibid., 63–64.

75. Stringfellow, *A Simplicity of Faith*, 126.

76. Ibid.

77. Ibid., 128.

78. Ibid.

79. Stringfellow, *Free in Obedience*, 49–50.

80. Ibid., 54.

81. Ibid., 55.

82. Ibid.

83. Ibid., 56.

84. Ibid., 57.

85. Dawn, *Powers, Weakness, and the Tabernacling of God*, 75.

86. Stringfellow, *Free in Obedience*, 57.

87. Ibid.

88. Ibid.

89. Ibid., 58.

90. Ibid.

91. Stringfellow, *An Ethic for Christians and Other Aliens in a Strange Land*, 98.

92. Ibid.

93. Ibid.

94. Ibid., 99.

95. Ibid.

96. Ibid., 100.

97. Ibid., 101.

98. William Stringfellow, *An Ethic for Christians and Other Aliens in a Strange* Land (Eugene, OR: Wipf and Stock, 1973), 19.

99. William Stringfellow, *The Politics of Spirituality* (Philadelphia: Westminster, 1984), 38.

100. Ibid.

101. William Stringfellow, *Dissenter in a Great Society* (New York: Holt, Rinehart and Winston, 1966), 137.

102. William Stringfellow, *An Ethic for Christians*, 18.

103. William Stringfellow, *Free in Obedience*, 64.

104. Ibid., 68.

105. William Stringfellow, *Imposters of God*, 8.

106. Ibid., 64.

107. Ibid., 70.

108. William Stringfellow, *An Ethic for Christians*, 77.

109. Richard Beck, *The Slavery of Death* (Eugene, OR: Cascade, 2014).

110. Ibid.

111. Stringfellow, *The Politics of Spirituality*, 44.

112. Stringfellow, *An Ethic for Christians*, 78.

113. Stringfellow, *Free in Obedience*, 69.

114. Stringfellow, *Instead of Death*, 21.

115. Ibid., 22.

116. Stringfellow, *Imposters of God*, 6.

117. Ibid., 9.

118. Stringfellow, *Free in Obedience*, 64.

119. Stringfellow, *An Ethic for Christians*, 32, 34.

120. Ibid., 149–150.

121. Ibid., 67.

122. Ibid., 51.

123. Ibid.

124. Ibid., 52.

125. Ibid., 68.

126. Ibid., 48.

127. Ibid., 50.

128. Stringfellow, *Free in Obedience*, 29.

129. Ibid., 76.

130. Ibid., 75.

131. Ibid., 75–76.

132. Ibid., 72.

133. Stringfellow, *Dissenter in a Great Society*, 142.

134. Stringfellow, *Free in Obedience*, 73.

135. Ibid.

136. Stringfellow, *Instead of Death*, 43.

137. Ibid., 111–112.

138. Ibid., 112.

139. Johnston, *Bombast, Blasphemy and the Bastard Gospel*, 181.

140. Stringfellow, *Instead of Death*, 111.

141. Stringfellow, *Dissenter in a Great Society*, 46.

142. Ibid., 46, 47.

143. Stringfellow, *My People Is the Enemy*, 42–44.

144. Stringfellow, *The Politics of Spirituality*, 34.

145. Stringfellow, *An Ethic for Christians*, 42.

146. Ibid., 45.

147. Stringfellow, *Free in Obedience*, 17–19.

148. Stringfellow, *An Ethic For Christians*, 45–46.

149. Ibid., 47.

150. Stringfellow, *Free in Obedience*, 22.

151. Ibid.

152. Ibid., 28.

153. Ibid., 40.

154. Ibid., 41.

155. Ibid.

156. Ibid., 42.

157. Ibid., 43.

158. Ibid., 44.

9 THE SUBVERSION AND RESISTANCE OF THE POWERS

1. Genesis 2:19–20.

2. J. Richard Middleton, *The Liberating Image: The Imago Dei in Genesis 1* (Grand Rapids: Brazos, 205), 204–212.

3. Genesis 17:5; Genesis 32:22–32; John 1:42; David Pawson, *Simon Peter: The Reed and the Rock* (Kennington, Ashford, UK: Anchor Recordings, 2013), 9–22.

4. University of California, Los Angeles, "Putting Feelings into Words Produces Therapeutic Effects in the Brain," June 22, 2007, *ScienceDaily*, https://www.sciencedaily.com/releases/2007/06/070622090727.htm.

5. Walter Wink, *Unmasking the Powers*.

6. William Stringfellow, *My People Is the Enemy: An Autobiographical Polemic* (New York: Holt, Rinehart and Winston, 1964), 2.

7. Ibid., 4.

8. Ibid., 129.

9. Dancer, *An Alien in a Strange Land*, 70.

10. Ibid., 74.

11. William Stringfellow, Memorandum, March 1961 (no recipient given) announcing his partnership in a new law firm. Box 5, William Stringfellow Papers, #4438, Department of Manuscripts and University Archives, Cornell University Library, 2.

12. William Stringfellow, *An Ethic for Christians and Other Aliens in a Strange Land*, reprint ed. (Eugene, OR: Wipf and Stock, 2004), 41.

13. Dancer, *An Alien in a Strange Land,* 79.

14. William R. Coats, "A Prophet of the Biblical World," in *Prophet of Justice, Prophet of Life: Essays on William Stringfellow*, ed. Robert B. Slocum (Eugene, OR: Wipf and Stock, 2014), 165–166.

15. Ibid., 166.

16. Ibid.

17. Ibid., 167.

18. Ibid.

19. William Stringfellow, *Dissenter in a Great Society*, 142–143.

20. William Stringfellow, "The Political Witness of the Church of Christ," *The Witness,* December 3, 1964, 8.

21. Marshall Johnston, "Bombast, Blasphemy and the Bastard Gospel: William Stringfellow and American Exceptionalism" PhD diss., Baylor University, 2007, 160–171.

22. William Stringfellow, *Dissenter in a Great Society* (New York: Holt, Rinehart and Winston, 1966), 162.

23. Ibid.

24. Ibid.,

25. Ibid., 136.

26. Ibid., 131.

27. Ibid.

28. Ibid., 132.

29. Ibid., 133.

30. Ibid.

31. Ibid.

32. Ibid., 121.

33. Ibid.

34. Ibid.

35. Ibid., 122.

36. Ibid.

37. Ibid.

38. William Stringfellow, *Imposters of God*, 39–40.

39. William Stringfellow, Dissenter in a Great Society, 110.

40. Croasmun, *The Emergence of Sin*, 47.

41. Ibid., 48–49.

42. Ibid., 49.

43. Eduardo Bonilla-Silva, *Racism without Racists: Color-Blind Racism and the Persistence of Racial Inequality in the United States*, 3rd ed., (Landham, MD: Roman and Littlefield, 2010), 8–9, quoting Croasmun, *The Emergence of Sin*, 49.

44. Croasmun, *The Emergence of Sin*, 49.

45. Bonilla-Silva, *Racism without Racists*, 8–9, quoting Croasmun, *The Emergence of Sin*, 49.

46. Croasmun, *The Emergence of Sin*, 49.

47. Ibid.

48. Ibid.

49. Ibid.

50. Ibid., 50.

51. Ibid.

52. Ibid.

53. Ibid., 51.

54. Ibid.

55. Ibid.

56. Ibid.

57. Ibid.

58. Ibid.

59. Ibid.

60. Ibid.

61. Ibid.

62. Ibid.

63. Ibid., 52.

64. Mary Douglas, *Natural Symbols: Explorations in Cosmology* (London, Barrie and Jenkins Ltd, 1973), 29. Thanks to Jon Tyson for this metaphor.

65. Alt-right and alt-left represent extreme ideologies on both sides of our political polarities.

66. Walter Wink, *Engaging the Powers*, 51.

67. Ibid., 85.

68. Patrick Oden, *Hope for the Oppressor: Discovering Freedom through Transformative Community* (Lanham, MD: Fortress Academic, 2019).

69. Mike Cosper, *The Rise and Fall of Mars Hill*, June 21, 2021–July 1, 2022, produced by *Christianity Today*, podcast, https://www.christianitytoday.com/ct/podcasts/rise-and-fall-of-mars-hill/.

70. Stringfellow, *Free in Obedience*, 63.

71. Sarah Pulliam Bailey, "Why Mark Driscoll's fall and Mars Hill's breakup issues a warning for megastar pastors," *Religion News Service*, November 5, 2014, https://religionnews.com/2014/11/05/mark-driscolls-fall-mars-hills-breakup-raises-questions-megastar-pastors/.

72. Mike Cosper, "Who Killed Mars Hill?" June 21, 2021, in *The Rise and Fall of Mars Hill*, produced by *Christianity Today*, podcast, https://www.christianitytoday.com/ct/podcasts/rise-and-fall-of-mars-hill/who-killed-mars-hill-church-mark-driscoll-rise-fall.html.

73. Ibid., 18:31.

74. Husna Haq, "Pastor reportedly buys his way onto New York Times bestsellers list," *The Christian Science Monitor*, March 7, 2014, https://www.csmonitor.com/Books/chapter-and-verse/2014/0307/Pastor-reportedly-buys-his-way-onto-New-York-Times-bestseller-list.

75. Kate Tracy, "Mars Hill Defends How Mark Driscoll's 'Real Marriage' Became a Bestseller" *Christianity Today*, March 7, 2014, https://www.christianitytoday.com/news/2014/march/did-mark-driscoll-real-marriage-earn-nyt-bestseller-status-.html.

76. Walter Wink, *Engaging the Powers*, 61–62.

77. Ibid., 62.

78. William Stringfellow, *Free in Obedience*, 55.

79. Graham Houston, *Leading by Example*, 13.

80. Mike Cosper, host, "Who Killed Mars Hill?" *The Rise and Fall of Mars Hill,* podcast, June 21, 2021, https://www.christianitytoday.com/ct/podcasts/rise-and-fall-of-mars-hill/who-killed-mars-hill-church-mark-driscoll-rise-fall.html.

81. Brandon Kiley, "Why the Mars Hill Faithful Have Started to Question Mark," *The Stranger*, July 30, 2014, https://www.thestranger.com/seattle/why-the-mars-hill-faithful-have-started-to-question-mark/Content?oid=20257920.

82. Ibid.

83. Ibid.

84. Ibid.

85. Ibid.

86. Ibid.

87. Ibid.

88. Ibid.

89. Mark Driscoll, "There is a pile of dead bodies behind the Mars Hill bus," Joyful Exiles, https://joyfulexiles.files.wordpress.com/2012/06/preaching-paul_edits1.mp3, accessed December 12, 2021.

90. Ibid.

91. Joanna Petry, "My Story," *Joyful Exiles*, March 19, 2012, https://joyfulexiles.com/2012/03/19/my-story-by-jonna-petry/.

92. Sarah Pulliam Bailey, "Exclusive: Mark Driscoll's resignation letter to Mars Hill Church," *Religion News Service*, October 14, 2012,: https://religionnews.com/2014/10/15/exclusive-mark-driscoll-resigns-from-mars-hill-church/.

93. Mars Hill Elders, "Seven Years Later: 18 Mars Hill Elders Issue Letter of Confession to Brent Meyer, Paul Petry, and the Church," *Joyful Exiles*, November 2, 2014, https://joyfulexiles.com/2014/11/03/seven-years-later-18-mars-hill-elders-issue-letter-of-confession-to-bent-meyer-paul-petry-and-the-church/.

94. Ibid.

95. René Girard, *The Scapegoat*, 207.

96. I developed this leadership matrix in conversation with my PhD supervisor, Phil Meadows.

97. This illustration was given to me by my PhD supervisor, Phil Meadows.

10 TOWARD A THEOLOGICAL REMEDY

1. Stanley Jr. Grentz, *Theology for the Community of God* (Grand Rapids: William B. Eerdmans, 2000), 2–3.

2. Wink, *Engaging the Powers*, 3.

3. There are others who have this same view. See David Bradnick, *Evil, Spirits and Possession: An Emergentist Theology of the Demonic* (Leiden, Netherlands: Brill, 2017).

4. Ibid., 8.

5. Ibid., 51.

6. Wink, *Engaging the Powers*, 51–52.

7. *Kenosis* essentially means "self-emptying." I will explore this in the next chapter when I look at a Girardian reading of Philippians.

8. N. T. Wright, *The Day the Revolution Began: Reconsidering the Meaning of Jesus's Crucifixion* (New York: HarperOne, 2018), 366.

9. See chapter two of this book.

10. See chapter three of this book.

11. Dietrich Bonhoeffer, *Creation and Fall Temptation: Two Biblical Studies*, reprint ed. (New York: Touchstone, 1997), 115.

12. Gerald F. Hawthorne, *The Presence and The Power: The Significance of the Holy Spirit in the Life and Ministry of Jesus* (Eugene, OR: Wipf and Stock, 2003), 137.

13. Ibid., 138.

14. Ibid., 139.

15. Susan R. Garrett, *The Temptations of Jesus in Mark's Gospel* (Grand Rapids, MI: William. B. Eerdmans, 1996), 117.

16. Ibid., 60.

17. Henri Nouwen, *The Selfless Way of Christ: Downward Mobility and the Spiritual Life* (Maryknoll, N.Y.; London: Orbis Books, 2011), 50.

18. Ibid., 52.

19. Ellul, *If You Are the Son of God*, 62.

20. Nouwen, *You Are the Beloved*, 6.

21. Henri J. M. Nouwen, *Bread for the Journey: A Daybook Of Wisdom And Faith*, Reprint ed. (San Francisco: HarperOne, 2006), 171.

22. Nouwen, *The Selfless Way of Christ*, 58.

23. Ellul, *If You Are the Son of God*, 65.

24. Nouwen, *The Selfless Way of Christ*, 64.

25. Ibid., 64–65.

26. Stringfellow, *Free in Obedience*, 75–76.

27. Stringfellow, *An Ethic For Christians and Other Aliens in a Strange Land*, 145.

28. Richard Twiss, *Rescuing the Gospel from the Cowboys: A Native American Expression of the Way of Jesus* (Downers Grove, IL: InterVarsity Press, 2015), 46.

29. Bob Goudzwaard, *Idols of Our Time* (Sioux Center, IA: Dordt College Press, 1989), 25.

30. David T. Koyzis, *Political Visions and Illusions: A Survey and Christian Critique of Contemporary Ideologies*, 2nd ed. (Downers Grove, IL: IVP Academic, 2019), 16.

31. Girard, Oughourlian, and Lefort, *Things Hidden Since the Foundation of the World*, 286–287.

32. Eduardo Bonilla-Silva, *Racism without Racists*.

33. Author adaptation of Galatians 3:26–28.

34. Stringfellow, *An Ethic for Christians and Other Aliens*, 142–143.

35. Scott Cowdell, *Abiding Faith: Christianity Beyond Certainty, Anxiety, and Violence* (Eugene, OR: Pickwick, 2009), 195.

36. The ideas in the paragraph were shaped by Robert Hamerton-Kelly, but ordered and considered differently. Robert Hamerton-Kelly, *Sacred Violence: Paul's Hermeneutic of the Cross* (Minneapolis, MN: Fortress, 1992), 165–166.

37. Ibid., 166.

38. Cowdell, *Abiding Faith*, 194.

39. Phil Meadows, "Making Disciples That Renew the Church," 2013, https://urc.org.uk/wtwresources/Making-Disciples-that-Renew-the-Church.pdf. (Phil Meadows was my supervisor for my PhD research.)

40. Ibid., 17.

41. Amos Yong, Vinson Synan, and Miguel Álvarez, eds. *Global Renewal Christianity: Spirit Empowered Movements: Past, Present, and Future*, vol. 2, *Latin America* (Lake Mary, FL: Charisma House, 2016); Vinson Synan, Amos Yong, and J. Kwabena Asamoah-Gyadu, eds., *Global Renewal Christianity: Spirit-Empowered Movements Past, Present, and Future*, vol. 3, *Africa* (Lake Mary, FL: Charisma House, 2016); Allen Yeh, *Polycentric Missiology: Twenty-First Century Mission from Everyone to Everywhere* (Downers Grove, IL: IVP Academic, 2016); Veli-Matti Kärkkäinen, *An Introduction to Ecclesiology: Ecumenical, Historical and Global Perspectives* (Downers Grove: IL: IVP Academic, 2002); Henning Wrogemann, *Intercultural Theology*, vol. 1, *Intercultual Hermeneutics, Missional Engagements* (Downers Grove, IL: IVP Academic, 2016); Graham Hill, *GlobalChurch: Reshaping Our Conversations, Renewing Our Mission, Revitalizing Our Churches* (Downers Grove, IL: IVP Academic, 2016).

42. Crouch, *Playing God*, 25.

43. Ibid., 45.

44. Dawn, *Powers, Weakness, and the Tabernacling of God*; Dan B. Allender, *Leading with a Limp: Take Full Advantage of Your Most Powerful Weakness* (Colorado Springs, CO: WaterBrook, 2008); Crouch, *Playing God*; Roy Kearsley, *Church, Community and Power* (Farnham, England: Routledge, 2009); Hardy, Whitehouse, and Yarnell, *Power and the Powers*. Henri Nouwen, *In the Name of Jesus: Reflections on Christian Leadership* (New York: Ballantine, 1992).

45. I will discuss this more in chapter twelve of this book.

46. Wright, *The Day the Revolution Began*, 368.

47. Alan Hirsch, *The Forgotten Ways: Reactivating Apostolic Movements*, 2nd ed. (Grand Rapids, Brazos, 2016). (See chapter seven. *Communitas* is where we move from just being community to being communities on mission.)

48. St. Francis of Assisi, *The Complete Writings of St. Francis of Assisi*, trans. Paschal Robinson (Philadelphia, PA: Dolphin, 1905), 54.

49. John Michael Talbot and Steve Rabey, *The Lessons of Saint Francis: How to Bring Simplicity and Spirituality into Your Daily Life* (New York: Penguin, 1998), 84.

50. Ibid., 244.

51. Adrian House and Karen Armstrong, *Francis of Assisi: A Revolutionary Life* (Mahwah, NJ: Hidden Spring, 2003), 9.

52. G. K. Chesterton, *St. Francis of Assisi* (Mount Pleasant, SC: Arcadia, 2019). This quote was on the back cover of the book.

53. Ibid., 15–16.

11   A NEW WAY OF BEING AND BELONGING

1. Larry Crabb, foreword to *The Connecting Church: Beyond Small Groups to Authentic Community*, by Randy Frazee (Grand Rapids: Zondervan, 2001), 13.

2. I believe that at the time of writing, this is the first published attempt to look at Philippians through a Girardian lens, so this is my experimental offering of which I gladly invite critique and dialogue.

3. Tom Corson-Knowles, "Stories Matter: Stories Are Important to Our Lives and Culture," tckpublishing.com, June 18, 2022, https://www.tckpublishing.com/stories-matter/.

4. Patrick Gray, *Paul as a Problem in History and Culture: The Apostle and His Critics through the Centuries* (Grand Rapids: Baker Academic, 2016).

5. N. T. Wright, *Paul: A Biography* (San Francisco: HarperOne, 2018). N. T. Wright, *Paul and the Faithfulness of God* (Minneapolis: Fortress, 2013). James D. G. Dunn, *The Theology of Paul the Apostle* (Grand Rapids, MI: William B. Eerdmans, 1998). Michael J. Gorman, *Apostle of the Crucified Lord: A Theological Introduction to Paul and His Letters* (Grand Rapids, MI: William B. Eerdmans, 2017). Michael J. Gorman, *Cruciformity: Paul's Narrative Spirituality of the Cross* (Grand Rapids, MI: William B. Eerdmans, 2001). Robert Hamerton-Kelly, *Sacred Violence: Paul's Hermeneutic of the Cross* (Minneapolis, MN: Fortress, 1992).

6. Although I remember this particular statement from a lecture in California, I do not remember the date and place. I believe anyone who reads N. T. Wright will pick up on this methodology in most of his works.

7. While Matthew 23:13 states this emphatically, a general reading of the Gospels reveals this understanding.

8. I borrow the wording "forgiving victim" from James Alison. James Alison, *Jesus the Forgiving Victim: Listening for the Unheard Voice* (Glenview, IL: Doers, 2013).

9. A reminder that I am looking at Philippians from a Girardian point of view, which I expounded in chapters six and seven of this book. Like other Girardian scholars, at this point, I am assuming the reader has absorbed that knowledge.

10. James Alison, "Belonging and Being Church: What's Catholicism All About?" September 10, 2021, https://jamesalison.com/belonging-and-being-church/.

11. This language is in common use in the US. For those in a different context, "deplorables" was used by Hillary Clinton to talk about conservatives in a negative way. However, some have proudly adopted the name for themselves against the "woke community": those who lean more progressive in their politics.

12. Ninjay K. Gupta, *Reading Philippians: A Theological Introduction* (Eugene, OR: Cascade, 2020), 14.

13. Peter Oakes, *Philippians: From People to Letter* (Cambridge: Cambridge University Press, 2001), 45.

14. Ibid., 49.

15. Ibid., 47.

16. Ibid., 75.

17. Joseph Hellerman, *Reconstructing Honor in Roman Philippi: Carmen Christi as Cursus Pudorum* (Cambridge: Cambridge University Press, 2005), 6.

18. Ibid., 10.

19. Ibid., 12.

20. Ibid., 35.

21. Ibid., 62.

22. Joseph H. Hellerman, "Μορφη Θεου as a signifier of social status in Philippians 2:6," *Journal of the Evangelical Theological Society* 52, no. 4 (December 2009): 781, https://digitalcommons.biola.edu/faculty-articles/163.

23. Hellerman, *Reconstructing Honor*, 109.

24. Alain de Botton, *Status Anxiety* (New York: Random House, 2005).

25. Ibid., vii.

26. Ibid., vii–viii.

27. Ibid., 5.

28. Ibid., 6.

29. Ibid., 8.

30. Ibid.

31. Ibid., 25.

32. Ibid., 31.

33. Ibid., 36.

34. Ibid., 43.

35. Ibid., 76.

36. Ibid., 82.

37. Ibid., 87.

38. What American businessman and politician Andrew Yang calls the "fourth industrial revolution" comes into play here, too. Elon Musk shares Yang's concerns about how, in the near future, artificial intelligence will cause a massive loss of jobs, leaving many unemployed and purposeless.

39. Hellerman, *Reconstructing Honor*, 108.

40. Ibid., 109.

41. Ben Witherington III, *Paul's Letter to the Philippians: A Socio-rhetorical Commentary* (Grand Rapids, MI: William B. Eerdmans, 2011), 97–103.

42. Witherington, *Paul's Letter to the Philippians*, 95–112; Corné J. Bekker, "Sharing in the Incarnation: Towards a Model of Mimetic Christology Leadership"; *International Journal on Spirituality and Organizational Leadership* 9, no. 2 (July 2021), 6; G. A. Kennedy, *New Testament Interpretation through Rhetorical Criticism* (Raleigh, NC: University of North Carolina Press, 1984); Michael F. Bird and Nijay K. Gupta, *Philippians* (Cambridge: Cambridge University Press, 2020). Nijay K. Gupta, *Reading Philippians*.

43. Markus Bockmuehl, "A Commentator's Approach to the 'Effective History' of Philippians," *Journal for the Study of the New Testament* 18, no. 60 (April 1996): 57–88. https://doi.org/10.1177/0142064X9601806003.

44. Ibid., 58.

45. Ibid., 73.

46. Ibid.

47. Ibid., 74.

48. Ibid.

49. Ibid., 74–75.

50. Ibid., 75.

51. James Alison, *Living in the End Times: The Last Things Re-imagined* (New York: The Crossroad Publishing Company, 1996), 55.

52. Ibid., 71.

53. Bockmuehl, "A Commentator's Approach to the 'Effective History' of Philippians," 75.

54. Ibid., 76.

55. Ibid.

56. Ibid.

57. Ibid., 81.

58. Ibid.

59. Ibid., 83.

60. Ibid.

61. Davorin Peterlin, *Paul's Letter to the Philippians in the Light of Disunity in the Church* (New York: E.J. Brill, 1995).

62. Witherington, *Paul's Letter to the Philippians*, 475; B. Mengel, *Studien zum Philipperbrief* (Tubingen: Mohr, 1982), 243; F.F. Bruce, *Philippians* (Understanding the Bible Commentary Series) (Grand Rapids: Baker, 1983), 138–140; Fred B. Craddock, *Philippians: Interpretation: A Bible Commentary for Teaching and Preaching* (Louisville, KY: Westminster John Knox, 1985), 69; Lynn H. Cohick, *The Story of God Bible Commentary: Philippians* (Grand Rapids: Zondervan, 2013), 398 (Kindle); Peter T. O'Brien, *The Epistle to the Philippians* (Grand Rapids, MI: William B. Eerdmans, 1991), 477–480.

63. Gordon D. Fee, *Paul's Letter to the Philippians* (Grand Rapids, MI: William B. Eerdmans, 1995), 391; G. Walter Hansen, *The Letter to the Philippians* (Grand Rapids, MI: William B. Eerdmans, 2009), 279–280.

64. N. T. Wright, *Philippians: Studies for Individuals and Groups* (Downers Grove, IL: InterVarsity Press, 2009), 55.

65. G. Walter Hansen, *The Letter to the Philippians*, 279–280.

66. Nils A. Dahl, "Euodia and Syntyche and Paul's Letter to the Philippians," *The Social World of the First Christians: Essays in Honor of Wayne A. Meeks* (ed. L. Michael White and O. Larry Yarborough) (Minneapolis: Fortress, 1995).

67. Hansen, *The Letter to the Philippians*, 284.

68. Nijay Gupta, *Reading Philippians*, 54. (The following are some Bible translations

that use the word *rivalry*: Holman Christian Standard Bible, Literal Standard Version, New Heart English Bible, World English Bible, Young's Literal Translation.)

69. Hansen, *The Letter to the Philippians*, 284.

70. Jean-Michel Oughourlian, *The Genesis of Desire* (East Lansing, MI: Michigan State University Press, 2010), 2.

71. Ibid. 12.

72. Ibid.

73. Ibid.

74. Mabvuto J. Phiri, "Scandal Must Come: Reconciliation as a Divine-Human Kenotic Event in World Immersed in a Culture of Violence and Death," Doctoral diss., (Boston College, 2013).

75. Oughourlian, *The Genesis of Desire*, 13.

76. I am including all anti-models Paul mentions in Philippians 3 as enemies of the cross, for whether they are the same or different groups, they all devalue the cross.

77. William Kurz, "Kenotic Imitation of Paul and of Christ in Philippians 2 and 3," in *Discipleship in the New Testament*, ed. Fernando F. Segovia (Philadelphia, PA: Augsburg Fortress, 1985), 103–126.

78. Oughourlian, *The Genesis of Desire,* 27.

12 THE SCANDAL OF IMITATING CHRIST

1. Nijay K. Gupta, *Reading Philippians*, 49–50.

2. Bird and Gupta, *Philippians*, 70.

3. N. T. Wright, *The Climax of the Covenant: Christ and the Law in Pauline Theology* (New York: T and T Clark, 1991), 84.

4. Joseph H. Hellerman., "Μορφη Θεου as a signifier of social status in Philippians 2:6," 780.

5. David Alan Black, "The Discourse Structure of Philippians: A Study in Textlinguistics," *Novum Testamentum*, Vol. 37, Fasc. 1 (Jan. 1995): 16–49. http://www.jstor.org/stable/1561235, 45.

6. Bekker, *Sharing the Incarnation*, 6.

7. Hellerman, *Reconstructing Honor in Roman Philippi*, 135.

8. Ibid.

9. Ibid., 110.

10. Timothy G. Gombis, *Power in Weakness: Paul's Transformed Vision for Ministry* (Grand Rapids, MI: William B. Eerdmans, 2021), 22.

11. Hellerman, *Reconstructing Honor*, 124–25.

12. Ibid.

13. Wink, *Engaging the Powers*, 61–62.

14. Gombis, *Power in Weakness*, 22.

15. Sarah Coakley, *Powers and Submissions: Spirituality, Philosophy and Gender* (Oxford: Blackwell, 2002), 11.

16. Gombis, *Power in Weakness*, 109.

17. This language of "becoming a nobody" is borrowed from a lecture I heard by Nijay Gupta.

18. Hellerman, *Reconstructing Honor*, 143.

19. Gombis, *Power in Weakness*, 57.

20. Hellerman, *Reconstructing Honor*, 154.

21. Ibid., 154–5.

22. Richard Bauckham, *God Crucified: Monotheism and Christology in the New Testament* (Grand Rapids, MI: William B. Eerdmans, 2002).

23. Ibid.

24. Hellerman, *Reconstructing Honor*, 166.

25. Michael Lee, *Revolutionary Saint: The Theological Legacy of Óscar Romero* (Mary Knoll, NY: Orbis, 2018, 87.

26. Ibid., xx.

27. Ibid., xvi.

28. Carolyn Kurtz, introduction to *The Scandal of Redemption: When God Liberates the Poor, Saves Sinners, and Heals Nations,* by Óscar Romero, edited by Carolyn Kurtz (Walden, NY: Plough, 2018), 2; Julio O. Torres, *Óscar Romero: A Man for Our Times* (New York: Seabury, 2021), 37.

29. Torres, *A Man for Our Times*, 48.

30. Ibid., 40.

31. Ibid., 37.

32. Ibid., 35.

33. Ibid.

34. Ibid., 36.

35. Brockman, *Romero*, 38.

36. Ibid., 38–39.

37. Lee, *Revolutionary Saint*, 5–6.

38. Brockman, *Romero*, 39.

39. Torres, *A Man for Our Times*, 61.

40. Ibid., 61–62.

41. Ibid.

42. Ibid., 63.

43. Brockman, *Romero*, 42.

44. Ibid., 15–16.

45. Ibid., 45.

46. Ibid., 42.

47. Ibid., 42–43.

48. Ibid., 43.

49. Ibid.

50. Ibid., 54.

51. Peruvian Gustavo Gutiérrez's book *A Theology of Liberation* was released December 1971 and was influential in Latin America at the time.

52. Brockman, *Romero*, 56.

53. Wilbert Shenk, "Why Mission to Modern/Postmodern Culture?" MP520, lecture. Pasadena, CA: Fuller Theological Seminary, School of Intercultural Studies.

54. Michael Lee, *Revolutionary Saint*, 46.

55. Ibid., 47.

56. Carolyn Kurtz, *The Scandal of Redemption*, 7.

57. Jon Sobrino, "A Theologian's View of Oscar Romero," in *Saint Oscar Romero: Voice of the Voiceless*, rev. ed. (Maryknoll, NY: Orbis, 2020), 31.

58. Óscar Romero, *A Prophetic Bishop Speaks to his People: The Complete Homilies of Archbishop Oscar Arnulfo Romero*, vol. I, trans. Joseph Owens, SJ (Miami: Convivium, 2015), 62.

59. Ibid.

60. Michael Lee, *Revolutionary Saint*, 47–48.

61. Ibid., 48.

62. Michael Lee, "The Liberation Spirituality of Oscar Romero," YouTube video. 1:09, March 1, 2018, https://www.youtube.com/watch?v=gWz0Um_0Eko&t=1331s.

63. *Saint Oscar Romero Voice of the Voiceless: The Four Pastoral Letters and Other Statements* (Maryknoll: NY: Orbis, 2020), 57–174.

64. Ibid., 51.

65. Michael Lee, *Revolutionary Saint*, 86–87.

66. Ibid., 87.

67. Ibid.

68. Óscar Romero, *The Violence of Love*, translated by James R. Brockmann (Maryknoll, NY: Orbis, 1988), 129.

69. Ibid., 140.

70. Ibid., 57.

71. Michael Lee, *Revolutionary Saint*, 53.

72. Óscar Romero, *The Violence of Love*, 124.

73. Robert T. McDermott, "In the Footsteps of Martyrs: Lessons from Central America," in *Romero's Legacy: The Call to Peace and Justice*, ed. Pilar Hogan Closkey and John P. Hogan (Lanham, MD: Rowman and Littlefield, 2007), 19.

74. Óscar Romero, *The Violence of Love*, 48–49.

75. Ibid., 22.

76. Jon Sobrino, "A Theologian's View," 41.

77. Ibid.

78. Ibid.

79. Ibid., 42.

80. Ibid.

81. Ibid.

82. Ibid., 42–3.

83. Sarah Coakley, *Powers and Submissions*, 38.

84. Óscar Romero, *The Violence of Love*, 132.

85. Ibid., 116.

86. Ibid., 46.

87. Michael Lee, *Revolutionary Saint*, 141.

88. Ibid.

89. Ibid.

90. Jon Sobrino, "A Theologian's View," 56.

91. Lesslie Newbigin developed the idea of the church as a sign, foretaste, and instrument. Lesslie Newbigin, *Lesslie Newbigin: Missionary Theologian: A Reader*, ed. Paul Weston (Grand Rapids, MI: William B. Eerdmans, 2006), 130–42.

92. Schweitzer, *Albert Schweitzer Thoughts for Our Times*, 51.

CONCLUSION

1. Roxburgh uses identity, telos, and work of the leader. Praxis is mentioned by others.

2. Croasmun, *The Emergence of Sin*.

3. Amos Yong, *In the Days of Caesar*; Amos Yong, *The Spirit of Creation*; David L. Bradnick, *Evil, Spirits and Possession: An Emergentist Theology of the Demonic* (Boston, MA: Brill, 2017).

4. David E. Fitch, *The Church of Us vs. Them: Freedom from a Faith That Feeds on Making Enemies* (Grand Rapids, MI: Brazos, 2019).

5. Koyzis, *Political Visions and Illusions*.

6. Harvey Cox, *The Market as God* (Cambridge, MA: Harvard University Press, 2016).

7. Nouwen, *The Selfless Way of Christ*; Smith, *Desiring the Kingdom*; James K. A. Smith, *Imagining the Kingdom: How Worship Works* (Grand Rapids, MI: Baker Academic, 2013); James K. A. Smith, *Awaiting the King: Reforming Public Theology* (Grand Rapids, MI: Baker Academic, 2017).

8. Helland and Hjalmarson, *Missional Spirituality*; Zscheile, *Cultivating Sent Communities*; Fitch, *Faithful Presence*; Finn and Whitfield, *Spirituality for the Sent*.

9. Smith, *Desiring the Kingdom*; Smith, *Imagining the Kingdom (Cultural Liturgies)*; Smith, *Awaiting the King*.

10. Lesslie Newbigin, *The Open Secret: An Introduction to the Theology of Mission*, Rev. edition. (William B. Eerdmans, 1995), 125.

11. Newbigin, *The Gospel in a Pluralist Society*, 227.

12. Source unknown.

BIBLIOGRAPHY

Achtemeier, Paul J. *1 Peter*. Edited by Eldon Jay Epp. Minneapolis, MN: Fortress, 1996.

Acolatse, Esther. *Powers, Principalities, and the Spirit: Biblical Realism in Africa and the West*. Grand Rapids, MI: William B. Eerdmans, 2018.

Adam, Peter James Hedderwick. "The Practice of the Imitation of Christ with Special Reference to the Theology of Dietrich Bonhoeffer." Durham thesis, Durham University, 1981. http://etheses.dur.ac.uk/7559/.

Alison, James. *Jesus the Forgiving Victim: Listening for the Unheard Voice*. Glenview, IL: Doers, 2013.

———. *Living in the End Times: The Last Things Re-imagined*. New York: Crossroad, 1996.

Allender, Dan B. *Leading with a Limp: Take Full Advantage of Your Most Powerful Weakness*. Colorado Springs, CO: WaterBrook, 2008.

Aniol, Scott. "Toward a Biblical Understanding of Culture." *Artistic Theologian*, October 31, 2012. http://artistictheologian.com/journal/at-volume-1-2012/toward-a-biblical-understanding-of-culture/.

Aristotle. *The Complete Works of Aristotle: The Revised Oxford Translation*, vol. 2, edited by Jonathan Barnes. Princeton, NJ: Princeton University Press, 1984.

Arnold, Clinton E. *3 Crucial Questions about Spiritual Warfare*. Grand Rapids, MI: Baker Academic, 1997.

———. *Power and Magic: The Concept of Power in Ephesians*. Eugene, OR: Wipf and Stock, 2001.

———. *Powers of Darkness: Principalities and Powers in Paul's Letters*. Downers Grove, IL: IVP Academic, 2009.

Ashford, Bruce, and Scott Bridger. "Missiological Method." In *Missiology: An Introduction to the Foundations, History, and Strategies of World Missions*, 662. Rev. ed. Nashville, TN: B and H Academic, 2015.

Ayers, Michale. "Toward a Theology of Leadership." *Journal of Biblical Perspectives in Leadership* 1, no. 1 (Fall 2006): 3–27.

Barrett, Lois. "Missional Witness: The Church as Apostle to the World." In *Missional Church: A Vision for the Sending of the Church in North America*, edited by Darrell L. Guder. Grand Rapids, MI: William B. Eerdmans, 1998.

Barth, Karl. *The Christian Life*. London: T and T Clark, 2004.

———. *Church and State*. Translated by G. Ronald Howe. Greenville, SC: Smyth and Helwys, 1991.

———. *Evangelical Theology: An Introduction*. Reprint ed. Grand Rapids, MI: William B. Eerdmans, 1992.

Barth, Markus. *The Broken Wall: A Study of the Epistle to the Ephesians*. Valley Forge, PA: Judson, 1959.

Bauckham, Richard. *God Crucified: Monotheism and Christology in the New Testament*. Grand Rapids, MI: William B. Eerdmans, 2002.

Bekker, Corné J. "Sharing in the Incarnation: Towards a Model of Mimetic Christology Leadership." *International Journal on Spirituality and Organizational Leadership*, no. 2 (July 2021).

Beely, Christopher A., and Joseph H. Britton Britton. "Introduction: Toward a Theology of Leadership." *Anglican Theological Review—A Quarterly Journal of Theological Reflection*, vol. 91, no. 1 (Winter 2009): 3–10.

Beilby, James K., and Paul Rhodes Eddy, eds. *Understanding Spiritual Warfare: Four Views*. Grand Rapids, MI: Baker Academic, 2012.

Bennema, Cornelis. *Mimesis in the Johannine Literature: A Study in Johannine Ethics*. London: T and T Clark, 2019.

Berkhof, Hendrik. *Christ and the Powers*. Translated by John Howard Yoder. 2nd ed. Scottdale, PA: Herald, 1977.

Berry, Steven E, and Michael Hardin. *Reading the Bible with René Girard: Conversations with Steven E. Berry*. Lancaster, PA: JDL, 2015.

Bevans, Stephen B., and Roger P. Schroeder. *Constants in Context: A Theology of Mission for Today*. Maryknoll, NY: Orbis, 2004.

Bird, Michael F. and Nijay K. Gupta, *Philippians*. Cambridge: Cambridge University Press, 2020.

Black, David Alan. "The Discourse Structure of Philippians: A Study in Textlinguistics." *Novum Testamentum,* vol. 37, fasc. 1 (Jan. 1995): 16–49. http://www.jstor.org/stable/1561235.

Bockmuehl, Markus. "A Commentator's Approach to the 'Effective History' of Philippians." *Journal for the Study of the New Testament* 18, no. 60 (April 1996): 57–88. https://doi.org/10.1177/0142064X9601806003.

Boers, Arthur, and Eugene Peterson. *Servants and Fools: A Biblical Theology of Leadership*. Nashville, TN: Abingdon, 2015.

Bonhoeffer, Dietrich. "The Church is Dead": A Lecture Presented at the International Youth Conference of the Universal Christian Council on Life and Work and the World Alliance for Promoting International Friendship through the Churches, Gland, Switzerland, August 29, 1932.

———. *Creation and Fall Temptation: Two Biblical Studies*. Reprint ed. New York: Touchstone, 1997.

———. *Discipleship*. DBW, vol. 4. Minneapolis, MN: Fortress, 2003.

Bonilla-Silva, Eduardo. *Racism without Racists: Color-Blind Racism and the Persistence of Racial Inequality in America*. 5th ed. Lanham, MD: Rowman and Littlefield, 2017.

Bosch, David J. *Transforming Mission: Paradigm Shifts in Theology of Mission*. Maryknoll, NY: Orbis, 2011.

Botton, Alain de. *Status Anxiety*. New York: Random House, 2005.

Boyd, Gregory. "Response to Walter Wink." In *Understanding Spiritual Warfare*, edited by James K. Beilby and Paul Rhodes Eddy. Grand Rapids, MI: Baker Academic, 2012.

Brockman, James R. *Romero: A Life*. Maryknoll, NY: Orbis, 2003.

Bradnick, David L. *Evil, Spirits and Possession: An Emergentist Theology of the Demonic*. Global Pentecostal and Charismatic Studies, vol. 25. Boston: Brill, 2017.

Branch, Taylor. *Pillar of Fire: America in the King Years 1963–65*. New York: Simon and Schuster, 1999.

Brownson, James V., Inagrace T. Dietterich, Barry A. Harvey, and Charles C. West. *StormFront: The Good News of God*. Grand Rapids, MI: William B. Eerdmans, 2003.

Bruce, F. F. *Philippians*. Understanding the Bible Commentary Series. Grand Rapids: Baker, 1983.

Brueggemann, Walter. *Truth Speaks to Power: The Countercultural Nature of Scripture*. Louisville, KY: Westminster John Knox, 2013.

Bruner, Frederick Dale. *The Holy Spirit—Shy Member of the Trinity*. Eugene, OR: Wipf and Stock, 2001.

Bultmann, Rudolf. "New Testament and Mythology: The Problem of Demythologizing the New Testament Proclamation (1941)." In *New Testament and Mythology and Other Basic Writings*. Translated by Schubert M. Ogden. Philadelphia, PA: Fortress, 1984.

———. "On the Problem of Demythologizing (1952)." In *New Testament and Mythology and Other Basic Writings*. Translated by Schubert M. Ogden. Philadelphia, PA: Fortress, 1984.

———. *Theology of the New Testament: Complete in One Volume*. New York: Prentice Hall, 1970.

Burridge, Richard A. *Imitating Jesus: An Inclusive Approach to New Testament Ethics*. Grand Rapids, MI: William B. Eerdmans, 2007.

Caird, G. B. *Principalities and Powers: A Study in Pauline Theology: The Chancellor's Lectures for 1954 at Queen's University, Kingston Ontario*. Eugene, OR: Wipf and Stock, 2003.

———. *The Language and Imagery of the Bible*. Philadelphia, PA: Westminster, 1980.

Campbell, Will D., Jimmy Carter, and John Lewis. *Brother to a Dragonfly*. Reprint ed. Jackson, MS: University Press of Mississippi, 2018.

Chesterton, G. K. *The Scandal of Father Brown*. London: Cassell, 1935.

———. *St. Francis of Assisi*. Mount Pleasant, SC: Arcadia, 2019.

Coakley, Sarah. *Powers and Submissions: Spirituality, Philosophy and Gender*. Oxford: Blackwell, 2002.

Cochrane, Arthur C. *The Church's Confession under Hitler*. Philadelphia, PA: Westminster, 1962.

Cohick, Lynn H. *The Story of God Bible Commentary: Philippians*. Grand Rapids, MI: Zondervan, 2013.

Commins, Gary. "Harlem and Eschaton: Stringfellow's Theological Homes." In *Prophet of Justice, Prophet of Life: Essays on William Stringfellow*, edited by Robert Boak Slocum. Eugene, OR: Wipf and Stock, 1997.

Cooper, John W. *Panentheism—The Other God of the Philosophers: From Plato to the Present*. Reprint ed. Grand Rapids, MI: Baker Academic, 2013.

Corson-Knowles, Tom. "Stories Matter: Stories Are Important to Our Lives and Culture." *tckpublishing.com*. June 18, 2022. https://www.tckpublishing.com/stories-matter/.

Cowdell, Scott. *Abiding Faith: Christianity Beyond Certainty, Anxiety, and Violence*. Eugene, OR: Pickwick, 2009.

———. *René Girard and the Nonviolent God*. Notre Dame, IN: University of Notre Dame Press, 2018.

———. *René Girard and Secular Modernity Christ, Culture, and Crisis*. Notre Dame, IN: University of Notre Dame Press, 2013.

Cowdell, Scott, Joel Hodge, Chris Fleming, and Mathias Moosbrugger, eds. *René Girard and Raymund Schwager: Correspondence 1974–1991*. Translated by Sheelah Treflé Hidden and Chris Fleming. New York: Bloomsbury Academic, 2016.

Cox, Harvey. *The Market as God*. Cambridge, MA: Harvard University Press, 2016.

Crab, Larry. Foreword to *The Connecting Church: Beyond Small Groups to Authentic Community*. Grand Rapids: Zondervan, 2001.

Craddock, Fred B. *Philippians: Interpretation: A Bible Commentary for Teaching and Preaching* Louisville, KY: Westminster John Knox, 1985.

Croasmun, Matthew. *The Emergence of Sin: The Cosmic Tyrant in Romans*. New York: Oxford University Press, 2017.

Crouch, Andy. *Playing God: Redeeming the Gift of Power*. Downers Grove, IL: IVP, 2013.

Dahl, Nils A. "Euodia and Syntyche and Paul's Letter to the Philippians." In *The Social World of the First Christians: Essays in Honor of Wayne A. Meeks*. Edited by L. Michael White and O. Larry Yarborough. Minneapolis: Fortress, 1995.

Dawn, Marva J. *Powers, Weakness, and the Tabernacling of God*. Grand Rapids, MI: William B. Eerdmans, 2001.

———. "The Concept of 'The Principalities and Powers' in the Works of Jacques Ellul." PhD diss., University of Notre Dame, 1992.

Doran, Robert. "René Girard's Concept of Conversion and the 'Via Negativa': Revisiting 'Deceit, Desire, and the Novel.'" *Religion and Literature* 43, no. 3 (2011): 170–179.

Douglas, Mary. *Natural Symbols: Explorations in Cosmology*. London, Barrie and Jenkins, 1973.

Dunn, James G. *The Theology of Paul the Apostle*. Grand Rapids, MI: William B. Eerdmans, 1998.

Edwards, Dennis R. *1 Peter*. Edited by Tremper Longman III and Scot McKnight. Grand Rapids, MI: Zondervan Academic, 2017.

Einstein, Albert and Leopold Infeld. *The Evolution of Physics*. New York: Simon and Schuster, 1938.

Elliott, John H. *1 Peter*. New Haven, CT: Yale University Press, 2001.

———. *A Home for the Homeless: A Social-Scientific Criticism of 1 Peter, Its Situation and Strategy*. Eugene, OR: Wipf and Stock, 2005.

Emery White, Dr. James. "The Pastoral Mess of 2016." *Crosswalk.com*. Last modified 2017. https://www.crosswalk.com/blogs/dr-james-emery-white/the-pastoral-mess-of-2016.html.

Gordon D. *Paul's Letter to the Philippians*. Grand Rapids, MI: William B. Eerdmans, 1995.

Finn, Nathan A., and Keith S. Whitfield, eds. *Spirituality for the Sent: Casting a New Vision for the Missional Church*. Downers Grove, IL: IVP Academic, 2017.

Fitch, David E. *The Church of Us vs. Them: Freedom from a Faith That Feeds on Making Enemies*. Grand Rapids, MI: Brazos, 2019.

———. *Faithful Presence: Seven Disciplines That Shape the Church for Mission*. Downers Grove, IL: IVP, 2016.

———. *The Great Giveaway: Reclaiming the Mission of the Church from Big Business, Parachurch Organizations, Psychotherapy, Consumer Capitalism, and Other Modern Maladies*. Grand Rapids, MI: Baker Books, 2005.

———. "The Other Missional Conversation: Making Way for the Neo-Anabaptist Contribution to the Missional Movement in North America." *Missiology* 44, no. 4 (October 1, 2016): 466–478.

Fodor, Jim, and Willard M. Swartley. "Christian Discipleship as Participative Imitation: Theological Reflections on Girardian Themes." In *Violence Renounces: René Girard, Biblical Studies and Peacemaking*, edited by Willard M. Swartley. Scottdale, PA: Herald, 2000.

Forbes, Chris. "Pauline Demonology and/or Cosmology? Principalities, Powers and the Elements of the World in Their Hellenistic Context." *Journal for the Study of the New Testament* 24, no. 3 (March 1, 2002): 51–73.

———. "Paul's Principalities and Powers: Demythologizing Apocalyptic?" *Journal for the Study of the New Testament* 23, no. 82 (July 1, 2001): 61–88.

Ford, David, and Rachel Muers, eds. *The Modern Theologians: An Introduction to Christian Theology Since 1918*. 3rd ed. Malden, MA: Wiley-Blackwell, 2005.

Frei, Hans W. *Types of Christian Theology*. Edited by George Hunsinger and William Placher. New Haven: Yale University Press, 1992.

Frost, Michael, and Alan Hirsch. *ReJesus: A Wild Messiah for a Missional Church*. Grand Rapids, MI: Baker Books, 2008.

———. *The Shaping of Things to Come: Innovation and Mission for the 21st Century Church*. Peabody, MA: Hendrickson, 2003.

Garrett, Susan R. *No Ordinary Angel: Celestial Spirits and Christian Claims about Jesus*. New Haven, CT: Yale University Press, 2008.

———. *The Temptations of Jesus in Mark's Gospel*. Grand Rapids, MI: William B. Eerdmans, 1996.

Gatumu, Kabiro wa. *The Pauline Concept of Supernatural Powers: A Reading from the African Worldview*. Eugene, OR: Wipf and Stock, 2008.

Girard, René. *Deceit, Desire, and the Novel: Self and Other in Literary Structure*. Translated by Yvonne Freccero. Baltimore, MD: Johns Hopkins University Press, 1998.

———. "Epilogue: The Anthropology of the Cross." In *The Girard Reader*, edited by James G. Williams. New York: Crossroad, 1996.

———. *The Girard Reader*. Edited by James G. Williams. New York: Crossroad, 1996.

———. *I See Satan Fall Like Lightning*. Maryknoll, NY: Orbis, 2001.

———. *Job, The Victim of His People*. Stanford, CA: Stanford University Press, 1987.

————. *The One by Whom Scandal Comes*. Studies in violence, mimesis, and culture series. East Lansing, MI: Michigan State University Press, 2014.

————. *Resurrection from the Underground: Feodor Dostoevsky*. Edited by James G. Williams. Translated by James G. Williams. East Lansing, MI: Michigan State University Press, 2012.

————. *The Scapegoat*. Baltimore, MD: Johns Hopkins University Press, 1989.

————. *Theater Of Envy: William Shakespeare*. Reprint ed. South Bend, IN: St. Augustine's, 2004.

————. *To Double Business Bound: Essays on Literature, Mimesis and Anthropology*. Baltimore, MD: Johns Hopkins University Press, 1988.

————. *Violence and the Sacred*. Baltimore, MD: The John Hopkins University Press, 1979.

————. *When These Things Begin: Conversations with Michel Treguer*. Translated by Trevor Cribben Merrill. East Lansing, MI: Michigan State University Press, 2014.

Girard, René, and Mark Rogin Anspach. *Oedipus Unbound: Selected Writings on Rivalry and Desire*. Stanford, CA: Stanford University Press, 2004.

Girard, René, Pierpaolo Antonello, and João Cezar de Castro Rocha. *Evolution and Conversion: Dialogues on the Origins of Culture*. London; New York: Bloomsbury Academic, 2017.

Girard, René, Jean-Michel Oughourlian, and Guy Lefort. *Things Hidden Since the Foundation of the World*. Stanford, CA: Stanford University Press, 2002.

Goheen, Michael W. "Historical Perspectives on the Missional Church Movement: Probing Lesslie Newbigin's Formative Influence." *Trinity Journal for Theology and Ministry* 4, no. 2 (Fall 2010): 62–84.

Gombis, Timothy G. *Power in Weakness: Paul's Transformed Vision for Ministry*. Grand Rapids, MI: William B. Eerdmans, 2021.

Gorman, Michael J. *Apostle of the Crucified Lord: A Theological Introduction to Paul and His Letters* Grand Rapids, MI: William B. Eerdmans, 2017.

————. *Cruciformity: Paul's Narrative Spirituality of the Cross*. Grand Rapids, MI: William B. Eerdmans, 2001.

Goudzwaard, Bob. *Idols of Our Time*. Sioux Center, IA: Dordt College Press, 1989.

Gray, Patrick. *Paul as a Problem in History and Culture: The Apostle and His Critics through the Centuries*. Grand Rapids, MI: Baker Academic, 2016.

Grentz, Stanley Jr. *Theology for the Community of God*. Grand Rapids, MI: William B. Eerdmans, 2000.

Guder, Darrell L., ed. *Missional Church: A Vision for the Sending of the Church in North America*. Grand Rapids, MI: William B. Eerdmans, 1998.

Gupta, Ninjay K., *Reading Philippians: A Theological Introduction*. Eugene, OR: Cascade, 2020.

Gutiérrez, Gustavo. *A Theology of Liberation: History, Politics, and Salvation*. Translated by Caridad Inda. 15th anniversary ed. Maryknoll, NY: Orbis, 1988.

Hamerton-Kelly, Robert. *Sacred Violence: Paul's Hermeneutic of the Cross*. Minneapolis, MN: Fortress, 1992.

Hansen, Walter G. *The Letter to the Philippians*. Grand Rapids, MI: William B. Eerdmans, 2009.

Hardy, Andrew, Richard Whitehouse, and Dan Yarnell. *Power and the Powers: The Use and Abuse of Power in Its Missional Context*. Eugene, OR: Cascade, 2015.

Haven, Cynthia L. *Evolution of Desire: A Life of René Girard*. East Lansing, MI: Michigan State University Press, 2018.

———. "The Evolution of René Girard." *America Magazine*. Last modified November 16, 2018. https://www.americamagazine.org/arts-culture/2018/11/16/evolution-rene-girard.

———. "What Was the Most Important Moment in René Girard's Life? 'Coming to America,' He Said." *The Book Haven*, January 20, 2016. Accessed December 3, 2019. http://bookhaven.stanford.edu/2016/01/what-was-the-most-important-moment-in-rene-girards-life-coming-to-america-he-said/.

Hawthorne, Gerald F. *The Presence and The Power: The Significance of the Holy Spirit in the Life and Ministry of Jesus*. Eugene, OR: Wipf and Stock, 2003.

Hellerman, Joseph. "Μορφη Θεου as a signifier of social status in Philippians 2:6." *Journal of the Evangelical Theological Society* 52, no. 4 (December 2009): 779–797. https://digitalcommons.biola.edu/faculty-articles/163.

———. *Reconstructing Honor in Roman Philippi: Carmen Christi as Cursus Pudorum*. Cambridge: Cambridge University Press, 2005.

Helland, Roger, and Leonard Hjalmarson. *Missional Spirituality: Embodying God's Love from the Inside Out*. Downers Grove, IL: IVP Books, 2011.

Hiebert, Paul. "Spiritual Warfare and Worldviews." Nairobi, Kenya: Lausanne Movement, 2000. https://www.lausanne.org/content/spiritual-warfare-and-worldview.

———. *The Gospel in Human Contexts: Anthropological Explorations for Contemporary Missions*. Grand Rapids, MI: Baker Academic, 2009.

Hirsch, Alan. *5Q: Reactivating the Original Intelligence and Capacity of the Body of Christ*. 100 Movements, 2017.

———. *The Forgotten Ways: Reactivating Apostolic Movements*. 2nd ed. Grand Rapids, MI Brazos, 2016.

Hirsch, Alan, and Tim Catchim. *The Permanent Revolution: Apostolic Imagination and Practice for the 21st Century Church*. San Francisco, CA: Jossey-Bass, 2012.

Hood, Jason B. *Imitating God in Christ: Recapturing a Biblical Pattern*. Downers Grove, IL: IVP Academic, 2013.

Hooft, W. A. Visser 't. *The Kingship of Christ*. New York: Harper and Brothers, 1947.

House, Adrian, and Karen Armstrong. *Francis of Assisi: A Revolutionary Life*. Mahwah, NJ: Hidden Spring, 2003.

Houston, Graham. *Leading by Example: Peter's Way for the Church Today*. Milton Keynes; Colorado Springs, CO: Paternoster, 2008.

Hunter, George G., III. *The Celtic Way of Evangelism: How Christianity Can Reach the West . . . AGAIN*. Nashville, TN: Abingdon, 2000.

Johns, Loren L., and James R. Krabill, eds. *Even the Demons Submit: Continuing Jesus' Ministry of Deliverance*. Scottdale, PA: Institute of Mennonite Studies, 2006.

Kaplan, Grant. *René Girard, Unlikely Apologist: Mimetic Theory and Fundamental Theology*. Notre Dame, IN: University of Notre Dame Press, 2016.

Käsemann, Ernst. "The Eschatological Royal Reign of God." In *Your Kingdom Come: Mission Perspectives*. Report on the World Conference on Mission and

Evangelism, Melbourne, Australia, 12–25 May. World Council of Churches, 1980.

Kaufholz, Eddie. "The Mega-Problem Behind the 'Falls' of Megachurch Pastors." *Relevant Magazine*, October 5, 2016. https://relevantmagazine.com/current16/mega-problem-behind-falls-megachurch-pastors/.

Kearsley, Roy. *Church, Community and Power*. Farnham, England ; Burlington, VT: Routledge, 2009.

Kell, Garrat. "A Pattern Among Fallen Pastors—Lessons for Us All." *Garrett Kell*. Last modified February 20, 2015. http://garrettkell.com/pattern-among-fallen-pastors-lessons-us/.

Kelly, Gerard. *Retrofuture: Rediscovering Our Roots, Recharging Our Routes*. Downers Grove, IL: InterVarsity Press, 1999.

Kempis, Thomas à. *The Imitation of Christ*. Translated by Aloysius Croft and Harold Bolton. Mineola, NY: Dover, 2003.

Kennedy, G.A. *New Testament Interpretation through Rhetorical Criticism*. Raleigh, NC: University of North Carolina Press, 1984.

Kenneson, Philip D. *Life on the Vine: Cultivating the Fruit of the Spirit*. Downers Grove, IL: IVP, 1999.

Kirwan, Michael. *Discovering Girard*. Lanham, MD: Rowman and Littlefield, 2005.

Koyzis, David T. *Political Visions and Illusions: A Survey and Christian Critique of Contemporary Ideologies*. 2nd ed. Downers Grove, IL: IVP Academic, 2019.

Kreider, Alan. *The Change of Conversion and the Origin of Christendom*. Reprint ed. Eugene, OR: Wipf and Stock, 2007.

Kurtz, Carolyn. Introduction to *The Scandal of Redemption: When God Liberates the Poor, Saves Sinners, and Heals Nations,* by Óscar Romero. Edited by Carolyn Kurtz. Walden, NY: Plough, 2018.

Kurz, William. "Kenotic Imitation of Paul and of Christ in Philippians 2 and 3" in *Discipleship in the New Testament*, edited by Frenando F. Segovia. Philadelphia, PA: Augsburg Fortress, 1985.

Kwon, Soon-Gu. *Christ as Example: The Imitatio Christi Motive in Biblical and Christian Ethics*. Acta Universitatis Upsaliensis 21. Uppsala, Sweden: Uppsala University Library, 1998.

Laws, Sophie. *The Epistle of James*. Black's New Testament Commentary. Carol Stream, IL: Tyndale House Publishers, 1993.

Lee, Michael. *Revolutionary Saint: The Theological Legacy of Oscar Romero*. Maryknoll, NY: Orbis, 2018.

———. "The Liberation Spirituality of Oscar Romero." YouTube video. 1:09, March, 1, 2018, https://www.youtube.com/watch?v=gWz0Um_0Eko&t=1331s

Lewis, C. S. *The Screwtape Letters*. New York: HarperCollins, 1996.

Lincoln, Andrew T. "Liberation from the Powers: Supernatural or Societal Structures?" In *The Bible in Human Society: Essays in Honour of John Rogerson*, edited by M. Daniel Carroll R., David J. A. Clines, and Philip R. Davies. Sheffield, England: Sheiffield Academic, 1995.

London Jr., H. B., and Neil B. Wiseman. *Pastors at Greater Risk*. Grand Rapids, MI: Baker, 2003.

Lynch, Chloe. *Ecclesial Leadership as Friendship*. New York: Routledge, 2019.

Lyon, Jo Anne, Margaret Diddams, Gary Walter, and Leith Anderson. "Independent Advisory Group Report," 2019. https://www.willowcreek.org/-/media/images/7-0-about/elders2019/iagreport-022819.pdf?la=en.

Mallow, Vernon R. *The Demonic: A Selected Theological Study: An Examination into the Theology of Edwin Lewis, Karl Barth, and Paul Tillich.* Lanham, MD: University Press of America, 1983.

Mark, Joshua J. "Monastic Orders of the Middle Ages." *Ancient History Encyclopedia*, June 24, 2019. https://www.ancient.eu/article/1407/monastic-orders-of-the-middle-ages/.

Marshall, I. Howard. *1 Peter.* Downers Grove, IL: IVP Academic, 1991.

Martin, Douglas. "Walter Wink, Theologian Who Challenged Orthodoxy, Dies at 76." *The New York Times*, May 19, 2012, sec. US. https://www.nytimes.com/2012/05/20/us/walter-wink-theologian-who-challenged-orthodoxy-dies-at-76.html.

Martin, Ralph P., and John D. W. Watts. *James, Volume 48.* Edited by David Allen Hubbard and Glenn W. Barker. Grand Rapids, MI: Zondervan Academic, 2015.

Maxwell, John C. *The 21 Irrefutable Laws of Leadership: Follow Them and People Will Follow You.* 2nd ed. Nashville, TN: Thomas Nelson, 2007.

McAlpine, Tom. *Facing the Powers: What Are the Options?* Eugene, OR: Wipf and Stock, 2003.

McClendon, James Wm. *Biography as Theology: How Life Stories Can Remake Today's Theology.* Reissue ed. Eugene, OR: Wipf and Stock, 2002.

McDermott, Robert T. "In the Footsteps of Martyrs: Lessons from Central America," in *Romero's Legacy: The Call to Peace and Justice*, edited by Pilar Hogan Closkey and John P. Hogan. Lanham, MD: Rowman and Littlefield, 2007.

McKnight, Scot. *The Letter of James.* Grand Rapids, MI: William B. Eerdmans, 2011.

Meadows, Phil. "Making Disciples That Renew the Church," 2013. https://urc.org.uk/wtwresources/Making-Disciples-that-Renew-the-Church.pdf.

Mengel, B. *Studien zum Philipperbrief.* Tubingen: Mohr, 1982.

Middleton, Richard J. *The Liberating Image: The Imago Dei in Genesis 1.* Grand Rapids, MI: Brazos, 2005.

Moreau, A. Scott, Tokunboh Adeyemo, David G. Burnett, Bryant L. Myers, and Hwa Yung, eds. *Deliver Us from Evil: An Uneasy Frontier in Christian Mission.* Monrovia, CA: World Vision International, 2002.

Moses, Robert Ewusie. "Powerful Practices: Paul's Principalities and Powers Revisited." PhD diss., Duke Divinity School, 2012.

Mottu, Henry. "Walter Wink and Theology," in *Enigmas and Powers: Engaging the Work of Walter Wink for Classroom, Church, and World*, edited by D. Seiple and Frederick W. Weidmann. Eugene, OR: Wipf and Stock, 2008.

Neufeld, Thomas R. Yoder. *Ephesians: Believers Church Bible Commentary.* Scottdale, PA: Herald, 2002.

Newbigin, Lesslie. *The Gospel in a Pluralist Society.* Grand Rapids, MI: Wm. B. Eerdmans, 1989.

———. *The Open Secret: An Introduction to the Theology of Mission*. Rev. ed. Grand Rapids, MI: William B. Eerdmans, 1995.

———. *Truth to Tell: The Gospel as Public Truth*. Grand Rapids, MI: William B. Eerdmans, 1991.

Nouwen, Henri. *Bread for the Journey: A Daybook Of Wisdom And Faith*. Reprint ed. San Francisco: HarperOne, 2006.

———. *In the Name of Jesus: Reflections on Christian Leadership*. New York: Ballantine, 1992.

———. *The Selfless Way of Christ: Downward Mobility and the Spiritual Life*. Maryknoll, NY: Orbis, 2011.

———. *The Way of the Heart: Connecting with God Through Prayer, Wisdom, and Silence*. Revised ed. New York: Ballantine, 2003.

———. *You Are the Beloved: Daily Meditations for Spiritual Living*. New York: Convergent, 2017.

Oakes, Peter. *Philippians: From People to Letter*. Cambridge: Cambridge University Press, 2001.

O'Brien, Peter R. *The Epistle to the Philippians*. New International Greek Testament Commentary. Grand Rapids, MI: William B. Eerdmans, 1991.

Oglesby, Les. *C. G. Jung and Hans Urs von Balthasar: God and Evil—A Critical Comparison*. cra vols. London: Routledge, 2013.

Olson, Roger E. "Evangelical Superstars and Why They Fall." *Roger E. Olson*, August 30, 2014. https://www.patheos.com/blogs/rogereolson/2014/08/evangelical-superstars-and-why-they-fall/.

———. "What's Wrong with Panentheism?" *Roger E. Olson*, August 7, 2012. https://www.patheos.com/blogs/rogereolson/2012/08/whats-wrong-with-panentheism/.

Oughourlian, Jean-Michel. "My Life with René." In *For René Girard: Essays in Friendship and in Truth*, edited by Sandor Goodhart, Jorgen Jorgensen, Tom Ryba, and James G. Williams. East Lansing, MI: Michigan State University Press, 2009.

———. *The Genesis of Desire*. East Lansing, MI: Michigan State University Press, 2010.

Palaver, Wolfgang. *René Girard's Mimetic Theory*. East Lansing, MI: Michigan State University Press, 2013.

Pasewark, Kyle A. *A Theology of Power: Being Beyond Domination*. Minneapolis, MN: Fortress, 1993.

Pawson David, *Simon Peter: The Reed and the Rock*. Kennington, Ashford, UK: Anchor Recordings, 2013.

Peterlin, Davorin. Paul's Letter to the Philippians in the Light of Disunity in the Church. New York: E. J. Brill, 1995.

Peterson, Eugene. *The Pastor: A Memoir*. New York: HarperCollins, 2011.

Phiri, Mabvuto J. "Scandal Must Come: Reconciliation as a Divine-Human Kenotic Event in World Immersed in a Culture of Violence and Death", Doctoral diss., Boston College, 2013.

Pulliam Bailey, Sarah. "Exclusive: Mark Driscoll's Resignation Letter to Mars Hill Church." *Religion News Service*, October 15, 2014. https://religionnews.com/2014/10/15/exclusive-mark-driscolls-resignation-letter-to-mars-hill-church/.

Ravitch, Dr Sharon M., and Dr J. Matthew Riggan. *Reason and Rigor: How Conceptual Frameworks Guide Research*. 2nd ed. Los Angeles: SAGE, 2016.

Ringe, Sharon H. "Walter Wink and Pedagogy," in *Enigmas and Powers: Engaging the Work of Walter Wink for Classroom, Church, and World*, edited by D. Seiple and Frederick W. Weidmann. Eugene, OR: Wipf and Stock, 2008.

Rollins, Wayne G. "An Overview of the Work of Walter Wink." In *Enigmas and Powers: Engaging the Work of Walter Wink for Classroom, Church, and World*. Eugene, OR: Wipf and Stock, 2008.

Romero, Oscar. *A Prophetic Bishop Speaks to his People: The Complete Homilies of Archbishop Oscar Arnulfo Romero,* vol. I, Translated by Joseph Owens, SJ. Miami: Convivium, 2015.

———. *Saint Oscar Romero, Voice of the Voiceless: The Four Pastoral Letters and Other Statements*. Maryknoll, NY: Orbis, 2020.

———. *The Scandal of Redemption: When God Liberates the Poor, Saves Sinners, and Heals Nations*. Edited by Carolyn Kurtz. Walden, NY: Plough, 2018.

———.*The Violence of Love*. Translated by James R. Brockmann. Maryknoll, NY: Orbis, 1988.

Ross, Bobby Jr. "Why Pastors Step Down." *ChristianityToday.com*. https://www.christianitytoday.com/ct/2011/julyweb-only/sexmoneypride.html.

Roxburgh, Alan. "Missional Leadership: Equipping God's People for Mission." In *Missional Church: A Vision for the Sending of the Church in North America*, edited by Darrell L. Guder. Grand Rapids, MI: William B. Eerdmans, 1998.

Roxburgh, Alan J., and Martin Robinson. *Practices for the Refounding of God's People*. New York: Church, 2018.

Roxburgh, Alan, and Fred Romanuk. *The Missional Leader: Equipping Your Church to Reach a Changing World*. San Francisco: Jossey-Bass, 2006.

Rupp, E. Gordon. *Principalities and Powers: Studies in the Christian Conflict in History*. London: Epworth, 1952.

Ryba, Thomas, and Vern Neufeld Redekop, eds. *René Girard and Creative Mimesis*. Lanham, MD: Lexington, 2013.

Samuel, Vinay, and Chris Sugden. *Mission as Transformation: A Theology of the Whole Gospel*. Oxford: Regnum, 1999.

Sauls, Scott. "The Plight of the Falling Pastor." *Christianity Today: Pastors*. https://www.christianitytoday.com/pastors/2016/june-web-exclusives/plight-of-falling-pastor.html.

———. "Thoughts on the Rise and Fall of Pastors." *Scott Sauls*, May 23, 2019. Accessed June 19, 2019. https://scottsauls.com/blog/2019/05/23/pastors/.

Schwager, Raymund. "Christ's Death and the Prophetic Critique of Sacrifice." *Semeia; an Experimental Journal for Biblical Criticism* (1985).

———. *Must There Be Scapegoats: Violence and Redemption in the Bible*. New York: Crossroad, 2018.

Schweitzer, Albert. *Albert Schweitzer Thoughts for Our Times.* Edited by Erica Anderson. White Plains, NY: Peter Pauper, 1975.

Seiple, D., and Frederick W. Weidmann, eds. *Enigmas and Powers: Engaging the Work of Walter Wink for Classroom, Church, and World.* Eugene, OR: Wipf and Stock, 2008.

Shellnutt, Kate. "Darrin Patrick Removed from Acts 29 Megachurch for 'Historical Pattern of Sin.'" *ChristianityToday.Com.* Last modified 2016. https://www.christianitytoday.com/news/2016/april/darrin-patrick-removed-acts-29-megachurch-journey.html.

Shenk, Wilbert "Why Mission to Modern/Postmodern Culture?" MP520, lecture. Pasadena, CA: Fuller Theological Seminary, School of Intercultural Studies.

Smith, James K. A. *Awaiting the King: Reforming Public Theology.* Grand Rapids, MI: Baker Academic, 2017.

———. *Desiring the Kingdom: Worship, Worldview, and Cultural Formation.* Grand Rapids, MI: Baker Academic, 2009.

———. *Imagining the Kingdom: How Worship Works.* Grand Rapids, MI: Baker Academic, 2013.

Smith, Mandy. *Unfettered: Imagining a Childlike Faith Beyond the Baggage of Western Culture.* Grand Rapids, MI: Brazos, 2021.

Sobrino, Jon. "A Theologian's View of Oscar Romero," in *Saint Oscar Romero: Voice of the Voiceless,* rev. ed. Maryknoll, NY: Orbis, 2020.

St. Francis of Assisi. *The Complete Writings of St. Francis of Assisi.* Translated by Paschal Robinson. Philadelphia, PA: Dolphin, 1905.

Stassen, Glen Harold. *A Thicker Jesus: Incarnational Discipleship in a Secular Age.* Louisville: KY: Westminster John Knox, 2012.

Steinmair-Pösel, Petra. "Original Sin, Grace, and Positive Mimesis." In *René Girard and Creative Mimesis,* edited by Vern Neufeld Redekop and Thomas Ryba. Lanham, MD: Lexington, 2013.

Stetzer, Ed. "Laypeople and the Mission of God: Part II—Reclaiming the Priesthood of All Believers." *The Exchange | A Blog by Ed Stetzer.* Last modified 2012. https://www.christianitytoday.com/edstetzer/2012/august/laypeople-and-mission-of-god-part-ii—reclaiming.html.

Stevenson-Moessner, Jeanne. *Overture to Practical Theology: The Music of Religious Inquiry.* Eugene, OR: Cascade, 2016.

Stringfellow, William. *A Keeper of the Word: Selected Writings of William Stringfellow.* Edited by Bill Wylie Kellerman. Grand Rapids, MI: William B. Eerdmans, 1996.

———. *A Simplicity of Faith: My Experience in Mourning.* Eugene, OR: Wipf and Stock, 2005.

———. *An Ethic for Christians and Other Aliens in a Strange Land.* Reprint ed. Eugene, OR: Wipf and Stock, 2004.

———. "Care Enough to Weep." Chicago: Box 7, William Stringfellow Papers, #4438, Department of Manuscripts and University Archives, Cornell University Library, 1963.

———. *Conscience and Obedience: The Politics of Romans 13 and Revelation 13 in Light of the Second Coming.* Eugene, OR: Wipf and Stock, 2004.

———. *Free in Obedience.* Eugene, OR: Wipf and Stock, 2006.

———. *Imposters of God: Inquiries into Favorite Idols.* Reprint. Eugene, OR: Wipf and Stock, 2006.

———. *Instead of Death: New and Expanded Edition.* Expanded ed. Eugene, OR: Wipf and Stock, 2004.

———. *My People Is the Enemy: An Autobiographical Polemic.* New York: Holt, Rinehart and Winston, 1964.

———. *The Politics of Spirituality.* Eugene, OR: Wipf and Stock, 2006.

Swartley, Willard M. "Discipleship and Imitation of Jesus/Suffering Servant: The Mimesis of New Creation." In *Violence Renounced: René Girard, Biblical Studies, and Peacemaking,* edited by Willard M. Swartley. Scottdale, PA: Herald, 2000.

———, ed. *Violence Renounced.* Telford, PA: Pandora, 2000.

Swinton, John, and Harriet Mowatt. *Practical Theology and Qualitative Research.* London: SCM, 2006.

Talbot, John Michael, and Steve Rabey. *The Lessons of Saint Francis: How to Bring Simplicity and Spirituality into Your Daily Life.* New York: Penguin Group, 1998.

Thurén, Lauri. *Argument and Theology in 1 Peter.* Sheffield, England: Sheffield Academic, 1995.

Tillich, Paul. *The Eternal Now.* New York: Scribner, 1963.

Torres, Julio O. *Oscar Romero: A Man for Our Times.* New York: Seabury, 2021.

University of California – Los Angeles. "Putting Feelings into Words Produces Therapeutic Effects In The Brain." ScienceDaily. Access November 27, 2021. https://www.sciencedaily.com/releases/2007/06/070622090727.htm

Van Gelder, Craig, and Dwight J. Zscheile. *The Missional Church in Perspective: Mapping Trends and Shaping the Conversation.* Grand Rapids, MI: Baker Academic, 2011.

Van Wyngaard, George. "The Public Role of the Christian Community in the Work of David Bosch." *Missionalia* 31 (April 1, 2011): 151–167.

Vaters, Karl. "Jesus and Crowds—An Unhappy Marriage." https://www.KarlVaters.com/jesus-unhappy.

Walker, Ken. "Is Buying Your Way Onto the Bestseller List Wrong?" *ChristianityToday.Com.* Last modified 2015. https://www.christianitytoday.com/ct/2015/januaryfebruary/buying-bestsellers-resultsource.html.

Walton, John H, and J. Harvey Walton, eds. *Demons and Spirits in Biblical Theology: Reading the Biblical Text in Its Cultural and Literary Context.* Eugene, OR: Cascade, 2019.

Webber, Robert E. *The Church in the World: Opposition, Tension, or Transformation.* Grand Rapids, MI: Zondervan, 1986.

Whitehouse, Richard, Andrew Hardy, and Dan Yarnell. "More Recent Approaches to Spiritual Conflict." In *Power and the Powers: The Use and Abuse of Power in Its Missional Context.* Eugene, OR: Cascade, 2015.

Wilson, Michael Todd, Brad Hoffmann, and Members of Caregivers Forum. *Preventing Ministry Failure: A Shepherd Care Guide for Pastors, Ministers and Other Caregivers.* Downers Grove, IL: InterVarsity Press, 2007.

Williams, Rowen. Foreword to *An Alien in a Strange Land: Theology in the Life of William Stringfellow,* by Anthony Dancer. Eugene, OR: Wipf and Stock, 2011.

Wink, Walter. *Cracking the Gnostic Code: The Powers in Gnosticism.* Atlanta, GA: Scholars, 1994.

————. *Engaging the Powers: Discernment and Resistance in a World of Domination.* The Powers vol. 3. Minneapolis, MN: Fortress, 1992.

————. *Naming the Powers: The Language of Power in the New Testament.* Philadelphia, PA: Fortress, 1984.

————. "Stringfellow on the Powers." In *Radical Christian and Exemplary Lawyer,* edited by Andrew W. McThenia Jr. Eugene, OR: Wipf and Stock, 2006.

————. *The Bible in Human Transformation: Toward a New Paradigm in Bible Study.* 2nd ed. Minneapolis, MN: Fortress, 2010.

————. *The Powers That Be: Theology for a New Millennium.* New York: Doubleday, 1998.

————. *Transforming Bible Study: A Leader's Guide.* Eugene, OR: Wipf and Stock, 2009.

————. *Unmasking the Powers: The Invisible Forces That Determine Human Existence.* Minneapolis, MN: Fortress, 1993.

————. *Violence and Nonviolence in South Africa: Jesus' Third Way.* Philadelphia, PA: New Society, 1987.

Wink, Walter, and Steven Berry. *Just Jesus: My Struggle to Become Human.* New York: Image, 2014.

Witherington, Ben, III. *Paul's Letter to the Philippians: A Socio-rhetorical Commentary.* Grand Rapids, MI: William B. Eerdmans, 2011.

Wright, Christopher J. H. *The Mission of God: Unlocking the Bible's Grand Narrative.* Downers Grove, IL: IVP Academic, 2006.

Wright, N. T. *The Climax of the Covenant: Christ and the Law in Pauline Theology.* New York: T and T Clark, 1991.

————. *The Day the Revolution Began: Reconsidering the Meaning of Jesus's Crucifixion.* New York: HarperOne, 2018.

————. *Evil and the Justice of God.* Downers Grove, IL: IVP, 2013.

————. *Following Jesus: Biblical Reflections on Discipleship.* Grand Rapids, MI: William B. Eerdmans, 2014.

————. *Jesus and the Victory of God.* Minneapolis, MN: Fortress, 1997.

————. *Paul: A Biography.* San Francisco: HarperOne, 2018.

————. *Paul and the Faithfulness of God.* Minneapolis: Fortress, 2013.

————. *Philippians: Studies for Individuals and Groups.* Downers Grove, IL: InterVarsity Press, 2009.

Woodward, JR. *Creating a Missional Culture: Equipping the Church for the Sake of the World.* Downers Grove, IL: InterVarsity Press, 2012.

Woodward, JR and Dan White Jr. *The Church as Movement: Starting and Sustaining Missional-Incarnational Communities.* Downers Grove, IL: InterVarsity Press, 2016.

Wylie-Kellermann, Bill. "Not Vice Versa. Reading the Powers Biblically: Stringfellow, Hermeneutics, and the Principalities." *Anglican Theological Review* 81, no. 4 (October 1, 1999). https://www.questia.com/library/journal/1P3-47298237/not-vice-versa-reading-the-powers-biblically-stringfellow.

Yong, Amos. *In the Days of Caesar: Pentecostalism and Political Theology*. The Cadbury lectures 2009. Grand Rapids, MI: William B. Eerdmans, 2010.

———. *The Spirit of Creation: Modern Science and Divine Action in the Pentecostal-Charismatic Imagination*. Pentecostal manifestos. Grand Rapids, MI: William B. Eerdmans, 2011.

Zscheile, Dwight, ed. *Cultivating Sent Communities: Missional Spiritual Formation*. Grand Rapids, MI: William B. Eerdmans, 2012.

Author Links

- /jr.woodward1
- @jrnseattle
- @dreamawakener
- jrwoodward
- jrwoodward
- manchester.academia.edu/JRWoodward
- jrwoodward.com

The V3 Movement Links

- theV3movement.org
- /v3movement
- linktr.ee/thev3movement
- @V3_movement

ABOUT THE AUTHOR

For over twenty-five years, JR Woodward has been passionately planting discipleship-fueled, movement-oriented, neighborhood-grounded churches seeking to be a foretaste of God's coming kingdom. He has helped start and multiply dozens of missional-incarnational communities from Blacksburg, VA, to Los Angeles, CA.

Woodward currently serves as the national director for the V3 Church Planting Movement, which helps to train North American and global church planters to embody a grounded spirituality, missional theology, and movement ecclesiology. He is the cofounder and codirector of the Praxis Gathering, an annual gathering for planters who want to grow in grounded missional practices.

JR cofounded and currently serves on the board of the Missio Alliance. He is an active board member with Reliant Mission, which serves almost nine hundred missionaries in North America and around the world. He also serves on the Fuller Global Mission Advisory Council, the Fuller Church Initiatives Board, Movement Leaders Collective Council, and the Kineo Board. He is a member of the Colloquium on Violence and Religion and is a junior fellow at the Manchester Wesley Research Centre.

Woodward is the author of *Creating a Missional Culture* (IVP, 2012) as well as coauthor of *The Church as Movement* (IVP, 2016). He has contributed chapters for *Sent to Flourish* (IVP, 2019) and 뉴노멀 시대 교회의 위대한 모험 (*The Great Adventure of the Church in the New Normal Era*, Institute for Church Growth, 2021). JR speaks at conferences and gatherings across the US and various parts of the world.

JR has served as an adjunct professor at Capital Seminary, Missio Seminary, American Evangelical University, and Central Seminary. He will be leading an upcoming cohort for the Doctor of Global Leadership at Fuller Theological Seminary. He graduated with a Master of Arts in Global Leadership from Fuller Theological Seminary and completed his PhD at the University of Manchester, UK.

In his spare time, JR loves to surf, travel, read, skateboard, and meet new people. He enjoys photography and film and attends the Sundance Film Festival whenever he can.

The **V3 Movement** is a training network that deeply understands the terrain of mission in the West. Every year, V3 coaches church planters, marketplace planters, and re-missioning pastors all over North America and the world—in places such as Seattle, Miami, Honolulu, Toronto, Los Angeles, New York, Dallas, Atlanta, Tokyo, London, Nairobi, and Yangon.

Research shows that church planters who engage in in-depth training experiences, alongside experienced coaches, are more likely to thrive in their efforts at church planting. This is why our cohorts provide strategic coaching as you journey through the formative phases of establishing a new church, a new business, or re-missioning an existing church.

Our training is holistic, communal, peer-based, practice- and process-oriented, and equips you in transferable tools for discipling your team. You will discover the grassroots work of movement: tight-knit community, life-forming discipleship, locally rooted presence, and boundary-crossing mission.

V3 Website: **thev3movement.org**
V3 App: **subsplash.com/thev3movement/app**

PRAXIS
GATHERING

The **Praxis Gathering** is a unique church-planting conference that is passionate about combining real-time practice, rich theology, and deep reflection. Annually, over 250 practioners from around North America gather together in a US city to learn and dialogue around the hands-on work of missional presence in our neighborhoods and networks. There is a movement afoot, calling us to rediscover the on-the-ground essentials for being the church. Gather with us to be equipped, nourished, and sent back into the world.

thepraxisgathering.com

Missio Alliance

The church is known for many things but not always for looking like Jesus. The world desperately needs individuals and communities whose lives testify to the transformative power of Christ's life, death, and resurrection. Missio Alliance exists to resource, gather, and embolden Christian leaders to reshape the church's witness in the world.

Through partnerships with individuals, congregations, schools, denominational bodies, ministry organizations, and networks, Missio Alliance addresses the most crucial theological and cultural issues facing the North American church in God's mission today.

Rooted in the global, biblical convictions and calls to action of the Cape Town Commitment, the ministry of Missio Alliance is animated by a strong and distinctive theological identity that emphasizes the integration of the following three essential aspects of kingdom living:

Formation: Advancing a way of being the people of God in the world that reflects our unwavering need for deliberate, inner work, which grounds us in God's loving, abiding, and transforming presence.

Justice: Advancing a way of being the people of God in the world that reflects our unwavering commitment to demonstrating God's justice that works toward flourishing for all humankind and points toward the future hope of the renewal of all things.

Mission: Advancing a way of being the people of God in the world that reflects our unwavering understanding that our identity and witness is found and expressed through our active participation in God's mission in the world.

To explore our growing library of articles, podcasts, and videos, **visit missio-alliance.org**.

ALSO BY JR WOODWARD

Creating a Missional Culture
987-0-8307-6679-3

The Church as Movement
978-0-8308-4133-2